Bernard Malamud

A Writer's Life

Bernard Malamud, by Karl Schrag, oil on canvas, *c.*1970, stretcher: 63.5 × 45.7 cm (25″ × 18″)
National Portrait Gallery, Smithsonian Institution

Bernard Malamud

A Writer's Life

PHILIP DAVIS

OXFORD
UNIVERSITY PRESS

OXFORD
UNIVERSITY PRESS

Great Clarendon Street, Oxford OX2 6DP

Oxford University Press is a department of the University of Oxford.
It furthers the University's objective of excellence in research, scholarship,
and education by publishing worldwide in

Oxford New York

Auckland Cape Town Dar es Salaam Hong Kong Karachi
Kuala Lumpur Madrid Melbourne Mexico City Nairobi
New Delhi Shanghai Taipei Toronto

With offices in

Argentina Austria Brazil Chile Czech Republic France Greece
Guatemala Hungary Italy Japan Poland Portugal Singapore
South Korea Switzerland Thailand Turkey Ukraine Vietnam

Oxford is a registered trade mark of Oxford University Press
in the UK and in certain other countries

Published in the United States
by Oxford University Press Inc., New York

British Library Cataloguing in Publication Data

Data available

Library of Congress Cataloging in Publication Data

Data available

Typeset by Laserwords Private Limited, Chennai, India
Printed in Great Britain
on acid-free paper by
Clays Ltd, St. Ives plc

ISBN 978-0-19-927009-5

1

In memory of Bernard Malamud

—'The Human Sentence'—

Preface

It was a graduation day at the University of Liverpool in the summer of 2002. After the ceremony I was talking to the biographer and literary critic Hermione Lee. Now Goldsmiths' Professor of English Literature at Oxford, she had once been a lecturer in the School of English at Liverpool and had come back on this day to receive an honorary degree. I said to her that I had seen an advertisement a few months earlier for a conference in Oxford on biography, featuring, amongst others, herself and the daughter of Bernard Malamud. Was Janna Malamud Smith going to write her father's biography, I asked, because I really wanted to read that book. She looked startled and said she had only just returned from Cambridge, Massachusetts, where she had spoken to the Malamud family. 'They are now looking for a biographer.' For years, since Malamud's death in 1986, the family had resisted the writing of his life. Now they were concerned that his name was fading, his readership and literary standing in danger of decline. 'Why don't you write it?'

I had written about Malamud in a book called *The Experience of Reading*, published in 1992 and again in an experimental mixture of literary criticism and short stories entitled *Malamud's People* in 1995. But I had been reading Malamud's work, with a passion, since 1969 when my schoolteacher, the novelist Stanley Middleton, told me to read *The Fixer*. I remember exactly where I was standing when a friend of mine told me that Malamud had died that day, and I thought, simply: I shall never meet him now.

The conversation with Hermione Lee was a moment of sheer chance. What followed from her suggestion and then introduction was a series of informal meetings with the Malamud family, first with Janna Malamud Smith and her husband David Smith in London, later on in that summer of 2002; then in the November, in the supportive company of my wife Jane, interviews with Malamud's own wife Ann Malamud, in Cambridge, with Tim Seldes (Malamud's agent and one of the literary executors) in New York, and with Paul Malamud, the son, over the telephone in Washington, DC. It was decided that I would indeed write the first-ever biography; that it would be primarily a literary life, as the life of Malamud indeed was; and that it would not be an authorized biography as such, but one written with the full cooperation of the family and estate, without censorship. Let me say here that

I am more than conventionally grateful for the generosity of Ann Malamud, Janna Malamud Smith, and Paul Malamud—who in their different ways have been equally and entirely supportive, whilst knowing all the time that not everything I was going to write would please them. But they knew I loved the work. I have thought of them while I was writing—a man from the wrong side of the Atlantic, given unlimited and unconditional access, always hoped he was doing justice to the project they entrusted to him. To them above all, as well as to Hermione Lee and Tim Seldes, I owe this book.

'Anyone turning biographer', wrote Freud, 'has committed himself to lies, to concealment, to hypocrisy, to flattery, and even to hiding his own lack of understanding: for biographical truth is not to be had, and even if it were it couldn't be useful.' It is a sentence that Malamud, a great reader of biographies, quoted twice—once in a paper he gave to a group of New York psychoanalysts on Walter Jackson Bate's life of Samuel Johnson; again in *Dubin's Lives* where it is said, in chapter 8, that that sentence of Freud's 'devastated' Dubin the biographer.

This particular biographer, myself, has had two aims in writing this book, Freud's warning notwithstanding. The first has been to place the work above the life—but to show how the life worked very hard to turn itself into that achievement. Too often where Malamud is still remembered, it is for a handful of great short stories; but wonderful as many of those stories are, I want most of all to make the case that Malamud himself most favoured—the case for the novels. But in any event I seek more recognition and more readers for Malamud in the future. In some concluding remarks made at the memorial service for Malamud in Bennington, Vermont, 17 May 1986, Claude Fredericks asked his audience to remember 'that we, as human beings, are, all of us, nothing other than what we think and that what we think are words and that the words *he* thought we still have, even though he himself is gone'. I have tried to do justice to those thoughts by doing something more than merely summarizing the works: in the case of *The Assistant* and *Dubin's Lives* they occupy whole chapters; elsewhere, distinct and often concluding or climactic sections.

Whether we are finally 'nothing other than what we think', I also wanted to tell the as-it-were *physical story* of Malamud's life, as a struggling and damaged, second-generation, self-made man in America. Thus my second objective has been to show serious readers all that it means to be a serious writer, possessed of an almost religious sense of vocation—in terms of both the uses of and the costs to an ordinary human life. When Stanley Eskin's wife Barbara asked Malamud if he was working on anything, his answer bore his characteristic mark: 'Of course; it's a way of life.' It was also a means of self-education, in the broadest sense: the story of learning from life and in art.

That is why this biography is called *A Writer's Life*—a writer concerned every day with creating what he called 'the human sentence'. That was the name of a course that Malamud the teacher once thought of putting on at Bennington College. For that is what Malamud mainly spent his life doing—trying to make his sentences into human sentences—and I attempt to show what he meant by that and how he did it, draft after draft. The 'human sentence' also gestures towards what Malamud said about his use of the prison motif, in his interview with Daniel Stern in the *Writers at Work* series for the *Paris Review* in 1984: 'Perhaps I see it as a metaphor for the dilemma of all men: necessity whose bars we look through and try not to see. Social injustice, apathy, ignorance. The personal prison of entrapment in past experience, guilt, obsession—the somewhat blind or blinded self, in other words. A man has to construct, invent, his freedom. Imagination helps. A truly great man or woman extends it for others in the process of creating his/her own.' The winning of freedom out of necessity was to Malamud also the winning of writing out of experience, of imagination out of memory. He always wanted to insist he was an imaginative and inventive writer, hiding the autobiographical origins of his work. But I believe he was a greater writer than he himself sometimes thought he was, precisely because of the tense closeness of the life and the work, and the struggle between them.

Therefore, despite Freud's warnings about biography, I think it is 'useful' to try to imagine how this man made himself a writer in the process of writing, in the act of transforming his own experience. In order to avoid as much as possible some of those biographer's 'lies' which are called paraphrases, I have tried wherever I can to follow the example of the great nineteenth-century lives of writers, by quoting Malamud's own words, as in surrogate autobiography, with relation also to the words of his family, friends, colleagues, and students. As such, this is indeed a collaborative work, indebted to all those who allowed me to quote what they gave me in memory of Malamud, through documents and in interviews.

Some of those encounters might make for wry short stories of their own. There was the man who, about to undergo angioplasty, still insisted on carrying out our interview from his hospital bed, whilst wired to every possible monitoring device. When he told bland, well-meaning untruths, who in the world of interviewers could help looking at the monitors and wondering what would happen if you said you knew he was lying? Or then again there was the woman, a former student, who really did not want to talk about herself and Malamud. But she was perfectly happy to tell me a thoroughly scurrilous tale about Malamud and one of her contemporaries instead. This in turn was adamantly—though not entirely convincingly—denied by the person concerned. And so on. The novelist Dan Jacobson told me I was visiting so many Jewish old-people's homes that I might as well stay put in one of them. But many of these interviews were rich experiences that were a privilege to share. Sometimes they mattered more at the time than the use I could subsequently make of them. At other times I found something important in the transcripts that I had not even recognized when we were speaking. For help with the arduous work of transcription, as well as for detailed advice and enlivening conversation, I owe much to Dr Sarah Coley. The names of the collaborators themselves—interviewees, librarians, donators of documents, correspondents by letter and e-mail—are listed, in gratitude for their trust and their effort, at the end of this preface.

Of course, I take sole responsibility for the form of this book and the interpretations, implicit and explicit, that result. But in terms of form, I need to make two points. Firstly, I often attempt in this book to create at least two directions: telling the story forwards, whilst also rendering it back again via Malamud's own memory of it. I have taken as my model here the form of *Dubin's Lives*, juggling between past and present, work and life, inside and outside the protagonist. Secondly, with regard to Freud's powerful warning against the biographer 'hiding his own lack of understanding', I have tried, again through form, to leave the gaps and the holes and the conflicting uncertainties open to the reader in the very midst of the gathered evidence. 'I did what I could' was Malamud's own habitual riposte.

That said, I remain painfully aware that what I have written is dependent on what writings have remained, on which surviving individuals I happen to have found, and on what those people have been able to recall, and willing to tell me, on and off the record. Such are the perils of a first biography, for all the assistance provided by Janna Malamud Smith's own memoir, *My Father Is a Book* (2006). When one of Ann Malamud's helpers took me to Mount Auburn Cemetery in Cambridge, I knew when I at last found the place which marked Malamud's ashes that the responsibility was a real and peculiarly intimate one, and that what was involved here was not simply the routine writing of an informative book. One day whilst studying the manuscripts at the Library of Congress I even received an unexpected e-mail from Bernard Malamud, which began 'As you may well imagine, I am keenly interested in your project'. It was signed at the end as from 'Bernard Malamud, Professor of Economics, University of Nevada, Las Vegas', but by then could have proved fatal.

Did Malamud himself want a biography after his death? Certainly in his lifetime, the stern and prickly, wily and reticent Malamud always sought to preserve his methods and his secrets. And if like Dubin at the end of *Dubin's Lives* he bequeathed to his daughter the role of writer, then part of Janna's inheritance was also expressed in her book *Private Matters* (Addison-Wesley, 1997):

I first began thinking about privacy when my father, the writer Bernard Malamud, died in 1986, and we were left to settle his literary estate. My mother sought opinions from me as she made her decisions. She had to decide whether to encourage or discourage people who wrote asking particular details of his life; whether to publish an unpublished manuscript or place it in an archive for scholars; whether to save all letters from his friends. Should she sell manuscripts or give them to the Library of Congress? Should any writings be sequestered until some time in the future or even be destroyed?   (*Private Matters*, 3)

'My mother pondered what to do when a biographer called.' I am not a biographer; I became one for this purpose.

But if he had not wanted a biography, why had Malamud once shown the biographer James Atlas into his study, opened his filing cabinet, and said that some day this would make great material for a biographer? He also told Toby Talbot after she had written *A Book about my Mother* (1980) that she should write his life some time. Daniel Stern recalled that Malamud inserted into the revision of the *Paris Review* interview a prying question that Dan had never even asked:

DS: What is the source of *The Assistant*?
M: Source questions are piddling but you're my friend, so I'll tell you. Mostly my
    father's life as a grocer, though not necessarily my father.

Even as a veiled tribute to his father, it showed in Malamud a characteristic ambivalence, a mix of revealing and concealing nervously intrinsic to his art.

I do think I know the sort of biography Malamud would not have wanted—the sort that left out or explained away his work. During the writing of *Dubin's Lives* Malamud records in a notebook a dream he had, in which he complained to his friend the sociologist Alex Inkeles, about any sociology that sought to 'explain all mysteries'. Explanations and definitions were too often reductive of life in ways that fiction emphatically was not. There was nothing Malamud hated more than feeling 'diminished': all his life had been a fight against that belittlement of meaning. It was fiction that provided the best *context* for human understanding—the discourse that could make the private public without violating or betraying it. There is a great ostensibly simple sentence in *The Assistant* which refers to the recidivist thief and liar Frank Alpine, the man who deep inside himself knew he had reformed in the end and wanted now to be known as a changed, good man: 'He could see out but nobody could see in.'

My own view is that any biography that seeks to 'see in' and thus do justice to Malamud should learn from the fiction, from its methods as much as its contents, and then direct its readers back towards it. Sometimes the lesser thing is temporarily necessary, precisely to reveal the greater by comparison.

I am grateful to the Harry Ransom Center, University of Texas at Austin for a Paul Mellon Fellowship to research the Malamud archive during the summer of 2005 with the help of my wife Jane Davis; to the British Academy for a grant to research the equivalent archive in the Library of Congress; to the staff at both archives; and to the University of Liverpool for funding and study leave. I am also indebted to Special Collections in Oregon State University for the Malamud papers, in Washington University in St Louis for the Howard Nemerov papers, and in the University of Calgary for the Clark Blaise papers; to the Berg Collection of English and American Literature in New York Public Library for the Malamud–Beck correspondence; to the Smithsonian National Portrait Gallery; and to Claude Fredericks and the Claude Fredericks archive at the Research Institute of the Getty Centre in Los Angeles. Sophie Goldsworthy at Oxford University Press backed this book from the very first, and Andrew McNeillie warmly supported it from then on, directing me to the ever-helpful and ever-patient pair, Tom Perridge and Jacqueline Baker, whenever I had questions about production. My thanks to the assiduous and kindly Charles Lauder Jr and Elizabeth Robottom in the final preparation of the manuscript. To save me from homesickness, my wife and son, Ben, gave up the summer of 2003 to travel America, east and west, whilst I carried out interviews on what they called the Malamud trail.

It is a pleasure to record the names of those who have helped me on that trail—marred only by the uneasy thought of the accidentally ungrateful omission of some name I should never have left out. There are also people whose papers I have found in archives but have been unable to trace despite my best efforts: if contacted, I am happy to make acknowledgement in any subsequent edition. Thus, sincere thanks go to Pat Adams, Minda Rae Amiran, James Atlas, Evelyn Avery, Jay Beilis, Ellen Belton, Lillian Ben-Zion, Clark Blaise, Joan Norris Boothe, Robert Boyers, Jay Cantor, Phebe Chao, Alan Cheuse, Suzanne Clark, Bonnie Coles of photoduplication services in the Library of Congress, Arnold Cooper, Bill Cooper, Susan Crile, Joan Crowell, Sheila and Sid Davis, Elena Delbanco, Nicholas Delbanco, Robert Dunn, Tiah Edmunson-Morton of Oregon State University Archives, Edward Engelberg, Victor Erlich, Stanley Eskin, Bob Farrell, Stuart Feder, Judy Feiffer, Alvin Feinman, Anna Fels, Elizabeth Frank, Helen Frankenthaler, Claude Fredericks, Laura Furman, Joan Gardner, Chester Garrison, Michael Garreffa, John Bart Gerald, Dr Isaac Gewirtz of the Berg Collection in New York Public Library, Stephen Gill, Robert Giroux, Celia Gittelson, Robinson Gomez of New York Public

Library Photographic Services, James Groshong, John Gross, Jean Haber, John Haislip, Marc Harrington, Peter Hayes, Didi Heller, John Henley, Preston Henley, Arlene Heyman, Joy Holland of Brooklyn Public Library, Glenn Horowitz, Sue Hovland, Warren Hovland, Doria Hughes, Laurence Hyman, Alex Inkeles, Bernadette Inkeles, Stephen Kellman, Karen Kennerly, Constance Kheel, Bruce Kirby of the Library of Congress, Joanna Kirk, Charles Kopelman, Doris Milman Kreeger, Leonard Kress, Patricia Lang, Nan Lehmann, Leonard J. Lehrman, Mrs Mickey Levine, Larry Lockridge, Linda Lowell, Harriet Lustig, Larry Lustig, Sylvia Malament, George and Ethel Martin, Pam Matz, Reinhard Mayer, Bruce McAuley, Lorena MacCafferty, Ed McClanahan, Ellen McCulloch-Lovell, Milt and Phyllis Meisner, Ellen Miles and Wendy Wick Reaves of the Smithsonian National Portrait Gallery, Ruth Morris, Bharati Mukherjee, Dan Myerson, Bill Needle, Brian Nellist, Edna O'Brien, Jules Olitski, Cynthia Ozick, Camille Paglia, Sarah Patton of Special Collections, Washington University in St Louis, Chris Petersen of Special Collections, Oregon State University, Bert Pogrebin, Letty Cottin Pogrebin, Katha Pollitt, Bill Potts, Katherine A. Powers, Marjorie Pryse, Bruce Reitz, Erica Rex, Lilly Rivlin, Roxana Robinson, Anne Roiphe, Betsy Rush, Burt Rush, Joel Salzberg, Beverley Sanders, Nelson and Olive Sandgren, Stephen Sandy, Virginia Sandy, Maggie Scarf, Peter Schrag, Suzanne Schrag, Tim Seldes, Susan Shreve, Martha Sermier, Barbara Herrnstein Smith, Apollonia Steele of Special Collections at the University of Calgary, Daniel Stern, Gloria Stern, Richard Stern, Dorothea Straus, Nina Pelikan Straus, Roger Straus, Enid Stubin, Dan Talbot, Toby Talbot, Janet Thormann, Marion Tigers, Tamas Ungvari, Anne Waldman, Katherine Wangh, Jenna White of Alumnae(i) Relations at Bennington College, Kate Hickler White, Sara Witter, Herb Wittkin, Philip Wofford, Richard Workman of the Harry Ransom Humanities Research Center, Peggy Worthington, Karen Wunsch, and Kathy Kohner Zuckerman.

Every effort has been made to trace and contact all copyright holders. If there are any inadvertent omissions or errors, the publishers will be pleased to correct these at the earliest opportunity.

Philip Davis
Liverpool, August 2006

Postscript: As I correct the proofs of this preface, it is a sadness—inextricable from the nature of this project—to read the names of those who have died since this book's completion. In particular I record the death of Ann Malamud on 20 March 2007.

PD

Contents

List of Abbreviations

CBM   *Conversations with Bernard Malamud*, ed. Lawrence Lasher (Jackson: University Press of Mississippi, 1991)

HRC   Malamud Papers, Harry Ransom Humanities Research Center, University of Texas at Austin [followed by box and folder numbers; thus: HRC 35.2 = box 35, folder 2]

LC   Malamud Holding, Library of Congress [followed by part, container and folder number; thus: LC I 38.3 = part I, container 38, folder 3]

MFB   Janna Malamud Smith, *My Father Is a Book* (Boston and New York: Houghton Mifflin, 2006)

MWB   *The Magic Worlds of Bernard Malamud*, ed. Evelyn Avery (Albany: State University of New York Press, 2001)

OSU   Bernard Malamud Papers, Special Collections, Oregon State University [followed by box number]

TH   *Talking Horse: Bernard Malamud on Life and Work*, ed. Alan Cheuse and Nicholas Delbanco (New York: Columbia University Press, 1996)

NOTE ON EDITIONS

For the novels, all editions refer to the first English edition.

For the short stories, the standard edition used is *The Complete Stories of Bernard Malamud*, ed. Robert Giroux (New York, Farrar, Straus and Giroux 1987; London: Vintage, 1998).

Thanks are due to Farrar, Straus and Giroux.

List of Illustrations

Chronology

26 April 1914   Bernard Malamud born in Brooklyn, New York, to Max (originally Mendel) Malamud (b. 1885) and Bertha (née Brucha Fidelman) Malamud (b. 1888), who had been married in 1910. There had been a stillborn child in 1912.

1917   Birth of brother, Eugene Malamud.

1920   BM attends elementary school, Cortelyou Road, Brooklyn.

1922   BM enters P.S. 181 in third grade. Family living above grocery store in 1111 Gravesend Avenue, in the Flatbush section of Brooklyn.

1928–32   Attends Erasmus Hall High School. Wins Richard Young essay prize for 'Life—From behind a Counter' (1932), which comes second in the national Scholastics Awards.

May 1929   Death in mental hospital of mother, Bertha, who had been admitted to King's County Hospital in 1927 and then transferred to a private mental hospital in Queens.

1931   Max Malamud marries Liza (Elizabeth) Merov.

1932–6   BM attends City College in Manhattan; receives BA (1936).

Works during the summers in Catskills hotels.

1936–7   Works at $4.50 a day as teacher-in-training but over next few years twice fails teaching exams to become a permanent substitute teacher.

1937–8   Attends Columbia University on government loan; finally gains MA (1942) with routine thesis on Hardy's *The Dynasts*: 'Thomas Hardy's Reputation as a Poet in American Periodicals'.

1938–9   Unemployed; odd jobs in factories and department stores; tutors German-Jewish refugees in English.

1939   First temporary teaching position, Lafayette High School, Brooklyn.

1940   Clerk, U.S. Census Bureau, Washington, D.C.

Begins to write seriously while at his work desk and publishes sketches of real life in *Washington Post*.

1940–8   Returns to Brooklyn to teach at Erasmus Hall High School; teaches evening classes there and at other New York City schools, whilst writing short stories during the day.

1942	Begins to write novel 'The Light Sleeper', completed 1948 but rejected by publishers and eventually burnt by BM in Oregon, (1951).
	Disliking stepmother, moves out of family home to lodgings in Flatbush.
1943	First short stories published: 'Benefit Performance' in *Threshold*; 'The Place is Different Now' in *American Prefaces*; 'Steady Customer' in *New Threshold*; and 'The Literary Life of Laban Goldman' in *Assembly*.
November 1945	Marries Ann de Chiara (b. 1917), whom BM first met in February 1942. Moves from Brooklyn to 1 King Street, Greenwich Village.
October 1947	Son, Paul Francis Malamud, born.
1948–9	Teaches evening classes at Harlem Evening High School.
	Also now has to teach during the day at Chelsea Vocational High School to maintain family.
1949–61	Moves to Corvallis, Oregon, to teach at Oregon State College: from instructor in composition, not allowed to teach literature for want of PhD; to assistant professor (1954); to associate professor (1958).
1950	Short stories published in major periodicals: 'Cost of Living' in *Harper's Bazaar*; 'The Prison' in *Commentary*; 'The First Seven Years' in *Partisan Review*. Followed in 1951 by 'The Death of Me' in *World Review*; and 'The Bill' and 'An Apology', both in *Commentary*, and 'The Loan' also in *Commentary* in 1952.
December 1951	Brother, Eugene, committed to King's County, the same mental hospital where his mother had been a patient; transferred to King's Park State Hospital and then to King's Park Veterans' Hospital and diagnosed as schizophrenic. BM returns from Oregon to visit, in June 1952; Eugene released home July 1952.
1952	First novel, *The Natural*, published by Harcourt, Brace and Company, editor Robert Giroux. Begun writing early 1950, finished in October 1951.
	Daughter, Janna Ellen Malamud, born in January.
	BM begins novel 'The Broken Snow', later 'The Man Nobody Could Lift', about a schizophrenic: Robert Giroux advises against publication (November 1953).
1953–4	Short stories published: 'The Girl of My Dreams' in *American Mercury* (1953), and 'The Magic Barrel' in *Partisan Review* (1954).
March 1954	Father, Max Malamud, dies of heart attack (first suffered heart attack in 1952 following Eugene's committal).

1955	Publishes *Kim of Korea*, a children's story written by Faith Norris, revised by BM, using assumed name 'Peter Lumn' as co-author.
	Short stories published: 'The Mourners' in *Discovery* and 'Angel Levine' in *Commentary*.
Autumn 1956–Summer 1957	Gains *Partisan Review* and Rockefeller Foundation fellowship in fiction; takes family to live and write in Rome; visits Austria and France.
	Short stories published: 'A Summer's Reading' in *The New Yorker*, 'Take Pity' in *America*.
1957	Second novel, *The Assistant* appeared: begun April 1954 completed June 1956 before BM's leaving for Italy, it was published by Robert Giroux now at Farrar, Straus and Company, after he was shocked to find it had been rejected by Harcourt Brace.
1958	'The Last Mohican' in *Partisan Review* and 'Behold the Key' in *Commentary*: both included in first collection of short stories, *The Magic Barrel*.
	Receives both Rosenthal Award from National Institute of Arts and Letters, and Daroff Memorial Fiction Award of the Jewish Book Council of America for *The Assistant*. Summer fellowship at Yaddo.
1959	Wins National Book Award for *The Magic Barrel*. Now allowed to teach literature, as well as creative writing, at Oregon State.
	Receives Ford Foundation Grant of $15,000, providing two years' free writing-time.
	'The Maid's Shoes' published in *Partisan Review*.
1961	Teaches creative writing at summer school at Harvard.
	Moves to teaching post in Division of Language and Literature at Bennington College, Vermont.
	Third novel, *A New Life*, published: begun December 1957, completed early 1961.
	'Idiots First' published in *Commentary*.
	Eugene Malamud again hospitalized, as suicidal, at Brooklyn State Hospital, early 1961 till August.
1962	'Still life' published in *Partisan Review*.
1963	More short stories published ('Suppose a Wedding', *New Statesman*; 'The Jewbird', *Reporter*; 'Life is Better Than Death', *Esquire*; 'Black is My Favorite Color', *Reporter*; 'Naked Nude', *Playboy*; 'The German Refugee', *Saturday Evening Post*) and collected in second volume of short stories, *Idiots First*.

'A Choice of Profession' published in *Commentary*.

Elected to American Institute of Arts and Letters.

Travels in England and Italy.

1965   Travels in Spain, France and Soviet Union.

1966   Fourth novel, *The Fixer*, published: begun October 1963, completed March/April 1966.

Visiting lecturer at Harvard 1966–8.

1967   Wins both National Book Award and Pulitzer Prize for *The Fixer*.

Elected member of American Academy of Arts and Sciences.

1968   Visits Israel in March.

'My Son the Murderer' published in *Esquire*; 'An Exorcism' in *Harper's*.

Film of *The Fixer*, starring Alan Bates.

1969   Fifth novel, *Pictures of Fidelman: An Exhibition*, published: six linked stories, three already published in *The Magic Barrel* (1958); and 'A Pimp's Revenge' in *Playboy* and 'Pictures of The Artist' in *Atlantic* (1968).

O. Henry Prize for short story 'Man in the Drawer' published in *Atlantic Monthly* (1968).

Malamuds move to Catamount Lane, Old Bennington, spending winters in Manhattan.

1971   Sixth novel, *The Tenants*, published: begun 1969, completed 1971.

Malamuds living in London from autumn for five months: BM writing short stories.

1972   Malamuds purchase flat in Lincoln Towers, Manhattan.

Short stories published: 'God's Wrath', *Atlantic*; 'Talking Horse', *Atlantic*; 'The Letter', *Esquire*; 'The Silver Crown', *Playboy*.

1973   Short stories published: 'Notes from a Lady at a Dinner Party', *Harper's*; 'In Retirement', *Atlantic*; 'Rembrandt's Hat', *New Yorker*. Collected in third volume of short stories, *Rembrandt's Hat*.

Eugene Malamud dies of heart-attack, October 30, aged 55.

1976   Receives the Jewish Heritage Award.

1978   ~~Visits Hungary~~

1979   Seventh novel, *Dubin's Lives*, published: begun February 1973, completed August 1978. Parts previously published in *The New Yorker* and *Playboy*.

Serves as President of PEN American Center, 1979–81.

1980   'A Wig' published in *Atlantic*.

Receives the Governor's Award from the Vermont Council on the Arts.

1981   Brandeis Creative Arts Award.

Fellow of the Center for Advanced Study in the Behaviorial Sciences, Palo Alto, California, (1981–2).

1982   Eighth novel, *God's Grace*, published: begun early 1980, completed early 1982.

            March: suffers stroke during heart surgery at Stanford, impairing ability to write.

1983   *The Stories of Bernard Malamud* published.

            Wins Gold Medal for fiction from American Academy and Institute for Arts and Sciences.

            'The Model' published in the *Atlantic*.

1984   'Alma Redeemed' published in *Commentary*; 'In Kew Gardens' in *Partisan Review*.

            Film of *The Natural*, starring Robert Redford.

1985   'Zora's Noise' published in *GQ (Gentlemen's Quarterly)*; 'A Lost Grave' in *Esquire*.

            Premio Mondello Prize in Italy.

18 March, 1986   Dies of heart attack in apartment in Lincoln Towers.

            Cremated: ashes buried in Mount Auburn Cemetery, Cambridge, Massachusetts.

1989   Unfinished novel *The People* (begun 1984) posthumously published by the estate with *Uncollected Stories*.

1997   *The Complete Stories* published, with introduction by Robert Giroux.

THE FIRST LIFE

1

◁◇◇◇▷

The Inheritance

26 April, 1984: Mother and Father

In notes for a speech to mark his seventieth birthday, 26 April 1984, Bernard Malamud recalled for his audience of family and close friends a story, set in 1934, about himself and his immigrant father, Max, a poor grocer.

> One day during the Depression, as I was lying in bed with a heavy cold, miserable because I had no job, he came up the stairs from the store, and after we had talked a minute, he took my foot in his hand and said 'mir soll scin far dir'—'I'd rather it were I than you'. I've always remembered that. (HRC 29.6)

Among the audience on that birthday was Malamud's friend and fellow-writer Daniel Stern. He recalled the story nearly two years later at the memorial service held for Malamud at the 92nd street YMHA in New York, 20 April 1986, a month after his death on 18 March: 'Mir far dir is the ungrammatical way it stayed in my mind—as a three word Yiddish poem.' It was Malamud's shorthand, said Stern, for what it meant to be 'human', a word he used and valued more than any writer Stern knew. In 'Idiots First' a father fighting for his retarded son cries to the force that would ruin them: 'You bastard, don't you understand what it means human?' In the Yiddish of Malamud's own father, heard in the very accent of the question, it meant a 'mensch'—not just a man or a human being, but a true upright person of moral intelligence and imaginative kindness. 'Mensch' was the highest compliment Malamud knew.

A few months after his birthday, Malamud again used that story of his father as mensch in an unusually autobiographical lecture he gave at Bennington College in the Ben Belitt Lectureship Series, 13 October 1984, entitled 'Long Work, Short Life'. This time the story went like this:

Once when I was twenty, he trudged up the hall stairs from his grocery stair one morning. I had a summer cold and was stretched out in bed. I had been looking for a job without success. My father reached for my foot and grasped it with his hand.

'I wish it was me with that cold instead of you.'

What does a writer need most? When I ask the question, I think of my father.   (TH, 32)

The resonantly half-hidden love that Malamud implies in those last sentences is itself related to the more inarticulate mixture of dourness and tenderness in Max Malamud himself. In its characteristic mix of reticence and confession, it is, moreover, a novelist's implicit form of thinking, achieved not so much through concepts as through people: 'I think of my father.' Repetition in Malamud does not mean merely repeating himself: he was finding new things to think or realize in his compulsive places.

But Malamud knew that 'mir far dir' was not just his father's saying. In September 1963 he was reading *Life Is With People*, a classic account of the culture of the Jewish shtetl, the small town or village in Poland and Russia that was to be destroyed in the coming of the Nazis. It was partly a preparation for beginning to write *The Fixer*, his Russian novel. But it also gathered in him the fragments of a broken tradition he had unknowingly inherited. 'For the first time,' Malamud wrote, 23 September 1963, 'I feel I have an understanding of the sort of life Popa and Mama lived before they came to America' (HRC 36.6). Amongst much else in the book he read this:

Paternal love is also expressed in worrying, which the father does in manly silence and the mother does with womanly worry. Worry is not viewed as an indulgence but as an expression of affection and almost a duty ....

The intensity of one's worry shows the extent of identification, another proof of love. 'Oh, it should have happened on me!' cries the mother whose child has hurt himself. 'It should be to me and not to you!' ... Even before anything happens, a good mother worries about it and there is magic in her worry. It not only proves her love but it may keep misfortune away.[1]

Malamud loved the memory of emotional tenderness in men, of inarticulate sweetness in the father. In reply to a letter from Elihu Armour, a fellow-graduate from Erasmus Hall High School in 1929, he sent a message to their contemporary Jim Oliva, whose father had run the local barber shop: 'Tell him I remember his father very well. Once he almost cut my finger with his straight razor as he was shaving me. He kissed the finger and I knew I was in the hands of a man who could not cut me, and whose kiss blessed me' (HRC

8.3). But these physical acts, the hand on the foot, the kiss on the finger, were from fathers in place of a mother. There was no mother to worry for Malamud in 1934.

Bertha (originally Brucha) Malamud had died in a mental hospital in 1929, after years of suffering from schizophrenia. Malamud remembered 'my father crying over her in the store on Gravesend Ave.' She was first committed to Kings County Hospital in 1927, where she was miserable; then, though Max could hardly afford it, he had her sent to a private hospital in Queens. 'She died, I think, in 1929 when I was just 15,' wrote Malamud, adding quietly, 'On Mother's day. May, 1929.'[2]

Two years earlier, the young Malamud, aged thirteen, had returned from school to find his mother frothing at the mouth on the clean kitchen floor, an empty can of disinfectant beside her. He had had to run for help to the local drugstore to save her. Bertha was hospitalized some time after the suicide attempt and never returned home.

Childbirth had been unkind to her. Malamud suspected that on each of three occasions she had suffered from what only in later years came to be recognized as post-natal depression. There had been a stillborn son in 1912. In 1914 the birth of Bernard may have damaged her left leg. At any rate the boy thought that he had somehow perhaps caused the injury. Yet he also felt shame in front of his friends to see his fat two-hundred-pound mother walking peculiarly, hat to one side, limping at crazy angles through the streets. Malamud never forgot a girl cousin 'telling someone' in his hearing of 'the way the car tipped when my mother got in it' ('Family History').

In 1918 the birth of another boy, Eugene, began the process of complete breakdown. The mother still functioned in a fashion: 'Eugene', wrote the older brother in 1951, 'may be said to have had a happy childhood:

> However, he was overprotected and 'over cared for'. Bertha slept with him till he was five or six, possibly more. She dressed him every day till he was in grammar school, even helping him on and off with his overcoat. Nor could she bring herself to wean Eugene from his bottle until he was five or six, and already the victim of ridicule by neighbors and relatives who knew of the situation. (HRC 20.2)

After the loss of this still-born first son, it was Bernie who became the privileged child. He was witty and bright, and loved school.

Worry may have been a traditional parental duty and a sign of love but Bertha's worries were not normal. She had been shy and nervous from the start—afraid to come in the house and meet Max's family—and later was scared of serving semi-strangers in the store. More refined than her husband, she became fanatically concerned with cleanliness. Later she thought people were talking about her, that a policeman was following her along the street, and (perhaps rightly) that the wife of Max's partner in the grocery store was stealing from the till. She was scared of the radio that Max brought into the house, and often kept to the back bedroom, door locked, the household gradually deteriorating with her, though she still kept the children obsessively clean.

Malamud had an index finger missing part of its tip from an accident when slicing meat for a customer, and there was a chipped front tooth that resulted from a tussle with Eugene. But the lasting scars came from losses and lacks. He once described to his daughter, Janna, how as a boy he was 'waiting with a friend for his mother to come down and take them to the movies':

> In spite of her having agreed to do it, she was too ill and couldn't leave the apartment. They waited with growing restlessness, and I'm sure, on his part, embarrassment. He'd promised his friend he'd get them in. Time passed; the movie started long before she came; I'm not sure she ever did.
>
> Throughout his adult life, Dad was absolutely, compulsively prompt. He never arrived at a train station or airport less than an hour early, often more. He became agitated, sometimes to the point of fury, if my mother held up their departure for a dinner party, and he was often the first guest to arrive. (MFB, 36)

Malamud was a time-haunted man, always feeling he was running from behind and having to catch up, yet always needing the sane reliability of order.

At a crucial point, two girlhood friends came to see Bertha, to join with Max in begging her to get well—to *try*, because the children needed her. But she made no reply, wept when she began to answer, and left the room to go upstairs again. Only Bernie could follow her, 'and she smiled in my presence, and wept because she hadn't talked to her dear friends whom she had known ever since they were girls' (HRC 33.8). In 1983, as part of his ageing efforts to recapture the family history, Malamud made fragmentary notes of a conversation he had with Anna Fidelman, his mother's kindly sister-in-law, about his mother's condition—notes floating out of the memory of the past, like the voices the mother heard, the sights she thought she saw:

> Someone comes into the store. Someone comes in and looks at her.
> She won't look into Anna's eyes.
> If you look out of window you will see a man watching me. He watches me all the time—wherever I go, his eyes follow me. (I don't want his eyes to follow you.) (HRC 20.4)

She feared the evil eye. She shouted at people in the streets. According to Eugene, 'mother said she was bit behind the ear by devils' (ibid.).

When Malamud was making notes on his friend Howard Nemerov's collection of poems *The Western Approaches* (1975), he suddenly sketched out in the midst of them a little frail poem of his own. Written more than forty-five years after her death, it was headed 'In the rain/MAMA':

> Don't go in the rain
> Not in the rain, my son, she said
> Or it will make you catch a cold
> You will get sick
> So don't go in the rain.
> Mama, when you died
> I walked in the rain.   (LC II 12.14)

'I walked in the rain' meant that finally no one could or even should protect him. To become a free man with even a normal life meant taking defiant risks and feeling the pain and the loneliness that went with them. It felt like necessary disobedience and yet was still a cry of lostness.

The little poem reappears in prose in chapter 2 of *Dubin's Lives* (1979): 'Don't go in the rain, Willie, not in the rain. You will catch a cold, the doctor will come, you will get pneumonia. Don't go, Willie, out in the rain.' Immediately preceding it, there is an account of Dubin's mother trying to commit suicide by swallowing disinfectant and the young Dubin, sent home from school early because running a fever, finding her lying upon the clean kitchen floor:

> He rushed downstairs to the drugstore and afterward induced vomiting by getting her to swallow the contents of a bottle of citrate of magnesia he had bought in panic.
>
> Yes, she whispered, yes, yes. She drank from the bottle as though famished, as though she had wanted all her life to drink the miraculous potion he served her. It would make her sane again, healthy, young—would restore her chance to have everything she hadn't had in her life. She drank her own everlasting hunger. When she recovered, her graying hair coiled in braids on her head, she promised she would never—never again.
>
> Willie, don't tell Papa I am crazy.
>
> Mama, don't say that.   (*Dubin's Lives*, chapter 2)

In the mother, there is desperate persistence of natural instincts in unhealthy contexts; in the son, the premature wounds of knowledge and responsibility. The vulnerable traits of his later life are here: the powerful intermingled language of thirst and hunger; the need for magic, or if not that, at least, a second chance. In the drafts, Malamud gives the son's final reply as first, 'Don't tell me any more. I'm only twelve,' and then 'I'm not bar-mitzvahed yet.'

There never was a proper bar-mitzvah, the ceremony that marks the coming of age of the male Jew at thirteen, by his reading a portion of the Law in the synagogue. In 1980 Malamud began working on a manuscript which he thought of as notes either for a memoir of what writing had meant to him, or possibly for a new series of short stories. It was entitled 'The Lost Bar-Mitzvah' and was never printed: 'When I was twelve,' it begins, 'one day I awoke frightened by the thought that I was doing absolutely nothing about my bar-mitzvah.' He should not have had to do anything on his own initiative:

> I reminded my father of my impending bar-mitzvah. 'Next year I'm going to be thirteen. The Jewish kids I know are getting Hebrew lessons, but not me. Do you want me to be bar-mitzvahed?' My father looked at me as if he was wondering why I was upset. He then said he wanted me to be, and promised to do something about it. I said I hoped it would be done right. My mother upbraided him for neglecting my religious education. He said he would take care of it. 'Times are bad,' he said, 'but I'll take care of it.' Yet as the months went by, he did nothing. He sat in the back of the store waiting for customers to enter—Not many did.   ('The Lost Bar-Mitzvah', HRC 33.8)

Though not an educated man, Max Malamud thought of himself as a socialist and a free thinker. He was not a member of the synagogue, did not believe in God, but wanted his son to make up his own mind. For the young Malamud this was not freedom, it felt more like not belonging. He carefully befriended Leon and Sam Snider, sons of a local Brooklyn tailor-turned-clothier who sold suits and rented tuxedos. With them he went to the synagogue, competing to see who could touch the Torah first, even though Malamud had no idea what it meant to touch the sacred scroll as it was paraded around.

> I decided to talk to a white-bearded old man whom I had seen praying at sundown, one Friday evening at the synagogue. I told him I was behind in my preparation for my bar-mitzvah and needed help. He asked me who would pay for the lessons and I hesitantly said my father would. The old man was a melamed, a Hebrew teacher, and he would teach me if my father promised to pay his usual fee for the lessons.   (ibid.)

All his life Malamud was proud that his name meant 'teacher', but generally a melamed was of low status, teaching basic Hebrew to an unwilling youth.

Though the father agreed to pay, the lessons went poorly. Malamud was starting from scratch; he did not even know the Hebrew alphabet. 'When I made a mistake the old man reached for his ruler on the table and struck the back of my hand. I was astounded, outraged. I did not cry but I cried out.' He was not used to such treatment. In later years Malamud told his own children that Max, though usually a soft man, had a bad temper. Once he chased the boy round the room with a broom until he hid beneath the bed; then, as the father tried to get at him, the huddled boy, who had a infection in his thumb, held out the wound he was trying to protect. 'The gesture characterized [him] … He believed he had suffered enough' (MFB, 24). Max did not have the heart to add to the boy's injuries.

The melamed would come to the store after school to give him his lessons, and sometimes the mother would struggle out of her bedroom and sit on the bench along the wall, watching and listening. Then there was less use of the ruler:

> 'Don't hurt his hand,' she said to the old man.
> 'You can't learn by dreaming,' he replied. 'When he doesn't learn I have to wake him.'
> 'Don't hurt his hand,' she said fearfully.
> When the old man was gone I told my mother I did not want to see him again.   ('The Lost Bar-Mitzvah', HRC 33.8)

Malamud knew he was loved by both of his parents, but with the hurt from the melamed went the last chance for a clearly defined birthright, to be ritually recognized and celebrated as a man.

Taking over from the old teacher, Max promised that he would bar-mitzvah the boy—'I know this stuff'—though the boy himself was doubtful.

> On the morning of the day I was thirteen years old, my father trudged up the stairs from the store with a pair of phylacteries in a blue cloth bag—I assume he had borrowed them from someone because I had never seen them before, and never saw them again. 'Today you are thirteen years. It's time for your bar-mitzvah.' He chanted the prayer in a sing-song. 'Blessed art thou Master of the Universe, who has made us holy by Thy Commandments, and has commanded us to wear the Tefillin.'
>
> He wound the Tefillin around my right arm and entwined them around my head and spoke the prayer again,
>
> 'Say the prayer like I do,' he said, and he recited it slowly as I spoke it after him, as accurately as I could until we both had said the prayers he had asked me to say.
>
> Then he kissed me and said I was bar-mitzvahed, and he went downstairs into the store, to wait on any customer who may have appeared.   (Ibid.)

But the boy-made-man had not had what Leon Snider had had. There was no ceremony, no presents, no raisins and nuts, or cakes and wine afterwards. Instead, he was to be forced into a more uncertain, partially formed manhood.

The man was most made in him at thirteen when he found his mother, a near suicide, on the kitchen floor and saved her. When she died two years later, his father did not tell Malamud how it had happened. Max got up 'frantically early' one morning and told Bernie he could not go to school 'because Mama was sick'. Eugene was sent off to school but the elder brother stayed in the store and 'in the afternoon a telegram came from my father to say that my mother had died' (ibid.). Later Max spoke vaguely of a sickness of some kind. Years after Malamud tried without success to find out the cause through calling up the medical records. It could have been a heart attack, since there was a history of high blood pressure, or the pneumonia she feared from the rain. But Malamud thought it was most probably suicide, perhaps through swallowing poison again. He had been the one who, aged fifteen, had had to tell Eugene, four years his junior. 'We took him for a suit on the day of the funeral, and while they were shortening the cuffs, we went outside of the store, and it was raining, and I told him. Then he said he knew—he guessed it, and I wanted to cry' (letter to Ann de Chiara, July 1942).[3] Within two years the father had re-married, without much joy.

> There had been no celebration for me, and here I was set adrift in the world to become a man and a human being on my own.
>
> I could not forgive my father.   ('The Lost Bar-Mitzvah', HRC 33.8)

'I feel I was gypped'—cheated from the very start—remained a characteristic thought and a repeated saying.[4]

But that was not the last word. There may be family quarrels and misunderstandings, write the authors of *Life Is With People*, but in the unwritten tradition 'human relations are expected to endure. There is seldom a final end to anything' (p. 304). Malamud ended 'The Lost Bar-Mitzvah' on this note:

> Years later, long after he was dead, I realized he had kept his promise to bar-mitzvah me. The ceremony was my own seeking—I like ceremonies. I sought it because I hadn't been satisfied that weekday morning before school when he took the phylacteries out of the cloth bag and uttered the words of prayer without song or dance.
>
> He had kept his promise but I found that hard to believe until I was a grown man and one day realized that he had given me what I had asked for, and I had not believed he had.   ('The Lost Bar-Mitzvah', HRC 33.8)

That phrase about not realizing it 'until I was a grown man' redeems the earlier 'set adrift to become a man'. This is a story of difficult growth and painful ambivalence, of second thoughts both on the page and off it, and of the inseparability in Malamud of what made and what marred him. It is the classic second-generation story of all that the American son found, lacked, loved, resisted, and resented in his immigrant parents.

Yet back at that seventieth birthday party in 1984, Malamud made only a little of all this: 'My mother was not a happy woman but she loved her children. She died young—in her forties. Having parents who were able to love their children was a lift to my imagination. I was from the beginning an imaginative child who told stories to express his feeling on life and the world.'

Instead of revealing more, he rather beautifully tied his story of his father's awkward tenderness to an account of his second family, though still sticking with that (for him) life-saving sense of 'imagination': 'One of the most imaginative things I ever did was to marry Ann de Chiara. We've had our ups and downs but have remained together sustained by love. A few weeks ago Ann, in sympathy, said to me "Mir soll sein far dir"'. Beneath 'in sympathy', he originally wrote: 'in relation to one disappointment or another' (HRC 29.6). For all the sympathy, this thin-skinned man never really got rid of those underlying disappointments or his toughened desire to hide them.

Although the Yiddish of 'mir far dir' linked father and wife together in this account, Malamud also knew that his atheist father had sat 'shiveh' over him—mourning and saying the prayer for dead—when in 1945 he had decided to marry an Italian Catholic in Ann de Chiara, rather than a Jewess. Imagination meant taking risks, walking in the rain, despite mother or father. The civil wedding of Ann de Chiara and Bernard Malamud took place in the Ethical Cultural Society in New York, 6 November 1945, another ceremony without frills or formal faith. Max was reconciled only when the grandchildren were born, Paul in 1947, Janna in 1952.

Ann Malamud herself remembers that her husband wrote his father a letter explaining why for the sake of his life he had to follow his heart, and that it was said that Max carried this letter about him throughout his life. In the same section of *Dubin's Lives* as 'Don't go in the rain', Dubin writes his father a note which Dubin later found on his person at his death: 'Dear Papa, How can a man be a Jew if he isn't a man? How can he be a man if he gives up the woman he wants to marry?'

December 1951: Mother and Father

Once before, outside the world of fiction, Malamud had described his beginnings, in a sort of family case-history he wrote with deliberate neutrality in late November or early December 1951 (HRC 20.2). The story goes like this:

Max, the father, was a grocer. He had come to America in 1905 or 1906 from Russia. He had had very little education, perhaps about the equivalent of a grammar school education. As a person he is a kindly man, tender, stubborn on occasions, good to his family though fundamentally unambitious. He is generally inclined to pessimism and in later years used to infuriate Bernard by his baseless pessimistic reactions to hopes and plans. In a way he is like a character from a Russian novel…. He had been very poor in Russia and apparently used to drudgery. His work in the grocery business was a continuation of that drudgery. He used to get up at six a.m. and work seven days a week, until about ten or eleven p.m., apparently the kind of life he was used to and the only kind he would respect.   (HRC 20.2)

Malamud's later notes from 1976 ('Family History') fill in the details. Max (originally Mendel) Malamud was born in 1885, the youngest of four closely attached brothers, with two older sisters and one younger. As a young man Mendel lived in a poor shtetl near Kamenets-Podoloski within the restrictions of the Jewish Pale of Settlement in the Ukraine. Amidst a rising tide of anti-Semitism and pogroms, he fled the country, hidden in a haywagon, to avoid conscription to the Russian army in the war against Japan. But his situation was not unusual. In the thirty three years between the assassination of the liberal Tsar Alexander II in 1881 and the outbreak of the First World War, one-third of all East European Jews left their homeland in the face of the harsher regime of Alexander III. It was a massive modern exodus. In 1880 there were 80,000 Jews in New York; by 1910, 1,100,000.

When Max got to America he joined his religious brother Dudye and his wife in a five-storey walk-up in Brooklyn. For some time he worked for another brother, Matis, now known as Morris Cohen, and his partner Isaac Schmuckler, selling butter and eggs to small stores. These two brothers in particular were keen to Americanize themselves, committed to the work ethic and the freedom to better oneself. But at some point Max fell out with Matis and eventually made common cause with Schmuckler's brother Ben to open a 'fancy' grocery store of their own on 15th Avenue, Borough Park in Brooklyn.

It was possible that Max had already met Bertha Fidelman, born in 1888, back in the old country, in Kamenets-Podoloski. One of four children, she was proud of coming from a finer family than his, her father having been the town's chief shochet (ritual slaughterer of meat), her grandfather a rabbi. Bernard Malamud was to be named after the father, Baruch. Only her brother, Casile, came over to America, working as a prompter in the Yiddish theatre; the parents and two sisters remained in the old country. Bertha badly missed her mother and would write tearful letters to her.

Introduced or re-introduced in Brooklyn, Bertha and Max married in 1910, the year she arrived in America, and lived first of all on Flushing Avenue, in a decent neighbourhold, mostly Jewish but also containing Italian and Irish families, on the edge of the Williamsburg section of Brooklyn. Max may have bought a grocery store as early as 1911 in partnership with a man named Britchky (LC II 11.14). Bernard was born in 1914, Eugene in 1917. In 1919 the young family moved to the rather superior grocery store on 15th Avenue. Within a year, however, the partner, Ben Schmuckler, had made off with all the money, or so Malamud believed, and Max had to sell up.

Helped by brother Matis, despite their earlier break-up, he bought another, much smaller store on 1111 Gravesend Avenue, so-called because situated near the cemetery to the east of Flatbush, with a new partner, Morris Wolin, whom Bertha also distrusted. When that too failed, he took another little store back in Williamsburg, the family living in Ellery Street, in a house (Malamud dimly recalled) 'with toilets in the hall'—only to move on to another in Church Avenue and East 4th Street, again with Wolin. This was again in the neighbourhood of Flatbush, in a more Gentile setting, consisting of mainly Irish and German families, with Jewish shopkeepers. By then, some time in the 1920s, Max had had enough of partners and decided to go it alone in Rogers Avenue and Albemarle Road, only to return finally to 1111 Gravesend Avenue around 1924–5. There Max set up a German-type deli, selling cheap canned goods, bread, vegetables, some cheese, and cooked meats. Unlike the Christian stores he stayed open on Sundays. Though now a seller of ham, he would close occasionally on Jewish holy days, just to show the Gentiles they were still Jews.

Burt Rush, a schoolfriend, described the store to Malamud's son, Paul, in an unpublished interview:

> The store was not unique—it was one of a group of row stores, typical of its kind, with a ground floor, and above that one or two floors with apartments. These were not very high buildings because the elevated train ran right past them, to the right of the roof. All that separated the building from the El was a sidewalk and a one-lane paved road, enough for a car to pass through with maybe a foot on each side, then you had these colossal iron and stone concrete pillars that supported the tracks. It was always noisy, and it shut out the sunlight.

There in the gloom of Gravesend Avenue the Malamuds remained, and though later the name was changed to McDonald Avenue, Gravesend was an apt title for Max's commercial career. Mrs Levine remembered Max and his second wife in 'a rather dreary and depressing store' in the early thirties when she was about ten years old:

I don't know how old they were then, but as a child they seemed older and very sad … My sister said that the woman spent a good deal of time sitting outside the store. The store had a long counter and a short counter, and they waited on customers at the short counter. They moved slowly and the prices were added up on a paper bag, which was usual at that time. Butter was cut from tubs in a case against the wall, and I vaguely remember bringing a can to have milk ladled into it.… The two of them never smiled and took care of business without much conversation between customers other than what was absolutely necessary. I remember high shelves with groceries, many of which had to be gotten down with a long pole.[5]

'It was not very good anywhere until the Depression,' said Malamud, adding laconically, 'then it was bad' (HRC 29.6).

It had hardly been idyllic even when Bertha had been alive and at home. 'Though our childhood was happy, because Max and Bertha were loving parents, it was meagre in terms of family life and things cultural.' Because they lived above and behind the store, there was an all-consuming store life rather than a family life. They ate in the back of the store: 'nobody starved', said Malamud, but at another level 'my hungers were already deep and endless' (HRC 33.8). Although Bertha devoted herself all too much to her children and rarely went out, the young Malamud as that 'special' child was trusted freely to wander the neighbourhood, a street boy. 'My life was laissez-faire, no orthodoxy, I had little direction at home—they thought I was a good boy and would turn out well' (HRC 29.6). But the parents' own social lives were empty; they never visited friends or mixed with other families, who were known as outsiders. [6]

There was some contact with the wider family. Malamud particularly remembered Frima (or Florence), his father's younger sister who was the lively comic vulgarian of the family. 'Once she met me on Church Avenue on Brooklyn as I waited for a trolley cart. She handed me an apple. "Eat," she said, "It's good for the bowels."' One of her best curses was 'Let her wash her feet and drink the water' ('Family History'). But best of all, from Malamud's point of view, it was the scatter-brained Frima, married but without children of her own, who 'seemed to have understood that Bern was special' (HRC 29.6). Bertha's brother Casile Fidelman, Americanized as Charles, believed that his sister 'had the capacity and imagination to live but that Max didn't'. The Fidelmans were involved in the life of the Yiddish theatre, Casile had written plays in Argentina before coming over to the States, and Malamud first thought that he had got his creative talent from that side of the family. It was Casile who believed that the young Malamud, aged fifteen, was destined for fame and fortune. It was Casile who listened to the boy when he was unhappy at home with a new stepmother, and later it was Casile who welcomed Malamud and his Catholic wife into his home when Max initially rejected his son for marrying out of the faith.

Inside the store it was a mainly Yiddish-speaking household. Max and Bertha confined their reading to the Jewish paper, *The Daily Forward*. There were no books or magazines in the house, Malamud recalled, save for some broken-backed works in Yiddish. No one read them to him and he never knew what they said. The parents resorted to speaking their native Russian to each other only when they did not want the boys to know what they were saying:

> She and Max had many quarrels some severe, principally, as I remember it, over where he spat, and how he went around before the children. Naturally, the children were frightened of these 'fights'. Once Bertha asked Bernard if he would go with her if she left Max. He wept, and she said, 'No no, my child.'
>   (HRC 20.2)

It is no wonder that Malamud came to admire D. H. Lawrence's *Sons and Lovers*, with its autobiographical account of the ill-matched parents, the rough miner with the sensitive lady who, like Bertha, seemed to have known a better life. A key sentence for Malamud was when Lawrence said of the father that he had 'denied the god in him' (HRC 20.5). The Brooklyn father was meant to be 'The Jew, The Man, the one who most literally is made in God's image' (*Life Is With People*, 296). Like Lawrence's Walter Morel, Max would spit on the floor, walk around carelessly in his longjohns. At home on Sundays, Malamud told Daniel Stern, all he could do was listen yearningly to someone else's piano through the living room window (TH, 12): 'I was moved by the music being played by someone in one of the houses nearby, perhaps a girl my age, and was hungry to hear more of it' (HRC 33.8).

Malamud's schoolfriend George Markowitz (now Martin) remembered how Max, a gruff, bald-headed man, heavy-set, illustrated 'the hardship of life, of a Jewish life': 'His father was—I didn't use the word then when I first met his father but now, looking back, the word I would use would be "dour". His father could look at things and say "What do you expect? Life is tough, full of hardship and you had to endure it and live through it"'.[7]

Malamud remembered his father lighting a long match and, as he watched it burn, praising Eugene V. Debs, the American socialist, for wanting to do something for somebody else besides himself, or reciting little verses he had learned in night school when he first arrived—then hastily lighting his cigarette at the very last second (HRC 33.8). But he was also the sort of man who often had to look away from what was around him. Eugene remembered him as Bernard did at the opening of the short story 'The Grocery Store': inattentive to the salesman's weekly offers, going off the point, closing one eye—then getting angry when the despairing salesman did not call back and dictating a hotly indignant postcard to the National Biscuit Company: 'Where is he hiding? Is he dead?'[8] After Max's death, Eugene wrote to Malamud, 24 September 1954 : 'Pa, he offered no one any help in understanding his needs'; and earlier on 3 April 1954: 'Had he learned better to express his love, perhaps we would all have been happy; or, instinctively was he asking us to discover for ourselves the love lying there, in his heart, real, strong and unshakeable, in spite of crises and recriminations' (HRC 13.1). Perhaps in such implicitness there was a test only a novelist had the imagination to pass. Indeed in a notebook used for the writing of *The Assistant* (then known as 'The Apprentice'), Malamud writes, on page 64, of his fictional equivalent of the family in the store: 'Poverty isolates. There is immanent love in this family—you can depend on it—but otherwise it is not there' (HRC 19.1). It could get lost amidst difficulties and buried in its unspokenness. Eugene also knew all about these emotionally complex, inarticulate family communications. He wrote out for his brother a piece of dialogue when 'Pop' was in hospital after a heart attack in February 1953—he died a month later:

E: Pa, does the light bother you?
P: Yes, it bothers me and so do you.
E: Excuse me (putting out light and leaving foolishly mortified).
   But the next day I said
   Pa, does the light bother you?
PA: No it doesn't bother me and you don't bother me.   (HRC 13.1)

This was a man who knew contrition.

But the store had narrowed and oppressed him, as the son acknowledged, and, without resources to find another life, the oppression was something he passed on:

> Both boys remember being belittled by him often—in the sense of his making light of their accomplishments. No harm was meant by him—it was just his nature. He pooh-poohed anything they accomplished, though secretly he seemed pleased. It was almost as if his attitude were: how can anything that comes from me possibly achieve anything? Not so direct as that—but such an attitude seemed to underly his deprecatory remarks. Things were 'good' for a while now and then, but never steadily so.   (HRC 20.2)

He was, Malamud concluded, 'a loving but unimaginative husband and father'. For all the hard-working stoicism, that word 'unimaginative' is a mark of what the son alternatively strove for, from imagination, in the face of this discouraging, fearful disbelief in life: a sense of what he habitually called 'possibility' or 'freedom'.

Yet Max Malamud was also a man easily moved and at his kindest when people were ill or in trouble. It was as a result of illness that at the age of nine Malamud was given *The Book of Knowledge*, a child's encyclopedia in twenty volumes. He had caught the pneumonia so feared by his mother. The doctor had been about to pronounce him dead when an injection of digitalis kicked in and the heart began beating again (HRC 29.6). In celebration of his recovery, the volumes were Malamud's first home-based introduction to the English-language world of knowledge and learning, as well as a rare present for the boy. They were Max's life-gift to him.

A first cousin, a daughter of Matis, Florence Hodes had seen something of this compassion in her uncle Max. She later told Malamud that she remembered his father as a man of high ideals, of a sentimental nature, who would sing sad Yiddish songs to her and recite poems. In the early days he had gone to night school, studying English, German, and algebra, where he was tutored by Ben Becker: 'My father loaned him money to go to Med. School. Dr Becker took care of my father in his last illness. He said my father wanted to die' ('Family History'). This was corroborated by another cousin, Mathis Silverman, who wrote to Malamud that, above all, his father admired education: 'What wouldn't he do for that magic thing *Education*? Why, he even befriended some strange fellow, a poor medical student, and actually helped him become a doctor. He helped him with paying his rent, buying those costly text books, and when he graduated, helped him establish himself in a doctor's office. He did all that while he himself was a hard labourer, working for his brother' ('Family History'). Malamud told Daniel Stern that for all the family poverty, in his house he 'never heard a word in praise of the buck' (TH, 12).

Florence Hodes also told Ann Malamud that Max was particularly kind to her on two important occasions in her early life. Once when she stole a small amount of money from her mother's purse, she confessed it to her uncle who told her not to worry, that he would put aside money for her to pay it back. Later, after the death of her mother she told him how upset she was by her father's plans to remarry and Max got Matis to agree to wait till Florence was in high school.

But what Florence found in Max as uncle the son did not always find in Max as father. Despite his own advice to Matis, for example, Max himself re-married. That second marriage seemingly did no one any good. Admittedly, Malamud was aged about seventeen when Max married Liza (Elizabeth)

Merov, but fairly or unfairly he hated his stepmother and blamed his father
for marrying her. When years later his own son Paul asked him if Liza had
done anything good for him, he thought for a while and could only say,
'She helped me get out of the house.' An unpublished short story written
around 1953, ironically entitled 'How I Got Rid of My Stepmother', offers
an uneasily black-comic account of how a father brings a new woman into
the home—in order to get the grown-up kids to leave it. But again the 1951
memoir puts it neutrally:

> For two years after Bertha's death ... Max cooked and he and Bernard cleaned
> the house. Later he remarried, a woman not used to his sort of life. She was a
> 'greenhorn', and did not know how to approach the children, nor they her. She
> devoted herself to the store. There was still no family life. However, it was her
> hard-headedness that pulled Max out of the economic rut he was in. Neither
> of the boys had any affection for their step-mother.   (HRC 20.2)

The hard-headedness may have been partly the sort of toughness that the
second wife Bessie shows in the wonderful short story 'The Loan' when she
won't let her soft baker-husband give precious money to an old estranged
friend because of the terrible insecurity of the past she has known in Russia, in
Poland, and in Germany. As a 'greenhorn', a recent immigrant who had not
yet learned the ways of her new country, Liza had her own troubled memories.
In Russia she had been relatively well off and married with children, but then
something awful had happened to her. Ann Malamud thought Liza's husband
and sons may have been murdered in a pogrom. At any rate, Eugene later
wrote to his brother, 1 January 1949, that 'Pa confessed that the menopause
began or was beginning when she first married him' (HRC 12.8). There were
severe mood swings, marital rows triggered by Max refusing to take her out,
then long depressive silences on her part. Eugene wrote again, 15 March 1950,
'I hope pop doesn't have to put his second wife in an institution. I think it
would kill him' (HRC 12.8).

It is no wonder that in later years Malamud was so glad of glimpses
of the normalizing of past family life further down the generations. Charles
Kopelman is the grandson of Anna Fidelman, Malamud's aunt on his mother's
side. He remembers the night before his own bar-mitzvah in January 1969
when Malamud was at the height of his fame:

> He came to the house on Friday night, alone, without Ann. My grandmother
> looked at him when he came in, just looked at him, and said, 'You need a
> haircut.' And he said, 'Okay, fine.' She took him into the bathroom and took
> off his shirt. He had no pretensions about him, with her, just to sit there in
> his tee shirt. He sat there in front of the mirror and my grandmother went in

and gave him a trim, neatened up his hair and everything for him, and he was chatting. I think a lot of what he sought from her was the maternal affection he didn't have himself, and didn't have with his stepmother, that my grandmother was able to provide for him. But that image of him getting his hair cut is kind of childlike, because his aunt said he needed a haircut and tomorrow's the bar-mitzvah.[9]

When some years later Charles and his brother Kenny met at a Christmas party at the Malamud apartment in New York, they kissed each other as they always did, but Malamud watching cried out, 'Look at that! I never—To see two brothers greet each other that way!' Their father had died when Charles was only eleven, and Malamud came to the house of shiveh and took the boy into the den and said 'If you need anything, I want you to know that you can ask me for that. I'll give you whatever it is that I can give you.' After the grandfather died and the building in which the widowed Anna lived was being pulled down, Malamud said to Jean who was Anna's daughter and Charles' mother: 'If you cannot afford to keep her, I will.' Still, both Charles and Jean regretted that Malamud never really brought his own new family in much contact with what remained of the Fidelmans. 'It does feel like very separate times that he spent with us.'

Even so, these were the easier forms of memory, alleviating his own pain through a parallel alleviation of others'. But there was something else that Malamud particularly remembered, which was more painfully to do with his father and money and family-honesty, and which requires careful unfolding.

In her own memoir, Malamud's daughter, Janna, recalls her father interrogating her about her taking some bread between meals, and her adamantly denying she had done so. She was aged only four. He told her the classic, exemplary American stories about the need for honesty: how the young George Washington said he could never tell a lie; how Abraham Lincoln working in a grocery store and accidentally overcharging a woman by a nickel or dime ran after her barefoot in the snow to return the money. At much the same time, she now thinks, her father was finishing *The Assistant* in which the grocer's daughter recalls her father, Morris, running two blocks in the snow to give back to a poor Italian lady a nickel that she forgot on the counter—almost foolishly for sheer honesty's sake. Morris was modelled on Max Malamud. It is a wonderful glimpse of Malamud almost simultaneously as father, as writer, as son—characteristically, the three all connected at the deepest level of his mind, but at every other level kept ever so slightly separate from each other.

But honesty was also a problem. 'As a young man,' writes Janna, 'my father may have wondered if Max-like honesty would entrap him in an equally claustrophobic life. Or his ambition could also have made him feel dishonest—the desire held as a false claim or as a filial dishonesty' (MFB, 14). In particular, she recalls how—as he also admitted in his interview with Daniel Stern—it bothered her father his whole life that the honest grocer-father had once cut the boy short and called him a 'bluffer' for lengthily elaborating upon a story which he claimed to be factual (TH, 26). This was the talent in which Bernie cleverly excelled—the gift of re-telling to the other children the stories he had seen at the movies, when they couldn't go, earned him popular attention and praise in return for his power of imagination. But here was blame for it from his own father, in the reductive complaint of the plain man. It was as though the gift of storytelling that led to his being a novelist—and eventually a novelist who could defend a poor grocer's honesty—might be founded upon something as bad as the capacity for lying.

But something worse lay behind that memory of his father calling him a bluffer for telling stories. On one of those small white pieces of paper that Malamud used to take notes, left unnoticed on his desk the day he died, is this tiny confession to be found among the Malamud papers in Austin, Texas:

> I went through a period of stealing quarters from his till. One Sunday he caught me and my shame [was] so great I wanted to die. Perhaps I was 10 then. At first I denied it. He called me bluffer and made me give the coins to him.   (HRC 20.3)

It was just another version of what Florence Hodes, and countless other children, had done, and in both cases the money had to be paid back. Schoolfriends who came from families far better off than Malamud's had noticed that Bernie always had anything from fifteen cents to a quarter in his pocket when they did not. '15 or 25 cents in a child's hand was a lot of money. You've got to remember that 25 cents bought 5lbs of potatoes in those days'.[10] This was a boy who was ashamed to bring his friends back to the store. But the money gave him some power, a sense of being able to buy things for his friends, a chance to impress the girls. 'I was sympathetic,' said George Martin, 'towards the things that he lacked, or that life didn't give him.'

But Malamud himself could not forgive it. If ever his father called him a bluffer again, it reminded him of how his stories were at some level a matter not only of showing off but of covering up. They were associated with need and guilt and theft and concealment. In particular, that shameful story of how he had been caught stealing sums from his own father, in that struggling and impoverished store, was not something he was ever going to pass on to his own daughter. Janna reports how in 1985 it was still painful

to him even to tell her of how he stole a movie advert from a nearby store
and placed it instead in his father's, to try to win some free tickets. She was
asking him for stories, trying to get him to think about an autobiography,
or leave matter for a biography. He stole some apples, he said, he sneaked
a free ride to Coney Island on the El. But, only minutes in, he had to ask
her to erase the tape on which she was recording what he confessed. 'Most
raconteurs, sixty years later, would have relished their own ingenuity, and
laughed. Yet it was almost unbearable for him to tell it'—partly because he
always wanted to be the father who could serve as a teacherly model; partly
because he always wanted to protect both himself and the family he had
made from the painfulness and shameful deprivation of the family in which
he had grown up; but also because he had 'an angry, deprived kid within
himself who wanted to grab what he knew wasn't his. And while his inner
life was hardly unusual, the persona didn't fit with his larger sense of who he
wanted to be. By the time I knew him, he was meticulous about paying what
he owed' (MFB, 56).

The memory went into the writing instead, in indirect and complicated ways which have to do with what Malamud loved most of all as a
writer—revisions and transmutations of the elements of his experience. It
was what he called, in the shift and turn of his many-sided family conflicts and ambivalences, 'combinations': 'I want constantly to surprise—not
astonish—the way life surprises in the possibility of its combinations'
(HRC 27.5). Autobiographical essence, he always said, not autobiographical
detail.

But, in its relation to his father, the writing came out of something closer
to a vision than merely a change of point of view. Hidden in the recording
of the interview on his sixtieth birthday that Malamud gave Daniel Stern in
1974 for the *Writers at Work* series of *Paris Review* interviews, there is a story
about the relation of son and father in the transcript of the tape that was
never finally put into print:

> I remember once having this experience, in walking past his store as he was
> sitting in it, and I could see all the way through the store, through the little
> window that had been cut into the wall at the back, and watching him sitting
> at a table, reading his newspaper, and I felt a strong throb of something for
> him.   (LC II 14.1)

Max had looked up hungrily, looking for a customer. It had often been that
way. When after Bertha's breakdown, Max could no longer get an afternoon
break upstairs to have what he called a 'driml', a little dream, he would take
a restless nap at the back of the store, listening out for the store door. Then

he would wake up, slap water on his face, and walk straight back into his daily nightmare: 'Sometimes no one was present when he entered. It seemed as if someone had been there and gone elsewhere—my father could not say' (HRC 33.8). At this time Malamud was at college, and now from somewhere more outside it all, he looked back in through the store window:

> and I felt, my God, here's this man sitting here 16 hours a day, waiting for someone to come into the place, what a shameful waste of life, and existence, and all that, and why does he do it? Why does he allow himself to be victimized in this particular way, and, you know, it's a form of imprisonment, and I was conscious of that, and I wanted better for him, you know, I really felt a strong sympathy for him. He was a good man, he was a nice man, he was a kind man, and I feel, you know, just eternally grateful to him.   (LC II. 14.1)

He was getting away from the store, walking past, only then to see it from outside and re-imagine it from within. In that confusing and painful mixture of pity and exasperation—'a strong throb of *something*'—Malamud 'wanted better for him'. But instead the son had to want better for himself: the imaginative sympathy and the countervailing need for distance, or even escape, went hand-in-hand. In notes for his memoirs that he was making in July 1980, Malamud writes of one potential theme above all others—himself as 'the observer of Max, Bertha, Eugene': 'Ambivalent, involved and fighting for objectivity, freedom'. He writes of 'the birth of compassion' with which, significantly, he puts the next word: 'sadness'. It was that shift of point of view to something he called more 'objective' which made him a writer. Torn between the rival claims of loyal affection and irritated judgement, Malamud had seen his father as if for the first time, as also a separate human being. It was another revised estimate.

'He called me bluffer.' In the writing itself, the memory went first of all into a prize-winning essay that Malamud wrote at Erasmus Hall High School in 1932, 'Life—From Behind A Counter'. In his youth he had had to work behind the counter. If he was slow, Max would get angry and shame him in front of the customers. Once a well-dressed woman humiliated him by letting him cut her one type of cheese and then claiming she had wanted another. His father, as he recorded it in 'Life—From Behind A Counter', did not come to his aid: the customer was always right. She left the shop with 'a very well enunciated and perfectly pronounced "Stupid"'. He was the clever boy; he didn't like this sort of serving. But he also learnt something:

> Samuel Johnson learned that it was good to be honest from his mother. A thick volume elaborating on the subject didn't teach him anything new. I learned

that it was good to be honest from my parents. But experience with dishonest people and the knowledge of the consequences of their dishonesty taught me more than a thousand books.

Those dishonest people included two kids who one day held up his father's store at gunpoint. Two detectives caught them months later on another job and brought them to the store for identification. A few days before the trial, however, the parents of the younger of the boys came to beg Max to drop the charge. He did so for one significant reason—because 'I guess my father thought of my younger brother and me'. About one year later, the boy came into the store and blushingly introduced himself. He had made good, he was going to be married: he thanked the grocer for giving him a second chance and said that he now realized what happiness was.

One day some time after—the essay reports—the meat salesman told the young Malamud, renowned as 'Der Schule Boy': 'I bet vat you see in vun day, undt vat you hear in vun day from dese people—you can write a leetle book about.' But the clever, ambitious young Malamud made a silent retort: that one day he could and would write a *big* book about such things. It would be called 'Life—From Behind a Counter'.

In fact it was called *The Assistant* (1957), a big book that arose out of the short stories that the Erasmus mini-manifesto helped encourage into existence—in particular, 'The Grocery Store' (1943) and 'The Cost of Living' (1950).

'I wanted better for him' is the key note to both. In the first, which remained unpublished until after his death, the grocer, Sam, and his wife quarrel in a failing store—'Please', she says haughtily, 'please, to me you will speak with respect. I wasn't brought up in my father's house a grocer should—you'll excuse me—a grocer should spit on me every time he talks'. Sam stomps upstairs for a sleep, only carelessly to turn on the gas fire without lighting it, with near-disastrous results that utterly affect the wife.

In the second, the grocer, originally from Kamenets-Podolski and again called Sam, faces with his wife the disaster of competition from a brand new grocery store right next door. What had he got for twenty-seven years of labour? 'The back-breaking sixteen-hour day like a heavy hand slapping, upon awaking, the skull, pushing the head down to bend the body's bones; the hours; the work, the years, my God, and where is my life now?' The couple sell up and leave the store to painful memories Sam cannot bear to look back upon.

Malamud told Michiko Kakutani in an article on 'Authors and Parents' in *The New York Times Book Review*, 16 August 1981, that he proudly mailed a copy of 'The Cost of Living' to his father when it was published in

Harper's Bazaar, in March 1950: 'We didn't talk much, but when I sent him the story it was a way of getting close to him, to show him what I could do. I think he appreciated it—writing to him was almost the new land.' Writing was a triumph of education—though really Max had wanted his son to be a lawyer. But writing also came out of the failures of speaking. Crucially, Malamud told his colleague at Bennington, Reinhard Mayer, that 'the particular voice he had in mind when he was writing, the particular English he wrote, was something that was in memory of the way his father spoke.'[11]

The storylines from both tales are combined in *The Assistant* with the story of Frank Alpine, one of two masked young men who first holds up the grocer, as in 'Life—From Behind A Counter'; but who in the second place secretly returns to work for the old man free of charge; only then, thirdly, to begin to steal back small change from the till. Max became Morris Bober. But Frank the deprived and hungry young man, the betraying stealer and liar, secretly comes out of that ten-year-old son who also wanted some cents in his pocket.

Says the grocer in Malamud's second draft of the novel, when Frank asks him why he doesn't try out a few sharp tricks on his customers, to increase his tender profits:

> 'Why should I steal from somebody that they don't steal from me?'
> Frank looked away.
> 'When you are honest your heart feels clean,' Morris said.
> 'I know,' said Frank.
> But he continued to steal. He would stop for a few days then almost with relief go back to it. There were times stealing made him feel good.   (LC I 2.2, p. 82)

Even in the draft, in all that lies beneath the final polishing, the structural paragraphing is quietly brilliant in giving a wincingly silent language to what is customarily hidden and denied. Frank is the bluffer and bad son par excellence. Like a part of Malamud, he 'knows' only in reverse, from the other side of the track where the heart feels not clean but dirty. Yet he nonetheless 'continues' in ways that both follow from and contradict what went before. He still tries to feel 'good' in a way that seeks with desperate emotion to avoid the moral meaning of goodness—but then 'he could not explain why, from one day to another, he should begin to feel bad'. Not knowing why was, for Malamud, where the art began.

Very late on in the composition of *Dubin's Lives*, at proof-stage, Malamud went back to Samuel Johnson, to whom he referred in 'Life—From Behind A Counter', to add this paragraph to the opening of chapter 9:

He remembered Dr Johnson in the marketplace at Uttoxeter, standing bare-headed in the rain where his father's bookstall had been. Years before, the old bookseller, ailing that day, had asked his son to go there in his place and his son refused. 'Pride prevented me.' Fifty years later Samuel Johnson, an old man, laboriously journeyed to the market and stood an hour in the rain by the stall his father had once used, to do for the dead man what he hadn't done.

It was another sign to his now dead father, in Malamud's secret language.

For *Dubin's Lives* finished what *The Assistant* began—Malamud's recon-ciliation with his equivocal inheritance. In 1979 Malamud dedicated *Dubin's Lives* to 'Max and Bertha, my father and mother' in memory and 'for Anna Fidelman' still living. It was a story of marriage and troubled middle age in a world grown far different from their own in the twenties. In a notebook which he put together between April 1970 and October 1971, in preparation for the writing of *Dubin* (then entitled 'The Juggler'), Malamud says of his protagonist on page 26, 'He is like his immigrant father—fearful in life (without knowing it) except that he has read some books. He is quite surprised to learn how close to his father's his nature is.' And on page 33 he speaks of himself as 'missing the feminine after the death of his mother and in a sense throughout his life' (HRC 19.3).

Moe Moss, an old neighbour from Brooklyn still living on McDonald Avenue, wrote to Malamud, 14 October 1963, having seen a picture of the now-celebrated author in the newspaper: 'Seriously, you look very much like "Max" when I first knew him.' On reading *Dubin*, he wrote again, 26 June 1979, 'Your dedication to Max and Bertha evoked memories of "gentle Max" standing behind the counter with his dreams of a socialist society' (HRC 9. 2).

5 November 1951: Brother Eugene

Malamud told Kakutani in 1981 that, some time after the publication of 'The Cost of Living', he received a note back from his father quietly signed 'Sam', the name of the fictional grocer, 'a touching acknowledgement that I'd written a story based on his own experience'. Eugene also wrote his brother that their father put the story away in a drawer but on hearing it described as a 'contribution' to the magazine was suddenly worried that Bernie wasn't paid for it. But the only letter that is in existence from 1950 and is signed 'Your father, Sam' is this in the awkward assertive pain of its broken English:

I think you did a foolish thing by moving away from us. If you can get a job in Bklyn as a regular teacher you will be better off. Any time any body who moves away from N.Y. state is sorry.[12]

Malamud had moved out of Gravesend Avenue into pleasant one-room lodgings in a tree-lined street in Flatbush in 1942; then he married Ann in 1945 and moved to King Street Greenwich Village. But this letter refers to the life-saving move all the way out to the west coast, to Corvallis where Malamud took up a teaching position in Oregon State College in 1949.

Worse followed this sad letter of severance. A letter of 5 November 1951 is simply signed 'With a broken heart':

My Dear Son Bernie,
I'm verry verry saury to tell you that Eugenes sickness went from bad to worse! Since you left from New York he was talken to himself all that time.

'Since you left'. The letter goes on in halting spelling:

October 30, 1951 he came from Dr Jolowicz and he stard to talk foolish things. So I called Dr Becker and Becker called Jolowicz and we decited that the best place for him will be the hospital.

Eugene was suicidal. In terms of links, it wasn't only that this Dr Becker was the student Max had supported long before. The sole hospital the doctors could get Eugene into was Kings Country—where Bertha, the mother, had first been taken.

Eugene himself wrote his brother three days later, on 8 November 1951, that 'since mom died maybe I have to die too, but I don't think that has to be so'. It is what Max was to call his 'Bad luck Story' (15 November) which he now related to the doctors, like a sort of Brooklyn Greek tragedy.

This is the reason why the memoir, which is the source of much that is known about the early life, was written by Malamud in November or December 1951. It was actually a long letter he wrote specifically to Eugene's doctors, to provide background family information to aid diagnosis. Written in the third person rather than the first, that is why it was so clinical. What it described was the mother's schizophrenia coming out all over again:

Almost from the beginning Eugene had difficulty in school. Bernard, who was bright and capable, aggressive and somewhat authoritarian, possibly because he was overpraised by his parents, made a name for himself in school, which his teachers tried to make Eugene live up to. Bernard was always the recipient of complaints about Eugene. From an early age he acted in loco parentis for Eugene. As a result, Eugene disliked and sometimes resisted school. Bernard had 'power' over Eugene and frequently used his younger brother as an errand boy. When Eugene protested, he was hit by Bernard.   (HRC 20.2)

'I looked after him when I thought of it,' he wrote later, 'but was short of patience and used to sock him in the back when he didn't do what I wanted. He cried. No one told me to cut it out' (HRC 33.8). The father was too much worried about his sick wife and his meagre business. In a letter dated April 1952 Eugene recalls Bernie wanting Eugene to hit him back—'that night when you told me you had hit me as a kid and that you were responsible for my trouble, which I don't think is true, but it was brave of you to welcome the blow' (HRC 12.10). One simple action could resolve nothing, said Eugene. In fact, the younger brother was to live on with all his mental troubles until he died of a heart attack in 1973.

'My trouble', as Eugene called it, had begun early. For Bernie, a trip to Coney Island on the El was 'an enormous adventure': 'The ocean (not the sea) moved me deeply' (HRC 29.6). But when Eugene travelled to Coney to go swimming, he always wondered 'whether I would return home alive or be drowned' (HRC 12.7, 3 November 1945). Even back in July 1942 Malamud was worriedly writing his future wife about years of Eugene's 'many silent fears':

> When he was about twelve, he spat in the gutter outside of a church. The boy he was with said he had committed a sin. He came home pale, but he didn't say any thing. At night when we were in bed, in the dark I heard him sobbing. I was about fifteen. I got out of bed and put my arms around his shoulders, and later he told me what he did. I said it wasn't a bad thing; then he stopped crying a little bit.

The memoir recalls:

> The first strangeness Bernard noticed about his brother was during Eugene's early adolescence. He would sometimes look sidewise at the window as if he was afraid of something outside of it. After a while this symptom and fear seemed to go away.   (HRC 20.2)

Nothing ever really went away. One of Max's own letters to Bernie, with the business going to hell and Eugene sick, ends with the sad factual postscript 'To day Jan 9th 1905 I Came to America 47 years ago'. As if to say: all that, for this to happen, and to happen twice. It is in these terrible loops, twists, and ironies that facts are turned into story, into memory and feeling.

The father's letters, kept by Ann Malamud in her flat, are often written in thick, heavily pressed pencil, on the brown paper that Max used to reckon bills and wrap packages in the store. 'When you talk to him you see he is a Sick Person'; 'any time I see him I go home with a Broken heart'; 'I don't think that he Will be all right Soon.' The man and his language are trapped in the situation of helpless quasi-objectivity, repeating and passing on hospital instructions: 'Don't send to Eugene Raiser blats or a knife. he is Not allowed to have Such thing You have to be very Carefull With Such Patients You can't Trust them' (7 January 1952). 'Bernie let me know if you Understand my writing if not I will have Somebody to write the letters for Me,' he writes on 15 November 1951, adding what might cause laughter if it didn't make for tears: 'I Asked Eugene how he spels psychiatrist and he speled that for me.' He adds: 'I talk to him like a good father can talk to a child I kiss him and I Bring to him Fruit and Cigarettes.' As Eugene had put it before his illness, 'Pa said he likes to capitalize the words because it makes them big and meaningful' (1 July 1950).

Some time late in 1951, Max writes this about money, the son who has gone away, and the anxious stepmother, with the pains and ironies unexpressed:

> Bernie if you thing that you Wont to See Eugene I thing that Christmas time you will be Able to make it, Don't worry for money. I will give a few Hundred Dollars more ... Don't let Leza Know about Money. Don't write anything about it. Don't worry about Money.

But Malamud did not come back at Christmas. In his new life, he had only two weeks off and one would have to be spent on the journey, he says in a letter of 28 November. Moreover, Ann was in the eighth month of her second pregnancy, with a young, often poorly boy also to look after. 'Your family come first,' Max replied, with approval, on 3 December, telling Malamud to come in June instead when he might be more useful. Three times a week the father struggled to travel out to the hospital. Eugene had asked for his brother only when he was first admitted. 'If Eugene was interested in you he would have asked for you', Max writes simply.

On 7 January 1952 there is this, painfully:

> Dear Bernie
> I saw Eugene Sunday he told me that he received writing paper and a Pen from you. But he trough Every thing out The Window. Wen I went home he saw me Standing Waiting Outside for Taxes he said To me through the Window Pop look here maybe you will find the Pen. I was looking But I Coulnt find her.

It is not difficult to imagine the novelist reading this, as though life had offered its symbols. It just had to be 'a Pen', the pen which the brother gave Eugene to write to him instead of his being there, the pen that was to keep Malamud out of Brooklyn even by writing of the place. And it also had to be a 'Window'. For it was through a window in the store that, in a sense, Malamud first really saw his father. And it was through a window in a mental hospital that Malamud last saw his mother, as Ann Malamud described it:

> One time his father took him to the mental institution. He did not go in to see her. Now I don't know whether it wasn't permitted, or what it was, but his mother came to the window, and they waved to one another and that was the last time he saw his mother.[13]

2

◄◇◇◇►

The Long Adolescence

The Brooklyn Education

A favourite Malamud sentence of Philip Roth's, from the collection *The Magic Barrel*, was 'A child throwing a ball straight up saw a bit of pale sky.'[1] That child, finding a sudden glimpse of light and space amidst narrowed circumstances, was also Malamud himself, as he put it in a letter to Sidney Richman, 12 May 1963:

> My response to nature was always strong. It was thrilling to go to Prospect Park in Brooklyn. When I was sixteen, at the invitation of a school friend, I made my first trip out of the city (except for an excursion to Bear Mt. or a flight when I was two or three and there was a polio epidemic) to the Adirondacks, and the effect of nature was overwhelming. (I took to Wordsworth with a wham in college. Shelley; Keats—he was my favourite) Obviously I was starved for beauty in my natural surroundings. (HRC 29.6)

One image this Wordsworth of Brooklyn remembered from his childhood was a dead horse, left to go stiff in the street until a policeman slashed open its belly to keep the carcass from swelling, and 'the river of water, blood and oats pouring from its belly into the gutter'.[2] Another he told to Bernadette Inkeles was of a tailor bending to measure him for a suit: 'The tailor was kneeling on the floor and he was measuring my leg from hip to ankle, and I was overcome with what this man's life was and felt that I had found my voice.'[3]

But what most helped to make Bernard Malamud was the excellent New York system of free public education. He was much praised in the Malamud household for being a good pupil, but he became glad of school precisely because it was not only away from home but a way out of it. Later, characteristically, the education that was to take him out of that Brooklyn home was also to take him back to it as a writer: 'In college I wrote in a letter to a friend, "Brooklyn you are the universe"' (HRC 31.6).

But it began with basic survival in the outside world. Miriam Milman (later Lang), a girlfriend in the 1930s, recalled in a unpublished memoir, 'The Young Malamud: Age of Innocence', that 'he once told me that, coming from a Yiddish-speaking home, he didn't speak English until he went to kindergarten'. There 'he caught on quickly that in order to survive, he had to talk like the other kids'.[4] He was embarrassed when he found that he said 'bandeet' instead of 'bandit', because his mother did (HRC 20.3). The only toy that Malamud could remember ever having was bought for him by his mother, a monkey that climbed on a stretched string; but she misread the name and called it 'a chiming' monkey (HRC 20.3). Later Leon Snider laughed at him when Malamud mispronounced 'erstwhile' as 'erstwise' (HRC 33.8). He had to develop a sharp tongue in defence.

His first, elementary school was on nearby Cortelyou Road, Brooklyn. There he first began to read the books he had never had in his house—*Robinson Crusoe*, *A Tale of Two Cities*, *Treasure Island*. The public library was a block away from the grocery store in what was still a semi-rural setting. But at school he enjoyed also the Alger adventure books for boys and the dime novels of sensation and escape, starring heroes such as Buffalo Bill, Nick Carter the master detective, and Frank Merriwell, who combined the brain of Einstein with the body of Tarzan (LC II 14.1). Whenever he could, the boy also turned his school assignments into stories. He was habitually telling stories to his friends, often from movies he had seen, always at 'dreadfully long length' (LC II 11.14). 'There was some kid in the neighborhood, named Georgie, who was a sucker for a story, and they used to use me to tell him ghost stories at night, and one of his reactions to the ghost story would be a low opening of the mouth in astonishment, and fear, and they'd hit him with water pistols' (LC II 14.1). In another version, it is Malamud himself who shot the pistol into the mouth which his literary powers had opened.

In third grade, he made up a story about the American freedom-hero Roger Williams, including an encounter with a bear, 'and a girl too', an Indian maiden. 'I came to class early one morning with it,' he recalled, 'The teacher was there alone and took it over by the window, read it, and said: "It's very good"' (LC I 50.3). Needy, he always worked for the opportunity of individual contact.

Aged 10, he wrote about a ship lost in the Sargasso Sea, before ever reading 'The Ancient Mariner': 'All I knew was that when in the story I needed the ship it was there, magically present, and on it I took the long ride through stagnant waters and land-locked becalmed poisonous seas.' That, wrote Malamud, was 'the gift' that had first come without the hard work that was to follow in later years. 'I owned these stories before I had to pay rent for using them' (LC II 11.14). In some notes written in 1980 he recalls that free gift:

> When I was a child, there it was, the thing was there. I had it. It came with me—an almost mystical feeling proclaiming my worth. I felt it when I washed alone. I felt it in school.
>
> (HRC 20.3)

George Markowitz remembered Malamud writing at the age of nine or ten: 'He was dead serious about it. He would keep on writing, though we used to laugh at him, scoffing, but not cruelly.' It was somehow understood among the schoolchildren that Bernie never talked about his home and rarely invited anyone back there. 'We were a kind of second family, like substitute brothers for him.'[5] It was to this group of friends, the 'old gang', that for all their youthful scepticism Malamud was to dedicate his short-story collection *Rembrandt's Hat* in 1973—Herb Wittkin, George Markowitz, Hans Kerber, who was a little boy from Germany, Gene Lewis, whose father was a night-school principal, and Ebba Jorgenson, a Danish immigrant who eventually married Gene but initially had a crush on Bernie. But Linda Lowell, a student of Malamud's at Harvard in 1966, knew a more prosperous contemporary of his who grew up in a doctor's family in Queens. Bea Kresge said of the boy from the small grocery store who believed he had a gift: 'He used to hang around the more affluent kids,' she said: 'He was a nothing.'[6]

By then, from about 1923, Malamud was at Public School 181 with those more affluent children. It was a change he referred to in some other notes on 'The life in school' written in the 1980s: 'First the school I feared, then the school I loved' (HRC 20.3). Herb Wittkin was a classmate who lived just three blocks away from the school in a middle-class, predominantly Jewish area. He recalled that it was a mystery how Bernie got enrolled in PS 181, the outstanding new school in the borough, for he lived five miles away from the school, outside the official catchment area. He may simply have been registered when the family were still living only a mile away at 2700 Albemarle Road. But from Gravesend Avenue the nine-year-old had to travel to school every day on his own, on a journey of forty-five minutes at best, involving two trolley lines.[7] The boy was already ambitious. PS 181 was known as a 'progressive' school, partly because it moved its outstanding students along faster than normal, partly because it offered an experimental challenge launched by a talented and energetic young principal. Dr Nathan Peyser hand-picked a high-quality staff, including among them some attorneys who were having problems finding jobs, partly because of a deteriorating economy but also because of their left-wing politics. The syllabus was demanding: unusually, for example, by the fifth grade the students were studying French. In his notes for a family history, Malamud described it as 'the most important school in my life'.

In an unpublished memoir, 'Bernie, The Early Years', Herb Wittkin comments on the young Malamud's capacity to form close relationships with his teachers at the school. 'All the teachers in the last three years at PS 181—Mrs McDermott, Mr Squires and Mrs Ahner—fell under his spell.' He took initiatives, he produced his own single-issue newspaper, with stories from classmates. He even went to Mrs McDermott's home, claimed to have found out all about her love life, and told the others. In an early 1930s notebook, now in the possession of his daughter, Malamud makes one of his characteristic lists—in this case of what seem to be about twenty mysteriously shameful incidents that took place from the age of six onwards. One is of lying to Mrs Snider, Leon's mother, when he was fourteen or fifteen; another at about the same age cryptically refers to 'looking at Mama with the match'. And at the age of ten or eleven there is this, concerning his teacher: 'Proposal to Hilda McDermott'.

Malamud wanted attention and, whatever the risk of later winces of guilt or shame, was unafraid of putting himself forward. He got privileges from the teachers and passed them on to selected friends. Mr Squires put him in charge of the mimeograph room, a closet on the ground floor, where Malamud would sit with Herb Wittkin, after the copying was done, talking about the female teachers and the girls, the two of them measuring their erections with a ruler. The young Malamud was otherwise physically awkward, and poor at sports: the future author of *The Natural* threw a baseball like a girl, said Wittkin. He couldn't have broken a pane of glass at twenty-five feet, but he would get Herbie to help him practise his pitching, for hours on end, punishing himself with unmerciful determination, and yet still he could not do the man's thing. Yet though unathletic, swarthily horse-faced, and short, he was good at attracting the girls: 'As with his teachers,' wrote Herb Wittkin in his memoir, 'Bernie's manner was direct, persuasive, gentle and seductive. In addition, he was, in those pre-teen times, somewhat more free-wheeling, more assured than the rest of us. He travelled alone long distances to school, seemed more liberated and much less concerned than we about parental restrictions.' He introduced Herb to girls, taking him everywhere as though he were 'Bernie's security blanket'. But what was attractive was the sense of vulnerability the boy conveyed beneath his apparent independence. To Miriam Milman, 'Bernie seemed like an orphan in need of family closeness.

He enjoyed stopping by our house of an afternoon to visit with anyone who happened to be around.' All the mothers liked him, for talking like an adult whilst appealing to the maternal: 'He'll get some place, that boy,' said Herb Wittkins's mother. Herb also remembered how, exceptionally, one Saturday evening in later years, the boys took their roving crap game to the room at the back of Max Malamud's store. Bernie's style of handling the dice was always to hold them between his hands chest high, with the palms flat 'as though in prayer, invoking the gods for the luck he needed'.

The whole cohort moved on to Erasmus Hall High School in 1928, though, significantly, Malamud placed it a year later in some notes: 'In 1929 I entered Erasmus Hall H.S., where I awoke to literature generally, music and writing. My mother died the same year' (HRC 29.6). Among Malamud's papers, there is also a brief personal memoir of Erasmus Hall by a contemporary, Herb Jacobson, dated 1 September 1976 (HRC 11.7):

> In the years I attended it, from 1928 to 1932, and for about the three hundred years previous to that, Erasmus Hall was a unique institution in the city's educational system. On Flatbush Avenue it faced, across the street, the ancient but still active Dutch Reformed Church, whose sturdy parishioners had founded the school before the English took it into their hands in 1660 to steal New Amsterdam from the Hollanders and change its name to New York.

It was handed to the city of Brooklyn in the late nineteenth century and, true to its Dutch and Anglo-Saxon tradition of education in aid of assimilation, was rebuilt in the early twentieth century to meet the new influx of immigrant children from Eastern Europe. A rambling wooden building stood in the centre of a block-deep quadrangle, but around this core an architect had newly constructed

> a huge 'American College Gothic' shell rivalling Yale University's architecture in magnitude and pretentiousness. Actually it was none too big to hold the products of the home-building explosion that took place in Flatbush in that era. With over 8,000 students, some of them banished to an annex in a newly constructed public school erected over an old Dutch tulip farm, it was, indeed, one of the largest high schools in the world.

Loyal to its classical traditions, Erasmus offered Latin and Greek, the only school in New York still to teach the latter. The boys wore conventional suits and red ties, the girls dresses with red ties in their hair, all well-mannered, orderly, and quiet in the corridors. It was the best school in the five boroughs of Brooklyn. The teachers were of high quality because increasingly with the coming of the Depression a high school teacher earned more money than many of the other professions. The father of one of Malamud's friends, Burt

Rush, was a lawyer by training but became a chemistry teacher. At a time when a secretary earned $12–15 a week, a teacher in training would earn $22.50, a permanent sub $42.50, and a regular teacher who had passed the qualifying examination was secure on $2,500 per annum (HRC 15.7).

Florence Ripley Mastin, then in her mid-thirties, taught English, was a lesbian and a poet. She taught students to write haikus even during the war with Japan. In 1950 Malamud sent her a copy of his prize-winning short-story collection *The Magic Barrel* with an inscription that she recalled, together with the face of her young pupil, in a poem entitled 'Rosemary' (as in *Hamlet*, for remembrance), dated September 16 1966:

> Boy, with the darkly sombre eyes
>   and the listening look,
> Most brilliant and the most remote
>   Of any in my class,
>
> Did the long injustice of the world
>   Strike early to your heart?
> You knew the bitter taste of life …
>   What could I give you then?
>
> When you were laurel-crowned,
>   You told me:
>
>   'Yours is the hand
>   that reaches for flowers
> and if there are none
>   flowers grow to be for your hand'
> Now from my cloistered room
> I send you rosemary.   (HRC 18.7)

Everyone who cared noticed the sad mahogany of those eyes. But 'brilliant' *and* 'remote' goes deeper. When, in maturity, he sent her copies of *Idiots First* and *A New Life*, she sent him back letters, signed 'with pride' in his achievements, quoting specific passages she liked. One was what Feuer says about young Ben Glickman, a struggling writer, in 'Suppose a Wedding': 'He doesn't tell me what he has suffered, but I can see in his eyes. He knows what life means.' This is Malamud, she says, a Malamud who makes her think of D. H. Lawrence's *Sons and Lovers*. Another was from *A New Life*: 'He would, as a teacher, do everything he could to help bring forth those gifted few who would do more than their teachers had taught.'

'What could I give you?': 'I was very fortunate in some of the teachers I had,' said Malamud, 'I began to read and write and cultivate myself for them' (12 May 1963, HRC 29.6). Nina Peilikan Straus, a former student

of Malamud's at Bennington, made notes of a conversation she had with
him in 1975, where he expressed gratitude for all that public education had
offered him through books. 'I was a poor boy without connections: I didn't
have money, I didn't have friends, I didn't have a sense of power. Reading
was the mode by which I felt self-important. Appreciation of literature
made me feel valuable, made me feel life was valuable: life in books lived
with intensity. Books were a matter of being moved. No sense of critical
intelligence operating when young. But a great sense of what the writer has
to give me.'[8]

Thus, for example, he came upon Hemingway. Looking back at his early
reading of *Farewell to Arms* and *The Sun Also Rises*, he told Nina Pelikan
Straus, 'It was less the subject-matter than the technique and the mood.
I never knew that devices of simplicity could be that strong.' Even in the
simplicity he sensed also what was hidden—in Hemingway's case, the fear
of death, for example. 'The usefulness of the indirect; this is what moves.'
He liked the strength involved in one's *not* saying what was on his mind,
where style offered 'a repressive dignity'. For the youthful Malamud had his
own shaming secrets in his mother's death: 'You couldn't speak about it,' he
told Nina, 'In order to escape being the victim of it, you ritualized it. You
obtained grace under pressure.'

But at first he was known not so much as a writer but as an actor in
the Erasmus theatre group which he kept going outside school after he
graduated. Besides the old gang who went on from PS 181, this was another
of Malamud's little groups. With a wide vocal range and mercurial shifts of
mood, Malamud did the voices, switched identities, enjoyed the attentions
of a beautiful red-headed fellow-actress, Rena Fradkin, and clearly loved
the general notice he aroused as actor and director. Even when he was only
helping out with the spotlight, the drama teacher, Matt Thrall, half-comically
called him the Light of her life. He would sometimes take Matt out, and also
another teacher, Clara Molendyk.

As a writer he first of all aspired to contribute to the school magazine, *The
Erasmian,* and eventually edited it for a brief period. But initially 'Dorothy
Kilgallen, the writer, journalist, and TV star, was the editor and turned down
my first story. She said "It's too morbid for the Erasmian." So I tried stories
with some comic aspect, in particular dialect pieces about a farmer visiting
the city' (LC I 50.3). He had always had a good ear. A fellow-Erasmian,
Ben Loeb told Paul Malamud that he remembering watching a baseball
game with his father at Ebbet's Field when Bernie leaned over to tell the
man in front that he could tell he was from Pittsburgh. Thus, three rather
ponderously 'light' accounts of 'the doings of Hiram' appeared in serial form

in *The Erasmian* for April, May, and June 1931. Hiram, a southern country hick, writes home to his friend Josh: 'Waal, here I am in Flatbush (which aint flat and which aint got no bushes) investigatin school conditions out here.' He concentrates on a school he mishears as 'Raspers Hall' and there he comes upon the statue recently erected in honour of the great Dutch scholar, Desiderius Erasmus (1466–1536): 'a new statoo of a man readin a book. His name wuz Raspers too. Someone said his first name wuz Deciduous.' Curious to see what book the statue was reading, Hiram gets a ladder after close of school and climbs up, only to have the ladder fall down leaving him alone and on high. At last reading the name aright, he ends up, like any good and grateful graduate before the alma mater: 'I slept in erasmus' arms fer a few days.'

But Malamud's real Erasmus saviour was another English teacher, young Clara Molendyk, who one day told the young Malamud that she expected to be remembered because of what *he* would accomplish. Miriam Lang told Paul Malamud in an unpublished interview:

> She saw in your father in high school what nobody else saw, and she encouraged him to write when nobody, nobody was giving him credit for his ability. Everybody at that time who knew your father heard directly from him that he was going to be a writer someday. We laughed—not at him—among ourselves, we said 'Where, how does he think he's going to be a famous writer.'

He had once boasted to another teacher, Ellen Batchelor in the English Office, 'I'll write the great American novel' (HRC 18.7), but, equally, was amazed when Clara said so. In 1983 Malamud told Miriam that in what he had accomplished, he had proved something both to Clara *and* to his own uncertain self, and 'if I could embrace her now, I would' (The Young Malamud).

Clara was only six or seven years his senior. She was a small, slender, slightly built young woman, who in the midst of her teaching attended graduate school several evenings a week to get a doctoral degree in history, writing a thesis on Charles Evans Hughes, Mayor of New York and later Chief Justice. But English was what she taught, and she taught quietly, without apparent personality or charisma, like a disguised or repressed person putting everything, with precision, into the book they were studying. As Miriam's younger sister Doris was to put it in 1984, 'Her special qualities did not impress themselves immediately; they emerged or unfolded, slowly, during the course of the term. But as they unfolded, their impact was the reverse of her quiet, soft-spoken, unemphatic, undidactic, outward manner. ... We reached out to her as if she was a repository of secret keys to the life of mind.'9

It was she who helped encourage 'Life—From Behind A Counter', the essay published in *The Erasmian*, February 1932, in which Malamud first found a serious subject-matter in the ordinary but still baffling dramas to be found in the Brooklyn universe: 'Mr Thompson is unemployed ... His wife still dresses lavishly ... Mrs Murphy's eldest son was arrested ... Her youngest is a policeman.' He could write about such juxtapositions. Increasingly, he could make it so that 'the immigrant world had to represent me' (HRC 27.5). The essay won the school's Richard Young Prize and, better still, second prize (Malamud instead called it 'some sort of prize') in the nation-wide Scholastic Awards sponsored by the Scholastic Publishing Company.

But among Malamud's list of shame in the early notebook is another veiled memory—'borrowing buck from Clara'. Clara was not rich; she came from a modest and strict home and a limited social life in Brooklyn, her father a bartender, her mother a housekeeper. Malamud was invited into her home and later brought along some of his friends. Looking back, Miriam wrote him on 26 May 1983: 'Uptight, inhibited, unable to express herself emotionally, why did she slip so easily into the lives of a group of young people quite different from herself and relate to them so well?' Miriam thought that 'in the emptiness of her personal life' Clara had 'a need to live through us' (HRC 9.1).

Later, Clara married Ben Edwards, also a teacher, and became Principal of Lafayette High School where eventually she got Malamud a temporary teaching post. No one in the Erasmus group had liked Edwards. 'Everybody was either hurt or disillusioned when she went off with him. Bernie most of all. He thought that this was a poor match. He wanted something better for her.'[10] Edwards was a drinker and Doris Milman thought it likely that Clara became one too, increasingly retreating from the friendship of her past students. The sad ending was one reason why in 1984 she and Malamud nominated Clara for an award from the National Council of Teachers for English. Malamud wrote how it would make him happy if she were to receive an award for awakening him to the pleasures of poetry and literature; she was

an unusual person: very well educated, interested in teaching, investing a good deal of intelligence and—when it comes to essences—concern and passion in her teaching. She was very fond of her students and made us feel expansive, free and useful. ... She read a good deal and loaned us books freely. Her home was open to us and we went there often. To this day (I am seventy and she is seventy-six or seven) I remember her father and mother, their interest in us, and the pleasure of their company.   (HRC 18.7)

It was part of that final settling of accounts that Malamud was working on throughout the 1980s.

On a visit to give a reading in Chicago in 1959, Malamud suddenly became angry when a young member of faculty, Ted Solotaroff, suggested that the portrait of Helen Bober—the daughter of grocer Morris in *The Assistant*—was a satire on the stereotypical Jewish belief in education. Six more credits meant a new life. 'Absolutely not!' cried Malamud, 'I would never satirize someone's quest for an education. Without my education I could never have become a writer.'[11]

Helen stood for something in the young Malamud. A notebook entry for the novel speaks of her need, in relation to the father: 'She senses that he has given up, lost whatever free will he has had. She wants to retain hers. In the end she feels she must make herself a better person through education to escape her father's passive acceptance and fate' (HRC 19.1, p. 153). But Solotaroff concludes of Malamud's indignation:

> His earnestness was both affecting and off-putting. It conveyed a sense of the unworldly will and integrity that created a Morris Bober and of the almost naïve sententiousness that must have gone over like lead in the Faculty Club.   (Solotaroff, 236–7)

He often had to face those intelligently sceptical, university put-downs. All that was at the heart of Malamud's battle to become an almost literally self-made man was still to some who had had it easier just too naïve or earnest or sentimental. Malamud was going to need a strong language to develop, express, and protect the beliefs of characters who were trying to raise themselves by their bootstraps.

The Romantic Youth

By the end of 1932 Malamud was enrolled in the City College of New York, from which he graduated with a BA in 1936. It was a let-down after Erasmus, partly because of the sharper bite of the Depression. He felt he was awakening to poetry, philosophy, the whole domain of knowledge but he did not think he was always well directed. He remembered one day looking around the college library, making plans to read it all, but felt depressed (HRC 29.6).

Earle F. Palmer, Professor of Rhetoric, was one of the teachers in English literature and composition who took an interest in him. A formal testimonial from Palmer at the end of the degree course speaks of Malamud having done 'superior work', showing 'original power, versatility and good taste' and 'the bearing of a gentleman'. 'He has had experience apart from writing,' Palmer added drily, 'and this I think invaluable' (HRC 15.7). Malamud had to work part-time in order to maintain himself. In an interview for the *City College Alumnus*, June 1959, Malamud recalled Palmer's written comment on a paper he had submitted: 'This work reminds me of two other of my students: Lewis Mumford and Irwin Edman'—Mumford a man of letters, writer on architecture, cities, and the history of technology; Edman a philosopher and poet. 'I couldn't walk home that night, I was up in the air. The reward, the richness, the revelation of that comment by Professor Palmer has never been duplicated.'

But it was Theodore Goodman who was the charismatic influence, and remained a friend until his death in 1952. If students offered flowery prose to Teddy Goodman, he would invite them to take it straightaway to the toilet. Smoking and flicking the butts out of the window, he told his class please not to bother him with their introspection. Malamud was intelligent enough to see that this was what he needed. It was what he meant when he later wrote to Sidney Richman about being a Romantic youth: 'As a child I was full of unexpressed poetry; as a youth I was a romantic. I beat myself into shape with a terrible will' (HRC 29.6). It was a great day when he was finally praised by Goodman for an unpublished short story called 'The Latecomers', about a young man caught slackening the clothing of a young woman who had fainted, and, again, later, for 'The Bill', a sad and lovely story on the risks of giving 'credit' to human beings, which became part of the *The Magic Barrel*. But what the formidable Goodman taught him, above all, was to work very hard to avoid what he called 'dishonesty'. Through his minute analysis of short stories, Goodman 'revealed the relation of story technique to meaning' and the test of oneself which writing constituted. Goodman was 'the first person to teach me how dishonesty revealed itself in writing, and how certain superficialities of personality transmuted themselves into superficiality of story conception' (HRC 33.2). 'Either you go in honest,' said Goodman, 'or you sink.' For a while after Goodman's course, all Malamud could trust himself to write were theatre reviews for the City College *Mercury*.

For 'dishonesty' was not simply to do with those earlier youthful acts of stealing or bluffing. It meant that deeper more involuntary falseness of undisciplined self-consciousness, of ego and immaturity and fantasy, which writing too often unwittingly released in the young writer. This was a falseness in which the unhappy Malamud was saturated, throughout the thirties and early forties, in his life as well as his writing. For his was a long adolescence, the adolescence of an unsynchronized mix of old–young man.

Looking back, Doris Milman, who became a child psychiatrist, spoke of her generation as one that was allowed a long time to reach maturity. Though family troubles shoved Malamud out into the world from an early age, it took time for him to find a place within it. The Depression extended and exacerbated the period of what only in retrospect might be called waiting and gestation.

At the time it felt more like waste and loneliness. He wrote Doris Milman in June 1936 that as he walked out of the college at three o'clock, he said out loud to Herb Wittkin, who laughed to hear it, 'I have been a college graduate for one hour. I've also been unemployed for the same amount of time.' To fill the void, 'I was spending too much time', he wrote in 'Long Work, Short Life', 'being in love.' In a draft he spoke of falling in love 'as an easy way of feeling good, when I wasn't writing' (TH, 29). Then he remembered, crossed out the word 'easy', and wrote on second thought instead, 'an *uneasy* way of feeling good, when I wasn't writing' (LC II 12.3). The death of his mother had left a hunger for women. Again, he cut this confession: 'I loved women. I couldn't think of anything more beautiful than women, anything that moved me more than the beauty of women. Besides, I had been a lonely boy and stayed lonely for years. That had something to do with coming from a family that wasn't much of a family' (LC II 12.3).

The great but hopeless passion had been for Miriam Milman, his 'Mimi', whom he first met in 1930 at Erasmus and at the Sunday-evening Jewish youth-group meetings at Temple Beth Emeth, Flatbush, to which Malamud used to go to in order to make friends. He would walk her home, she recalled in her memoir:

> On the way, he liked to clown with the irrepressible spirit of a Groucho Marx, ad-libbing melodramatically in iambic pentameter alternating with a convincing Hebrew chant. Between laughter and embarrassment, I'd try to hush him, for fear of what the neighbors might think.

She told Paul Malamud that his father's sense of humour seemed to come from being hurt. 'Drooling on Mimi', aged twenty, was another on Malamud's list of humiliations.

They dated when Malamud went on to City College. He told her that after he brought her home from a date, or sometimes when she had been out with someone else, 'he would station himself across the street from our house and look up at the windows of the front bedroom I shared with my sister'.

Then Miriam herself left for college, at Wellesley, where young women had their eyes on a future closer to Harvard than to Brooklyn. She was out of Malamud's league and getting more interested in Ben Loeb, an Erasmian student who had gone on to Cornell and then Harvard but in the vacations still lived near the Milman home. Malamud had already tried shocking her with his maturity—taking her to a risqué play, waving a condom in her face, but 'never really coarse in word or deed, just immature, like a small boy trying to make an impression by behaving outrageously'. While she was away he doggedly saved up the little bits of money he had, in order that on her return at Christmas 1934, he could take her for a formal evening-out—borrowed tuxedo, corsage and taxi, the theatre followed by dancing afterwards. Miriam carelessly left the expensive orchid on her window-sill where it blew off. It looked as if she had thrown it into the garden to die. Years later it made her think when Frank Alpine in *The Assistant* found at the bottom of the garbage a carved rose he had given to Helen.

Eventually, Malamud proposed marriage, without any means of support save his dream of becoming a prize-winning novelist. They had visited her cousin, Sidney Kingsley, who, in his late twenties, had recently won the Pulitzer Prize for his first play: 'After we left, Bernie was silent, but I sensed as though he had uttered the words, "Some day I'm going to win the Pulitzer".' Years later in Oregon, his daughter would hear him muttering still in front of the shaving mirror, 'Some day I am going to win' (MFB, 20). Predictably Miriam turned down his proposal. She aspired to be a writer, not a writer's wife. 'Despite my attempt to let him down gently, Bernie was hurt to the point of tears. Accustomed though he was to mask his feelings with wry humor, this time he couldn't rely on that defense.'

This was not the first proposal he had made. It had happened two or three years earlier when another of the clever, more affluent girls he took out at Erasmus went away to a prestigious residential college. He was very sensitive about having to stay behind and work his way through City College. Hannah Needle, whom Malamud first knew from Miss Mastin's English class, went away to Vassar in 1932, at the same time as Malamud had to commute to City College. He came to visit Hannah in Poughkeepsie during her freshman year and proposed. 'Neither of us was ready,' Hannah thought, but 'it hurt me to see him so upset.'[12] But in a notebook entry for 14 May 1935, Malamud remembered she had said to him, 'You work life; you don't live it.'

Harriet Lustig was at Erasmus when Malamud came back there in 1935 as a temporary student-teacher, and he introduced her as a favoured and talented student to his theatre group. She remembers him around this time as slight, just under 5 foot 8 inches, not sturdy or happy or healthy-looking, with a long thin face, sallow complexion, and a heavy growth. He talked to her once about Miriam—he was hurt and stricken and he felt poorly treated. What should he do? he asked this inexperienced fifteen-year-old schoolgirl. He said he would show Miriam by becoming a writer.[13]

By late 1934, smitten with Miriam at Wellesley, he had also taken to writing to her clever seventeen-year-old sister, Doris, as his confidante. Doris Milman kept the letters from the twenty-year-old Malamud. They read painfully: Can Doris write to Mimi and find out for him when she is due home from college? It's wonderful to have a friend at court. Thanks for all the little hints you gave—for everything you told me. Thanks for arranging about the flowers: Mimi wrote that she liked them. I know I sound like a weakling. Doris, darling, I'm so hurt, you're the only one I can tell it to, the only one who can understand the quality of my pain. It all seems so hopeless, so abjectly hopeless. I went over to Ebba's: they were so nice to me, put on the radio, made me dance, gee if Ebba only knew all she was doing. We can't blame Miriam if she doesn't love me. My spring is going to be so empty—alone—without her. I know that I am going to laugh at this in the future. Please forgive my babblings and don't think less of me because of them.

The letters to Miriam herself must have sounded even more vulnerable. Years later Malamud phoned and asked her to return them. He sounded rather taken aback when she said she had already thrown away everything from that time. But in 1963 he told her he was grateful she had got rid of them: 'Sometimes I shudder at what a romantic kid I was.'

Yet the letters that virtually ended the relationship in 1935 still survive, carefully transcribed by Malamud in his 1930s notebooks. 'Written at Wellesley, Wednesday April third. Received by me Friday, April fifth' is this from Miriam:

> Bernie, when I said I liked you I meant it sincerely—and it's the kind of feeling that's indestructible. I guess it isn't love—I only wish it was, because love is very beautiful ... I guess it sounds like 'Can't we be friends' but it's really not as trite as all that. It's an indefinable relationship, much deeper.

His answer, written immediately on receipt April 5, tries hard, beneath its literary defence, to be magnanimous:

> Perhaps it is better so; you've always been a 'mansion unpossessed' and I've always been unsatisfied. Now, at least, there is a certain calm satiety in finality.
>
> I'm glad, both for your sake and mine, that you've had courage enough to stop my being a source of uneasiness to you.

There have been two Miriams in his life:

> To one, whom I loved, who is dead, except as she lives in me, I say—
> Good Bye.
>   'Fare thee well, and if forever—
>   Forever fare thee well—!'

To the other, with whom I have been less intimate, but whom, never, perhaps I shall come to know better—you have always been a very lovely person. Here, then, to that 'undefinable relationship, much deeper!' It will always be a pleasure to be your friend.

In fact, he began to look for 'his' Miriam elsewhere.

One place to meet women was at the Catskill holiday hotels where he worked in the summers between 1932 and 1936 to fund his studies. Another item on his list of shame must refer to his serving as a waiter: 'Bawled out in Pine Hill dining room', followed by the cryptic memory-note 'Job: you stink'. On the other hand, Miriam said he wrote her boastfully of his 'honoring with his body' one of the lonely women, in the woods. In the summer of 1935 Malamud was writing and acting in skits and stand-up comedy routines, the actor-entertainer trying not to think. The letters he was sending were mainly to Doris, from the 'Forest and Stream Club, in the heart of the Green Mountains', and mainly sorrowful. At once raw and flowery, they speak of his continuing misery after the failure with Mimi—but also of an affair with a lonely twenty-six-year-old teacher-clerk called Rose:

> I did it because I wanted to get it done with the first time. I was cold, deliberate, probably the worst horrible lover she has ever had. Without love, it is absolutely meaningless. I doubt if I shall ever indulge again in that way.

Then in the very next letter:

> I told you about my first experience, my second was somewhat like that one too. The result is my second experience became my last one.

'I take it that you think I have become Rake no. 1 of the whole god-damned universe,' he added. But he insists that it is not so. He is well below par for this camp—and will remain so because of these 'new experiences' and the adjustment of his personal 'philosophy' in the light of them:

> I'm glad I had them because now I know myself better. I know myself well enough to feel sure that any experience I may have in the future will evoke my deep disgust—unless there is actually a feeling of love between myself and the girl. I know she will have to be pleasant, intelligent, clean, personable and self-respecting if I am to undergo the act with any amount of joy. I know also that she must have all of my respect and that we must both be very honest with each other. There will be no using people as 'means' in my life.

This is the philosophy of Kant—'each person is an end in himself'—in the earnest hands of a young Malamud who still in 1935 was a long way from Goodman's requirement of being 'very honest'.

Even in 1966, at the height of his success, students in his writing class at Harvard were startled and baffled to hear Malamud speak of a stuck-up girl who had rejected him in youth, only to end up marrying a bra-manufacturer instead (Lowell). It was Miriam, who had married Ted Lang: his businesses included lingerie.

But back in the Catskills in the following summer of 1936, one year on from his rejection, he seemed at yet another end of the road, following his graduation from City College. Still immersed in the adolescent group, Malamud was writing rather preachily to Doris about her relationship with Burt Rush—how Rush had become over-dependent on her, how she had outgrown him, and was about to part from him. Analyzing it over, thinking of 'the-pain-to-come for Burt' of which Burt as yet knew nothing, Malamud himself knows plenty from his own relation to Mimi and feels a disturbing 'vicarious pain':

> What happened to me was easily explicable. But when the same thing happens to Burt (he's dead now and doesn't know it); and it happens through, or because of, *you*, I begin to mistrust and question uneasily. The more so, because you are you. You're Doris, so physically beautiful, so mentally fine, so spiritually lovely. You're Doris, whom I've loved as sister, mother, friend and human being. You're the same girl whom I've loved with such impersonal personalness.

In this messy flow of ill-formed emotions, the identities and roles are getting blurred and so are the boundaries. He writes to Doris that his feeling for her is as comprehensive 'as Andromache's love for Hector: "Thou art to me father and lady mother, yea, and brother, even as thou art my goodly husband"'. At much the same time, there in the Catskills, he can 'drink of the warm coolness of Mae, the gentle naivete of Adele, Elsie's happy loveliness, and of Marian's grace and charm'. And he was all too interested to hear that Mimi was unhappy in her new relationship with Ben Loeb and it was coming to an end.

The warning signs were there, and late in December 1936 the situation came to the boil over the play put on by that lingering group of Erasmus graduates whom Malamud gathered around him. As director, Malamud had spectacularly lost his temper with George and Gene because he thought they were putting their crap games and social gatherings before the serious business. There was a further row with the beautiful, histrionic Rena who was possessive towards him, though they were no longer involved, and jealous of his kissing another girl in the kitchen. Doris accused him of 'astounding behaviour' in falling out so bossily with all his friends. In the course of a nine-page letter—a painfully rationalized list of issues offered partly in apology, partly in justification—there is this under item 3 headed 'You', the following subsections to explain the tension that came about:

> C) Because you prevent me from acting as a man to you, and treating you as a woman. You are adolescent and show it by falling for H.R. and by your inability to handle men with poise. I will say that you can handle boys.
>
> D) Because I'm damn-fool enough to kiss you on the cheek or on your forehead—as if I were your grandfather.
>
> E) Because I'm making a hypocrite of myself—by trying to make Rush fall out of love with you, while I am falling in love with you.

Man, boy, adolescent, grandfather, Burt or Bernie: nothing is stable. His faults, he says, are not simply those of 'wrong-doing'; they are signs of 'incompletion', in the self-conscious want of sufficient life.

There is item after item in this long list of reasons for behaving badly. There was the problem of being unemployed—frustration, lack of money, being unable to go out, haggling with the family, and 'hearing my dear sweet kid brother say—"Bern, you can have part of my allowance (a pittance) because you always gave me money when I wanted it"'. There were physical problems—pains in the left kidney and left lung, stomach aches and digestive difficulties—which he associates with irregular habits and a physical readiness for marriage and its orderly routines. But perhaps within all of them, there is another underlying motivation: 'a subconscious desire to arouse sympathy for myself. I know that you worry about me and I like it. I love it when you write me letters telling me that you've noticed such and such a thing about me yesterday ... so why don't you marry me and still worry about me.'

Nothing came of it. Doris showed the next letter to Miriam, and Miriam angrily wrote in the margin, 'Trying to make a case out of nothing, as usual', 'misquoting as usual, quibbling', 'smug dope', 'words, words, words!' Howsoever the relationship with Doris was patched up, it was another cause for shame. Forced back into retreat, Malamud resolved again to take 'the long view' and somehow continue his intolerable waiting. Meanwhile he took a job in a yarn factory and readjusted to the short term.

Yet the notebooks chart the continuing late-adolescent indignities, sorrows, and anxieties. Some of the entries are literary quotations. Some are ideas for short stories and novels—beginning, say, with a mother's funeral, or this for 4 December 1938: 'The death of a father scene (why does that idea persist). The father talks about the loss of his first wife, the boy's mother (whom he didn't mention much since the years of her death) dead since 20 years. He talks long about her; then thinks he hurt her on the wedding night.'

Other notes are more the autobiography untransmuted. He analyzes his terrible need to belong—the 'social climbing', the clinging to educational institutions and books, the need to be 'one of the boys', the search for a woman's love. The date 14 August 1938 has him sitting on a bench on Columbia campus, again hopelessly waiting for Miriam, who like him was now engaged on an MA course:

> and the thought came to me how much I didn't belong, and how much I wanted to belong.
> A few days later, I thought of my relations with Irene W. and of how much I wanted love—one belonging to someone. The desire which Freud classifies as one half of life's desire, the other half being ego and the realization of the reality principle—is probably the cause for my falling so hard in a minor sort of way for D.B.S last June.

'So hard' but also 'in a minor way' Just about sums it all up. It wasn't quite real, he didn't expect it to be, yet he was still going to push at it to see if indeed it was real in any way. Irene W seems to have been a married woman whose husband was impotent: Malamud used to watch her slip hanging on the washing line. D.B.S. was Dorothy Shapiro in whose sister, Helen, he also showed an interest. Later still, there was also a Janice: 'I wanted very much to love her. It was *the way out*. At first I thought she would be difficult to get. But she wasn't and in about five weeks, my feelings for her literally stopped dead, leaving me ashamed and, for a while, worried.' He was worried about unfeelingness in himself. And then there was Horty Batchker who seemed to offer him 'the vision of a prosaic life. The school teacher with a decent salary. The comforting wife etc', but he didn't really want that either.

Teaching and Clerking

Even the prosaic idea of school-teaching had become a problem. Twice he failed a teaching exam. Remarkably, the first time that he flunked the teacher-in-training exam (as he wrote to Doris from the Catskills) was not because of lack of knowledge but through poor use of English. He had decided to simplify and ended up listing too many things instead of elaborating on them. 'I feel now like a strong man who has been bowled over, and has picked himself up to laugh at the puny force that overturned him.' But his next paragraph is more honest:

> Of course, what really hurts me more than anything is to have my friends really misunderstand what happened. 'Did you hear, Bernie flunked his T. and T.,

yet Zilch passed'—etc. etc. I never flunked any important exam in my life before ... and I'm sorry for my father who was hurt. Yet, even he realizes that the whole thing was a fluke.

But he failed the substitute's exam a second time. There were orals and his mentor said Malamud had failed because he had a sibilant 's'. There was a glut of teachers, and examiners may well have been encouraged to be extra strict. But whatever it was, it meant that, without the qualification, Malamud could never get a permanent teaching job in the public school system and could earn only about $4.50 a day.

When he had been a young sub, the girls had clearly loved him. He would stand at the front of the class, he would walk around, serious and interested. Beverly Miller (then Goldman) wrote him a letter, 14 March 1970: 'I even remember your being ill, and a few girls and myself went to your boarding house and found you quite neglected. We went down and bought some things for you. I don't remember if we have ever dated' (HRC 7.7). Carolyn Anderson, taught by him as a thirteen-year-old in Erasmus, met him again years later in Bennington: 'Thin young English teacher ... I wonder if you remember your brown tweed suit? ... You came to my desk (I always sat somewhere near the front, it seems) and told me I was becoming a very beautiful young lady .... I could almost recall your inflection when you used to call me "Carolyn" ' (20 August 1968, HRC 7.8).

He had enrolled on an MA at Columbia by taking a government loan. Burt Rush was there full-time and Malamud would sometimes borrow Burt's room on campus, to have somewhere to go. The work felt routine, and so was the eventual successful dissertation, finally submitted in February 1942, 'Thomas Hardy's Reputation as a Poet in American Periodicals'. He had begun by telling himself that 'what I was doing was worthwhile; for no one who spends his nights and days devoted to great works of literature will be wasting his time as a writer' (TH, 27). But increasingly he began to feel it was 'close to a waste of time' (HRC 33.2). The final dissertation, though industrious and dutiful enough in its research into reviews of Hardy's poetry, is a wholly secondary and almost anonymous piece of work. It has no quotations from the poems themselves.

But the lack of a permanent, regular teaching position meant that amidst all the odd jobs that he had to undertake in factories and department stores in 1938 and 1939, scouring the loathed job agencies on Sixth Avenue, Malamud also happened upon some hack work that became surprisingly important to him. After advertising on noticeboards, he began to tutor German-Jewish refugees in English. Hannah Needle recalls how Malamud, with his gift for mimicry, made a good story out of a little lady supposedly coming up to him after a lesson: 'Tell me, teach, which is right to say—"piss" or "shit"?' Malamud cautiously replied he was unsure what she meant. The lady replied, 'I never know whether to ask for a "piss" of paper or a "shit" of paper.' But actually the tutoring was serious and painful, with surprising implications for those problems of identity and belonging that Malamud had channelled so unsuccessfully into 'love'.

His tutees were mainly middle-aged intellectuals who had had distinguished careers in Europe and were of a status, sophistication, and education far above Malamud's experience. But they were now exiles left fumbling for thoughts in a barely known language. 'To many of these people,' he was to write in the short story, 'The German Refugee', 'the great loss was the loss of language—that they could not say what was in them to say. You have some subtle thought and it comes out like a piece of broken bottle.' Their problems affected Malamud because he was not only a lonely man of words himself, struggling in the Depression, but also an equivocal fellow-Jew, without much in the way of Jewish knowledge, faith, or identity, who now suddenly saw what being born Jewish might mean in the dangerous world of the thirties.

One of his pupils was Paul Schrag, a wealthy and highly cultured young international lawyer, who wanted to be a writer and a painter as well as a lawyer, and already knew considerable English. His brother was Karl Schrag, the artist, who also became a friend. Malamud helped Paul perfect his language, but the lessons continued long after, partly because Schrag enjoyed the literary conversations they turned into being, and partly because he knew Malamud needed the money. His wife, Susan, recalled that they had never met that type before, an intellectual poor person. The young Malamud seemed nervy, drinking milk to help settle his stomach. They would talk about European culture, Mann and Freud and Chekhov and Dostoevsky, while in return Malamud put Paul onto American literature, especially Sherwood Anderson's *Winesburg, Ohio*. He would also read the Schrags his own stories, though privately they did not think very much of them. Later, in gratitude, he gave Paul the manuscript of his first commercially published story, 'The Cost of Living'.[14] It was not until 20 November 1957 that Paul could write to Malamud to say that on reading *The Assistant* they had found 'the young man whom we met nearly 20 years ago—writing his story as he lived it' (HRC 9.4).

Another highly educated tutee was Kurt Pinthus, a literary man, who later wrote in a testimonial, 'Despite my age of about fifty at that time and my very poor knowledge of English, Mr Malamud drilled me so well that soon I was able to lecture in English' (HRC 29.6). Their friendship persisted into the

1950s, by which time the spectacularly disorganized Pinthus, having long since escaped Malamud's discipline, was five years behind in his correspondence, the reading of a Malamud short story still high on his list of things-to-do.

But the most memorable of all the pupils was Dr Friedrich Pinner. Pinner was an economist, aged fifty-five, who had been financial editor of the *Berliner Tageblatt*, and had written a successful anti-war novel after World War I. With his wife he had fled to The Hague, and when Hitler invaded the low countries, had gone on to the States via England, hoping to re-build his career in finance and investment. 'At the beginning of the lesson,' wrote Malamud, 'I look into his eyes to see how uneasy and pained he is.' Gradually as a careful Malamud gets him interested, Pinner's eyes clear:

> then they cloud again when I've caused an idea to rise in his mind, and he can't find the right word to give it expression. I wait—he thinks long, then comes up with several substitute words. I answer, reading into his remarks what I think he meant, and his eyes brighten again—because he has communicated with me.   (Notebooks)

Pinner worked hard: he would read the articles in *The New York Times* that Malamud recommended and would prepare a long list of words for which he needed definitions. But the talk was often depressing: 'You yourself, my dear Mr Malamud, have told me that these are times of transition. You said the world would not get rid of this blackness for fifty years' (Notebooks). Burt Rush told Paul Malamud the dark conclusion to the story of Pinner when America in turn entered the war. Then when he again lost all his European clients and contacts from the world of finance, 'he just couldn't face having to start over again in another country and he and his wife turned on the gas and committed suicide'. He remained in Malamud's mind, finally emerging in the transmuted account of a suicide in 'The German Refugee' in 1963.

But in 1940, after a year of substitute teaching under Clara Molendyk in Lafayette High School in Brooklyn, unsure whether he wanted to continue in that way, Malamud passed Pinner on to Burt Rush, and took a temporary position as a clerk in Washington, DC. Help was needed in processing the national census conducted that year. Malamud had taken some civil-service exams which allowed him to become a postal clerk or letter-carrier. 'This is mad, I thought, or I am. Yet I told myself the kind of work I might get didn't matter so long as I was working for time to write' (TH, 27–8). He got a promotion at the end of three months on to a salary of $1,800 for the year.

> April. In Washington D.C. now—I can understand now why Pinner became so sick with melancholia not so long after he came to this country. Just not

knowing a city was enough to make me feel lonely ... Imagine what it must feel
like to be driven out of Germany.   (Notebooks)

But at least he was imagining. And he was writing again—short sketches,
or what he called 'mood pieces, about all I was capable of at that time', which
he sent to the *Washington Post*. The job was not demanding: if he worked
fast he could finish the day's work by lunchtime and after that 'kept my head
bent low while I was writing short stories at my desk' (TH, 28). He wrote
over twenty such pieces, nine or ten of which were accepted. They fetched
five dollars each, but it was seeing them in print that raised hope (HRC 33.2).

One was entitled 'The Refugee' and tells of a man like Pinthus or Pinner
whose English was somehow always at its worst in the mornings—because
'I guess in my sleep I become entirely German'. 'Sunday in the Park' was a
vignette of a lonely young man who is a newcomer in the city, desperately
glad of anyone to talk to. In 'The People's Gallery' the same youth watches
ordinary people looking at the works of art, loves the democracy of it, and
closes with a man standing before a Rembrandt self-portrait, looking at the
eyes 'sad, with a kind of softness', as though amidst all the sunshine and
laughter of the world around they were Rembrandt's 'biography'. Another
sketch, entitled 'Vacancy', is about the friendless young man eagerly learning
of a new occupant moving into his block of flats, but only ever hearing him.
Indeed so lonely was Malamud himself that he began to take an interest in
an equivalent writer-aspirant, another regular contributor to *the Washington
Post*, with a female name. Eventually he got up sufficient courage to write her
care of the newspaper, and ask for a date. But when they met, the woman
was in some way crippled or deformed or burdened, and Malamud quickly
made off, his fantasies crushed. It was the basis of 'The Girl of My Dreams',
published in 1953.

But at this time the best of his writing was in 'Armistice', a genuine short
story, which brings together the grocery store and the state of the Jews in
Europe by means of the radio to which Max Malamud would listen with
drawn face, hearing Hitler 'crackling across the ocean, threatening, taunting,
berating the Jews' ('The Lost Bar-Mitzvah', HRC 33.8). In 'Armistice' the
world news terrifies Morris, a widower-grocer, which in turn upsets Leonard,
his clever fourteen-year-old son. It is like something large—the fall of civilization itself perhaps—registered within somewhere small—a common
store. The day that France falls, Morris is enraged to see the pleasure on the
face of Gus, the meat-salesman. For a second there is a violent mini-war in
the shop itself, with Leonard caught in the middle as the war's frightened
peace-maker:

'You Nazi, you,' Morris shouted angrily, coming from behind the table. 'You, Nazi! You don't deserve to live in America!'

'Papa,' cried Leonard, holding him, 'don't fight, please, please.'

'Mind your own business, you little bastard,' said Gus, pushing Leonard away.

A sob broke from Leonard's throat. He began to cry.

Gus paused, seeing that he had gone too far.

Morris Lieberman's face was white. He put his arms around the boy and kissed him again and again.

'No, no. No more, Leonard. Don't cry. I'm so sorry. I give you my word no more.'

Gus looked on without speaking. His face was still red with anger, but he was afraid he would lose Morris's business. ... He threw the basket into his truck, got in, and drove off.

As he rode amid the cars on the avenue, he thought of the boy crying and his father holding him. It was always like that with the Jews. Tears and people holding each other.[15]

Malamud had put the image of the twosome into the mind of the enemy and kept it there, just about protecting themselves from what all around was still condemning them.

The representation of home in 'Armistice', achieved as it was away from Brooklyn, was a surer and more objectively rendered sadness than the Washington loneliness of the present described more frailly in the other sketches. But Malamud was not wholly alone in Washington. Ben Loeb told Paul Malamud about the genesis of 'The Girl of My Dreams', because it was with Ben of all people that Malamud was rooming. Loeb was the clever, more extrovert young man who for a little while had taken Malamud's place with Miriam and ended his thin chances. At Erasmus he had always thought that Malamud, with his writerly pretensions, was a phony. Now, with the extra tension over Miriam in the background, it was not long before a bitter quarrel broke out. Armed with his student psychology, Ben Loeb went after Malamud verbally in a clash of egos that tore Malamud apart.

And Malamud let Ben do it, as though he needed, wanted, and was even interested to hear it all. The 1930s notebook, as usual, made a rational list out of Ben's accusations. Thus, item by item: Exaggerated ego, the result of an inferiority complex; use of knowledge for show, in order to compensate; talking too much and boasting and dramatizing; tremendous ambition disguised as some lonely search for belonging and tradition.

Next section: the causes of these traits. They were to do, said Ben, with Malamud's childhood; with social inferiority and being ashamed of his parents; with lack of sexual experience; with never having the things that others could afford; with wanting everyone to like him. Thus Malamud, he said, romanticized his suffering and failure. He made grand stultifying claims for his writing, with the corresponding fear of never being any good at it. It all made for a narrow kind of living, filled with psychosomatic symptoms, without room for joy. Malamud had found the category marked 'lost generation' and was satisfied to hibernate inside it.

Finally, Ben Loeb's solutions were equally brutal: fight the symptoms, especially the egoistic self-assertion; forget the novel, write only objective pieces for magazine; have the sexual relationships with women in place of the fantasy, and take more physical exercise; stop being like Clara Molendyk and drop the correspondence with adolescent school children. It was as though everything that had sickened Malamud about himself in his long adolescence had been waiting for something like Ben Loeb's sudden, sickened articulation from outside.

Thinking it over in the notebook, Malamud still hoped to heal himself by writing a novel. 'I still would like to write if I can. I wonder if it's worth trying. I must live as I write—or I'm sunk' (Notebooks). Somehow he had also, he knew, to live better, in order to write honestly. It seemed a vicious circle. For no one, certainly not Ben Loeb, told him how good 'Armistice' was, though Loeb was partly responsible for urging the *Washington Post* pieces into existence. Malamud himself never reprinted the story. It was left to Robert Giroux to spot it much later for the posthumously published *Collected Stories* of 1997. But Giroux did not spot Malamud himself until 1950. 'Nobody came,' wrote Malamud's admired Thomas Hardy, in *Jude the Obscure*, 'because nobody does.'

Yet one night in Washington, 'a young man in my twenties I lay at an open window watching the stars', after rainfall, and suddenly, he says in this note, he felt moved and blessed to be a writer (HRC 20.3). He had been 'laboring in vain for hours attempting to bring a short story to life':

> Then I experienced a wave of feeling, of heartfelt emotion bespeaking commitment to life and art, so deeply it brought tears to my eyes. For the hundredth time I promised myself that I would someday be a very good writer. This renewal, and others like it, kept me alive in art years from fulfilment. (TH, 28)

He was still waiting 'for the true writing life to begin'. It was a Wordsworthian moment for a young man who, as Malamud later said, could also have remarked like Kafka in his own mid-twenties: 'God doesn't want me to write, but I must write' (TH, 28).

The Long Courtship: Ann de Chiara

Malamud returned to Brooklyn late in 1940 to teach at his old school, Erasmus High, by evening, but to write by day. He was also to take temporary teaching work at Lafayette. On 30 June 1940 he wrote to Vivian Stein. She was going to marry his friend Alan Rothenberg, who, fourteen years her senior, had been her teacher at Erasmus, and Malamud felt the contrast:

> Within the last six weeks, four women, with whom I, more or less seriously (mostly more) went out, have announced their wedding dates. One I loved deeply; one I loved for a moment; two I tried very hard to love—they've gone now. There is no feeling left now—that is, nothing intense, but it was like having the past torn from my life.[16]

The second was probably Hannah Needle who married Joel, another of the Rothenberg brothers whom Malamud befriended partly also to get to know the father, Simon, a psychiatrist. The first of course was Miriam Milman. She met Malamud on Church Avenue some time after her marriage to Ted Lang and invited him to the apartment they had just moved into, with its own study, built-in bookcase, and work desk for Miriam. Malamud looked round and said, 'Oh God, I'd give anything for a room like that' ('The Young Malamud'). Now Vivian Stein was about to be married. He remembered Vivian five years earlier, 'dissatisfied and not happy'. What might five more years bring to him?

Malamud first met Ann de Chiara in February 1942 at a party given by Ruth Batchker, sister of Hortense, at the family apartment in Manhattan. Ruth had told Ann of an interesting young writer, and though Ann danced all night with someone else she noticed him sitting staring at her with 'soulful eyes'.[17] As her daughter writes, 'the twenty-five-year-old Ann de Chiara was a very pretty woman: five foot three, thin, full-chested, with fair skin, brown eyes, and shiny brown hair that waved slightly below her ears' (MFB, 66). Born in New Rochelle of Italian immigrant parentage, warm and vivacious, she was what Malamud was later to call 'an Italian beauty'.

When she was only two years old, her father had left her mother, Ida, for another woman, an American. The girl lived with her mother, her uncles, and her grandfather in a bustling, hospitable house. Ida's father was a strong and austere patriarchal figure, an enlightenment atheist who held the moral reins of his nominally Catholic family. He believed only in Nature. Ann remembered him making her take hold of a snake when she was four or five, because she was so afraid of it. He once slapped her for breaking off a twig of a horse chestnut tree with new buds on it, but could not sleep all night for having struck her. 'I'll always take care of you,' he would say after his daughter had been deserted by her husband, but he died when Ann was seven.

With the loss of husband and then of father, Ida became increasingly subject to periods of anxiety and depression which were a burden upon the daughter. 'As a very little girl, a three-year-old,' writes Janna Malamud Smith, 'my mother more than once had to coax the hysterical, despondent Ida out of committing suicide. They'd be alone. Ida would be crying frantically on the bed, threatening to kill herself. Her daughter would have to offer her up cause to continue' (MFB, 106).

Later, when Ann was seventeen and at college, her mother remarried—to Gino (Gennaro Barbieri), a musician, a conductor, and expert in opera, who increasingly over the years was forced to earn his living by giving singing lessons. It was a house of music, and, with Ida's gift for cooking, of warm hospitality. Ann herself found a cultural mentor in an Italian intellectual twenty-five years her senior, an engineer who had left Italy because of his opposition to Fascism. Domenico Citanna (called Citty) was passionately interested in books, particularly Russian writers, in theatre, in concerts at the Met, taking Ann under his wing from the age of thirteen. She loved him for it and he loved her, but with caution and scruple, deciding not to ask for her hand because of the age difference.

Naturally fluent in Italian, having lived in Naples for a year in 1926 after her father's desertion, Ann graduated from Cornell in 1939 with a degree in French, having spent her junior year, 1937–8, in Paris. Some idea of her romantic vitality, her youthful capacity for excited joy is given in an account of 'what Paris meant to me', written at his own request for a Malamud who had known little outside Brooklyn:

> It was getting away from everything that is known and familiar, and venturing into the unknown. At the same time, it meant seeing a city, a country which I was familiar with in my reading and studies ...
> The reality was even more exciting than the imagined picture. Never will I have such a feeling of exhilaration ... It was a fulfilment of a vision of beauty. It was a new freedom, an adventure away from the affection and worrying of parents and families. It was also an escape from a past which had not anywhere near lived up to my romantic dreams. I had been a self-conscious, unpoised, timid (sexually) adolescent. In France, I blossomed. I adjusted. I had fun. I thrilled with the joy of living. ...
> Perhaps this letter also tells you why, since then, I have always wanted to reach a kind of peak—which I know I will never again experience. After

the heights which I achieved in that year, it is difficult to be satisfied—in a
way—with less exaggerated emotions.   (28 February 1944)

In similar vein, Malamud loved to hear that the legendary tenor Enrico Caruso
had ridden in the family car to Ann's christening. It was a romanticized taste
of culture and glamour that seemed to open up the world for enjoyment.

Ann's father came back into her life on her return to New York and the
Depression. A successful distributor of marine steam valves, he had helped
finance her year abroad, but now urged her to obtain a good permanent
job. 'He was not a violent man but he banged the desk, and he might even
have cracked a glass on his desk, in trying to tell my mother that I really
ought to become more independent and leave the nest.' Throughout the
early to mid-1940s she worked for the Madison Avenue advertising agency
Young and Rubicam on market research, earning $25 a week and living in an
apartment in the Ansonia Hotel left her by Gino and Ida when they went to
Florida.

This was a young woman who had an image of strong men with 'character',
men who had their own separate ends and beliefs, and often an independent
commitment to a cultural vocation. But she had also had powerful experiences
of being let down by men, and not just her father. She had been engaged to
a lively and attractive young musicologist of Scandinavian background called
Hal, who had been getting his Masters in Music at Cornell and was later
to write a book on Sibelius. Ironically, the night she met Malamud was the
day that Hal married Ann's successor. When Ann and Hal were together,
Bernadette Inkeles recalled, there was a New Year's party at which Ann
became very disturbed and publicly angry with Hal because he had appeared
dressed up as a woman. His mother was a drinker and much later he became
one too. But it was he who broke up with Ann. And thereafter, as with
her feelings after Paris, there was, it seemed, to be no equivalent Romantic
thunderbolt:

> I had my doubts about my relationship with Bern. It was not a stroke of
> lightning. It wasn't one of those things where I was so crazy about him from the
> beginning that there was no reasoning left. I had had that kind of experience. I
> cared about him—but it was the kind of loving that was on and off. I always
> had a lot of respect for him and his integrity. He had character. But it was a
> gradual coming to care.   (Ann Malamud)

Even so, by May, Malamud was writing her love letters from his newly
rented room in a pleasant house in Marlborough Road, Flatbush:

> What does it mean when, increasingly, you find yourself thinking about one
> girl; when you read, and the words are woven into thoughts of her; when you

work, and her image, like light falling upon darkness floats into your mind;
when you rest, and her presence is with you?

What does it mean when, in memory, you hold her beautiful body in
your arms and rekiss kisses: when you constantly hear her voice, see her face,
remember her laughter, tell her loveliness and take quiet pride in her wisdom—

What does it mean?   (28 May 1942)

Sometimes she would come over to Flatbush to watch him teach; they would
eat at Sears' or Oetgen's and drink tea in his room; go to the theatre or meet
each other's friends; writing or telephoning each other during the week.

Yet the question 'what does it mean?' began to take on a harder edge.
The problem had to do with Malamud's commitment to his work. He could
not long continue with the thought of her in the midst of his writing. The
relationship with Ann became swiftly implicated in his struggle to get right
in the writing *and* in the living *and* in the juggling balance between the two.
In retrospect, in 'Long Work, Short Life' (1984), Malamud was to put it as
explicitly as he had dared to think:

> What about marriage—should I, shouldn't I? I sometimes felt that the young
> writers I knew were too much concerned with staying out of marriage, whereas
> they might have used it, among other things, to order their lives and get on
> with their work. I wondered whether I could make it a necessary adjunct of
> my writing. But marriage was not easy: wouldn't it hurt my career if I urged
> on myself a way of life I could hardly be sure of? One has a gift—therefore
> he's better protect it from those who seem to be without a compelling purpose
> in life. Many young women I met had no clear idea what they wanted to
> do with their lives. If such a woman became a writer's wife, would she, for
> instance, know what was going on in his thoughts as he worked in his sleep?
> Would she do her part in keeping the family going? I was often asking myself
> these and related questions—though not necessarily of someone who might
> answer them.   (TH, 28–9)

It is the voice of the traditional male, in all the potentially chilling language
of 'using' marriage and making it an 'adjunct'. But what he recalled was not
simply a calculated 'Wouldn't it hurt my career?' Rather, he remembered
something more fearful and complex: 'Wouldn't it hurt my career *if I urged on
myself* a way of life I could *hardly be sure of*?' What saves this from being no
more than cold selfishness was Malamud's life-long belief in the obligation to
one's talent—even though that talent and that egoism were always in danger
of becoming confused. He had staked his sanity on that talent—necessarily
before it could be proven; even though it might not exist. And now the act
of faith involved severe costs as well as fearful risks. It demanded a resistance
to arguably easier human needs, to the warmth of sexual yearnings, and to

the emotional desire for a partner and a family. It risked the sacrifice of a
normal human life in tough protection of the vulnerable gift. The ostensible
coldness was also a passionately austere commitment to survival as a writer,
with survival as a man following hard upon it. To be a writer might be
a romantic delusion. But for Malamud it felt almost anti-romantic in the
thought-demanding claims that writing was rawly making upon him.

Ann de Chiara half-saw, and was half-persuaded to see, how (as she herself
put it) 'you must achieve your own conception of success—which for you is
being a writer—or you will not be contented nor will you be able to content
any one else you live with' (19 July 1943). Even in pre-feminist terms, it was
tough for her because what was required was a young woman with a sense
of 'a compelling purpose in life' which nonetheless she was to put, not into
herself, but into being 'a writer's wife'. The demand was outrageous—unless
she was the one willing to fulfil it. It was selfish and pompous—but less so
if the talent was both struggling and exacting. Yet Ann was a young woman
from a relatively advantaged family, having gone to a good college, who could
assume she had prospects with regard to social status, wealth, or marriage. 'It
is very brave of you,' she recalled a friend saying to her as the relationship
developed, 'But, you know, you're very attractive. You don't have to marry
a Jew.' But religious difference was not the issue. It was rather that she was
confronted by a demandingly serious and rigid young man who had not
accomplished anything significant in life and whose prospects looked very
limited. Nor was hers a consuming passion, by the light of her past love. The
issues and doubts were worked out and struggled over in the course of time.
It was to be a long courtship that took nearly four years.

A postcard of 2 August 1943, written from a summer writing retreat at
Brant Lake near Gene Lewis and his family, makes clear the fussily mundane
and listed demands that were awaiting Ann:

> Please send me some envelopes large enough to mail out manuscripts in.
> Also two soft pencils with erasers on them. I haven't got the crackers or the
> shirts yet, but I expect to receive them in this afternoon's mail.
>
> I'm a little worried about leaving any completed chapters around here. If I
> sent you one, could you have it typed for me in a week? Please don't say yes if
> you can't. I know you haven't a typewriter now, and I don't want you to stay
> overtime at the office. However, if you do think you can type a chapter now
> and then, I'd like you to do it *within a week* after I send them. It makes me feel
> bad when you leave them lying around untyped.

His daughter remembered a car accident in slippery ice in 1968. Even though
it was Thanksgiving, he had insisted on getting in a morning's writing.

Irritably she was giving her father his lift to college, the precious manuscript on the back seat, when the car skidded and hit a tree. As they escaped with cuts and bruises, in shock, the first words Malamud could utter were, 'Where is my manuscript? Where is my manuscript? I need my manuscript' (MFB, 234). Everything was dedicated to the manuscript. 'Writing is an intense experience. You do it twenty four hours a day, no matter what,' he wrote to Ann, 15 August 1943, 'You must understand that and be lenient with me.'

Yet his concern about the scale of his demands and his anxiety as to his own emotional capacity were genuine. By November 1942, he is writing to Ann in fear of the sexual and emotional commitment that is going on alongside the commitment to the writing, a fear that was not wholly or comfortably selfish:

> The first thing is that I feel miserable about having hurt you. I never never want to do that. I fought very hard against finding myself in the position where I would have to hurt you. You know how hard I fought: I even went to a psychiatrist to have him tell me that there was hope. I tried everything.
>
> I've not grown up; I can see that. For some reason which I can't explain well, I want to be free. It's got something to do with my writing. I've seen so little, done so little. I want to do and see; I want to get the urge out of my system before I think of settling down. I'd hate to be in the position of breaking up a marriage to satisfy this sort of wanderlust

But the writing—the part of him that would not allow himself to be shackled—was also inhibiting this freedom to do and see. Going to a psychiatrist was a huge step for someone who was desperately private, always saving his experience for his writing. Ann Malamud recalled:

> There was a period when we were courting when Bern worked for a few months in a war materials factory because he felt he had to make some sort of contribution and also, I think this might have coincided with the period when he was in severe anxiety, which was one of the things that delayed our marriage. He went to a psychiatrist for a couple of months. The diagnosis was a kind of depersonalization, it was called, where he felt he could not love. It also had a lot to do with his work—and with words, the relation of language and feelings, the difficulty of writing about emotions without emotion.

He could write the words for the feelings, but he could not feel them. It is as his novel protagonist was to put it in *The Tenants* (1971): 'What have I done to myself? So much I no longer see or feel except in language. Life once removed' (p. 107). This was a climax in the story of the search for all that Goodman meant by that apparently simple word 'honesty'.

In November 1942 Malamud also proposed a break from the relationship: 'I know that I shall never meet a finer, more honest, more lovely, more understanding woman than you. That's why I fought against myself as hard as I did.' He feared unfairly leading her on, out of his sexual and emotional needs. Yet by July 1943 the on–off pattern is clear: 'You brought up marriage in your last letter', he writes: 'impossible to think of a division of my energies', 'immediate marriage, therefore, is out of the question', 'get married when I am far into the book so that I know, no matter what new changes I am undergoing, I shall not give it up', 'otherwise won't be able to live with myself, nor will anyone be able to live with me', 'you know the kind of man I am; you must give me spiritual elbow room', 'I said before, we'll be married, at the latest, by next June'.

They were not married by July 1944. One of Ann's letters offers a snapshot of the continuing tension, caught in characteristic little ways: 'Please don't let small details worry you. And when you get off the train in New York I expect to be greeted with a good-natured smile, and not a frown of anxiety caused by the fact that your luggage is scattered, or something' (4 August 1943). The mutual sensitiveness jarred on each other. He sounded grumpy and distant on the phone, or brief and dry by letter. She did not understand how he had found it difficult to use the telephone as a kid and this was a carry-over. She left his untyped manuscript lying around, or did not seem to realize in her demandingness how tired and worried he was made by the effort of writing. Then there were all the fiddly details of his diet. He needed looking after: he wanted his graham crackers and his 'Social Teas' cookies for a stomach ulcer serious enough to grant him 4F exemption from military service. It was the result of nerves, as well as a long history of irregular and skimpy meals taken between customers at the back of the store, especially in the years immediately following the death of the mother. But Malamud was mortified when the local druggist said to him, outloud for all around to hear, that his stomach problems might well be psychosomatic.

But the writing was making progress. In 1942 he was writing short stories such as 'Spring Rain', or 'The Place Is Different Now', or 'Benefit Performance': 'I laughed. I could hear my own voice in it from the beginning, so there was no need to borrow other voices' (LC II 1.1). It was the voice of the disadvantaged. There is in these tales a father who can only say at night in his sleepless thoughts what he cannot say in the day. There are those two sons of Mrs Murphy in 'Life—From Behind A Counter', one a ruined thief, one an unforgiving policeman. There is also a kindly barber who gives a free shave to the thief who was once a friend to his lost son: scraping the tough stubble that hasn't been touched for a week, the barber daydreams of his own boy coming home some day and—quiet detail—his at last being able to 'kiss him on the cheek'. There's an unemployed and ageing Yiddish actor, his wife and daughter at work, who opposes the girl's relationship with an uneducated young 'plum-ber'. But the young suitor shouts back that at least a plumber 'could support a wife and don't have to send her out to work for him'. And already with these stories the pattern is set: there is revision and revision. It takes at least three drafts, he tells Ann, for a short story.

His bedsit routine was firm: bed at 11.30, get up at 8.15; wash, breakfast, read *The Times*, begin work by 10 until 12.30; shave, eat, read for an hour, back at work by 2.30; quit at 5, shower perhaps, read or listen to music until 5.40 and then dress to go to teach evening class; back by 10.20, drink milk, read again, wash and go to bed (letter to Ann, 4 November 1943). He is looking for at least five hours of writing a day, though sometimes he cannot really manage it, idles over his desk or has to sleep in the afternoon. And there are also simple delighted reports of being able to mend someone's washing machine, selling a story just when money was low, being able to master a switchboard, or a spell as an air-raid warden. He told Principal McNeill of Erasmus that class sizes are too big and instructed some administrator at Lafayette on what constituted fair teaching hours: 'Would you ever believe', he writes Ann, 'I was a timid little boy?' There are a couple of scripts accepted for the Bulldog Drummond detective stories on the radio, for good money, more than $100 each. But, for all the struggle, he was averse to writing what would merely sell: 'He really was so much moved by his own ideas and his own imagination. I can remember when an uncle of mine said, "Bern, why don't you write some pot-boilers and make some money, then you can write serious books." For him this was a ridiculous idea' (Ann Malamud). Increasingly, precious time was to be spent not even on the short stories but a big, autobiographical novel entitled 'The Light Sleeper'.

They wrote to each other about the relationship between Levin and Kitty in Tolstoy's *Anna Karenina* and their struggle to get it right. But the next crisis came soon after his letter of July 1943 insisting upon delaying marriage—and perhaps in reaction to it. Ann was now helping type out his drafts and, in the course of so doing, had begun to make suggestions. Characteristically, Malamud never accepted them, yet ended one letter earlier in 1943 by signing himself 'The guy who doesn't mind being criticized by you.'

But he could never really be that guy. As he said to her, he was 'abnormally sensitive about myself and my work' (24 July 1943). So it was that on 14 August 1943 Ann unwittingly went far beyond herself in an extraordinary seven-page letter of criticism. She had been reading the revised first chapters of his novel and, without his consent, had showed them to her friend Bernadette Inkeles. 'I don't set myself up as a super critic,' she says, but five people—the two

Schrag brothers and Paul's wife, Susan, herself and Bernadette—had now read the work and agreed on its deficiencies. 'Let me enumerate the things that struck me,' she goes on: 'lack of an encompassing emotion', 'unnecessary detail', 'the result is clumsy', 'in a most unsubtle manner', 'much below the usual quality of your work … in the *longest* sentences I have ever read'. She does praise an older part to do with Ben, the protagonist, reminiscing about his childhood and his mother, and talking to his father. But then she criticizes a long conversation with an older teacher about Man and the War, which is not interesting enough:

> If you cannot bring in a subject of that kind without treating it in a more subtle or 'original' manner, if you cannot bring in a new idea or a new angle, then don't have a long discussion of it. The remarks you have to make, Bernie, forgive me, but they are 'old hat'. Bernadette also brought this up. It's a lot of conventional and re-hashed ideas on the subject.

All his life Malamud was worried about his intellectual standing, doubting the adequacy of his education and his capacity for ideas. If she wasn't attacking him for holding her off, she was attacking the work that he claimed was responsible for it.

And Malamud had to read that Bernadette agreed ('she does a bit of writing herself'). Ann needed the judgements of others, in a mixture of fairness and insecurity: 'Don't be angry because I discussed it with Bernadette. I was excited about it, and I felt I must let someone who feels un-involved in the whole pattern read it. I was also afraid that my having read it in another form might have created a notion of it in me that was inflexible and that maybe I couldn't readjust myself to a new way of starting the book.' Janna Malamud Smith says it was characteristic of her mother to 'brace her view by citing someone else who shared it. "So and so and I agree," she would say' (MFB, 68). From childhood, she had respected strong men. But it made her nervous when she sensed weakness in her man, and when she felt insecure and fearful, her way was often to lash out in criticism. But even as she goes on remorselessly, she is also somehow trying in this tangle of feelings to be selfless and helpful. Her fear was: was he botching the work for her sake? 'You have the talent and the will, Bern, but what's wrong? Is it that you are in a hurry to get through?':

> Don't be; I don't care if it takes you *4* years instead of *2* as long as it's good. You simply must not look on the book as a means to an end; it is an end in itself. You must not see it in the light of your relationship with me; learn to separate these 2 parts of your life as much as possible without allowing them to become problems for each other. If you cannot be 'my feller' or my husband and write

a book at the same time, and you must make these two elements in your life conflicting, then I am going to stop seeing you. You must realize yourself as a writer.

The last sounds like Malamud himself. But in the knot of emotions, 'I am going to stop seeing you' was hardly reassuring. For all her talk of separating the writing and the living, even worse are the two paragraphs that follow, in connecting them:

> As to your obsession with detail—is not that a reflection of your own life? Please try to minimize details—in spite of your diet.
> As to the lack of an encompassing emotion, which is reflected in the dryness of some of your writing—is that also a reflection of your life? B[ernadette] remarked that your approach to love is 'clinical'. Quote and unquote!

She ends: 'I know that this letter will seem *scathing* to you. But I had to express myself completely and uncompromisingly once and for all. Meanwhile you must not be discouraged.'

It was hardly encouraging. Malamud's response is dated the same day, August 14:

> Dear Baby,
> If there is one thing that I have learned from sad and bitter experience, it is that a writer should ask for no opinions until he has completed his first draft of his entire novel. For the second time my morale has been smashed, and I'm trying to put together the pieces so that I can go on without trying to recast my idea still another time.

The first time had been at Paul Schrag's house the previous May.[18]

Ann must have already communicated something of what she thought over the telephone because he speaks of going on writing into the early hours after her call—'on sheer will because my heart was in my boots and I was fighting despair every minute I wrote'. If the whole thing is wrong, that leaves him agonized at the thought of still another start. She may be wrong. He must go on, anyway. Then he manages this sentence, which he underlines: 'Now, Annie, this is not your fault and please don't feel bad.' It was, he goes on, 'just poor policy of me to ask an opinion so early in my work'. It is a harm which 'I've wrought upon myself.' That was the end of Ann's criticisms.

But what he had wrought was a situation in which it was Ann who became the more reluctant party. The final crisis came in late 1944, early 1945, when she writes him that she thinks she no longer loves him, because it has gone on too long. He replies that even though it is he who is saying it, it is also he who also knows her: she is wrong—'you mustn't think that your love for me is gone'. And he risks saying that she no longer understands herself:

I have told you what you are suffering from: dissipation of energy; lack of a focus for life. To a large extent, that is my fault. I have been most prodigal of your love. Now I am on my hands and knees, trying to collect the substance I wasted.   (24 January 1945)

For once he is writing hard in his letters. 'I'm suffering for my blindness,' he says, adding subtly, 'and I should like to spare you the same suffering in the future'. 'If you deny me now, you will have a rock in your heart for the rest of your life.' But also frankly giving no inch, he adds in a separate paragraph: 'Though my heart wants you with a single purpose, I must repeat again what marriage will mean for you. Though I love you and shall love you more, most of my strength will be devoted to realizing myself as an artist.' She will be called upon, he says solemnly, 'for all the love, patience, courage, understand-ing—and paradoxically—selflessness that you are capable of bestowing'. It was the last of Bern's famous lists, for the while. It was hardly wooing talk, but it stuck to a sort of truth even when he did not want to lose her, and she could not say that she had not been warned. They were to be married later that year.

The tenderness that had always been a part of the relationship now surfaces ever more clearly in almost courtly manner. In a letter 7 February 1945 he writes: 'Dear Annie, Tonight, three years ago, we met. Many lovely memories have come to me today as I sat here working.' For some time, without much spare money, he had been saving quarters in a jar in order to buy her a really good wedding ring. The ring she got from Georg Jensen the jewellers had a lovely design of lilacs, and cost over $40 rather than the usual $10. But Ann had to pick it out herself, along with a girlfriend: 'Bern had nothing to do with it. He hadn't the time.' Thus, on that double-note, ended the curious near-four-year courtship, with the marriage in November 1945.

But Vivian Stein, who had eloped to marry to Alan Rothenberg in 1940, left behind with a relative of hers a curious account of the wedding. First, it had to be delayed a week because no one had told the couple that the law in New York State required them to have an examination to prove that they did not have venereal disease. Then Alan Rothenberg, acting as best man, was told that his wife Vivian was not invited. Malamud said it wasn't a real wedding, in the sense of a fancy affair. The best man was expected to get the couple to the New York Society for Ethical Culture for the legal ceremony, because he had a car. Ann was accompanied by her grandmother, a little old Italian woman dressed completely in black from head to foot, and by an aunt, but by none of the rest of her family. It was almost farce, Alan told Vivian:

The two women got into the car and just sat in the back of the car crying from the moment they got in until the moment it was all over. Alan was driving and

Ann sat in front with Alan, and Bernie sat next to her, and they were driving to wherever it was—and Ann turned to Alan and said, 'Oh, my God, Alan, why am I doing this? What am I doing? Why am I doing this? I'm not sure I should be doing this', and she got very upset and Alan got terribly embarrassed—he didn't know what to do or what to say, and Bernie was kind of sitting there looking very embarrassed and not saying anything also, not knowing what to say, and finally Alan in desperation turned to her and said, 'Well, for heaven's sake, look, if it doesn't turn out there's always divorce'. But she just kept sort of carrying on, and the two other women were in the back of the car crying

Malamud told Danny Stern that he liked his comedy, like that of Charlie Chaplin, 'spiced in the wine of sadness' (TH, 19). But he couldn't have written this himself.

Claude Fredericks found Ann Malamud suddenly remembering some of this one day in 1970. '[She] poured out her life to me, the older man she'd known and adored and given herself to (he refused her) at 18, the boy she'd been engaged to before she married Bern, the advice the minister at the Ethical Culture society where they were married gave her about marriage, warning her she'd meet men handsomer than Bern, that there were grave differences—he poor & she with money, he Jewish she Italian—that had to be bridged—('And he was right, he was right' she said).[19]

What Malamud was writing and continued to write was 'The Light Sleeper', a novel about a depressed young man seeking to find himself, whilst waiting to be called into the army. The notebooks refer to scenes—'chapter 1 in the toilet', 'reflections on death of a child', 'the cat and the kittens', 'the slip—Irene', 'potency'. The correspondence with Ann refers to a train journey taken by the protagonist and a girl like Miriam Milman, talks with an older teacher, and family memories. When it was eventually completed in 1948, it was sent out to publishers by Malamud's new agent Diarmuid Russell and rejected six times.

The readers' reports give some sense of the nature of the book. Dudley Cloud for the Atlantic Monthly Press reported on the work's 'anguish and loneliness'. 'There is too much introspection', without enough drama or straight narrative; the protagonist was not likeable, and the language—'the strange, clipped writing, laden with nouns, elliptical, as it tries to capture Jewish accent and idiom'—was too difficult to follow (LC I 56.7, 14 October 1948). Pascal Covici reported somewhat more sympathetically for Viking Press on 26 October: 'Mr Malamud has certainly poured into these pages all he ever felt and thought and dreamed of, but it seems to me with no sense of selectivity, restraint or discipline. The novel is obviously autobiographical ... A great deal of work went into this, all the brooding of many years and it would sound cruel to tell him to put this away and start all over again, but that is what he should be told' (LC I 56.7).

The conclusion was that it would be better to write a new novel than to try once again to revise this one. 'I don't care if it takes you *4* years instead of *2*,' Ann had written in that terrible letter of August 1943, 'as long as it's good': it took more than five years, the writing going on for two or three years *after* the marriage—and still it wasn't good, the criticisms of Ann and the others horrendously justified, it seems, after all.

In an account of 'Creative Career' written in the early 1950s, Malamud looked back on the place of 'The Light Sleeper' and made his acknowledgement of all the criticisms he had received, to no apparent end:

> Soon I embarked upon a long autobiographical novel—a mistake. I knew little about novel construction, and it would seem to me now, less about the man I was writing about. But I struggled on, unwilling to abandon the book because I felt it was bad to give up on the first one. The writing, after three false starts, dragged on for five years. Ultimately, after I was married, I completed the book. Diarmuid Russell, who had become my agent, was willing to try it on about five publishers. I tried another half dozen or so and that finished it.   (HRC 33.2)

It felt very bad to him that it had got nowhere, for all the years and all the pain it had caused both him and Ann, separately and together. In retrospect, it can be seen that those years were looking for the expression they found in *The Assistant* in 1957 and The *Magic Barrel* in 1958, ten years away in the slow, complicated chronology of Malamud's development. But the feeling resolutely remained in Malamud that had he stopped at some point during all that time and left 'The Light Sleeper' unfinished, he might never have carried on as a writer—and certainly not as writer with such a hard-won apprentice's experience of writing a long fiction:

> My only triumph was in completing it after so many years of toil. However, I knew, from all the reading and writing I had done during those years, that I had learned something about writing. I could tell from the way certain pages of the manuscript read. There were many pages that had an existence apart from me.   (HRC 33.2)

He had learned to move beyond short stories in the difficulty of getting from scene to scene and relating the years to the days that seemingly formed them. Yet there is no surviving manuscript of 'The Light Sleeper' and consequently no way of being able to detect what pages possessed that different quality, transmuted beyond autobiography.

Bernadette Inkeles remembered the newly married Malamuds living in 1 King Street, Greenwich Village, and how she and Alex temporarily house-sat for them. The manuscript of 'The Light Sleeper', wrapped in brown paper, was in the living room on the top of a tall bureau by a window with a clear drop beneath it. 'Obviously the most important thing of all is the manuscript,' Malamud told them. In case of fire, they were carefully to drop it out of that window.

But in his new life in Oregon towards the end of 1951 or the beginning of 1952, Malamud had finally taken the much-revised sheets of 'The Light Sleeper' out of the house into the backyard, where there were wire brackets and containers for the burning of trash. There, with his four-year-old son, Paul, excitedly beside him, he deliberately burned the manuscript.

THE SECOND LIFE

3

◄◄◈◈►►

Oregon

Forward: 1 King Street, Greenwich Village to Corvallis

In New York in 1952 Malamud chanced upon Ben Loeb. There followed a
correspondence which summarizes how far Malamud felt he had come since
the turbulent days with Loeb in Washington in 1940. Ben Loeb recalled it
for Paul Malamud in an unpublished interview:

> In 1952, I wrote him apologizing for bad things I must have done in relation
> to him, and his answer was, 'I was no lilly then. I think what has made me
> liveable-with is my wife, the kids, providing an open wound of love, a certain
> amount of success in my work, and a lot of reading in Freud and neo-Freudians.
> However, like all men I have very rough edges still, especially a touchy ego that
> has become an intellectual as well as an emotional problem to me.'

One of those neo-Freudians was Henry Stack Sullivan, who believed that
analysts should help their patients think about their recurrent mistakes and
then devise experiments that shifted these patterns. Another was Karen
Horney, who showed how the need for safety, for protection of the ego,
could itself create neurotic egoism. The intellectual problem was 'The Light
Sleeper': autobiographical writing was too tied up with the ego to be fully
creative. But Malamud's phrase 'an open wound of love', combining ardour
with vulnerability, speaks of his own experiment in defiance of his egoistic
defence mechanisms: the emotional commitment to marriage and children.

In the ancient Jewish tradition described in *Life Is With People*, an individual
is never fully adult until he or she is married: Malamud knew it intuitively.
Alongside the fear that marriage would take over his life was a competing
need for the order it could provide, and Malamud had found in Ann a
woman who would be content to make him and his work the centre of her

household. But it *was* an experiment that went deeper than convenience: to Malamud at the age of 31, after all the romanticism of a long adolescence, marriage was a classic form of life which required discipline and the capacity for learning. Ben Loeb also quoted from another letter he received from Malamud in February 1954:

> Yes, I have changed. The fires of experience burned out much of the worthless ego. Writing helped. I wrote an unpublished first novel, which taught me a lot about myself—at times I thought too much. I read heavily in Freud, discerning all sorts of insights. Then I read the neo-Freudians, Harry Stack Sullivan and lots of abnormal psychology and I began to have some idea where and why I had gone astray. My wife's genuineness as a person helped me to analyze and to achieve certain changes. Naturally, I don't pretend to have licked myself into the best possible shape—there are still habitual, nasty ego responses. But I know what I want myself to be and try hard to be it. Having the children helps too. One wants so much for them, he learns to think secondarily of himself. Then, too, the lessening of economic frustration and some success on a prestige level as a writer was good. I am thankful I could change.

Marriage challenged the ego with love. The registering of a finally unascribable gratitude in that last sentence is also part of this sense of a new life and a second chance.

It is this period, from 1945 to 1952, which marks the formation of a second life for Malamud in his thirties: the marriage in November 1945, the birth of son Paul in October 1947, the great move west to a post at Oregon State College in 1949, the birth of daughter Janna in January 1952 after a previous miscarriage, and also finally in the summer of that year, the publication of the first novel, *The Natural*. It was a change of condition: he was no longer Brooklyn's Bernie; to Ann he was Bern.

After that protracted courtship, the first stages of marriage were accompanied by quiet surprises and gentle healings. In July 1946 Malamud returned home ahead of Ann from a first visit to her mother Ida and stepfather Gino in California. Alex and Bernadette Inkeles came over to supper with him alone in the King Street apartment. He writes to Ann, 'I missed not having you. For the first time with another couple around, I felt that I was sort of incomplete without my wife.' He adds a few simple sentences for Ida, thanking her for the warmth with which she had received him: 'If my mother were living she'd kiss you for being so kind.' Ann Malamud recalled how her mother loved Bern. When she had her depressions, he would take her out and walk with her.[1] The depression was another link with his own mother.

But in 1946, there were still two major problems facing the couple. One was to do with Malamud finding time to write while also having to earn a living wage. The other was the decision whether to have children. The two, of course, were inter-related: if Ann gave up her job at Young and Rubicam, the pressure on Malamud would mean his having to teach during the day, as well as the evening. Between 1943 and 1945 as a single man Malamud earned between $1,700 and $1,8000 per year, mainly from teaching at Erasmus. In 1946 Ann brought in over $3,100 and the couple were earning $4,500 between them. With the cost of medical insurance, Malamud would have to do twice as much teaching in the past if they were going to survive on his income alone.

But the larger and more secret consideration was not financial but biological. Given the mental instabilities in both families, but particularly on the Malamud side, what were the chances of a child inheriting a tendency for manic-depression or schizophrenia? One of the reasons that Malamud had been reading the neo-Freudians, Henry Stack Sullivan and Karen Horney, in the 1940s was that both of them rejected the idea that schizophrenia was biologically determined and contested the view that little or nothing could be done by psychiatric means. Malamud had been worried about his own state; Ann in particular was worried about a future child, with Malamud often reluctant to talk about it; and before them both was the deteriorating example of Eugene, Malamud's younger brother.

Yet they went ahead and had Paul in 1947. Soon after the delivery, Malamud writes to his convalescing wife, from school 'as the boys are writing':

> I'll never forget how radiant you were during your pregnancy and what a joy it was each night to hold you in my arms in bed. Though the privacy of two is gone, I look forward to your return so that I can once more lavish upon you les tendresses you always call forth.
>
> Grow strong, darling, and bring home our little boy who must add to our happiness because there will be that much more love.
>
> Yours forever,
>
> Bernie

It is a part of his new appreciation of experience that, without conflict or deprecation, he can acknowledge what is gone even as he celebrates what is gained. And with that gain also came reconciliation with his father. Ann was glad of it: 'When Paul was six months old, he and his wife came over and brought gifts. Liza was the one who had that kind of tender style, because he wouldn't have known what to buy for a gift. I do know that, when we were living in Oregon, apparently without Liza knowing, he had saved money for us after I had my daughter. And he sent us the money, a couple of hundred dollars that he had set aside, for a washing machine.' It was still not an easy adjustment for the new parents. Paul cried every night for the first few months, the mother nursing him every couple of hours, the father walking the floors with him or rocking him in his crib. They sang a particular popular song to put him to sleep: 'I've just told every little star | Just how sweet I think you are | Why haven't I told you?'

Yet for all his hard-won delight in new fatherhood, Malamud did have to take on teaching-work during the day as well as the evening, with less and less time for his writing. In 1947 on the basis of his published stories, he was invited by the directors of Yaddo to spend the summer working on his novel, at the artists' colony in Saratoga Springs. But family and economic circumstances meant he could not take it up. In 1947 and 1948 the family income fell to $2,500, and with medical insurance and doctor's bills, they were about $1,000 short of covering their annual expenses and having to borrow. Malamud had never earned more than $90 in any year for his writing, and now he was earning nothing that way. More teaching was taken on to get the income up to around $3,400. Joseph Driscoll, President of Chelsea High School, offered a snapshot of Malamud as a hard worker, teaching at his school in 1949:

His free period was spent in the library reading. I found a book he had been seen with. It was 'The Fall of Angels' by Anatole France, a model of prose style. He lived quietly in the neighborhood and on fine spring afternoons his wife wheeled a carriage and small baby to the park opposite the school. At dismissal, they greeted one another tenderly and walked up the avenue toward home.

(HRC 29.6).

As a writer Malamud had begun making a small reputation for himself. In Greenwich Village he was befriended by the novelist Mike Seide because Seide admired his short stories. To Malamud, Seide was extraordinary in his risky idealism and perfectionism—he would not finish a first draft and then revise, but fight to get everything out completely and finally the first time, though it might take him years. Years later Malamud put up $5,000 to help get the long and long-awaited thousand-page novel finally published. In Greenwich Village writers and painters began to become the people to whom he could speak more unrestrainedly. They knew and shared the inner dramas of the vocation. Yet for the moment the vocation was hardly sustainable.

Then came a major initiative. With the advice and encouragement of Alex Inkeles who was now teaching at Harvard, the Malamuds consulted a reference book containing the names and addresses of all the colleges in the country and picked out the likeliest possibilities. This was a boom time in

1. Malamud's mother, Bertha Malamud, née Fidelman (1888–1929) (left) and one of her sisters

2. Malamud's father, Max Malamud (1885–1954) with grandson Paul (b. 1947)

3. Site of family store, on 1111 Gravesend (later McDonald) Avenue in 1915, then a pub before Max Malamud bought it *c.* 1924

4. Family store (marked by vertical arrow), partly obscured by the El (1947)

5. Malamud's own drawing of the store, during the composition of *The Assistant* and marked as owned by Morris Bober

6. Erasmus Hall High School

7. Bernard Malamud (left) and Herbert Wittkin graduating from City College, BA, 1936

8. Malamud (right, in hat) in the Catskills, 1936

9. Ann Malamud
with son Paul in
New York, 1949

10. Malamud reading to son Paul in Corvallis, *c.*1951

see him. He went numb too. He wanted her but the barriers made a terrible
construction: She was Jewish. The mother would throw a fit, and maybe Morris.
Adele had plans, he sensed from the way she lived, for something big. He
had not even nothing--had held up her old man, and despite his [bleeding]
conscience, was stealing from him. How complicated could impossible get?

He saw only one way through the impossibility, beginning by relieving himself
of the oppressive load on his heart for the crime against Morris, by telling
him that it was he who had done it. If he could bring himself to do that, and
Morris accepted his explanation and solemn apology, he thought some of the
other things--granted that Adele fell for him, which was a hard thing to grant--
would in time take care of themselves, although he did not underrate the
difficulties. The confession had to come first. From the minute he entered
the grocery store on the night of the holdup, he knew that for whatever wrong he did he would
suffer until he absolved himself by vomiting up the deed in words, an act
basically repugnant to him, yet one from which, squirm as he would, he could
never escape. It became increasingly clear to him, in the store,
that he had known this for ages. It was something that came wrapped up in his
whole life; knowing that somewhere along the line, no matter what he had
previously got away with, or what dumb luck had thus far kept him out of the
clink, he would, though his gorge was thick with shame, have to say to some
stranger that he had done him a great wrong. Yet when the time came to say
it, when, shortly after the holdup, he was alone with Morris in the back of
the store, and strove with himself to spill it then, he lost his courage. He
failed because he feared the consequences, afraid, once he got started confessing,
that he would never leave off, afraid Morris would not understand; so he had
substituted a sort of indictment of his life, one which only partially expressed
what he felt about himself, arousing the old Jew's sympathy; and then he went
away, more or less contented--temporarily it turned out, because the need to

11. First typed draft of *The Assistant*

The end of ~~January~~ THE YEAR gave nothing to it. The sky was dark, barren, often broke into snow. The wind ~~was~~ ACTED still like an ax. She ~~looked at~~ AWOKE TO each monotonous day with dulled feeling. Then one Sunday afternoon the sun broke out of prison, the day thawed; winter let up for an hour and she went walking. She thought of the season of flowers and discovered a smile on her strange face. A warm breath of air was enough for inspiration. She equated nature with love and was suddenly grateful for living. But then the sun ~~felt~~ SANK behind clouds and it snowed steely pellets. She returned home, frozen. He was standing at Sam Pearl's corner but she didn't see him. He felt bad. He wanted her but the facts made a terrible construction: She wasn't interested. She was Jewish. The old dame would throw a double fit and Morris another. And he sensed that Helen, from the way she walked, had plans for something big in her life, not him. He had nothing--a backbreaking past, had ~~held up~~ her old man, and despite a scratchy conscience, was stealing from him too. How complicated could impossible be?

He saw only one way of crawling through this stone knot, and ~~that was~~ to start by getting rid of all the extra weight he was carrying around on his conscience for holding Morris up, by admitting to him that he was one of those who had done it. It was a funny thing about that: he was in a sense not sorry that they had stuck up a Jew--What was a Jew to him?--but he hadn't expected to be sorry that he had picked on this particular one, Morris Bober; yet he was. He hadn't minded, if by mind you meant in ~~thought~~, but what he hadn't minded didn't seem to matter; what mattered was how he felt while doing it, and after; and he felt bad. When Helen was around he felt worse.

The confession would have to come first--this was what stuck in the neck. From the minute he had followed Ward Minogue into the grocery, he had got this sick feeling that he would someday have to vomit up in words, no matter how tough or disgusting it was to do, the very thing he was then doing. He felt, in some appalling way, that he had known this long before he had entered the store, before he had met Minogue, or ~~had~~ come to New York; that he had known

12 a

12 a–b. Same passage as in no. 11, revised in second draft of *The Assistant*

8-6

ever since he was a kid ~~that~~ he would someday, through a throat swollen with
shame, eyes in the dirt, have to say to somebody, some poor son of a bitch, that
he had done him a dirty wrong, otherwise the wrong would rot in his memory.
This feeling had lived in him, he thought, like a habit, a thirst, a goddamned
need to get rid of everything that had happened yesterday--for whatever had
happened had happened wrong; to confess it out of his system and bring in a
little peace, a little order; to change the beginnings, beginning with the past
that always stank up the now--to change his life before it choked him. to death.

Yet when the time came to say what wrong he had done Morris, when he was
alone with him that ~~December~~ November morning in the back of the store, as they were
drinking coffee that the Jew had ~~offered~~ given him, and the impulse came on him to
spill it now, now, he strained to heave it out, but it was like throwing up your
whole life, with the broken roots and blood; and a fear burned in the pit of his
stomach that once he got started confessing he would never stop; so instead, he
said a few hurried things about how ass-backwards his life had gone, which
only partly said what he wanted to say. He had worked on the Jew's pity, and
gone away contented for the time being, but not contented long, because soon
the need to say it returned again, and he heard himself groaning, but the groans
were not words.

Frank argued with himself that he had done right in not saying more than
he had. Enough was too much, and, anyway, how much of a confession was the Jew
entitled to for eighteen or nineteen lousy buck, he had taken and put back into
his cash register drawer, and for the knock on the head he had got from Ward,
who Frank had come with unwillingly? Maybe willing, but not to do what had
finally been done. That deserved some consideration. Furthermore, he had
pleaded with the bastard not to clobber Morris; and also lately had turned him
down when he cooked up this idea of another stickup against Karp, who they
were out for in the first place. That showed his good intentions for the future.
And who was it, after all was said and done, that had waited around shivering

13. Same passage from *The Assistant* with second typed draft now written out again in longhand

14. Malamud in Assisi, 1957, photographed by son Paul

15. Bernard Malamud, by Rosemarie Beck, 1958 (also in colour on cover)

But if he loved her why was it so?

If, ecstasied out of his senses he let down his guard--was leapt on by fate--
Lord help Levin.

But suppose he looked her, knew at least, why?)?

Yet why if he loved *her* loved he? Because she had, one unforgettable
day, given herself to a city boy in a forest, an act of imagination he
insisted on forever paying for? And for the continuance of her generosity in
bed (was the ~~guy~~ *one* on top ~~(not so)~~ *ours* ganerous?), taking serious chances (he chanced
as much)? Or was he moved to love her because her eyes mirrored Levin when
he looked? Or to drag truth closer--because he was compelled by some law
of his being to be in love with her honest, open, vulnerable, sad, intelligent
self; the beauty she created in his eye? Neither questions nor answers made
much difference now, for he recognized fait accompli when he looked it in the
face. Who was he kidding, or what pretending to hold off or dress in camouflage
~~color~~ "The truth is I love Pauline Gilley." He was moved deeply by his confession, ~~so he was timed~~ exalted. What an extraordinary *human* thing--to be in love.
Truly a miracle. "Pauline, I love you, need you, never leave me." As he walked
~~in~~ the streets ~~in a falling rain~~ *UNDER A FULL MOON* he felt he had recovered youth and freedom.
The world changed as he looked; he knew it *it was night & close* would and wasn't afraid.
Courage!--you love. He loved what he looked on, life, could not understand--
the ~~same time~~ *while* he did--why he had ever denied ~~it~~ *love*. He thought of his years of
misery as though they had endured only minutes, black birds long ago flown
into night. Gone for all time. He had made too much of then in memory and
not enough of possibility, ~~crystallizing in~~ new forms forever. Love was etern-
ity. He beheld in the eye of heaven the rose of love. (Oh my *ever* romantic soul,
despite the shit I've lain in)...But he had long ago told himself ~~anything~~
that when he came again to this point--better whom. He had been as a youth
vulnerable, ~~romantic~~ *to feeling*: whatever was beauty was more beautifuly than it was; what
was love, more lovely; what tragic, ~~greater than~~ *immense order it wasn't* tragedy. Afterwards he
groped in the dark for reality, the blinded Levin. Therefore he had many times
warned himself, harden, kid, toughen--especially in love, for love as ~~excess~~ *because*
~~nohense of~~ *immense* feeling, cripples. Let love live in Levin, not he in *love*. ~~Let him love~~

A drowning man, ever drowning, he saw the world from under the sea. It was
not the world, it was the sea. He lived ~~in~~ strangeness. Like someone choking
himself for not feeling the more he choked the less he cared. If he kept on there
would be no problem. He thought of finishing himself off, wandered in an anguished
daze for hours at a time in downtown streets, his eyes glazed when he gazed in glass,
undecided whether to dive into a river or whiskey glass. His ~~tortured~~ tortured
thirst was thick as toothache. What sweet, what deliriously sweet release to drink
and forget, to pour the searing stuff down his sick throat. To feel the sodden
spirit soar. To be in peace not Levin. To stink in the gutter but be satisfied.
He looked long in every brown-bottled tavern as he staggered along, drunk with
emptiness, wrenching harder each place he had to pass ~~. In indecison and despair he dragged himself to the next.~~ At last he entered and
stood at the bar. "What'll it be?" said the hairy bartender. Staring at his thick
mustache, Levin muttered, "Love," and fled.

Sitting in the dirt under a bridge of rattling boards, dust sifting into his
hair whenever a car rumbled overhead, Levin, the machinery of his existence creaking, in some private place within, reasoned thus: that he, again in the grip of a
nervous reaction that he had once before in his life severely experienced, did not
presently desire her, does not diminish her value as a person, woman worthy of his
love. She has a woman's beauty. She has grace and loveliness. I know when I
look at her in spite of what I don't see. She has a mind, she has character.
I respect my history with her. What I had with her from forest to toushanan was unique;
it may never again be as it was but I respect what it was. I have no cause to
stop loving her, granted I have loved, and this I now grant. I have loved her;
she was my love. Her love for me was good once, it can't be bad or useless for
little or no cause.

He tried then to say that time alters things, everything changes, to
give himself grounds for escape, for if the change produced incompatibles, he

17a

was an honest man ~~even~~ when he ran. He sought again for grounds for escape so
he would once more be free to roam unbound, unburdened, where fancy fancied; but
when Levin rubbed his beardless face he (instantly) recalled his love for her, she
whom he had fought himself to cease loving.) He had loved her, this was the premise.
The one you chose was the one you had to live by. If you chose the wrong (premise)
you were done to begin with. You were all your life in jail. You cheated yourself
of the short freedom you had, the little life you had to be alive in. [If he had
loved, why should he love her less?] She was his love, changed by it as he by hers.
She is for me. I can go to her and be loved. ~~I am loved, this is the difference~~
from last time. [I'm responsible for her in love with me.] I made it so. What she
gives I must.

He said it many times. What had happened had happened against the will. No
matter how much he had gone through, what renounced, to what degree banished, or
misused, or failed feeling, if Pauline loving him loves, Levin with no true cause
not to, loves her. I won't lose what I have unwillingly lost. I will love, if necessary, without feeling. I will wait for it to return to me. [A tree can grow out
of a broken root.] Perhaps it's only a season gone, I'll wait for it to return.
What has happened to me can only be a temporary thing. Maybe it's a test of love,
to hold on when I want most to let go. Love if it is love is forever. I'll make
it be what it must be. I'll marry her.

Having reasoned thus, he cursed reason.

They talked, that night, in a field. It was cold, the clouds low and foggy,
the moon, when it shone through, high and unfamiliar. They both wore coats. Levin
was his numb shattered self. Pauline rubbed her cold nose agains his rigid jaw.
Her hair was scented. He could smell. She teased him to kiss her and he kissed
her when she teased. She was bright with plans for them. He had come with one of
his own: delay, forstall, ~~████~~ postpone telling Gilley. He still hoped to serve

17b

feeling or none? Although he had asked her to tell Gilley nothing, she was,
after all, alone from here on in, possibly frightened of what had to be done,
certainly disturbed by it. He felt for her a ~~sort of~~ ~~sheer~~ pity, not enough
to give him relief, but at least a response.

He lived for days in a sterile (salty) country. Everdrowning Levin saw the
world from under the sea. It wasn't the world, it was more of the sea. He
lived in it as a ~~lone~~ fish, poking ~~into salty bubbles~~, his own invention.
Until Gilley appeared with hook, line, and sinker. He then became this half-
dead thing choking itself for not feeling, the more he choked the less he
cared. He thought of finishing himself off, wandered in an anguished daze
for hours at a time in the downtown STREETS, his eyes glazed when he gazed in
glass, not knowing whether to dive into the river or a whiskey bottle. His
tortured thirst was thick as toothache. What deliciously sweet release to
drink and forget, to pour the ~~searing~~ WHISKEY ~~liquor~~ down his white-hot throat.
To feel sodden spirit soar. To be in peace not Levin. To stink in gutter,
satisfied. He cast lovesick looks at each brown-bottled tavern he staggered
EACH PLACE HE PASSED. HE DRAGGED
by, drunk with emptiness, wrenching harder against himself on his rectangular
circle, until broken by weariness, he went through a door and stood at a bar.

"What'll it be?" said the hairy bartender.

LEVIN STARED
~~Staring~~ at his thick mustache, ~~Levin muttered~~, "Love," he muttered, and fled
~~And fled.~~

Sitting in the dirt under the rattling boards of the old river bridge,
sweat clinging his face
dust sifting into his hair whenever a car rumbled overhead, Levin, the machinery of his existence badly creaking, in a private place in the mind put
things in place thus: he, again in the grip of a [nervous emotional] reaction
(for whatever cause) that he had once before in his life severely experienced,
person
did not presently desire her, did not diminish her [as a woman] worthy of his
love. [She had in her way her value. I know when I look at her in spite of
I CANT BLAME HER FOR WHAT'S HAPPENED.
what I don't see. I also respect my history with her. What I had from
forest to frustration was unique, worth having, I respect what it was. If
I could have it again I would want it again. I have no cause now not to love

her, granted I loved, and this I must grant. I loved her. We loved.

This was the premise. And the premise one chose was what he must live by.
If you chose the wrong one you were done to begin with. You were in jail with
your life. You cheated yourself of the short freedom you had in the world,
the little of life to be alive in. He tried then to say that time alters
things, premises wear out, change produces change, incompatibles. He hunted
reasons for escape, to go where he pleased, unbound, unburdened, where fancy
fancied; but when as he touched his beardless face he returned to the premise.
It was unalterable; they had loved. She was his love, changed by it only as he be
hers. What had changed beyond that wrongly willed, then unwilled. A man
sentenced to death may regain his freedom; so may love or it isn't love to
begin with. No matter how much he had suffered, what renounced, to what
degree misused or failed feeling, if Pauline loving him loves, Levin with
no true cause not to, must love her. He would love if he had to, without
feeling. He would hold on when he wanted most to let go. He would compel
love to be what it must be.

Having reasoned thus he cursed reason.

They talked that night in his car, parked on a dark country road with
fenced fields on both sides. Levin had for a few hours felt some relief at
a decision taken, and had even begun, he told himself, to anticipate seeing
her. But after he had picked her up on a corner near her house, as they were
driving, her head against his shoulder, her scent warm--he could still smell--
he had to admit it was bad again. He felt, although she sat
at his side, her body touching his, as though he were in another room,
READY TO SPEAK getting out of the house. The anticipation he thought
he had had, had gone out of him like a flight of birds sucked by some force
into an underworld; or maybe blown the other way, scattered and lost in the
sky, his feeling for her--and himself--swallowed by the winds. He was afraid
to tell her that. He wanted to preserve her image of him as a man, but he felt

17d

18. Malamud and Paul in Vermont, 1961

university instruction because the troops were returning from the Second World War, many of them without a degree, and the government provided the opportunity for them to go to college at the expense of a grateful nation. Higher education was beginning to become mass education, and this meant a shortage of university teachers. For the first time in his life, the economic situation was in Malamud's favour. Though he had no PhD, he did have the MA which—though at the time it had seemed increasingly a waste of effort—was just sufficient a qualification.

Ann Malamud typed out 200 standard letters, applying for a chance at a job. Few replied but one was Dr Sigurd Peterson, Head of the English Department, Oregon State College. It wasn't a university, but a cow college of 6,000 students—endowed by the state to further practical agricultural education in particular, with the liberal arts left very much in the background, as its name 'the Lower Division' accurately suggested. On 15 April 1949 Malamud returned the official application form, together with a photograph and 'a memorandum setting forth something about my preparation and background and my ideas on the teaching of Freshman Composition' (OSU 3.4). He heard nothing despite a promise of a decision in June. He wrote again on June 22 and finally received an offer by telegram on July 29. He only had one other offer—from a college in New Mexico. The Malamuds chose Oregon State for being closer to Ann's mother. Malamud sent Peterson a number of worried questions about housing, syllabus, and general conditions. He knew nothing: 'Does the Corvallis climate call for any special clothing?' (30 July 1949). Peterson replied advising the purchase of a gabardine overcoat for the rain. Finally in August 1949 the Brooklyn city-boy set off alone to the small rural town of Corvallis—population 16,000—to try to sort out the housing situation, whilst Ann waited in her mother's house in California, with young Paul.

The Depression was over. A genuine New Deal was coming through, and the fifties was a time of new opportunity for the Malamud generation. Salaries were not high, but goods were cheap, life was brightening amidst new building and fresh decorating, education was flourishing, and after an age of austerity people began to enjoy a social life. Malamud's initial salary was $3,600. In 1949, 1950, and 1951 he also began to make money from his writing, about $300 each year.

'I should like very much to teach in a college or university which encourages creative work among members of its faculty,' Malamud had written, hopefully, in the biographical data attached to his application (OSU 3.2). Yet it was not an altogether ecstatic beginning for the Malamuds in Corvallis. Oliver Lawrence, a colleague, recalled Malamud being shown round a beautiful house for rent which he found simply too large for the family needs—whereupon one of the two elderly lady owners, when asked for further suggestions of where to look, said to Bernie: 'Why don't you ask some of your people to help you?' Your people meant Jews.[2] From Los Angeles Ann wrote him not to be concerned that his worried letters might depress her:

> when it comes right down to it, all that you describe is much as I had pictured it, including the housing problems and the probable mediocrity of the English dept. We had our eyes rather well open about this move. If there is any disappointment it's over the fact that summer school is out & so is the Ph.D, if you want it. However, you may be able to get a summer school job elsewhere, perhaps in Cal. And as I discussed with you a Ph.D from Oregon would probably not be worth much.

'I was nakedly without a Ph.D' (TH, 5). And without a Ph.D he was allowed only to teach English composition, not literature. He taught freshman classes to the future engineers, agriculturalists, foresters of Oregon—where composition meant grammatical exercises, reports, and letter writing. At the national level, after the war the country was badly in need of graduates to rebuild industry and drive on the economy. At the regional level, OSC was state-funded to serve the local community. It was a technological environment.

Charles Crow, a friend from New York who had been a teacher of composition after leaving the army, gave Malamud advice on textbooks in the hope that the college would tolerate a liberal attitude to grammar. But Peterson and his head of composition, Herb Nelson, were old-fashioned sticklers for neo-classic 'rules': when to use 'shall' as opposed to when to use 'will' was what counted. The students were to be taught to write, not to think, whereas in his 'Ideas on Teaching Freshman Composition in College', written in application for the post, Malamud had insisted 'Understanding the ideal is the beginning of its use'.[3] At their first meeting Herb Nelson simply gave Malamud a few minutes on the basic requirements, then said he was late for a golf game and went off down the hall practising his swing. Shep Levine, a painter who was head of art, told Paul Malamud in an unpublished interview that the 'long-term hacks' in the English Department of the fifties, ill-equipped to cope with anything literary, made sure that the larger classes and the most marking and paperwork were given to the more talented younger faculty. But in the face of all such discouragement Crow insisted:

> Don't feel too much alone in an academic desert of 'practical' instruction. The humanities are retreating everywhere. That is largely the fault of administrations,

not of students. Despite the dumbheads among students, I daresay there are now more American students thirsty for the humanities than ever before, though most of them don't know it. How could they? (9 January 1950, HRC 8.3)

Yet if the students wanted to gain a full degree in the liberal humanities, they had to transfer to the nearby University of Oregon at Eugene. It wasn't long before Malamud was complaining about Oregon State losing its best arts students to their rivals.

Malamud teamed up in particular with Chester Garrison, an ex-army man from New Jersey, who acted as a calming but loyally supportive presence:

Bern stood out as a New Yorker. He was outspoken, as New Yorkers are, compared to people in many other parts of the country. I think out here it's desirable, or was desirable, that one be nice and not seek confrontation and think things over before kind of maneuvering for a position; but if Bern saw something was wrong, he spoke out immediately at meetings, or if it was an administrator, he spoke out immediately to that administrator.[4]

Malamud would ignore or complain about departmental regulations, particularly if they got in the way of his writing time. Sometimes he would amuse himself with practical jokes. Oliver Lawrence recalled a nervous moment at home when he was not sure whether to offer round alcohol in front of Herb Nelson, given that Sigurd Peterson was a devoted abstainer and alert to reports. But Malamud encouraged him: 'And *how!*' he had responded when Oliver Lawrence had privately asked him in advance whether he drank beer. When Lawrence finally plucked up courage to offer the beer around, Malamud was first in line: 'The sonofabitch smiled sanctimoniously and said, "No, thank you."'

But the most notorious college incident occurred one Governor's Day. On such occasions as part of the celebrations, the Recruiting Officers' Training Corps, the college military unit, would march up and down the football field before the dignitaries and faculty assembled in the stands. But one year in the very early fifties, at the time of the Korean War, a ragbag protest group held a counter-march in front of the Governor, bearing placards against the ROTC. It was led by Lester Eugene Lundahl, a quiet poet, in his first year as an instructor in the English Department. An embarrassed Herb Nelson immediately fired Gene Lundahl that Friday evening, on the pretext of smoking in the classroom. Lundahl went to Malamud, in no way a protest marcher but the natural supporter of the young and the powerless. Malamud, as usual, went straight to the Dean and the President. Groshong, an Oregon-born colleague preferred to work through the departmental committee. By Monday the man was restored for a year, though Groshong believed that it was working through the proper channels that had achieved it. Malamud told Herb Nelson he had 'a heart of corn flakes' (MWB, 8). As he neared retirement, Peterson remarked to Groshong of Malamud, 'I'll get rid of him if it's the last thing I do.'[5]

If Malamud looked down on the philistine parochialism of the college and felt out of place—'one foot in a bucket' (TH, 6)—Ann too was unhappy and struggling to adapt at home. Paul was susceptible to bronchial problems and had an allergy to house dust. He missed six weeks of schooling when he developed scarlatina, and a paediatrician was worried that it might have affected his heart. These were real concerns, but both the Malamuds were anxious parents anyway, without secure models from their own past. In addition, the rented housing situation caused tension, the first house no more than a cabin, but the next an improvement—a simple two-bedroomed ramshackle house on the street that led into campus. By the end of the first year Ann had a stomach ulcer. It was not until 1955–6 that they bought their first house, at her insistence, for $12,750 at 445 N. 31st Street. In 1949 Corvallis was slow, easy-going, parochial, and blandly uncultured: 'Many of the streets, even major ones, were still unpaved and there wasn't a single traffic light in town. There were no art galleries, only two or three depressed movie houses, little music, no theater.'[6]

Malamud began to set up evening classes in creative writing for local residents. Gradually, with the help of a ginger group of friends—Chester and Louise Garrison, Faith and Tom Norris, and Warren and Sue Hovland—he helped form the Foreign Film Society, a Great Books reading group, a Liberal Arts lecture series, an arts theatre group, and a chamber-music society.

Moreover at home Ann was becoming a good cook, and was helping to establish the sort of social life, amongst other young faculty, that Malamud had never really known before. 'Some of my earliest memories', writes Paul Malamud, 'are of dinner parties. My mother would laugh and refer to Corvallis as "the centre of the universe—ha ha", meaning that it was almost like that, then, for a little while.' Malamud himself seemed to his young son in the early 1950s 'a vast presence', 'a happy academic': 'He had a heavy blue-green beard shadow, and wore rimless spectacles. He was fond of Shetland sweaters and corduroy jackets. He was professorial, given to orderly thought and habits.'[7] Behind it all was the security of marriage, after the past insecurities of both of them. As Ann wrote him on their fifth wedding anniversary, 6 November 1950, using their pet-names:

My dearest Bunny,
    It seems as though we've *always* been together, and yet it does not seem like

five years. Now quite what all this means I'm not sure—but I do love you, maybe *that's* it!

Baby

It was a new life. For all the initial disadvantages and the gradual adjustments, the life-story was now part of the western rural world of Oregon—of a kind of American life foreign to Malamud. For whereas before in the big city Nature had been for this Wordsworth of Brooklyn no more than a small break in the clouds, or a walk in the local park, there was now opening out all around and above the small-town parochialism sudden huge panoramas of great skies, coastal beaches, and forests. The small town of Corvallis was set in the midst of the wide Willamette valley of farms, forest, and sawmills, of hills of dark green Douglas fir trees and golden-brown fields of wheat or grass, with the Cascade Mountains to the east, the Coastal Range to the west and the Pacific Ocean a two-hour drive beyond. The initial settlers were French trappers working for the Hudson Bay Company, leaving a few names on the land before moving on—hence Corvallis, heart of the valley. There was still a wildness, an other-worldliness, about the place: in that sense, at least, this was a larger world. Elizabeth Henley was a poet who came to teach at OSC in the mid-fifties and could still feel the land's history, almost geologically, the tracks just beneath her feet, barely yet built over by the latest pioneers: 'Old streets in many an eastern town | Are cobbled and bricked streets yet; | But the streets of a western city changed | Before a child could forget'.[8]

But only Malamud's later language can recreate the emotional effect it had on him. His old English teacher Florence Ripley Mastin wrote out in a letter of 13 December 1961 to Malamud two passages from *A New Life* which particularly marked the sense of a startling, educative change in a newly arrived Easterner who, 'although he had lived little in nature, had always love it' (NL, 8; HRC 18.7). One was of the little Chaplinesque man with his gabardine and umbrella:

> If it was raining he went under his blooming black umbrella. Usually the morn-ing was overcast between wettings, the moving sky continuously surprising. Overhead the clouds rolled dark; ahead thinning through shades of grey to an accident of gold. To the north above the dark green hills a moody blue. In the west white steam shrouded the mountain tops. Depending on the direction he looked, above could be gold, black, silver, grey. He had never in his life gazed so long at sky ... (NL, 97)

It is no longer even '*the* sky', but richer, looser, and wider than that in its changing surprises. The other passage was again of surprises (a favourite Malamud word) despite disappointment with the cow college:

Within a week men on tractors were harrowing the burnt fields, and the rich brown earth looked newly combed and awaiting planting. The sight of the expectant earth raised a hunger in Levin's throat. He yearned for the return of spring, a terrifying habit he strongly resisted: the season was not yet officially autumn. He was now dead set against the destruction of unlived time. As he walked he enjoyed surprises of landscape: the variety of green, yellow, brown, and black fields, compositions with distant trees, the poetry of perspective. Without investment to speak of he had become rich in sight of nature, a satisfying wealth. In the past he had had almost none of this, though in winter he had tenaciously watched the frozen city trees for the first signs of budding; observed with reluctance the growth of leaves; walked alone at night close to full-blown summer trees; and in autumn followed dead leaves to their graves.

(NL, 62–3)

Not wishing now to force the rhythm of things but see what there was to see outside himself, nonetheless the man was still looking for his own new spring.

And yet another part of the life-story—the part underlying the tense deliberations about whether to have children—still remained back in Brooklyn, like a dark wintry alternative. For Malamud's decision to leave for Oregon was what also helped precipitate his younger brother Eugene into mental breakdown and hospitalization—and Malamud knew it. It was the other side of his own new life, and in a sense paid the price for it.

Backward: Eugene's Story

The life of Eugene Malamud was the elder brother's alternative story. It was like that almost from the start. Bernie had been good at school; but Eugene could not live up to what his elder brother had achieved. He got into trouble with his teachers, and stayed on at Erasmus Hall only at his brother's and father's insistence. Afterwards, disheartened by the Depression, Eugene said he was 'afraid' to go out and look for a job. At the same time, at another level, he began to develop a strong political sense, indignantly championing the ideal of a better life for the 'common man'. But mainly he still stayed home all day. If his stepmother nagged he walked out, hanging around with unemployed friends on street corners. Otherwise he stayed in his room, reading or listening to the radio. Something of the fecklessness of it is caught in the short story 'A Summer's Reading', which was printed in the collection Malamud dedicated to Eugene, *The Magic Barrel*.

Malamud himself continues the story in his letter of late 1951, written to provide background information for Eugene's doctors:

He began giving up his friends as they got jobs and drifted off to work. Eugene
continued to stay home. He was beginning to have a reputation as a recluse.
Friends continued to look him up and occasionally he went to parties with
them. He seemed to have no interest in girls. Both he and Bernard were
very much embarrassed once when Bernard, by accident, came upon Eugene,
masturbating. Bernard was disturbed by his brother's hermit's life and probably
nagged the boy. He had no realization till years later that Eugene needed
psychiatric treatment.   (HRC 20.2)

Even in its strength, the relationship was shaped by all that happened to the
parents and the need for surrogates: 'Bernard's fatherly feeling to his brother
was extremely strong. He tried up to build up his "kid-brother's" confidence.
Possibly Eugene responded with a son's love.'

Eventually with a few other local boys Eugene joined the Civilian Con-
servation Corps set up by Roosevelt to get the unemployed working on
the land. Sent out to Idaho, he bravely adjusted to this life, though he felt
lonely. 'He always had courage, something Bernard always respected him
for'—especially given the fears with which Eugene had to contend. Yet when
Eugene got back, it was only to return to his room, and he was 'almost glad'
when he was drafted for military service in 1942.

It was Eugene who had been called up for military service, not Bernie. The
older brother was excused, classified 4F, unfit mainly because of his stomach
condition. His teacher status may also have helped, and so (if he mentioned
it) may his brief consultation with a psychiatrist when first courting Ann. It
was early in 1942 when Malamud received a letter in which Eugene, on active
service, asked his brother to understand it if he had to do something drastic.
Malamud wrote Ann:

> My poor pop would just about die if anything happened to Euge. Last time he
> was here he sat heavy in his chair, his brown eyes filled with tears and sadness,
> saying, 'Oh, if they would only take me in his place, I would go with joy. My
> life is over; his has not begun. Oh, if he were here, I would put my arms around
> him and kiss him.'

'Mir far dir', me in your place. But it couldn't be Max, and it wasn't Bernard:
it had to be Eugene. In relation to Bernard, Eugene did not want it otherwise.
'Did you read or hear that they are going to de-classify men in 4F and charge
them,' he wrote his brother on 25 April 1942 'If you get into the army, I think
it will be the last straw' (HRC 12.7). It wasn't true; it was part of Eugene's fears
('I threw away a Jewish prayer book, and calendar, and I was afraid to do so').

At first Malamud thought of writing on Eugene's behalf to his officers or to
a chaplain. For want of anything else, he always tried to write encouragingly

to Eugene about his return. But in the letter of 25 April Eugene said that there could be no real return to what had been: either he would die in the war or come back a wreck. He served for four years, including 21 months overseas in the Pacific, at Hollandia, Biak, New Guinea, and the Philippines, and saw Hiroshima after the bomb. 'Later he was honorably discharged as a private first class' (HRC 20.2). He had been sent to a rest camp with what they called 'battle fatigue'.

But there was little actual contact with the enemy. Once he shot at a Japanese soldier and was horrified by what he had done. Eugene was in no sense a fighter:

> To fight one must have the will and spirit to do so, but I never had any courage, nor ever will. ... I am a man without spirit, without hope, and without faith. How can I live. Again I say I wish that I had never been born.   (Ibid.)

The discipline bothered him: he had trouble with some of the sergeants over him, and he hated the tedium. 'He found it extremely difficult to do such a comparatively simple thing as roll a pack,' Malamud wrote, 'He had a friend or two in his outfit but generally he was a lone wolf and probably considered a little strange. He read a lot and wrote many letters' (HRC 20.2). 'I can almost taste the sweet remembrances of life as an individual,' Eugene wrote Malamud, 16 September 1945, 'and these succulent memories sustain me. I hope it isn't too long before we can clasp each other's hand' (HRC 12.8). 'But if and when I get home,' he added in a letter of October 1942, 'I'm afraid I'll be afraid'.

Malamud takes up the account in his letter to Eugene's doctors:

> When he came home he was dearly welcomed by his father, step-mother and brother. For a time he was afraid of what it would be like looking for a job. He began to fall back into his solitary life. Bernard had left the house in 1941 to live by himself and he was now married and living in N.Y.C. He got Eugene an appointment for a job with a friend, but Eugene never showed up. That was one of the patterns of his life—Bernard digging up job opportunities and Eugene never taking them.
>
> Finally Eugene found himself a job, as a checker and stock clerk at Namm's, in Brooklyn. He was happy about this, Bernard too.
>
> For the first time in his life Eugene had a decent amount of money to spend on himself. He made friends in the store and visited bars with the boys, played softball with them and talked union politics. He was soon made assistant shop steward, and later became one of the union representatives who bargained with management. His attitude to his employers grew truculent. He honestly felt they were unjust to their employees. Once or twice, now, he went out with girls from the store—usually timid or unhappy girls.

About once a week, sometimes oftener, he visited Bernard and his wife. Bernard's wife liked and respected Eugene. He liked her. When their son was born Eugene was delighted. He enjoyed the child from its infancy. Though he found it difficult to shop for gifts (Gifts were never exchanged or ever given on birthdays in Max's house) he did manage to buy the baby a toy bus that the baby enjoyed very much. Eugene liked to play with the baby.

(HRC 20.2)

By 1948 Eugene was undergoing psychoanalytic sessions, arranged by his brother. The analyst was Dr Ernst Jolowicz, a sixty-year-old German refugee who was to suffer two minor strokes and thus be unable to keep up regular sessions. Eugene did not like the alternative man. About this time he took a vacation from the department store, always a difficult time for him, and never returned to work. Then things got bleaker. He thought everyone was talking about him; he stopped reading because he was beginning to hear the words as voices; he developed severe insomnia, particularly after being unjustly warned one night by a policeman not to loiter outside his own house. Increasingly he suffered from bad headaches, especially, noted Malamud 'when he attempted something formerly pleasurable' (HRC 20.2).

Everything that had helped keep Bernie together—work, books, discipline, routine—were somehow not there for Eugene. 'Trivial incidents were magnified by him': he bumped his head on the bus and thought the driver had made it happen because he didn't like the way Eugene had dropped his nickel into the slot (HRC 20.2). To Eugene, Bernie was the one who previously had helped keep such things in true proportion. When he was a child, he had cried for being caught spitting in a gutter outside a church till his brother had comforted him. 'I know it is difficult,' Malamud wrote him 15 October 1951, 'but I hope you will try a little to forget the thought that people wish you harm. It's been my experience that *most* human beings haven't the energy to go round hating others.' At times the constant counsel made Eugene angry. 'Personally,' he wrote on 5 July 1951, 'I think you and Liza calling me mentally ill all the time does me harm and keeps me in fear.' But mainly Eugene believed what he had written in his war-time diary—that Bernie is 'a port in a storm and a great intelligent person who guided me through the storm; he gave me direction and balance and if it weren't for him I would be a rudderless boat' (HRC 12.8).

Only now Bernie was away, leaving Eugene with 'a sense of being a complete failure with only blind alleys facing me' (11 September 1949). Malamud wrote back, sounding discouraged with his own situation in Oregon ('which Pop confused with Oklahoma'). But Eugene replied on 14 September, 'Your school isn't Harvard but it may have little pleasures that will delight' (HRC 12.8).

Eugene loaned him money to help get started out there. But with his brother having departed

> Eugene entered another period of difficulty. At work—he wrote Bernard—he felt he was disliked first for his union activities, then as a person. He wrote that he was suspected of homosexuality by people at work and by some in the neighborhood.   (HRC 20.2)

This was the dispassionate account Malamud offered the doctors. But Malamud had had a harder time explaining it to Eugene direct. On 9 October 1951 Malamud offered his justification, just a month before the hospitalization on 3 November:

> As for your finding out that I was human, all to the good, even though it cuts down, in your mind, the measure of my sympathy. To be an effective man, to provide for my family and do my work—the writing I had to do—it was best for me to leave New York. That this should hurt you was, as you describe it, a bad break. Frankly, except for you and Pop, I felt no attachment to the city. I had thought about what going away would mean to you and it worried me a good deal but I figured that you were in Jolowicz's hands and would be helped by him. I had no idea that he was sick and would be unavailable to you at a time when you needed him. That too was a bad break. You deserved better.
>
>   True, I left. But I left unwillingly. And no matter what you think, my sympathy for you is unending.   (HRC 36.5)

Malamud talks hopefully of buying a big house somewhere, if he can get a decent sum for his new novel, so that eventually Eugene can join his family and live with them. It always worried Malamud when things went wrong and he was not there. His father had had to have an eye operation in July 1951 and Malamud had written Eugene that he wondered if it was somehow a result of his not being there.

By 27 October Eugene was writing to his brother in the third person, as if he were indeed a case:

> Then there is Eugene who for a long time was afraid of himself and life because from an early age he was sexy, but because he hung around the house he was afraid of his passion because it was directed towards his mother and father and brother, which wasn't nice; so he suppressed it and the knowledge made him bashful. He tried to remain a baby so that he wouldn't lust towards his family, especially his mother who returned his love. So his father and brother must have resented him, hated him, and he thought this was because of his secret lust for them and he was ashamed of it.   (HRC 12.9)

With nothing in his life, everything was going on in his head. His brother was like a father to him, but now the re-direction took brother and father into a terrifying inner world.

Finally on 3 November Eugene came home from a visit to Dr Jolowicz, talking to himself. 'I assumed, mistakenly, the burdens of the Lord God Jehovah,' he wrote apologetically to his father, a month later, 'I was a foolish masochist, so foolish that I almost destroyed my life.' Max had been very frightened that November night. Delusional, paranoid, and suicidal, Eugene was committed to hospital. 'He wanted to see his brother' (HRC 20.2). Simply factual, it was one of the saddest sentences Malamud ever wrote.

Jolowicz's diagnosis was all too clear. On 3 December 1951 he concluded: 'He was full of paranoidal ideas and delusions so that any new idea was immediately incorporated into his distorted philosophy … This is in my opinion a case of "process schizophrenia": that means that other than psychological factors determine the course of this illness.' Then again he writes on 3 March 1952: 'The diagnosis has been always clear: a serious schizophrenic psychosis. The prognosis has been always poor as far as a cure was concerned' (HRC 36.7). It was inherited. No matter what Malamud had done, even if he had stayed in Brooklyn, the breakdown was likely to happen. Yet it hardly helped Malamud to think it: what for him was mitigation, for Eugene was a life sentence. Malamud was always worried about the genetic inheritance: when he suffered heart flutters in 1951 it was Eugene's turn to try to be reassuring, insisting Bernie had not inherited 'pop's heart' (5 July 1951).

Eugene was transferred from King's County, where his late mother had been placed, to King's Park State Hospital, 19 November 1951, and then to King's Park Veterans' Hospital in December, where he was declared an incompetent person by the Supreme Court, 21 May 1952. 'Mama did what a mother always does,' Eugene wrote his father, 'she saved my life and made me want to live' (December 1951). But if the dead had influence on Eugene's mind, the living could not get through to him. Max initially went every Sunday to visit, struggling out to the hospital on Long Island, leaving the store at 8, arriving at 11, leaving for home at 2, but by January it was getting harder and harder for him. He needed to apply for a pass, each time, to take his son outside for a walk. Eugene was infuriated that his father, bothered by the paperwork, trying to live in the present, would never get the pass in advance.

On 14 March 1952, the father wrote Bernie that he was delighted to receive a photograph of baby Janna, born in January, glad too that 'You Solt the Novel but you don't tell us how Much Money Your are Getting'—all good news from Oregon. Then he added that he himself has been upstairs with a cold but 'will be all right in a few More days'. In fact the 'cold' was a heart attack, and Max did not tell Bernie about it until he came to New York in the summer—partly to see Eugene for the first time prior to his release from hospital in July, partly to publicize *The Natural*. When he learnt that it had not been a cold, Malamud wrote Ann, 24 June 1952, 'You can imagine how I felt.'

And all the time between the hospitalization in November 1951 and Malamud's arrival in New York in June 1952, Eugene wrote his brother letter after letter. 'I see now why I should not have gone to psycho-analysis, but I had to know & did know. Unfortunately it led me to my mother who was in King's County. I wonder whether I have to die because she did; it may be so' (8 November 1951). 'I am in a nuthouse and I wander about it all as day passes day … A kid stands right near me and looks at this and people come to look out of the window and I try in spite of that to read and write. Do you see my problem, do you see how I must live? … Bernie am I nuts?' (undated). Eugene was scared that he was speaking his inner thoughts out loud; that he was repeating himself endlessly without knowing it; that both the doctors and his brother were urging him to change religion because being Jewish meant being neurotic. He also feared that he was being used for the purposes of sexual experiment, that he had been hospitalized because he was too sexual and had abnormal sexual powers. Now at last he had opportunities for sex but only to stimulate hospital patients.

'As I see it I am through—hopelessly insane' (8 November 1951). 'I must ask you to forgive me for acting as I did, which I know you will … It is a small thing besides my agony, the agony of being locked up' (9 January 1852). 'Bernie, did you ever cry out "He shall be destroyed"?' (12 March 1852). 'Bernie, I need you. I need you here' (5 May). And there was also this on 1 January 1952—so intelligently and helplessly frightened and angry: 'this letter is sadistic, designed to break your heart and I should hope that it does.' By April he is writing in guilt of his bad letters, 'I feel as though I menace you.'

Yet Eugene was allowed home in July 1952. There had been some sort of remission; he was well for a while, then slowly relapsed. 'Pa tells me that you've gone back to your old habit of sleeping during the day and remaining awake at night' (12 December 1952, HRC 36.5). Malamud writes to his father urging upon him the importance of letting Eugene have some control of his own money, in order to take his measure of adult responsibility: 'he was always treated as a baby' (9 November 1952). But in March 1954 Max died of a heart attack, the first real warnings of which had appeared in the attack of 1952. Eugene and Liza carried on living together in the store until she died of a stroke in 1967, where thereafter he lived on alone.

Every week, or at least every fortnight, for twenty years Eugene wrote his brother, and his brother wrote back. From the beginning Malamud had encouraged it: 'You don't know how much I miss your weekly letters. I don't care what you right [sic] about, even if "there is nothing to say", so long as I feel in communication with you. That has always meant a good deal to me and I sincerely hope, to you' (18 September 1951, HRC 36.5). He hoped the writing would help, at first as therapy, perhaps later only as company.

To read through the hundreds of Eugene's letters over thirty years, now lodged in the Harry Ransom Center, University of Texas at Austin—with the tone and content and even handwriting suddenly changing just before each of Eugene's renewed attacks of illness—is piteously to witness an intelligence compulsively grinding itself small for want of substance to communicate or life to lead. 'If trying to understand were all, you would be a free man', Malamud had written him at the onset of the crisis. But it was not to do with understanding. Re-reading some of this correspondence in 1959, Eugene himself appreciated what it must have been like for his brother to have to receive and reply to all that he wrote, year after year: 'It surprises me at your patience, since you carried your own heavy burdens and still do, accepting these letters' (10 May).

Ever increasingly and at great length Eugene had nothing to say: 'I hate to close, for I feel near you when I communicate with you' (15 July 1962); 'I have little to say these days, so it is hard to write a letter about nothing. I am doing my best.' There was little to do, beyond the guilty pleasures of masturbation: 'In bed I must do something, this seems the best, only I couldn't or shouldn't concentrate on myself. But this is fun, it must be done and it will help' (HRC 13.5). In his youth Eugene had read much, and written one or two stories, but like some parody-figure of his own brother, he considered himself a fake. In one of his private notebooks for 1960 he says, 'I often wish I hadn't started this diary, that I had no need for it, that I just lived as everyone lived. Yet hasn't writing been my salvation, as I make clear the muddle, try with words as accurately as possible to describe my state of mind which keeps up, my mind does, all day long' (HRC 37.1). As Eugene sat there writing, he was like his brother, the successful writer whom he admired and envied, only living in some terrible parallel universe. 'If I used all that energy at home to create instead of to destroy, I would have a book perhaps coming out as Bernie has, and it is never too late. I may not be a writer, but I was always better than I thought I was' (2 April 1952).

Yet as Malamud wrote at the top of one of the pages in Eugene's notebooks, when he read the entries shortly after Eugene's death: 'Delusions about genius, voices that are sick supporting this delusion, and good sense mixed with it.' He had long known that his relationship with Eugene was something like that of the saved to the damned—where the saved could imagine just how close the one could be to the other. Back in 20 September 1952, after the publication of *The Natural*, he was explicitly writing to Eugene about what was to be his next work, a sixty- to seventy-thousand-word novella provisionally called 'The Broken Snow'. It was a study 'somewhat realistic but not totally so (because art has more than realism)' of a man who is 'on the verge of mental illness, who manages to shake himself out of it through having to perform a difficult service, on a lonely farm during a snow storm, to a sick woman and her child' (HRC 36.5). It was clearly modelled on Eugene, shared with Eugene, to be written in hope for both of them.

'It will be, I think, a realistic study of the onset of a schizophrenic experience upon a man whose particular burden is a guilty intent, which one day assumes the form of a desire to murder his brutal drunkard of a father' (HRC 33.2). Horrified by this desire, the man flees home during a snowstorm, and ends up across the bridge in a remote farmhouse almost buried in the snow. There he has to try to keep alive a young woman, fighting a possible miscarriage, as well as her five-year-old stepson sick with pneumonia—the pair of them abandoned by the husband and father on his discovery of the pregnancy. Malamud writes in outline:

> There is no food or water in the house, nor light nor heat. The man is therefore confronted with an agonising task which he can understand and respond to only at intervals. Once he unwillingly, fearfully, hopelessly takes upon himself its solution he has, obviously, to contend not only with physical conditions but also with his own delusions, hallucinations, fears, and inertia. In the end, after he does manage to save them all—mostly during his short period of lucidity—in pain and error, he confesses to the woman his previous evil intent, only to discover that he has a priori expiated his guilt.   (HRC 33.2)

'One's service to others', wrote Malamud, 'somehow enlarges the area of freedom' (HRC 33.2). This was the extreme schizophrenic version of what the responsibility of marriage might make for. 'Bern really was basically so sensitive himself,' Ann Malamud said. 'Sometimes I think the very sensitive people straighten themselves by helping others. It makes them feel stronger too, I think ' (Ann Malamud).

It became 'The Man Nobody Could Lift'. But it did not do what Malamud had wanted. It failed 'because I allowed the point of view to be the man's. The focus was blurred' (HRC 29.6). His editor, Robert Giroux, advised against publication. Though he called it a remarkable study of 'a man's immersion into insanity', he thought that the use of material which was 'totally and unrelievedly clinical' meant that it 'somehow loses vitality' (20 November

1953, HRC 10.8). Giroux recommended included a shortened version in a collection of short stories. It was only in 1997 when Giroux edited the posthumous *Complete Stories of Bernard Malamud* that the first chapter of 'The Man Nobody Could Lift' was published as 'A Confession of Murder': 'He walked as if he were dragging a burden. The burden was the way he felt.' His brain felt like a rock: 'If it got any heavier, he would keel over in the street and nobody'd be able to lift him.'

Malamud could not lift Eugene, in art or in life. By 1960 Eugene was deteriorating towards another crisis, partly brought on by looking for a job. He told Malamud it was he who was the genius and claimed his brother was just looking after his own interests, getting daughter Janna to lie to Eugene over the telephone. On 26 July, Malamud writes, 'My phone has never been tapped in all my life and I am sure it never will be. I can say the same for yours, and I hope you will believe it. Nor am I not allowed to inform you of anything.' He added, as though trying to instil his own will into him, 'You are now fighting courageously to get over this illness, trying hard to see through the confusion to the truth of reality. This is a great battle, and I know you will ultimately win, as you did once before … I admire your courage. I believe in you' (HRC 36.5).

But early in 1961 Eugene was back in hospital, Brooklyn State, and undergoing electrical shock treatment by February. In May he was still hospitalized and tried to hurt himself. Malamud visited in the summer before he took up a new post at Bennington. 'Same old story again', wrote Eugene in the pencil the hospital allowed him. He did not know whether to send his letters but 'Bernie tells me I should' (HRC 13.3). Malamud wrote in reply to one of them about the relation of writing and mental illness, 'No, I'm not one of those who believes a man becomes a writer as a result of his sickness' (9 July 1961). Eugene had fears about homosexuality and one of the doctors; he apologized for having bad thoughts about his brother; he accepted he was not a genius. A kindly cousin, Marshall Malament, wrote Malamud on 6 May 1961, 'He goes for walks everyday and sometimes lands near Erasmus Hall HS trying to recapture the happier boyhood days.' But those days had ended, Eugene believed, with the death of his mother, and then began the irrational thoughts and sexual disturbances.

Eugene was allowed home in the August, provided he attended an aftercare clinic daily throughout 1962. Malamud kept on writing about the need for a part-time job, the possibilities offered by Fountain House and its clubhouse self-help programme, urging routine, the use of an alarm clock, anything. He speaks from his own experience which is also partly Eugene's: 'I would be having a rough time without a routine' (30 April 1963); 'though I like travelling, it's always something less than easy for me—I think as a result of our terribly restricted life as children' (26 July 1965); 'We were the children of immigrants—poor immigrants and, let's face it, with all their good will, almost ignorant' (25 November 1965).

In 1967 Eugene was again suicidal, asking Mickey Platt, the family lawyer, about the possibility of electrocution by putting a wet finger in a light socket, and also requesting a gun. 'You are brave,' Eugene would write back to his brother, 'you have your own sufferings yet not a peep' (30 August 1967); 'I like the things you do. They seem wonderful to me' (11 September 1967, HRC 13.5)

Like his father, Eugene finally died of a heart attack in 1973, aged 55, twenty-four years after Malamud left. Malamud wrote some notes for what he wanted to say at Eugene's funeral, and these included notes of Eugene's own, some self-exhortatory and not unlike something Malamud himself might have written: 'Believe in your health, believe in everything good. Believe in health. It can come'; 'Oh God, please save me from my bondage. Look at [Robert] Frost's background. These are poets; they understand each other and themselves'; 'Objectivity is the goal. Those who can, grow. I tried to imitate a rational person but it didn't work' (HRC 20.2). Malamud wrote: 'Freud said, perhaps in a pessimistic moment, the purpose of life is to endure. Eugene tried to keep himself going.' Thus he would get up late, make breakfast, buy his milk and bread and cigarettes, while helpers such as Mickey Platt, or Murray and Marshall Malament helped out with other shopping, managing finances, and providing simple company. He watched televison, read the newspaper, liked talking on the telephone, was glad to hear news of his relatives, and went to his doctor. That was it.

> That's not much to do with your life. He was a wounded man trying to keep going. He did so for many years. He had very little, perhaps some small pleasures. But he had courage. He wanted to live. He wanted to be well. He wanted a better life. Rest in peace, my dear brother.   (HRC 20.2)

Yet what Eugene wanted, and what Malamud had wanted for him, was perhaps more than their own father had hoped or managed.

The speech was written, but Malamud did not attend his brother's funeral. Murray Malament ('that kind good man' as he was called in the notes) read the eulogy for him. For Malamud had been admitted to hospital with suspected heart trouble. Eugene died on Tuesday 30 October, Malamud was admitted to Mount Sinai the very next day, 31 October, and was released 5 November. It was almost for him as it had been for Max in 1952, with the heart attack that followed Eugene's breakdown.

What's New?—Forward and Back

'The hope of the world lies in new life,' Eugene had written Malamud, 26 January 1952, on the birth of daughter Janna. Whatever was happening in Brooklyn, it was the past life. As Malamud was to put it, at the opening of what was originally the third chapter of his Oregon novel, *A New Life*, 'What new with Levin in the September weeks before classes began?'

John Eriksen, a student in 1949, remembered Malamud as a strange man leaning forward on the lectern, on the very first day at OSC for them both: 'It has been brought to my attention that many of you people here today are practicing celibacy. I have nothing against this practice and will not penalize you for it.' Malamud pointed a finger at the gigglers: 'I have documents in my possession that show that each one of you back there matriculated within the last two weeks. One as recently as this morning.'[9]

The Department was lodged in one of three tin-roofed Quonset huts, converted army barracks left over from wartime. From 1949 the new working life for Malamud was divided between teaching organized for Mondays, Wednesdays, and Fridays, and writing on Tuesdays, Thursdays, and Saturdays, sometimes sneaking half of Sunday, though increasingly Ann tried to get him to leave Sundays clear for the family. Because there was no room at home, he wrote in the English Department, shutting if not locking the door, declining to break for coffee with the others, the odd man out who refused interruptions and pounded away at his work. Ann became famous for bringing Malamud his lunch there: 'I would take Janna in her stroller and Paul. I would pass by his window and hand him a paper bag with a sandwich in it and fruit. And it became a local lore' (Ann Malamud). When the building was not heated, he wrapped himself in a blanket and carried on. His next-door neighbour, Faith Norris, remembered hearing him recite dialogue to himself as he wrote it—'whispering if the character was supposed to whisper and shouting if he was to shout'.[10] He was in fact so rigid in his work schedule that eventually, when he was getting well known for the discipline of his writing, the word went around the department that he had told Ann, pregnant with their second child, that in no circumstances was she to bear the child on Thursday, a writing day. Ann denied it. Certainly there was no open-door policy when he was writing. A student late for a consultation would find the door locked. Colleagues would have to shout through the door if they dared and might be given a strict couple of minutes on the other side.

Malamud's obsession with punctuality was notorious. In the mid-fifties, Alex Inkeles introduced him to Victor Erlich, an expert on the Slavs, then teaching in Seattle: the three men eventually formed 'The League of Lopsided Men', qualification dependent on a physical incapacity for any handyman chores. But the problem, from Malamud's point of view, lay with Victor's wife, Iza, who would become so absorbed in the conversation that dinner at the Erlichs was never served on time and sometimes not served at all. The first time he encountered this phenomenon, Malamud became more and more uneasy, until he began to tell one of his well-prepared stories. It was about a German plane getting into trouble over the Atlantic ocean. Malamud was well into his account, when he looked at his watch and said, 'I'll finish telling the story after we get something to eat.'[11]

One former student remembers what it was like to be taught freshman English by Malamud in those early days, and how he was also allowed to teach a seminar on creative writing after the publication of his first novel. Lorena MacCafferty was at OSC from 1951 till 1955:[12]

> During my freshman class, Mr. Malamud had just completed *The Natural* and was receiving the galley proofs from the publisher. He would read us the sexy bits with an obvious glee because the students from Oregon were easily shocked. It was obvious he hated teaching us, and he certainly could be forgiven.

Lorena found herself, to her surprise, the smartest among the bored or stupid:

> At first I would eagerly raise my hand to answer his questions. When, as invariably happened, no one could answer, he would then say, in a long-suffering voice and with his eyes closed, 'Miss MacCafferty, would you please tell the students the answer'. As you can imagine, the rest of the class loathed me all the more. ... Still, Mr. Malamud was not a good teacher. Any teacher who has such disdain for his students that they are all too aware of it cannot be a good teacher.

He found the students too naïve, too uncommitted, and unambitious. In *A New Life* Levin, despite this, tries to change as a teacher: 'He had allowed his disappointment in their mediocre work, their sameness as people, to sour him against them, though this bothered him in afterthought' (NL, 236). But for Lorena MacCafferty it was a somewhat different story in the creative writing seminar during her senior year:

> There were just ten students in the class, so we got a lot of feedback from Mr. Malamud. He still seemed appalled at our cavalier attitude to education, but he treated us as adults with minds that might be developed—with a great deal of work. I remember writing a short story in this class in which I wanted the protagonist to sit down and play a piece on the piano. Being

particularly ignorant about music, I went down the hall in my sorority and asked a music major what piece a good, but not great, student pianist might be playing. She suggested the raindrop prelude. I put that in my story. Malamud praised the story and in particular the use of the symbolism of the rain. That seemed rather funny to me—that he would have believed it was symbolism when it wasn't. Of course, since then I have learned a lot more about writers and how symbolism appears, seemingly from nowhere, in their work.

Malamud was seeking imaginative richness wherever he could find it. But Lorena MacCafferty noted other things going on in his literature classes—for example, in competition with Herb Childs, the department's no-nonsense literary scholar and expert on Emily Dickinson:

> I wrote in one place that I was fascinated by Dickinson's poem that ends with the line, 'I'm Wife! Stop there!' since she herself had no knowledge of married love and probably was, in fact, a virgin. Malamud called me into his office. This was a little scary because he had a reputation of chasing women students around his office, and even worse. Whether he actually did this or whether it was just vicious gossip, I don't know. However, it was 1955, and if a teacher were to sexually harass a student, the student would certainly not report it, so I was nervous. He asked me about the notebook entry I made regarding Emily Dickinson. He said I must know that Emily Dickinson had been raped by her father and had probably had other sexual experiences as well. I was shocked, as I was meant to be. Although I suppose he could have been right, I have not read any reference to these allegations about Dickinson. I think it was just a way of getting back at Dr. Childs. I also remember Dr. Childs making disparaging remarks about Malamud's tendency to find symbolism everywhere. 'Sometimes a story about an old man and the sea is just a story about an old man and the sea,' he said.

Malmud must have made up the Dickinson story. 'Whether deserved or not, however, we students felt Malamud was obsessed with sex in literature, and found it to be the driving force in every piece of writing we examined. We, of course, were also obsessed with sex, but not comfortable with older adults making such a big deal of it.' Judy Rycraft Juntunen gave the reporter Tom Bennett a similar account of being taught by Malamud in 1958: 'I found him intimidating. He was so formal and so very knowledgeable, and we were so dumb, so unsophisticated. We were shocked by his interpretations of things we had missed in the textbook. It was the first time I heard the word "homosexual" spoken out loud.' His colleague James Groshong recalled that Malamud would ask his students about their sex lives.[13] But Lorena MacCafferty concludes, from her own view of Malamud's new life:

The picture I am left with of Malamud is of a very unhappy man. I know his wife was with him there, but I felt he was also a lonely man. I think he felt Oregon was a foreign country.

He wanted to get back to the city and the east and his milieu, she believed, and did so as soon as he possibly could. Certainly he spent part of the summers of 1952, 1954, and 1958 alone back east, and for a year, from summer 1956 to summer 1957, the Malamuds as a family lived in Italy as a result of his winning a *Partisan Review* fellowship to support the writing of fiction. Oliver Lawrence remembered a colleague telling him of an evening at the Malamuds' house after Lawrence had left in 1952: 'As I recall, Stan and Ann and Bernie were in the bedroom. Bernie, it seems to me, was in bed. He was quite depressed. Ann may have phoned Stan and asked him to come over, I can't recall. I do remember Stan's saying that Ann, terribly upset for Bernie, said, "But Bernie, where would we go?" Or there's no place left to go.'

It was the writing routine that kept him sane. The writing half of the Oregon regimen was fixed early on. On writing days Malamud would rise at 7.30, exercise for ten minutes, wash, eat, and be at his desk by 9; eat lunch in his office at 1, or sometimes go home till 2, then write again until 4 or 4.30—mainly revising the page or (at very best) two pages completed in the morning. Then he would return home, read his mail and newspaper, and take a short nap; family dinner at the table by 6.15, chatter with the children, help with homework. There was no television allowed in the house. After the children had gone to bed, he would talk with Ann, listen to classical music, and read for three hours until 12, usually half the time on fiction, half on non-fiction often connected with his novel.[14]

'Even if he didn't know what he was going to say,' his friend Chester Garrison recalled, 'He would sit at his desk—he told me this—he would have paper and pencil in front of him and then suddenly a word or two or phrase or sentence might wander in' (MWB 20). There was an initial reading over of yesterday's work and then a sentence would get him going. Later, Ann would type it up for him to revise on the typed page, or to write out again in his own hand, from script to type and back, again and again. Malamud described to his publishers the process that went on behind the office door, because the actual daily working life of a writer was something austerely interesting to him:

> I was becoming excited at the way in which I could put a story together. I would sit at my desk in the morning without a suggestion for a story and at the end of the day I had two or three. Then I would choose the one that bit hardest and spend a day or so inventing some sort of plot. If the plot came easily, it

was usually good; if not I had to abandon it usually and work on another idea. Having constructed a plot, I would then start the story, writing each paragraph over and over until I was satisfied, before I went to the next. Some writers can write a quick first draft—I can't. I can't stand rereading a first draft, so I had to make each paragraph as good as it could possibly be at the time. Then when I had the whole story down, I found I could revise with ease.   (HRC 29.6)

Malamud was always concerned with what people could 'make of themselves'. This was his making of himself, until at the end of the so-called first draft (which was really the umpteenth draft of each paragraph) he could bear to see it and know he was a writer. Up to that point, he was always only becoming a writer again and again. It meant finding a way for the writing to take *its own* time—not just repeating the recalled events of autobiographical time but, day after day adding layer after layer, until, unharassed, it had an independent life and a time band of its own. 'Work slowly. Don't push tomorrow in today,' he urges himself in a later notebook (HRC 19.5). If he anxiously rushed the writing and left it inadequate, the present compulsively ate up its own possible future. But if he stayed with it and found its rhythm, independent of the memories it was drawing upon, then the present created a tomorrow for itself which transmuted and redeemed all his yesterdays.

Thus locked inside his rigid time-structures, Malamud found something rather extraordinary happening to him in the different dimension of time that existed within his own head. There he found himself going back to Brooklyn, for all that he was learning much about a different America. 'I was overwhelmed by the beauty of Oregon ... and the new life it offered, which I lived as best I could as I reflected on the old':

almost without understanding why, I was thinking about my father's immigrant life (how he earned his meagre living and what he paid for it) and my mother's (diminished by fear and suffering) as perhaps matter for my fiction. In other words, I had them in mind as I invented the characters who became their fictional counterparts.   (TH, 6)

'I tried all sorts of things but at last resolved to do simple stories about simple people. I did about ten of these, concerned mostly with Jewish and Italian storekeepers and their three-walled, plate-glass-windowed world. About six of the stories sold, the first to *Harper's Bazaar*, the second to *Commentary*, and the third, to my surprise, to *Partisan Review*' (HRC 29.6). These were, respectively, 'The Cost of Living', 'The Prison', and 'The First Seven Years'—followed soon after by 'The Death of Me', 'The Bill', 'An Apology', and 'The Loan' of which the first was published in *World Review* and the other three in *Commentary* again—all in a great release of creative energy in 1950 and 51 forming the core of the collection *The Magic Barrel*, published in 1958.

They are short stories given form by the amount of money owed or lost or stolen, by the number of years wasted or still required. But this ostensibly materialist form—what one reviewer was later to call Malamud's account book or testament of failure[15]—is played off against an anti-materialistic content characterized by sudden generous shifts into illogicality. Danny Myerson was a learned young Jew who in later years would often help Malamud with information about his religion: what he loved about the stories were those moves that could only come in life's *second* place, because they were in spite of that first self from which one normally lived.[16] Thus in 'The Prison' there is a storeman who unexpectedly discovers that he does not want to catch the little girl shoplifter, after all; or in 'The Bill' the debtor who doesn't repay in cash but, too late, in unspoken contrition instead: 'His throat had turned to bone.' In 'The First Seven Years' Feld the shoemaker doesn't want Sobel, his immigrant assistant, even to think of marrying his adored nineteen-year-old American-born daughter, Miriam. Sobel is a great reader of books who has been working on a pittance for the last five years, a bald thirty-year-old aged by his past. 'She will never marry a man so old and ugly, like you,' cries the father bitterly at the climax. Sobel bursts into tears.

> Watching him, the shoemaker's anger diminished. His teeth were on edge with pity for the man, and his eyes grew moist. How strange and sad that a refugee, a grown man, bald and old with his miseries, who had by the skin of his teeth escaped Hitler's incinerators, should fall in love, when he had got to America, with a girl less than half his age. Day after day, for five years, he sat at his bench, cutting and hammering away, waiting for the girl to become a woman, unable to ease his heart with speech, knowing no protest but desperation.
>
> 'Ugly I didn't mean,' he said half aloud.
>
> Then he realized that what he had called ugly was not Sobel but Miriam's life if she married him. He felt for his daughter a strange and gripping sorrow, as if she were already Sobel's bride, the wife, after all, of a shoemaker and had in her life no more than her mother had had.

That ugly 'young man but old' is a version of Malamud. Of that immigrant world, half-remembered and half-imagined in all its disadvantages, he said: 'it had to represent me' (HRC 27.5). But it is the sudden and almost involuntary emotional effect of Sobel upon Feld, the father, which is so powerful. 'Ugly I didn't mean': the insight into what he did mean by it comes on second thought, creating a saddened kindness out of the painful reaction against unkindness, recent and one's own. In such ways, Malamud believed, it was always to be asked of the writer: 'How much feeling have you got in your heart?'—not least a writer who had had trouble about the relation of words and feelings in his earlier life (LC II 13. 10). Sobel had already waited five years. Wait another two years until she is twenty one, says the father reluctantly, and then you can ask her—making the biblical seven years in all. The following day Feld sees his assistant back at his usual seat, silently recommitted to waiting, 'pounding leather for his love'. That last is just the sort of phrase Malamud would work at his revisions—Sobel's prosaic version of work beating itself into love poetry.

In his own work, in these ways, said Malamud, 'I began to have more confidence in what I was doing'; 'I felt my imagination was stronger than I had thought' (HRC 29.6).

However powerful or successful, the short stories were never sufficient for Malamud, but were written, increasingly, during the time between novels. Writing in a notebook, 'Story Ideas—Oregon' as his own most exacting critic, he unsparingly asks himself why he has not yet succeeded in writing a first-rate story, long or short. One reason is 'the tremendous influence of Naturalism on me (a habit) which in a sense traps my not profound intellectualism, and my not too imaginative (original) imagination.' His dialogue 'imitates life rather than takes on a life of its own'. 'Plot leads me by the nose,' he complains: 'I work very close to movement.' Everything is too linear, too horizontal.

'What shall I do?' The subject-matter 'must be closer to primitive life'. The moral must come 'as revelation'. There must be 'more inner connections' in the layered technique of the work. The dialogue must reveal character and 'be used as counterpoint—for music':

> I must experiment. I must express my self—my belief in life. I must work to handle material originally—original form. I must try symbolism. I must work for art. I must work *harder*. I must hit my highest possible level.
>
> (5 August 1949, HRC 22.2)

All these 'musts' were directed towards the novel that was to come after 'The Light Sleeper'. For even in that failure he had learned about moving from writing short stories to writing novels, as he indicates in a letter to his fellow-author J. F. Powers, 15 June 1954:

> I was much interested in your saying, about your novel, that you had some difficulty getting from scene to scene. I had a similar difficulty at one time—I would imagine any short story writer would when attempting a longer work but then I discovered some of the delights of sheer narration; and how, in synoptic

writing, one may really wind into strongly emotional scenes—much stronger,
I would think, than if immediate scene throughout; and the opportunities for
changes of pace and the introduction of harmonic and contrapuntal matter to
enrich the whole. ... You may be surprised by the instrument you find yourself
playing.[17]

The Natural was to be more primitive, more experimentally imaginative,
more compressedly synoptic and symbolic, more musically layered with inner
narrative connections and counterpoints and changes of pace, more revelatory
of emotion and belief.

'The Light Sleeper' had ended in ashes in a backyard of Corvallis. A second
novel was the real test of whether the years spent on it remained wasted
or could be reclaimed. Whether the first attempt had been published and
changed the author's life, or, unpublished, had been destroyed or hidden away,
it was the second novel that obliged the writer either 'to fight success'—like
the glamorous Mailer after *The Naked and the Dead* in 1948—or to fight
'failure'—like Malamud for whom nothing ever went right first time out.
Either way, as Malamud wrote in some notes in 1974, it was the austere
second attempt that made any writer have to dig in and fight 'his own nature'
to see if his career could be sustained (LC II 11.5). 'Some are born whole;
others must seek this blessed state in a struggle to achieve order.' Malamud
was one of the others, not the first but the second-born:

> That is no loss to speak of; ultimately such seeking becomes the subject matter
> of fiction ... Who am I, and how can I say what I have to? He reads his sentences
> to see if his words answer the question.   (TH, 5)

There was an interview with Alex Hamilton of *The Guardian* on 6 March
1972 which started with the subject of loss and ended going back to *The
Natural*. Throughout your work, said Hamilton, some precious piece of
art-work, a manuscript, a painting, or a sculpture, is mutilated or destroyed,
sometimes but not always by its creator. Why so?

> Malamud replies that he knows only that when he was a student he was
> enormously moved to learn that Carlyle's *The French Revolution* had been
> burned in John Stuart Mill's grate by his maid. Just why an idea stays with a
> person is hard to say, perhaps the whole concept of the loss of a life's work is
> very dramatic. Again, T. E. Lawrence forgetting *Seven Pillars of Wisdom* on a
> train seemed an insurmountable loss.

But Hamilton noted that both instances were accidents, and that in both
cases the authors heroically rewrote their work from scratch. Yet when in
Pictures of Fidelman the protagonist loses his essay through theft, or daubs

over his own painted masterwork, or when in *The Tenants* the Jewish
and black novelists are both bereaved in the loss of their writing, then,
says Hamilton, it feels more like 'avenging chances'. 'Hard to say what it
ties up with,' replied Malamud, 'It might tie up with a loss of my own.'
What might that be? asked Hamilton—now reaching that point in an
interview where Malamud characteristically became cagey, if not irritable,
in his unwillingness to allow amateur psychoanalysis of himself to be an
'explanation' of his work:

> Well, this is my right to use the imagination in a way that satisfies an aesthetic
> need and represents a metaphor for some psychic quality I refuse to describe.
> Well ... but let it go at that.

These are the classic, by then well-honed Malamud defences—words such
as 'dramatic', 'imagination', and 'metaphor' insistently fending off the autobiographical reduction. But Hamilton did not let it go. Not even knowing
about 'The Light Sleeper', he went on correctly pointing to the fact that
any novel Malamud had started he had completed; nothing was lost or
unfinished. But Hamilton added: although Malamud started telling stories
at the age of 8, didn't he really begin only at 35 with his first novel *The
Natural*?

> 'Yes,' and pauses. 'Maybe the loss is the loss of years. Having begun then—this
> is a guess—when time mattered, the loss of five years or so might be more than
> the loss to someone who started in his early twenties.'

In *The Natural*, Hamilton notes, Roy Hobbs, a natural sporting genius, loses
over fifteen years before he gets back into baseball, by making a comeback
at the age of 34. That is Hobbs' rewriting of his equivalent of a lost script.
Malamud for a moment got interested, but then smiled, 'Well then, you play
with that.'

Malamud himself had begun making notes for the second novel in New York
in October 1948, and began writing in Oregon in early 1950. 'I felt ready for
another novel, subject to one restriction; it was not to be autobiographical; it
was to be an imaginative, invented work. I was impressed by Eudora Welty's
remark to writers: dare to do. My book was to be a sort of imaginative
dare. I'd fly out and see how far I could go' (HRC 29.6). This was *The
Natural*, finished in October 1951, after just two main drafts, taking a year
and a half.

In ordinary life it did not look as though Malamud was flying. Paul
Malamud, in a manuscript novel entitled 'White Piano, Black Piano, Brown

Piano', offers a semi-fictional account of what it took even to catch a train, to visit his grandparents in California. Malamud is Bob, Ann is Mimi, seen through the eyes of Paul as Eddie aged seven.[18] It is 1954 but with roots still set deep in the anxieties of the thirties:

> 'Come on,' Bob said succinctly, and tensely. 'Let's go.' Eddie loved to travel, and couldn't understand why everything that made him happy seemed to make his father tense.
>
> The conductor put down the footstool. Mimi smiled and thanked him as he handed her up into the car. Bob nodded and grinned at Eddie, who climbed up afterwards. Eddie looked round anxiously, afraid his father might somehow get left behind, but Bob determinedly lugged the heavy suitcase right up, then stumbled down the stairs again to pick up the other two, rushing back, trying to swing them up onto the train, with an awkward forced motion. Eddie knew his father was not athletic, and tended to be worried about missing things that were about to start.

Bob's movements were awkward, unlike the cowboys Eddie sometimes managed to get a look at on someone else's television. It seemed odd to see the father, an indoors' type, lifting anything at all. Eddie connects it with his father being Jewish—'perhaps Jewish men didn't exercise very much or become athletes'.[19] In real life (where Chester Garrison saw Malamud mowing the lawn—once), Ann was always trying to get Paul to stop reading and go outside and play baseball, but Malamud, she thought, was 'much more understanding and sympathetic' to the delicate kind of child Paul was:

> I would have liked a strapping boy, you know, who was tough, and Paul was not. Between my own anxious and depressive mother who had these cycles, and the fact that Bern's mother was schizophrenic, and Bern's brother, I think I was always worried about this, about emotional issues.

At any rate, to the impatient little Eddie in Paul's fiction, the father 'always seemed so slow to want to do something that was fun, as if he really didn't like fun'. He could get angry quickly but also quickly forget about his anger, 'as if his own anger made him tired'. At home, in his routines, he was solid, reassuring, with a kind of quiet, sad dignity. The mother was changeable of mood in less predictable ways, and 'sometimes her worries made Eddie worried, and sometimes they didn't'.

In the train's dining car the mother orders steak, the father lamb, and it is decided that Eddie should have spaghetti:

> His parents sat and talked quietly about how enormously expensive the dining-car food was—and his mother tried to decide whether it would be any good or

not. 'Well, it will be a surprise,' she said finally, with the sunny tone of voice she had when she was amused.

'How is your lamb? she asks Bob, when it arrives:

'Well, it's okay,' Bob chewed slowly. 'It's not bad.' He stoically gulped some ice water. 'The potatoes are a little … skooshy.' Eddie's father was an English teacher, and he liked making up words.

With that glimpse of the writer, what we have in all this is the Malamud who mainly followed Flaubert's dictum: 'Be regular and orderly in your life like a bourgeois, so that you may be violent and original in your work' (Notebook, 47; HRC 19.5). But the awkward Brooklyn boy who threw the ball like a girl, and the protective Oregon father who didn't mind that his son wouldn't go out and play, was to write the great all-American baseball novel, *The Natural*.

In a scratch contest, while their train is halted, Roy Hobbs, an unknown young pitcher on his way east for a trial, does battle with the Whammer, the thirty-three-year-old leading hitter of the American League.

The first ball spins off Roy's fingers like a white bird, suddenly dipping out of view. The second, looming like a planet about to hit earth, the Whammer aims to smash into dust, but again misses. The Whammer is 'oddly relieved': he has just one shot at it now, all or nothing, his back where he likes it against the wall. But he looks up at the young pitcher and suddenly experiences a dipping 'moment of depression'. Roy's coach and mentor, Sam, suddenly feels an unexpected pity for their adversary, even for a split-second hoping that the idol won't be toppled by his boy. But within another second the Whammer has 'regained confidence in his known talent and experience and was taunting the greenhorn to throw'. These fleeting emotions are like tensely unstable predictions of what all the potential parallel lives might be like, on the other side of the decisive moment:

> The third ball slithered at the batter like a meteor, the flame swallowing itself. He lifted his club to crush it into a universe of sparks but the heavy wood dragged, and though he willed to destroy the sound he heard a gong bong and realized with sadness that the ball he had expected to hit had long since been part of the past   (*The Natural*, 32)

This is clearly not the simple baseball novel of Ring Lardner or Heywood Broun. The language is poetically thick with resonance in words such as 'club' (rather than 'bat' as he first wrote it), 'meteor', and 'universe'. In the intensification of the moment, the dimensions of space and time are

alternately slowed and then accelerated, suddenly expanded and contracted
again. And it is that sort of compression and then release of energy that
Malamud is after in the physics of his verbal revisions. He starts by writing
'The third ball slivered [to] at him like a streak of lightning, no, like an
exhilarating meteor, the flame eating itself'; then he characteristically shortens
and tightens the sentence, eliminating the obtrusive correction ('no') and the
repeated simile. You get one shot at it. In his typed-up first draft, Malamud
wrote: 'he heard a gong bong and knew that the ball he had expected to see
had long since been lost in the past'. But on the typed page—and this is
what Malamud mainly did with his life—he then inserted in pencil 'realized
with sadness' instead of merely 'knew'; raised the stakes by replacing 'see'
with 'hit'; and, most important of all, hardened 'had long since been *lost in
the past*' into 'had long since been *part of* the past'—the warrior's future
now as entirely lost behind him as the ball is. Within one decisive second, the
Whammer is suddenly, in that defeated sadness, years older and, even as the
ball goes past, is made into the past himself. 'The Whammer understood he
was, in the truest sense of it, out.' In this novel, the ebb and flow of strength
and self-confidence, the mysteries of being in or out of form, feel like types
of life or death.

In that 'truest sense', the meanings lie in a charged area created somewhere
in between the realm of magic, the world of gods and heroes, and the science
of the physical universe. It is a drama which has what Malamud called 'a
magic feeling', sport transformed into some myth it recalls without ever
ceasing to be physically itself. For the contest marks, he says in his notes,
'the central confrontation between two forces', batter and pitcher, hero and
adversary, good (your team) and evil (the adversary), with high and low
culture thrown together in Malamud's mix:

> The confrontation is like the jousting of knights in a tournament, or like the
> toreador with a bull.
> There is a quality of expectancy about it. One watches, waits, identifies
> with the hero, and sees it, and in a single blow of a bat—the weapon—or
> the knight's lance, or the bull's horns—and the drama is visible to all—in
> the open.   (LC II 1.10)

Behind *The Natural* is Malamud's reading of Jessie Weston's *From Ritual
to Romance*, behind which also lies J. G. Frazer's *The Golden Bough*—both
books vital to the writing of T. S. Eliot's *The Wasteland*. They contain
accounts of primitive myths which can be recreated by certain rituals, their
memory triggered by certain words. Malamud knew what he was doing in
this: baseball becomes one of those ancient rituals.

In the midst of writing the novel, he responded thus to Paul Brooks of Houghton Mifflin, 3 July 1950, who sought to buy the option for $250:

> You might like to know that my novel, which I am 5000 words into, is called The Natural. It is the story of an enormously talented baseball player (it is not a 'baseball novel') who does not comprehend what it is to be a 'hero' nor understand the responsibility thereof; on another level it is the story of a man who has been 'wounded' but does not understand the meaning of the wound and so 'has' to be wounded again. And on a lightly shaded symbolic level—which will not hinder story pleasure for those who can't see the light tracings of other meanings, but will deepen it for those who can—it is the story of perhaps another Gawain, who failed.   (LC I 55.4)

In the legend of the Grail, Sir Perceval or Sir Gawain seeks to rid the land of its infertility by means of a test and a mission. The wound or sterility of a king—the Fisher King (here Pop Fisher)—causes the land (or team) all its problems. The wound of the hero goes with the effort to redeem both himself and the world. As he writes and rewrites, Malamud works very hard to create density of meaning, constantly writing in his own margin: 'build', 'develop', 'go deeper'. For what so much of the mythic background does is twofold—first, it yields Malamud a sense of form, of keying into an underlying world-view, a resonant traditional story, lodged beneath it all; second, it gives him the confidence to enrich and deepen the meaning by revision, knowing there is always more behind it all that he can tap into. But what Malamud means by symbolism still depends upon the use of a literal and physical naturalistic basis in story, in character and in emotion—such that 'in one thing we see more than one thing: we see a thing plus an idea' (LC II 11.5). The 'idea' is not so much conceptualized as felt almost physically, and then realized emotionally. When at a crucial moment the batter swings mightily and misses, when the pitcher finds to his horror that the power he has released has been banished into outer air, these are indeed like sudden blows and wounds.

Pam Metz, a student of Malamud's at Harvard, said that if you watched a baseball game on the television with Malamud, what he was really good at was telling you what made a particular moment biographically crucial in the life of, say, Luis Tiant, the Redsox pitcher.[20] But Malamud only regained his youthful interest in baseball for an ulterior reason, when Jackie Robinson broke baseball's colour barrier by becoming the first negro to play for the Brooklyn Dodgers. His protagonist Roy Hobbs is a 'natural' genius, something like Bobby Feller, a speedball pitcher from the sticks whose father used to catch his pitching every night after work. But he is also one of those heroes who threaten to ruin their talent through human flaws—like Babe Ruth, sent to a Catholic orphanage by his own parents, who consumed so much in his subsequent neediness that he ate his way into hospital; or Shoeless Joe Jackson who allegedly fixed the 1919 Chicago World Series for the Black Sox against his own team, the Chicago White Sox. These personal stories and ulterior reasons were Malamud's real interest: 'The original decision to work with symbols came after I had read practically every baseball novel written by decent writers and they were all woefully thin, because baseball in itself is a not very important phenomenon' (LC I 56.8).

The first forty pages of the novel are a prologue, entitled 'Pre-game' which ends prematurely with the young hopeful, Roy Hobbs, being shot in a hotel room by a young woman, Harriet Bird, who is madly destructive of heroes. It was what had happened to Eddie Waitkus, a first baseman for the Philadelphia Phillies, at the hands of Ruth Ann Steinhagen in Chicago in 1949. But the book restarts after a gap of fifteen years: only now, because of the wound, Hobbs is no longer a pitcher but, like Babe Ruth, is turned hitter. Malamud loved the time gap and what it asked of the reader imaginatively, when most might have preferred a simple ongoing chronology. It was the form's invisible 'idea': what William James calls a 'once-born' soul now having to refind his destroyed genius the second time around.[21] His own agent Diarmuid Russell did not like it, but Malamud said of its purpose:

> at the outset let me say, in connection with the use of symbolism, that I am not afraid to have the reader feel that he is being told a story. I know this technique would bother some editors but it doesn't bother me. I like the way some sculptors handle stone—so that you get the feeling of the stone despite the form of the object they have wrought. Moreover, I feel that once you get hold of the reader's imagination via the creation of real people, he will take anything, within reason, that the writer gives him. …
>
> Now it was my purpose to take Roy Hobbs through a lifetime in the opening chapter. My theory is that many people have two lifetimes to live—the lifetime of childhood to youth time, when our first mistakes, you might say, are made for us by others; and the second lifetime, when after the defeat of the idealized self, we become adult through suffering and taking on mature values.
>
> (LC I 56.8)

Thus as Malamud himself pointed out, in both lives there is a woman, first the evil one, then the good, who interrogates the sporting hero as to his deeper purpose in life. Harriet Bird asks him if there is anything more to him than his ambition to be the best in the game. 'Is that all?' she repeated. 'What more is there?' (*The Natural*, 35). Iris Lemon tries to tell him that the failures and sufferings in one realm may make for a better person in a wider sphere.

As Malamud wrote to Ann, 30 July 1950, as he built up his drafts: 'Now it has to develop vertically, in terms of characters, as well as move horizontally.' Iris herself urges this extra dimension upon Roy.

All this is what makes for the density that Malamud had wanted in the Oregon notebook: underlying connections and counterpoints between different parts of the books, so that the second part of the book does not just come after the first, horizontally, but is textually laid over it. Yet ironically Roy himself does not allow time to see this: for him the second life is not a new life in itself; it is an existence still in chase of the lost first one, in a bitter and desperate game of catch-up. He does not understand the potential moral form, the second meaning, within which his story is being told. For still he cannot realize, as Malamud can, those meanings *within* baseball for which the life of baseball, like any life, is itself only vehicle and metaphor.

For Malamud himself the second life went on within the act of revision, often when most apparently simple or basic. When Hobbs complains about his life not turning out the way he had wanted it to, Malamud first writes Iris's reply thus:

'Whose does?' she cruelly asked.
But her eyes were deep with tenderness and he lost the fear to speak.

But by the final revision he writes it as one paragraph, different levels hidden within the same line:

'Whose does?' she said cruelly. He looked up. Her expression was tender.

(Ibid. 157)

The egoist in Malamud knew it had sometimes been as hard for him as it was for Roy Hobbs, to see from someone else's point of view whilst in the midst of his own. The existence of other people baffled such men, and if it came, came as a shock. And Malamud the writer still could not always get in the two viewpoints simultaneously at the very first draft. He needed revision—to have imaginative room for another dimension, and imaginative time for another person. Then he could make art, correctively, out of the failings, mistakes, and difficulties of life's first draft. 'I have succeeded in afterthought. I connect revisions with reformation' (December 1965, HRC 20.9).

'How can I say what I have to? He reads his sentences to see if the words answer the question' (TH, 5). What makes Malamud a good reviser is that he is a good reader of his own work. Roy Hobbs is always on some speeding train, always eating and eating, an action man without a spiritual language, lacking anything inside himself to replace his speed and need, in its self-consumption. But as Malamud read his own first draft, he began to note in the margin how, in counterpoint to the book's restless movement, Roy 'always stops every once in a while' (LC I 31.1, revised first draft, p. 51), as if he can't believe where he is or still does not fully belong there. It is these alternations between pressing on and momentarily stopping and going back in memory that Malamud creates and develops in his revisions—behavioural structures which are for him a symbol and for Hobbs an inarticulate sign. Malamud had read Melville's *Billy Budd* just before starting *The Natural*: what the two books share is not only a mythic sense of the elemental fight between the simple uneducated innocence of a 'natural man' and the evil underlying the civilized world, but also a protagonist's stuttering incapacity to get powerful inner feelings out into words.

He relishes what in a retrospective justification of *The Natural* he called 'the obstruction to clear meaning' both in the novel and in the life it is depicting (LC II 11.5). It was obstructions or obstacles that got him away from working too close to simple linear narrative movement. The idea was made explicit to him by the short-story writer Eudora Welty when she wrote of how some writers seems to be 'obstructionists', 'as if they hold back their own best interest'. Yet they do so, argued Welty, in order to enter 'another world' where there are no blatant qualities and where beauty itself 'is associated with obstruction—with reticence of a number of kinds' (LC II 11.5). Such writers, hiding their deepest thoughts, eschew the easy, open ways of life. It is like what Memo says when she, the second of the novel's destructive women in succession to Harriet, compares Hobbs with her former lover, Bump Bailey, previously the team's star player:

> Even when he played ball, there was something carefree and playful about it. Maybe he went all the way after a fly ball or maybe he didn't, but once he made up his mind to catch it, it was exciting how he ran and exciting how he caught it. He made you think you had been wishing for a thing to happen for a long time and then he made it happen. And the same with his hitting. When you catch one, Roy, or go up to hit, everyone knows beforehand that it will land up in your glove, or be a hit. You work at it so—sometimes you even look desperate—but to him it was a playful game and so was his life.
>
> (*The Natural*, 120)

It is Bump who is more 'natural' here, the figure of magical wishes who still retains the easy freedom and chance romance of the unpredictable game. But Roy has raised himself to another level, to a professional dedication in his second life itself the equal of his talent in the first. And with that increased inevitability in his play, there is at once a loss of spontaneous life and the gain of intensely narrow prowess. Though writing *The Natural* surprised and excited him, in his own way Malamud was already taking the disciplined route, unable to rely, he thought, on the free gifts of imagination when artists like Saul Bellow were more 'natural' than he could ever be. What lies behind Memo's criticism of Roy, as compared with Bump, are hidden things like Hannah Needle's words when she rejected Malamud's hasty marriage-offer: 'You work life; you don't live it.' It was another obstruction he stored, used, and transmuted in order to recreate 'the same thing in different worlds' (TH, 16).

As he puts it in a cryptic note made while writing *Dubin's Lives*: 'One must transcend the autobiographical detail by inventing it after it is remembered' (LC II 1.5). To do this, to get away from 'The Light Sleeper', and forget in one life in order to remember in another, what Malamud needed was form to give that second existence in the book a genuinely autonomous life. It is not that *The Natural* is 'really' about the autobiography of Malamud as twice-born soul, in his own vocation as writer. That is just one of the secondary hidden meanings, the subtexts, that help to generate the work's resonance. For that matter, *The Natural* is not 'really' about baseball either. For this novel suggests that the content of *all* lives is really no more than a metaphor for what they are endeavouring to overcome or trying to stand for: that is the implicit 'idea', the symbol which the life is seeking for itself.

In that repeated search, Bump Bailey is like a reincarnation of the Whammer in Roy Hobbs's mind. But Bump is also like an alternative version of Roy whom Roy seeks to replace both in the team and in the affections of Memo, herself a replay of Harriet as opposed to Iris. When at the end of the novel, Hobbs strikes out against a new pitcher significantly named Youngberry, it is as though what he once did to the Whammer is now happening again to him. Sometimes Hobbs hits the ball as if it were something he hated, watching it soar as though it were a thought:—it was spinning away in circles when 'he never really liked the sight of a circle' (*The Natural*, 158). But the novel is full of cycles and circles—repeated mistakes, the same thing happening in different circumstances, the life of one character going into another—yet always there is the attempt to win some changed outcome out of the repeated human material, potential constantly seeking or losing some embodiment for itself in the genetics of this world.

For example: Memo had once gone in the dark to Hobbs's room, tricked into thinking it was Bump's, and only afterwards discovering, with disgust, that it wasn't. Thereafter Roy finds: 'It was a confusing proposition to want a girl you'd already had and couldn't get because you had; a situation common in his life, of having first and then wanting what he had had, as if he hadn't had it' (Ibid. 110). The sentence isn't there until the second draft when Malamud can sense it for his character implicit within the shape and sequence of the story he has created. One can see him in the drafts getting the sentence to say itself, in the shape it had to.

These shapes are also formed into longer narrative stretches. One night Memo, with Roy beside her, is driving along too fast. The car seems to hit something or someone, but Memo does not stop and persuades Roy not to either. It may be an illusion of trees in moonlight, but Roy thinks it was a boy coming out of the wood with a dog. Later, there is no sign on the car and, on the return journey, no sign on the road. Malamud first writes: 'he felt a terrible pain in his gut yet *at once* remembered there had been no sign of blood on the bumper and fender when he had looked'—and then writes in, above 'at once', *'simultaneously'* instead (LC I 30, 113). Malamud always wants the two possibilities held together in solution, at the same time. Then Hobbs breaks the spell, splits, and has to go one way, only to find the other way coming back at him later, without progress. The next day he looks in the papers for a report of a hit-and-run accident on Long Island, and there is no sign there either.

But what did not seem to happen at one level comes back in a different dimension, in metaphysical form. There follows a slump in Hobbs's batting form. He is not a thinker. Only from the run of bad form does he begin to suspect that somehow there is something wrong with him. In some other internal world, the boy who was run over was symbolically his lost younger self.

Yet there is also another boy, a real physical one, who was hurt in an accident in the street and is lying in a hospital with a broken skull, losing the will to fight. In the first draft it is even more pointed: this boy was run over in the city, and the driver didn't stop. To rouse him, his father promises the son, an avid baseball fan, that his hero Roy Hobbs will hit a home run for him at the next game. It is in the very midst of Roy's slump. 'Why did you promise him, and why did you tell me?' cries Roy. In the game that follows, in every strike, at every inning, Hobbs fails to deliver, the begging father desperately looking on.

Then a woman, in her thirties, stands up in the crowd and bows her head. In the first draft nobody knows why; some think she has got confused about the end of the inning. But gradually in the rewriting the embarrassing strangeness of it increases until eventually her insistent silence makes itself articulated: 'she stood there, so cleanly etched in light, as if trying to communicate something she couldn't express' (*The Natural*, 147).

In every sense, the woman, alone, is standing up for Roy Hobbs—what Malamud always wanted for himself. She rises again after strike two against him. 'Then it flashed on him the reason she was standing was to show her confidence in him. He felt surprised that anybody would want to do that for him' (Ibid. 149). The home run he can now hit restores the sick boy, as though expiating his offence with Memo.

When he speaks to the woman later, it is clear that her showing 'confidence' in him, giving him renewed confidence in his own powers, is related to something whose real and more ancient name is belief. This is Iris: 'I hate to see a hero fail. There are so few of them ... Without heroes we're all plain people and don't know how far we can go':

> 'I felt that if you knew people believed in you, you'd regain your power. That's why I stood up in the grandstand. I hadn't meant to before I came. It happened naturally ...'
>   'Were you praying for me to smack one over the roof?'
>   'I hoped you might become yourself again.'   (Ibid. 155–6)

She speaks a language he needs to learn, though it is hard to come by. For she is his chance of what she herself finally calls 'a second life'—in one of Malamud's most crucial formulations, found by him only at the very last moment, in galley proof: 'We have two lives, Roy, the life we learn with and the life we have after that' (Ibid. 159).

Iris too had a first life. She is already a mother, after one bad sexual experience with an older man who half-forced himself upon her in a park. 'You are really the first,' she whispers to Hobbs. His story is saying to him, if he could hear it, that he ought to marry her. Yet just as he is about to consummate the relationship, she blurts out that she is also a grandmother, then he stops, then carries on and finishes anyway. Hobbs was brought up by his grandmother because his parents were no good. When she died, his father—who at least had taught him baseball—put him, like Babe Ruth, into an orphanage. Now he deserves better, he thinks, than to be tied to a grandmother. It is like a much more serious version of the ungenerous disappointment in 'The Girl of My Dreams': *this was she*. He stared unbelievingly, his heart a dishrag.' He cannot get out of his circles.

Some reviewers thought the women in the book should have been more realized: in a letter to Robert Giroux, Malamud said that Roy would not let them be (9 February 1952, HRC 10.8). Others said that it was hard to feel pity for Roy. But at each crucial point in the novel 'Roy' is also momentarily all that he could have been, and all that again and again he does not make himself be, as he lapses back into what he has become. It belongs with what Malamud was trying to tell himself in a note he wrote after 'The Light

Sleeper' in the effort to get away from the dead facts of autobiography: 'A good way to see the possibilities of any single person in a book is, so to speak, to know him inside out. If the mind first conceives him as a "good" person, let the imagination play upon the idea that he is a "bad" person and see what happens to the story then' (HRC 22.2). 'I hoped you might become yourself again,' said Iris. In the worst old habitual version, he does become himself again.

It makes him so sick he will have to retire after just one season of his comeback. That is why he agrees to throw his final match, for the future money he will never otherwise earn. Only at the last moment in the last innings does something in him make him change his mind, want to save the game for its own sake. 'Only a homer, with himself scoring the winning run, would truly redeem him' (*The Natural*, 215). This is what baseball offered that modern life apparently never did: one dramatic moment in which to change the years, the patterns of a whole lifetime. He swings at the new young pitcher, misses, and in that moment knows that it is too late, he has learnt nothing from the past, and now must suffer again.

It is a little boy, again, who comes up to Roy and demands of him what, in baseball legend, Shoeless Joe Jackson was said to have been asked by an equivalent young believer after the fix:

'Say it ain't true, Roy.'
        When Roy looked into the boy's eyes he wanted to say it wasn't but couldn't, and he lifted his hands to his face and wept many bitter tears.   (Ibid. 234)

In the world of possibilities that lies behind this one, every success could have been a failure at another level, every failure a success. Malamud knew that knife's edge. So much in Malamud is about the loss of the heroic and the attempt to regain it albeit in smaller, more ordinary forms. Without heroes, said Iris, we don't know how far we can go. The final bitter tears, so like those of Isaiah or Peter, are in memory of that lost possibility in the world. 'The end may never be reached, never fulfilled ... Although there are many who do not believe that it exists, still, it exists as a possibility, and possibility is necessary to man' (TH, 187).

Robert Giroux, editor in chief at Harcourt, Brace and Company, had first written to Malamud on 6 November 1950. Giroux was the quietly great talent-spotter: his list came to include Robert Lowell, J. D. Salinger, Flannery O'Connor, Elizabeth Bishop, Thomas Merton, Jean Stafford, and John Berryman. Malamud came to him recommended also by Catherine Carver who admired a short story not yet published called 'The Magic

Barrel', and by Alfred Kazin, who knew Malamud was writing a novel about baseball. Kazin was another clever Jewish boy from Brooklyn, born in 1915, who had been in one of Malamud's literature classes at City College, but, unlike Malamud, had achieved enormous success, as a man of letters, as early as 1942. In his letter Giroux praised the stories he had recently read in *Commentary* and the *Partisan Review*, 'The Prison' and 'The First Seven Years', respectively, and wanted to know if there was a novel in progress. Malamud replied at once, and Giroux said he was interested in seeing the baseball novel and keen to publish a volume of short stories. 'We prefer to publish a writer, rather than a book', he wrote (13 November 1950, HRC 10.8).

The telegram from Giroux—'We like The Natural enormously and want to publish it'—arrived on 7 January 1952, with further letters to follow containing readers' suggestions for rewrites, some of which Malamud accepted, most not. *The Natural* was published in July. 'Now I join the sacred company', he wrote Ann only half-wryly from New York (4 July 1952), where he was visiting Eugene in hospital, seeing his book launched, meeting up with old friends, and making new literary acquaintances.

The personal responses he got from friends in New York were mixed. Discouraged, he wrote to Ann, July 26, 'I know well that the book is no masterpiece but it is clever entertainment and says something to perhaps simple people.' Perhaps that is why he was later to write a talk entitled '*The Natural*: Raison d'être and Meaning' in belated defence of the book, citing Katherine Ann Porter, Alfred Kazin, Saul Bellow, and Irving Howe amongst those who thought he had made a success of it. Bellow had written him a note, 28 July 1952, saying that every page of *The Natural* showed unmistakeable signs of 'the mind and touch of a real writer'. But the reviews themselves were mixed and brief—many complaining of the mix of the fanciful and the realistic.[22] But Harry Sylvester in the *Sunday New York Times Book Review* saw that Malamud was an original with a mission, and in a review headed 'Baseball à la Wagner' in the *American Mercury* for October, Harvey Swados praised the novel's use of different levels to reach 'an audience ranging from lowbrows to highbrows'. Later, in 1955, Leslie Fiedler was to complain about the stupid neglect of *The Natural*, because of the sheer imaginative outrage it had offered.

Yet thus in 1952 Malamud at last made four figures from his pen, earning royalties of $1,225, rising to an income from writing of nearly $2,700 in 1953. But the great moment had been the first meeting with Giroux in his office at Harcourt, Brace. As Giroux put it in the elegy he delivered at the 92nd street YMHA (20 April 1986), printed by Glenn Horowitz:

When we shook hands, and I said 'I greet you at the beginning of a great career,' he replied 'Emerson to Walt Whitman.' I knew I had found a friend as well as an important writer.

As for Malamud, surprised by his own imagination, 'I walked around, a free man' (HRC 29.6). He thought that, imaginably, there might still be a third life for Roy Hobbs. 'Perhaps', he put it to his agent, Diarmuid Russell, 23 October 1951, 'there is yet another chance ... in the sense of there being three strikes to every time at bat' (LC I 56.7).

4

◄◇◇◇►

The Assistant

'A Belated Novel of the Thirties'

In truth, Giroux was not wholly persuaded by *The Natural*. 'I wasn't convinced when Kazin brought in the first book. The first book is always a gamble. Bern needed a success and wanted a theme which would be successful. Baseball was the great American sport. All kinds of gifts that he had, he put in to that book, but the baseball setting was artificial. It wasn't something genuine, that came from the heart.'[1] It was the grocery short stories that Giroux believed in as truly natural to Malamud.

All Malamud needed, felt Giroux, was encouragement: the great reviser did not want or need much editorial help, but he was always anxious. That is why Giroux knew he was taking a painful risk in urging Malamud not to try to go ahead with publishing 'The Man That Nobody Could Lift', the novella based on Eugene's schizophrenia. 'In terms of your own career, I hope you will put it aside', he wrote Malamud, 20 November 1953. It would not meet the expectations *The Natural* had established. 'It grieves me to send you so negative a letter,' he went on, 'but I assure you that this advice comes out of my very high regard for your writing and my belief in your future career. Don't think too harshly of me.'

Malamud respected and trusted Giroux, and Giroux respected and understood Malamud. 'Malamud wanted success for himself; he wanted to show that a person whose beginnings were so bad—as the world looks at it—could really become as good as anyone else, or better than anybody else. His beginnings haunted him as they did me when I was trying to make a living.' Giroux was a Catholic but was born in the same year as Malamud, like him struggled through the poverty of the Depression in New York, and also had a brother in a mental institution.

Yet in 1955 Malamud seemed to have lost this supporter. Giroux left Harcourt for Farrar, Straus and Company, in frustration at Harcourt's refusal to let him sign up Salinger's *Catcher in the Rye*. He was sorry that he could not take Malamud with him, but the contract which Giroux himself had drawn up tied Malamud to Harcourt for his next work.

But Harcourt rejected it. Malamud phoned Giroux, telling him they had turned down his new book. Giroux couldn't believe it: 'You mean they've rejected your stories?' 'No, it's a novel called *The Assistant*. Would you like to read it?'[2] 'It was the luckiest thing in my life,' Giroux recalled, 'when Harcourt Brace turned it down. They were so stupid.'

The rejection letter from John H. McCallum, Vice President of Harcourt, and directed initially to Malamud's agent, Diarmuid Russell, counts as a classic in publishing history—31 May 1956:

> We have come to the reluctant conclusion, after a number of readings and a great deal of discussion, that we are not prepared to publish Bernard Malamud's THE ASSISTANT. There is much that is excellent in this new novel of his, but on the whole we find it more unsatisfying than satisfying; we believe it would not be a step upward from THE NATURAL.
>
> I realize this decision may well mean that we shall lose Malamud, and this I regret, for many of us here were and still are enchanted with his first novel. May I say, then, that if THE ASSISTANT is not placed with some other publisher, we should be happy to have a chance at his *next* novel.
>
> Believe me, I *am* sorry about this one.

Just as bad, Pascal Covici from The Viking Press also 'wanted very much to like' the novel but felt that it 'just doesn't come off. There are some moving episodes, but the whole is not convincing. I see no sales, and I don't believe it would get favourable critical attention.' By October 1977, as Malamud himself noted, the total printing of *The Assistant* in all editions came to 1,190,000 (LC I 53.2).

To Giroux in 1956 *The Assistant* was the novel that the real Malamud had been waiting to write, the one that was implicit within the short stories and turned them into rehearsals for itself. It was originally called *The Apprentice*. As Malamud wrote in a brief addendum to the Norwegian edition:

> The apprentice character interested me, as he has in much of my fiction, the man, who, as much as he can in the modern world, is in the process of changing his fate, his life. This sort of person, not at all complicated, appears for the first time in my writing in the short story 'The First Seven Years' (included

in my first story collection *The Magic Barrel*) and I thought I would like to develop the possibilities of his type. The refugee shoemaker in the story becomes the Italo-American assistant, Frank Alpine, whose way of achieving his spiritual freedom is to adopt the burdens of a Jew. The grocery store background came from 'The Cost of Living', another short story written in the early fifties ... Morris Bober resembles Sam Thomashevsky, though his fate, I should think, is more moving because he helps call it down upon himself, whereas Sam is the victim mostly of economic circumstances. Thus from these two stories came the store background, and characters, who were to become Frank Alpine, Morris Bober, and Ida and Helen Bober. (TH, 86)

The store had been the prison from which Malamud had wanted to escape via his education; but now, in his very writing, he went back into it. This characteristic turnaround was a second-generation achievement: what at first in its shaming banality had seemed to be below literature could be made into literature's own subject-matter. It was the new-world continuance of the work of nineteenth-century European realism, of the novel in the hands of Tolstoy and George Eliot, making not heroic but ordinary life the subject of great literature. Years after its publication Malamud received from Evelyn Avery the sort of fan letter, concerning *The Assistant*, that most pleased him:

At age 19, as a Brooklyn College English major reading Puritan prose above a depressing grocery store, I felt trapped, both intellectually and emotionally. My friends were middle-class Jews; my courses emphasized British and early American literature. In the late 50s 'immigrant' was a pejorative word, while 'ethnic' was largely unknown. Imagine my joy and relief when I stumbled upon *The Assistant* and discovered I was not alone. More important, I realized that there might be some meaning to my father's misfortunes and my mother's hard life. Perhaps, I thought, they were not complete schlemiels, for like the Bobers, my parents' decency, in part, had kept them poor. (HRC 8.3)

Yet when people are young, says the grocer's daughter in the novel, they feel that when they get up in the morning, wonderful things might happen: 'That's what youth means and that's what I've lost. Nowadays I feel that every day is like the day before, and what's worse, like the day after. ... I want a larger and better life. I want the return of my possibilities' (*The Assistant*, 42). When Malamud returned to the store for fiction's rescue-work, he also made Helen Bober the mark of his own desire to leave it. That is the richness of his ambivalence.

There was also a richness to be found amidst the deprivation. *The Assistant* was what Leslie Fiedler was to call 'in a strange way ... a belated novel of the thirties', written nearly twenty years later (*Reconstructionist*, 24 (21 February 1958)). In an interview he gave in 1979, Malamud remembered seeing men at the beginning of the Depression queueing for a free cup of soup, people trying to make a living out of selling apples in the street, a long breadline one Christmas in the midst of Times Square, himself saving a nickel by walking two or three miles rather than take the subway home. From the Wall Street Crash in 1929 the Depression took ten years—a virtual generation—out of people's lives, often the lives of those who had had hardly had a decent beginning anyway. By 1932 manufacturing output was just half of what it had been three years earlier; unemployment rose to 15 million, at its worst comprising up to 30% of the workforce. 'Of course it influenced my social thinking, but not in a violent way. It was that I wanted a good life to any member of our society ... for people to have jobs and whatever items they needed to carry their lives out, and a little comfort' (HRC 31.4). It was the world that Alfred Kazin summed up in *A Walker in the City* (1951) with the anxious question his non-English-speaking mother would ask his house-painter father, each time he returned from the labour pool in front of the Brooklyn Municipal Bank: 'Geyst arbeten?'—will there be work this week? Max Malamud read *The Daily Forward* in Yiddish and dreamed of equality, but individual shopkeepers could have no active relation with the collectivism of strikes and unions. It was personally and emotionally, not politically, that Malamud's grocers belonged to the tradition of Jewish socialism.[3] Al Marcus, for example, is the paper products salesman who regularly calls on Bober. Al has cancer and is one of the few who has sufficient money put by to stop working, but he won't make it easy for death to find him wasting away at home:

> No matter how bad business was, Morris tried to have some kind of little order waiting for him. Al would suck on an unlit cigar, scribble an item or two in his metal-covered salesbook, then stand around a few minutes, making small talk, his eyes far away from what he was saying; and after that, tip his hat and take off for the next place. Everybody knew how sick he was   (*The Assistant*, 82)

In an interview with Michiko Kakutani, Malamud argued: 'The good thing about the Depression was everything went down to bedrock. Experience that deprives you of something can make you realize what it is that you need most, and it sends you inward, and that to a writer is important' (*New York Times*, 15 July 1980). It was as though seeing life reduced to that humdrum 'bedrock' yielded a better insight into its intrinsic nature—into the thing itself, as in the slow, bare, struggling motion of Wordsworth's beggars. In the first draft Malamud had written that Al Marcus made small talk, 'his eyes blank': it was in the second draft that he turned it into 'his eyes far away from what he was saying'. Something imaginatively deeper, more autonomous and mysterious was offered, even to the minimal life of a passing minor character. Malamud's gift is like Morris always trying to have 'some kind of little order waiting for him'.

'Some of my knowledge of Jewish past came to me, of course, through the immigrant Jews of New York, those who visited our house to sit and talk, or came to my father's place of business to sell him something and talk; and those whom I saw on the streets and in the trolley cars.' But Malamud had had to get over something: he was, he admitted, 'often not comfortable with them until I taught myself to understand' (TH, 188). When his son Paul asked him what it had been like, Malamud said that people in Brooklyn, when he was a child, were in every sense from a different world—not cultured, not articulately interesting, men talking mainly about cars and baseball and money. Over his lifetime, he said, in the rapid acceleration of American history as though a hundred years could pass in two decades, people had become astonishingly better looking and better educated. But Malamud had taught himself the subtext of this uneducated, unattractive lower class he had wanted to quit: 'They spoke then without voices, with their hands, eyes, even with inert bodies. If you were alive, could you hide it? They couldn't' (Ibid. 189). He learnt that overflowing language which burst out of the very force of their lives. In 'Take Pity' a salesman tells the recording angel how eventually he had used all his persuasive skills to urge a poor grocer not to buy more goods, but to sell up the whole business:

> This he finally agreed with me, but before he could go in auction he dropped dead.'
> Davidov made a note. 'How did he die?' ...
> 'From what he died?—he died, that's all.'
> 'Answer, please, this question.'
> 'Broke in him something. That's how.'
> 'Broke what?'
> 'Broke what breaks.'

This was the Yiddish–English amalgam that was in memory of the way his own father spoke. The second language of the son of immigrants with the original Yiddish still hanging around it, this was what Malamud called Yinglish which 'gets you English as if it is spoken for the first time'.[4] It is not the language of conceptual explanation. It is a language of happening—'broke'—reaching that deep implicit level *prior* to articulate thought, which later thought itself comes out of. 'What' it is that breaks is thus found only in the telling of its breaking; wherever Al Marcus really was is only describable as 'far away from what he was saying'. It was an inward language so broken and compressed as to become almost bedrock poetry—made witty and alive even in suffering, sad with the inventive inner spirit of comedy itself.

Malamud learnt the underlying characters of that language: the need to be safe, secure, and settled; the hard search for a living 'starting with nothing and living on it for a long time'; the sheer terror of going to the wall and being unable to provide even the basics for one's own family; the constant worries about health; the fear that assimilation might also be a form of betrayal; the complex concern passed on to the children, 'to give them the absolute best, yet afraid once the opportunity came to do so, of giving more than one should to the point of eliminating the necessity of struggle, and thus depriving the children of the means to protect themselves in the future' (TH, 188). But what he remembered above all was 'an emotional people' possessed of an old gentleness that was 'a miraculous transfiguration of the bitter experiences of the past'. For the needy boy in a struggling home, baffled or deterred by the appearance of the people outside and 'often not comfortable with them until I taught myself to understand': 'It was a magical experience to come into their homes and be loved' (Ibid.). He adds: 'To learn from love of one's own, to love other children is not as easy as it sounds.' He was one of those other children. It was those miraculous or magical emotional 'transfigurations' that later he wanted to recreate in his own fresh language.

That is why on its first page *The Assistant* has a ten-year-old girl enter the grocer's shop:

> 'My mother says,' she said quickly, 'can you trust her till tomorrow for a pound of butter, loaf of rye bread and a small bottle of cider vinegar?'
> He knew the mother. 'No more trust.'
> The girl burst into tears.
> Morris gave her a quarter-pound of butter, the bread and vinegar. He found a pencilled spot on the worn counter, near the cash register, and wrote a sum under 'Drunk Woman'. The total now came to $2.03, which he never hoped to see. But Ida would nag if she noticed a new figure, so he reduced the amount to $1.61.   (*The Assistant*, 7–8)

Even the negatives have positives hidden within them: it is 'no more trust' (instead of the more mercantile 'no more credit'); it is, beautifully, 'never [even] hoped'. The note 'Drunk Woman', set down as though by another recording angel, is literature at its bare minimum. Even the kindness of giving feels more like reluctance and repentance on his part ('the girl burst into tears')—like weakness or folly requiring concealment in a form of collusive cheating ($2.03 reduced to $1.61, neither of which will be paid). The grocer sees even Nick, his own lodger, surreptitiously going to the cheaper competition across the road. Later Nick's wife, Tessie, comes into the store:

> 'Please give me twenty cents' ham for Nick's lunch tomorrow.'
> He understood. She was making amends for Nick's trip around the corner that morning. He cut her an extra slice of ham. (Ibid. 26)

In financial and mathematical terms that 'extra' is poor business, but a good language with an austere inner richness, whether Tessie quite understands it or not. This was the equivocal 'good thing' about the Depression: what's left by what is taken away.

History, said Malamud, may be swallowed into the past but it is a past that then lives on in its people, instinctively. That is why, as he later made explicit, he could still hear behind the immigrant language of the Depression echoes of a long Jewish history. That which takes away also gives insight. Yet, equally, whatever is given has its cost and pain and burden. This instinctive double sense in Malamud had its roots, as he himself gradually discovered through his reading, in the drama of Judaism itself:

> When I think of the history of the Jews, of which they are understandably so conscious, I think of the triumph of insight and value that makes their lives so basically rich (in a sense life made rich by what they give it) although the primal knowledge is that life is tragic, no matter how sweet or apparently full. ('Imaginative Writing and the Jewish Experience', TH, 186)

The tragedy 'centers around that which is given'. And what was originally given was recognition of there being but the One God. Yet this was a belief that combined the gift of chosenness with the demand of utter obligation. Thus the drama began:

> The highest gift is given, and to affirm its endless value, it is taken. Or to put it another way, because the gift is pure and man is not, the gift, paradoxically, is a punishment; yet the punishment renews the extraordinary value of the gift. (Ibid.)

There is Exodus and then there is the Return. The Temple was meant to last forever, but when the recalcitrant children of Israel strayed from the Law, despite the warnings of the prophets, then Jerusalem fell. The Destruction of the Temple meant Exile: the empire of David and Solomon was dispersed. Yet, though the outer holy place was lost, God still retained the underlying covenant within, demanding its inner renewal in every individual soul instead:

> as if it were foreordained that the truest learning must be of suffering, because in suffering the self is contemplated as it has never before been

contemplated, and it is the self that is at fault—we may call it—for not being the
God-self.   (Ibid. 187)

After the Exile, therefore, there came the period of expiation through
cleansing of the self—until, of course, that renewal also fell back into the
old weakening of ideals and the return of sin. In all these cycles of repeated
renewals and repeated falls, the great modern version of exile for Malamud
was the diaspora, the gathering of lost and persecuted tribes struggling in the
America of the Depression. It is no longer Arthurian legend informing a story
about baseball. It is the drama of Jewish history as a universal human pattern
that lies behind the little world of 1930s Brooklyn with its poor displaced
immigrants.

'Material for Shaping, Reshaping'

Writing to J. F. Powers, 13 July 1954, Malamud described his struggle with
what became *The Assistant*—a struggle which arose from its subject-matter
being so deeply familiar to him:

> I have set myself an average of a page a day of writing and do just about
> that, though I am not, of course, in the rereading, pleased with each page.
> I think I know a little too much about what I am writing and tend to rely
> more on memory than on the imagination that I am more comfortable with. I
> love magic, and imagination is magic. The trick, of course, is to find its secret
> sources. Let us say that I am seeking and will continue to seek.[5]

To find those secret sources and turn memory back into imagination,
Malamud needed both formal obstacles and reinvented patterns.

The major patterns of adding and subtracting, of exile and return, are
created in two structural inventions in the novel's first three chapters.
Characteristically of this great Jewish novel, they come with the arrival of a
non-Jew. The first pattern lies in the figure of return. Of the two masked
young thieves who mug the Jewish grocer, one returns to the store to help
out for nothing, in secret reparation. The 'thief'—Frank Alpine, an Italian
American—goes back, disguised now as the 'assistant'. But in realist or even
recidivist counterpoint, the second movement is that even while Frank brings
extra custom into the store, he also, in this second life of his, begins to hold
some money back, take some more out of the till, like a thief again. There
is still an increased profit, Frank tells himself. In the first draft it is even
said that stealing felt to him secretly like 'a kind of creativity'.[6] Yet at the
same time, in further complication, it is also the case that, like the grocer

noting down the hopeless $1.61, Franks keeps a conscientious note of his own deficits, and hides the record for deferred future repayment in his shoe. As often when contradictory things happen almost simultaneously in Malamud, it is revision that enables him to do seemingly in one fell swoop what actually took him two stages: the detail of the card of reckoning kept in Frank's shoe is explicitly added after the first draft. In an early version Malamud even has Frank stealing from his own father. But in all versions Frank was dumped in an orphanage at an early age like Roy Hobbs, and was thus perhaps doomed—he himself half wants to think—from the very beginning.

Aged ten, feeling deprived or tempted, Malamud had been caught pilfering quarters from his own father and wanted to die for shame. From 1943 onwards, the older Malamud, like the son of a grocer, kept meticulous accounts, and continued to do so in his wealthier days, obsessively copying out and checking in longhand the figures his agent and publishers were giving him, to the nearest cent. Both parts went into the making of Frank Alpine, but both were now transfigured. Writing was the stealing Malamud did now.

Malamud began writing in April 1954 and finished in June 1956. The 'first draft' was typed out by Ann from the scribbled original that Malamud always destroyed; then was revised by hand, and typed up again. As in one of Malamud's account books, the chapters are dated at their commencement and their completion. It took him 189 working days to write 239 pages in first draft. He was not exaggerating when he spoke of a page or a page and a half per day. The first draft was then further revised in the course of Malamud writing it out again by hand. The second draft he typed out. The third he wrote first by hand and then typed out—and from that typed copy Ann typed the final draft. Then there were further changes made in the galley proofs. As Giroux wrote on 2 April 1957, the cost of the proof corrections was $401.05, reduced to a bill to Malamud of $300 against royalties, because 924 lines had been altered at that late stage (LC I 51.4). (After this Malamud shrewdly negotiated contracts that required him to pay for alterations only when in excess of 15% of the total cost of composition, the norm being 10%. By the time he was writing *Dubin's Lives* he had given himself scope for 20% (LC I 53.2).)

It was this minute obsessiveness that made Malamud often quote Valéry on a work of literature never being finished, only abandoned.

QUESTION: How long do you wait between the first rough draft before you read it again and are you ever struck with despair when you re-read it?

MALAMUD: I despair in reading almost any first draft. First draft is the time of hypothesis—you try to make it into a life or a representation of a life. Therefore, you are making mistakes, sometimes overdoing it, as you do the fiction.

And on reading it over, you can see all the mistakes at once, and the idea
is not to be overcome by it. Say, okay, I'm going at it again, and don't recoil
at it.   (TH, 128)

The writer faces and overcomes those mistakes. But actually with Malamud
over 60% of the novel is usually in place after the first draft. It is rare thereafter
that very much is moved about: chapter order will not alter; scenes, often
marked off by a single line-space, will very seldom be transposed. Instead
space will either close and tighten, or open up for something that was waiting
to get said in earlier draftings. By the time the novel is published, Malamud
will usually have taken out the numbers of the chapters in order to keep the
movement more fluid yet abrupt, the transitions subtle in a more blindly
felt rhythm. But if the reader turns to the space, the capital letter, which
signals the opening of what used to be headed, say, Chapter Nine, the second
paragraph in the final version is still what was the second paragraph in the
first draft, about spring on its way; or the chapter's second scene will begin
with Frank hearing Morris coming down from his bed; and so on. For such
a big reviser, nothing largely fundamental ever changes: rather, everything
is done to lock the novel into its constituent paragraphs. It was then, when
the template was more or less complete, that the main revisionary work went
on. The remaining 40% of the work is done, minutely, at the level of the
sentence. As one of Malamad's Corvallis friends, the painter Nelson Sandgren
put it, recalling their shared conversations:

> He was very interested in little things and little transactions, and quiet little
> thoughtfulnesses that occurred between people. If he saw a little girl fall down
> and a little boy come and help her get up again, that would interest him a
> whole lot more than some business transaction that might engage a couple of
> lawyers. I saw one day on the sidewalk—I have a notebook and I carry a pen
> usually—some bird poop and I looked because it had a fantastic shape to it.
> I thought, 'People will think this is odd but I have to draw that.' So I stood
> there and drew these shapes, which I have still in my notebook. That's the sort
> of talk or story Bernard would enjoy exceedingly.[7]

'More detail,' Malamud would urge in his own margin, knowing that it was
also symbolically more than squalid detail, and often more in fewer and fewer
words, compressed ever closer.

The text evolved but Malamud knew, broadly, what he was after. In a
notebook which he compiled after writing his first draft and in planning for the
second, Malamud ends by thinking back to *The Natural* in comparison: 'This
book is realistically wrought; its magic, then, must lie in the surprises wrought
not by event but by personality.' But he also adds, 'Perhaps the important

thing in the book is NOT so much the realization of the individual destinies as the relationships.' And, what is more, the magic must also come from 'a magic of style' achieved in revision by 'winnowing, making crisp, vitalizing, making new' (HRC 19.1). When the story, despite partial efforts, seems to be about nothing changing, again and again and again, then these three alternative interests—personality, interrelationships, and style—are what count.

For example: one moment Malamud paused over when checking his first draft consisted of a mere phrase about Helen (then called Adele), and the wrong start she finds she has made with her love life:

> Virginity she had thought she had parted with without sorrow, yet was surprised by torments of conscience, or was it disappointment at being valued under her expectations? (*The Assistant*, 17)

What Malamud hesitated over was the formulation 'parted *with without sorrow*', perhaps no model for Herb Nelson's composition classes at Oregon. Yet he then ticked 'with' and 'without' in confirmation, perhaps for Ann too as typist. Helen regretted the loss of her virginity to Nat Pearl that summer, and yet a few months later in the fall (goes the first draft) she 'found herself alone in the house with Nat and had again given in to passion'. But the creative language Malamud was after had to be more internally charged, less horizontally ongoing than that. In the second draft, Malamud wrote instead that she 'had done again what she had promised herself she wouldn't': thus 'how could you undo what you had done again in the fall, unwillingly willing' (Ibid.). This is personality baffled by itself, and style accordingly densened in the thick of the self-contradictions. That then is the magic Malamud is looking for: not mere polishing, but the work that raises and realizes what before may have been little more than a paraphrase of the imagined life. In his last illness Morris dreams of the son, Ephraim, who died young. 'Why didn't you stay alive?' he shouts in the first draft. In the second: 'Stay alive,' he cries after him, instead.

A few words changed everything, particularly when they suddenly interlinked like poetry in the midst of prose. A similar little thing happened in the second draft when Frank has taken over from Morris in the store and, indeed, has almost become Morris in being trapped there:

> 'Dear Jesus,' he said to himself, 'Why am I doing this for? Why am I killing myself [inserted: so]?' He gave himself many unhappy answers, the most satisfying being that while he was doing this he was doing nothing worse.
>
> But then he took to doing things he had promised himself he would never again do. He did them with a sense of self-repulsion, and a dread of what he would do next. On three different nights he climbed up the airshaft and

crouched under the bathroom window, waiting for Helen to come in for her
shower   (LC I 2.2, pp. 270–1)

There are changes that Malamud will make here. He won't let himself have
two attempts at 'Why' in the first paragraph, or both 'self-repulsion' and
'dread' in the second. He will change the 'most satisfying' answer to a rueful
'*best*' answer to set off against 'doing nothing *worse*'. But what Malamud does
tick are those four forms of 'do' at the end of the first and the beginning of
the second paragraph. 'While he was *doing* this he was *doing* nothing worse';
but he also 'took to *doing* things he had promised himself he would never
again *do*'. Then two more: 'He *did* them ... with a dread of what he would
do next.' Though finally he felt he could omit that fourth 'do', Malamud
knew he had worked himself into the novel's human complications when the
sentences began to thicken and bind themselves in this way. 'The real: how
thick, thin, extensive' Malamud wrote in some notes on writing (LC II 13. 11).

But the layers build up in other dimensions too. Helen is surprised by
her own contradictions, but in 'doing again what she had promised herself
she wouldn't' she is for once like Frank who repeatedly 'does things he had
promised himself he would never again'. This is what Malamud means by
relationship—not only at the explicit level of story, as to what might happen
between Frank and Helen, but also implicitly in terms of this secret connection
or partial similarity known only between writer and reader. In his notebook
he summarizes for himself four almost musical variations working through
the characters: Morris: 'Escape from economic prison'; Frank: 'Seeking for a
moral self'; Ida: 'Escape from insecurity'; Helen: 'Seeking the valuable life'
(HRC 19.1). The young seekers are types of Malamud; the older escapees
types of his worn-out parents. Yet in the cross-currents of the novel itself,
Frank's account of his poor life reminds Morris of his own: 'I am sixty and he
talks like me' (*The Assistant*, 37); but meanwhile Frank himself is frightened
by the hunger in Helen's eyes which 'he couldn't forget because it made him
remember his own' (Ibid. 59). As though he too were a thief, Morris secretly
withholds money from the till to pay Frank sufficient to try to stop him from
stealing, while, increasingly, Frank becomes Morris buried alive in the store,
in order to try to pay for Helen's release from it at college. Life keeps taking
different shapes in and between them all.

What is more, the human elements of the story get repetitively worked
and reworked in the course of the story itself. Later in the novel, after he wins
Helen only to lose her again by his bad behaviour, Frank goes back to having
to sneak dirty glimpses of her washing herself in the shower. In the raw first
draft Malamud writes:

He was filled with a [sudden—delete?] choking hatred of her, and felt it would give him a satisfying pleasure to tear her body apart; to destroy the firm breast he had kissed, and foul the soft place between her legs he was now cast out from. He hated her for having loved him. To be forced to live in everlasting desire of what he had once had, and lost, was the most inhuman thing that could happen to a man. (LC I 1.5, p. 247a)

The commas between 'had and lost' in that last sentence are added in pencil. The second draft, unusually, is worse, as Malamud hesitates over omitting the vicious wish to 'hack her flesh apart' and at the end writes: 'To be forced to live in desire of what he had *once* had was the worst thing that could happen to anybody' (LC I 2.1, p. 271). But the underling of 'once' does not quite achieve the structural magic it feels for. That is why the final version works hard to come out as:

He ached for her, for the flesh he had lived in a moment. Yet he hated her for having loved him, for to desire what he had once had, and hadn't now, was torture. (*The Assistant*, 218)

'What he had *once had, and hadn't now*, was' is the inner shift Malamud was looking for, stronger than merely 'lost', because now it syntactically reveals a life in utterly wrong chronological and moral order. The simpler and better moments have been lost in passing: for 'the flesh he had lived in a moment' (so transiently fusing together 'lived in' with 'in a moment') is a final rewrite of the second draft's 'in whose soft sweet flesh he had lived for a brief moment'. Just after this in both first and second drafts, there is another cyclical-type tangle about Frank swearing to himself that he would 'never spy on her again', because it smeared him with 'filth' or 'shit' or 'slime', *but* 'the next day he could hardly wait for night to come so he could see her again/climb up the airshaft again'. In the final version it is again abbreviated in Malamud's art of taking away: 'he swore to himself he would never spy on her again, but he did.' In the store, in all versions at this point, he also, significantly, takes to cheating the customers again too. Then (once more in all versions) there is a later sentence, usually in a separate paragraph, about how one day suddenly Frank gave up on spying on the girl and 'went back' to being honest in the store. But in the final version Malamud puts the following second and third clauses into that sentence: 'Then one day, *for no reason he could give, though the reason felt familiar*, he stopped climbing up the air shaft to peek at Helen, and he was honest in the store' (Ibid. 214). That is to say: when Malamud does add rather than take away, the added something—'*for no reason he could give*'—actually subtracts from over-easy meaning.

It is such formulations as '*for no reason he could give, though the reason felt familiar*' that offer a form of thinking so deep, so implicitly registered, and so precisely minute that it hardly ever gets discussed as such. Writers cannot talk *about* it afterwards but must *do* it in the moment of its happening, in the tight verbal spaces that the work allows. Here, moreover, such writing recreates the blind thinking that goes on inside bedrock creatures who can barely get out of their lives, are unable to think in advance or from above, but stumble along within strangely familiar locked and repeated structures. As Malamud says of Frank in his notebook, he is 'a man whose fate repeats itself'; 'He doesn't know what he wants. His feelings guide him'; 'He comes to Morris hoping he will break the cycle of his fate' (HRC 19.1).

On the lookout for some alternative to the cycle, Malamud thus writes in the notebook: 'The confession a way?' In the first draft confession is 'what was left of a childhood habit' and is explicitly Catholic: 'to kneel before the priest and spill out his guts' (LC I 1.5, p. 137). For Frank the first move towards the disciplined side of Malamud, and the formed life that went with it, might be through telling it all. It was like a way of formally stopping, in order to start again differently, rather than continue along the same old conveyor-belt. Writes Malamud in the notebook: 'Because it will satisfy a basic need … starting things from the beginning … the confession rooted in the desire to change his life, beginning with his past life' (HRC 19.1).

But Malamud can only activate his ideas or symbols through the emergence of very particular syntactic forms and verbal patternings. Looking back at the first draft Malamud finds a clue in a short sentence of realization deep in the midst of a paragraph: 'The confession had to come first' (Illustration 11). Frank thinks: if he can only bring himself to confess to Morris that he was one of the men who robbed and hurt him; if he could also confess that he was still pilfering from his till; if Morris can only forgive him for both failings; *then* there might be a chance for something to happen with Morris's daughter—despite family opposition, if she would only fall for him. 'If, if, if' desperately for the fantasy future; but 'The confession had to come first.'

In the second draft Malamud therefore makes that sentence 'The confession had to come first' the beginning, not the middle of a paragraph, for Frank to try to build on the short thought and not let it go: 'The confession would have to come first—this was what stuck in the neck' (Illustration 12a). It needs to stick. Then, in the struggle for form, Malamud also takes another, later sentence from the midst of the first draft: 'Yet when the time came to say it … he lost his courage' and now he makes that into the start of a second new paragraph, showing the contours of Frank's characteristic relapse. But above all in that second draft he takes the hint from his notebook's repeated use of the word 'beginning': 'starting things from the beginning ... beginning with his past life'. At the end of the paragraph commencing '[So] The confession would have to come first' and just before the paragraph following 'Yet when the time came', he inserts this:

> This feeling had lived in him, he thought, like a habit [with claws], a [stupendous] thirst, a godamned need to get rid of everything that had happened yesterday—for whatever had happened had happened wrong; to confess it out of his system and bring in a little peace, a little order; to change the beginnings, beginning with the past that always stank up the now—to change his life before it choked him.　　(LC I 2.2, p. 91; Illustration 12b)

When he writes out that second draft in longhand (Illustration 13) he will cut the plural 'beginnings' and then has just what he wants—'to change the *beginning, beginning* with the past', thus matching what goes with it, 'for whatever *had happened had happened* wrong'.[8] 'Compressionism' or the compressed sentence, said Malamud, was his alternative to 'the abstract thinking, the conceptual thought, I find much more difficult': 'I come forth to the metaphoric and the symbolic ideas' (TH, 127). These compressions mark the moments when what could have been fluid has become stuck ('happened *wrong*') or what has been stuck could be made possible again ('beginning with the *past*'): the life-stuff is densely there in the midst of the sentence awaiting its shape. You can see the life's raw material in search of its shaper:

> I think of the self, the self's spirit, as material for shaping, reshaping, in much the way a sculptor may do it, and what if he can do it for himself? Sometimes I ask myself what in particular happens to those who become conscious of their lives as stuff that can be shaped. Not everybody thinks of life in this way. Now if you want to call that attitude Jewish, you can, but I think I got it out of literature—or at least affirmed it in literature—my sense of what people, over and beyond the necessities of existence, are trying to do with themselves, particularly as you come across it in Russian literature. Through the major Russian novels of the nineteenth century perhaps more than others, you meet unforgettable human beings trying to understand why they are what they are, trying to find some experience that will open the doors of possibility and give them the kind of satisfaction they want out of life.　　(TH, 142)

That's why Helen has Frank read the Russians, Tolstoy and Dosteovsky, above all. They are novels, she had explained to him. 'I'd rather read the truth,' he said. 'It is the truth', she replied (*The Assistant*, 91). When a young colleague at OSC asked him if he had Dostoevsky's *Crime and Punishment* in mind in writing *The Assistant*, Malamud replied, only half-comically, 'Maybe Dostoevsky had me in mind,' as Frank had thought.[9] 'At times, as the clerk sat late at night, a book held stiffly in his reddened hands, his head numb though he wore a hat, he felt a strange falling away from the printed page and had this crazy sensation he was reading about himself' (*The Assistant*, 100). Within the ostensibly small and ordinary setting of *The Assistant* is hidden the big near-religious claims that Malamud made for the real value of books, including his own. 'As if—according to her—you could read in them everything you couldn't afford not to know—the Truth about Life' (Ibid. 99). When Malamud turned the novel into a screenplay in 1969, it was potentially the most literary use of film imaginable: scenes in absolute silence, lonely close-ups of eyes and faces, the use of split-screen juxtapositions of characters, dreams, and memories passing like slides, and—not least of all—quotations from books. As he put it in his notes: 'Since the novel is about self-education via books, there may be paragraphs from books: Bovary, Anna Karenina, Crime and Punishment. Photographing the moving page. Possibly we can use this device at the end with the Bible, possibly talking to self' (LC I 46.1). In the changed 'proportions' for the film, it was Frank who was even more emphatically the central character: 'communicating aloneness and loneliness: the single self speaking of the single self'. 'Bring all you've got,' Malamud urged the imagined actor of Frank, 'Bringing it up from the deepest part of the self' (LC I 46.1).

'But take away Malamud's culture', said one Malamud's former students, 'and Malamud is Frank, whose wound of longing and pain becomes associated with sexual desire. No culture, nothing: just a lot of desire. Comparing Tolstoy's Anna Karenina and Flaubert's Madame Bovary as though they were real women, Frank says Anna "was more interesting and better in bed". All these sorts of frenzies are percolating through the morality and discipline of Malamud himself. And they don't belong anywhere. They are just there—chasing around.'[10]

Frank would love the lawless shortcut, the stolen dollar or the quick lie—the unearned simple add-on that for once in his life would enable him to get ahead of the game. But being a chancer never helps him find his way; it is somehow not the law, or the truth, of his life. On the other hand, change is very hard in this book. Confessing is a risk but one that is all too easily deferred, as the repetitions show—'to spill everything now, *now*' (*The Assistant*, 85); 'if he only once—*once*—did the right thing—the thing to do at the right time' (Ibid. 87–8). Malamud works hard on Frank's simultaneous need for and fear of such confession: it 'was like tearing up your whole life, with the broken roots and blood; and a fear burned in his gut that once he got started saying the wrongs he had done he would never leave off' (Ibid. 85). What's left of him if he confesses that all he has been was bad? The language is frighteningly precise. How can you 'change the *beginning, beginning* with the past' (Ibid. 84) if you fear that once you 'got *started*' confessing, 'you would *never leave off*'? What happens if he confesses everything and yet is not forgiven? 'People forgave people—who else? He could explain if she would listen. Explaining was a way of getting close to somebody you had hurt; as if in hurting them you gave them a reason to love you' (Ibid. 159). It is the child's way: love me most for what I do wrong; that would prove love indeed. But to be better he has to risk looking worse than the people around him ever thought him, and everything then rests upon their mercy. If he cannot believe they will forgive him, or if he does not confess everything but instead makes one thing stand for others that are worse and unspoken, then it would be better to keep quiet and stay hidden, not as good as he could be, but not as bad as full confession would make him realize he was. 'At the same time'—that crucial phrase in Malamud—'a foreboding crept into him that if he said nothing now, he would someday soon have a dirtier past to reveal' (Ibid. 88). It is that word 'soon' in relation to an ever-building 'past' that is powerful: he is reluctantly looking forward to an awful looking back, worsening all the time. It is a life in terrible shape. 'How ass-backward his life had gone' (Ibid. 85). Again and again Frank will warn himself not to lie to Helen, not to spy on her. But the time of regret all too foreseeably ahead is never as real to him as is his neediness now.

It is only through various painfully worsening repetitions of itself that the novel's content begins to discover a new form from within. That revised form comes personalized through Frank; it is characters that make theme and form real, human, living, emotional in Malamud. 'In the end,' wrote Malamud of Frank in his notebook, 'he seeks to conquer his formless life—to give it form, meaning—by destroying the effect of the past on him' (HRC 19.1). 'Destroying': it is that tough. To create a new life means first destroying the old one, without guarantees as to what will follow.

'Not Interested in the Beautiful People'

No thematic underpinnings, no manuscript subtleties were of any use if finally the work was not humanly moving—and often in unexpected ways in the midst of the ostensibly small or ugly. On 20 January 1959 Malamud wrote a Mrs Zolderman: I'm not interested in "the beautiful people"; 'I'm interested in the human being, and his fullest representation in art. If beauty is there, it is in the realization of the character, in the fulfilment of his truth' (LC II 1.1).

Yet in his *Assistant* notebook, Malamud urges himself into the harsh and the ugly. He does it with Frank: 'Don't be afraid to make him unattractive.' He does it with Morris: 'More sour. Keep him from being too much of an angel'; 'He may be good but he is not totally adequate'; 'All his life—the Jew's fear—he will not be allowed to live his life.' He knows that Ida, Morris's wife, is 'the unwilling sharer of Morris's fate,' a 'Cassandra, co-sufferer'. He toughs it out with Helen too in relation to her father: 'She senses that he has given up'. 'In the end she feels she must make herself a better person through education to escape her father's passive acceptance of fate'. He adds: 'Bitch if necessary', 'has become without knowing it a denier of life and love?'

Malamud needed both elements. When Frank did get his first sight of Helen in the shower, 'instead of the grinding remorse he had expected to suffer, he felt a moving joy' (*The Assistant*, 72). That's how the novel has something in it more complex and unpredictable than over-literal moralism. The undeserved joy comes from the undiminished beauty of the right and good thing, found even in the wrong place by the ugly viewer. Malamud was interested above all in the combinations of the tough and the soft, in the hard-earned transformations of the ugly into the beautiful, in the difficult synchronization of right thing, right time, and right place.

Thus at Morris Bober's funeral, the oration is delivered by a rabbi who admits he never knew the man who never came to his synagogue. Yet he beautifully praises Morris for what he has heard of his honesty, his industry, his care for his family, and his endurance. The grocer ran two blocks in the snow to give back to a poor Italian lady a nickel she forgot on the counter: he could have waited till she came in the following day, but he didn't want her to worry. He caught his final illness shovelling away snow outside his shop, though he was selling up, though it was a dead day without customers any more, though he was old and tired. His wife said it would kill him, but he said, 'It's Sunday, it don't look so nice for the goyim that they go to church.' Was this man who lived and worked among Gentiles, who sold pigmeat and never kept the formal laws, truly a Jew?

> Yes, Morris Bober was to me a true Jew because he lived in the Jewish experience, which he remembered, and with the Jewish heart. Maybe not to our formal tradition—for this I don't excuse him—but he was true to the spirit of our life—to want for others that which he wants also for himself. He followed the Law which God gave to Moses on Sinai and told him to bring

to the people. He suffered, he endured, but with hope. Who told me this? I know. (Ibid. 207–8)

But alongside it, in counterpoint, runs Helen's reluctant but corrective judgement, subtracting away:

He's overdone it, she thought. I said Papa was honest but what was the good of such honesty if he couldn't exist in the world? Yes, he ran after this poor woman to give her back a nickel, but he also trusted cheaters who took away what belonged to him. (Ibid. 208)

He was no saint, but even in his goodness 'he was in a way weak'. He died in part because, when he thought he had finally sold the store, he found that after so many years imprisoned he was frightened of leaving it. Malamud hated the way his own father's fear and disappointment never let life become what it might. Helen complains with an intelligence which, like so much, was lacking in her father:

I didn't say he had many friends who admired him. That's the rabbi's invention. People liked him, but who can admire a man passing his life in such a store? He buried himself in it; he didn't have the imagination to know what he was missing. He made himself a victim. He could, with a little more courage, have been more than he was. (Ibid. 208)

Yet one of those liars and cheats that Morris trusted was Frank Alpine. And what remains to be seen in the remainder of the novel is whether that trust was finally as misplaced as it looks to be at the time of the funeral; or whether Frank of all people could have that 'imagination' and 'courage' to redeem both himself and the memory bequeathed him by Morris.

Still, even amidst this silent critical orchestration, the burial service itself continues movingly:

As the rabbi prayed over the empty grave … Helen rested her head against the coffin held by the pallbearers.

'Good-bye, Papa.'

Then the rabbi prayed aloud over the coffin as the grave diggers lowered it to the bottom of the grave.

'Gently … gently.'

Ida, supported by Sam Pearl and the secretary of the Society, sobbed uncontrollably. She bent forward, shouting into the grave, 'Morris, take care of Helen, you hear me, Morris?'

The rabbi, blessing it, tossed in the first shovelful of earth.

'Gently.'

Then the diggers began to push in the loose earth and as it fell on the coffin the mourners wept aloud. (Ibid. 209)

It is clear from Malamud's marginal notes, where he carefully tracks and choreographs the real-life time the novel is taking, that *The Assistant* opens in November 1947 and that this funeral takes place in April 1948—Morris dying ironically just as spring follows the hard winter. In the manuscripts there is also, at the top of the page, another series of dates which refer to the time it was taking Malamud to write the book. These six months of novel-time take him, in the first draft, about 170 days of writing, roughly the same number of days, between May 1954 and April 1955, as though in the name of realism the writing kept time with what it was rhythmically re-enacting.

Moreover, what Malamud wrote in April 1955, in imagination of April 1948, was based upon what had actually happened in July 1952, as he describes it in a letter from New York back home to Ann in Corvallis. Malamud was in New York to see Eugene in the mental hospital, for the first time since his breakdown, and to witness the launch of *The Natural*. The letter is about the death of his late mother's brother, Casile Fidelman, in his daughter Jeanie's house:

> After I awoke my father came up and said, today we must go to a funeral. I said, whose. He said, Casile is dead. He died of a heart attack. My father cried.
>
> The services were short—in at one p.m., out at one fifteen. Jeanie was grief-stricken but controlled. As they were praying at the grave she [put—deleted] rested her cheek on the coffin, as if it were against his face, and said papa papa papa over and over again. Gently, she said, when they were lowering the casket into the grave, gently, gently, gently.   (15 July 1952)

In the second draft of *The Assistant*, Malamud takes the daughter's 'gently, gently, gently' which he has used one word after another in the first draft, and now uses it instead in different paragraphs to measure the descent of the coffin into the earth. He also puts in and later takes out again the phrase 'as if it were her father's face she was touching'—as though he had his own letter by him. The relation between Jean and her father had been, as Malamud acknowledged, the basis of both 'Suppose a Wedding' and 'The First Seven Years', short stories in which a father opposes a young girl's marriage to an older man. But the letter of 15 July 1952 goes on also to record how a friend of Malamud's late mother, Bertha, was also at Casile's funeral, widening the resonance:

> She went with my father and me down aways to hunt for my mother's grave. We didn't know her exact plot and for a while I was worried because it meant so much to my father to see it. I wanted so much to find it and then I did. My father came over and he wept and asked my mother to take care of Eugene.

Then Jeanie said in Yiddish, Bertha take care of us. My father was surprised when I showed him on the stone that mama was only forty-one when she died.

'Morris, take care of Helen.' Max himself did not die of his own heart condition until March 1954, a month before Malamud began writing *The Assistant*.

Such is no more than part of the hidden background story of the writing of the novel. And there are probably a hundred more unfound memories massed behind the writing, which would tell a similar tale of the emotional experience that Malamud brought to that test of emotion which he was carrying out in *The Assistant* itself. All his working life he was to be told that he was a writer more of the heart than of the head, that his danger was that of sentimentality, of soft Jewish nostalgia. Yet here at Morris's grave, he was testing the value of the grocer's good heart and the status of the feelings felt for Morris at the funeral. In the notebooks Malamud was asking by the end of the first draft if Morris was a person of little value in the world: Morris himself seemed to think so ('What happens to him is, generally, bad; therefore he can't be very good; i.e. valuable'), and so perhaps did his daughter ('She senses that he has given up, lost whatever free will he has had. She wants to retain hers').

But Malamud insisted: 'I have not given up the hero—I simply use heroic qualities in small men' (HRC 27.5)—in underdogs, losers from the lower classes, people gone badly wrong. Likewise, therefore, great and almost heroic changes are hidden and found within the minutiae of manuscripts, loyal to realism in struggling depiction of the ordinary. Throughout the novel Morris and Frank have always needed each other not only as people but also at another level, more ambivalently, as mutually checking representatives of the gentle and the transgressive. It is left now to Frank, like a prodigal son, to redeem Morris's trust and complete Malamud's test. *The* assistant, *the* apprentice, must become *the* grocer: it is no longer about persons, or individual protagonists the size of Saul Bellow's Herzog, but about a personal commitment to roles, functions, the *formal* responsibilities that require consistent small daily actions to fulfil them. At the risk of repeating Morris's fate, Frank must set himself to make the classic moral virtues vital to him, their attainment near-heroic.

Such things are dismissed or resented only by those who have never felt what the want of disciplined morality means. Malamud himself needed the threat and temptation of Frank's lawlessness to feel afresh why the law was necessary. It is what drew Malamud to the work of Nathaniel Hawthorne: namely, that it was to those who broke the letter of the law that the law's spirit was then most freshly and painfully revealed, even from the wrong and fallen side of it. But Morris is not an orthodox or an intellectual Jew: all he can say to Frank is that a Jew must believe in the Law, and as for the Law: 'This means to do what is right, to be honest, to be good. This means to other people. Our life is hard enough. Why should we hurt somebody else? For everybody should be the best, not only for you or me' (*The Assistant*, 115).

Yet the realization of what 'this means' can only happen when Frank is as close as he can be to wrecking his second chance. The worst comes when he forces himself upon Helen, knowing his time with her is running out because Morris has caught him taking out of the till money which, ironically, he had put back in there minutes earlier. Frank saves Helen from rape at the hands of Ward Minogue, the youth who had led Frank into raiding Morris' store in the first place; but then, in his desperate desire, Frank does to Helen what Ward had tried to do, as though he were still no more than just another version of him. One of the greatest moments in Malamud occurs when Frank realizes what he has done to Helen and to love, and cannot let himself off any more:

> He planned to kill himself; at the same minute had a terrifying insight: that all the while he was acting like he wasn't, he was really a man of stern morality.
>   (Ibid. 160–1)

'Like he wasn't, he was' is another of those great Malamud mid-sentence movements, to and fro 'at the same moment'. Tiny, it is really a huge shift. His is not to be a life of more and more, but less: a life already committed to restrictions however much he had resisted it. All the years he had fleeing from judgment, he had not known that the judgment, the standards, were really his own. Stealing, getting things, had felt good, but always, significantly, he had felt bad later. And so it had gone on formlessly, the trying to feel good instead of being it; then the attack of conscience held back till as long as possible afterwards: like two lives alternately in time because he could not hold them both together in one. One half-life must go. He had not known that the bit of him that condemned himself was not part of the condemnation but potentially the self he could rescue and be rescued by.

Like a character out of Dostoevsky, he is surprised that after forcing himself upon Helen, there is no formal punishment. There is nothing immediate or physical that follows, his usual terms for reality. Instead it is a personal and a secret matter which anyway has been partially overtaken by the emergency of Morris's final illness. 'He had expected that punishment to be drastic, swift; instead it came slowly'—or as Malamud has it in the first draft, 'it came as the slow death of tomorrow'. But in revision he adds to 'it came slowly' two further clauses: '—it never came, yet was there' (Ibid. 168). In that revision, for Frank as much as for Malamud, reality is no longer simply a factual, physical event ('it never came') but is transformed, is metaphysical, moral, even in the eyes of a common man: 'yet it was there'.

But Helen cannot know or care that he is a different person, and he himself is not sure he will remain so.

> How could she know what was going on in him? If she ever looked at him again she would see the same guy on the outside. He could see out but nobody could see in. (Ibid. 171)

Only a novel could see in: 'I'd rather read the truth.' 'It is the truth.' 'Those books you once gave me to read,' he says to her as she ignores his penitence, 'did you understand them yourself?'

But in the ordinary world he has to create and establish that truth, he has to live out his formal role as 'the grocer', 'the provider', day after day after day, by absolute internal consistency, when all around might not only be doubting him but be plausibly right in doing so. The aim is to keep business and family going, without thanks, and finally give something back to Morris, do something for Helen by paying her way to college. It is a fairy tale, Catherine Carver complained, as an invited reader of the final text; but Malamud replied, 'Sure ... but fairy tale grounded in the uncompromising reality of the store: flowers grow anywhere' (HRC 4.11). For it goes on too long to be a source of comforting pride to him; the work is too wearying and too close to despair, flogging the old self to death, for it to remain a subtle selfishness in him or to create a burden of obligation upon her. It is not that these equivocal and recidivist things are not there in the human mix; it is rather that long time and hard work take him ever increasingly, even hopelessly, beyond them into a new sort of dogged unconsciousness, feeling bad even in being good. 'She passed without a word as if he didn't exist. He didn't' (*The Assistant*, 169). Malamud austerely loves what time and work can do. They make reality of the golden law that the rabbi praised in Morris, to want for others what he wants for himself—where, for Frank, serving others is the only way to make solid and external what he can make of himself.

And Helen's own achievement is to begin to recognise, with some hard-won objectivity, this commitment to sheer function and action in him, precisely because of what he knows he has done to her. One day in January 1949, nine months after her father's death, she sees Frank in the store, just as Malamud once saw his own father from outside the window, not seeing her, exhausted:

> It came to her that he had changed. It's true, he's not the same man, she said to herself. I should have known by now. She had despised him for the evil

he had done, without understanding the why or aftermath, or admitting there
could be an end to the bad and a beginning of good.

It was a strange thing about people—they could look the same and be
different. He had been one thing, low, dirty, but because of something in
himself—something she couldn't define, a memory perhaps, an ideal he might
have forgotten and then remembered—he had changed into somebody else,
no longer what he had been.   (Ibid. 219–20)

Jay Cantor, Malamud's best pupil during his brief time teaching at Harvard,
wrote that Malamud's people have to find their hidden Law, not straightfor-
wardly but as though from back to front: 'A sense of that task comes strangely
first from a mournful recognition of one's failures, one's limitations—the
themes one has left unrecognized or unfulfilled. Guidance comes, that is to
say, from guilt—the memory of regret and failure, that speaks, in pain, the
moral law.'[11] 'All the while he was acting like he wasn't, he was really a man
of stern morality.' What moved both Frank and Malamud himself about
Anna Karenina was when, towards the very end, Levin realizes that all the
time he has been despairing over the meaning of life, he has been living well,
marrying happily, but thinking badly. 'I was astonished,' says Tolstoy's Levin
in Malamud's imagined film, 'that in spite of the utmost effort of thought
along the road I could not discover the meaning of life, the meaning of my
impulses and yearnings.'

Out of the recognition of what the law is for him comes that self-control
and the sheer power of will—often so dull and wearying in Malamud
himself—which Frank himself at one moment can call beautiful. He was
moved by the austere word 'discipline', once spoken to him by Helen herself,
and its paradoxical relation to freedom: 'the beauty of a person being able
to do things the way he wanted to, to do good if he wanted' (*The Assistant*,
145). '*This* is what it is about—the great insight', writes Malamud excitedly
in the notebook, as though Frank, 'I have been living my life without will.
I must live now with the will or I am useless, finished' (HRC 19.1 notes
on chapter 8). These words—will, discipline, freedom—are nothing in the
way of amazing new ideas, without the experience and without all the other
smaller, creative words from the writer, that makes them an achievement. In
'Imaginative Writing and Jewish Experience', Malamud spoke of the Jews as
the embodiment of that sort of living ethic, its meaningful form continually
lost and renewed, dulled and reshone, in the centuries of their history: 'An
antique spirituality, an antique morality of surpassing beauty and importance
because it is a tie to God himself, lives in the Jews' (TH, 188).

That is why, stunningly, at the very end of the book Frank has himself
circumcised and lives as a Jew—in formal testament to his second life, as an

embodiment and symbol of the ancient value of law, as a personal tribute to what has helped remake him. It is Frank Alpine who first utters, at Morris's funeral in the first draft of *The Assistant*, one of Malamud's most famous, enigmatic sayings: 'Everybody is a Jew but they don't know it.' Malamud cut it from the novel but used it in interviews.

Afterwards: 'Imagining Jews'

In a letter of 30 November 1965, Philip Roth wrote Malamud that he had been teaching his students *The Assistant*. They told him Morris Bober was 'a failure' (HRC 16.6). Roth asked them to define failure. One who had never been an English major? One who made no money? When he next teaches the book, Roth says, he will take a cash register into the seminar and every time he gets a poor answer, ring up 'No sale'.[12]

But by 1974 Philip Roth wrote rather differently, in an article on 'Imagining Jews' in the *New York Review of Books* (3 October 1974). It is a defence of *Portnoy's Complaint* (1969) in its violation of the code of Jewish respectability which Roth felt he had had to fight, even in himself, as a student in the fifties. It was a 'rather priestly' literary education, dedicated to the literature of 'moral seriousness'—where the word 'moral', said Roth, masked a callow and inflexible naivete.

In turning on the fifties, Roth also turned on one of his own father-figures in literature. Malamud's *The Assistant*, he argued, re-enforced the stereotypes of Jew as virtuous victim, Gentile as lustful wild man. Morris Bober by his example of passive suffering transforms the young thieving Italian Frank Alpine into another imprisoned Jewish shopkeeper, and this soft goodness is called redemption—though it is achieved by the symbolic force of circumcision, upon the very organ with which Frank had attacked Helen. It is as if the grocer said, 'Now suffer, you goy bastard, the way I did.'

Roth enlists Norman Mailer as Cavalier to Malamud's Roundhead, roman-tic redskin to Malamud's classic paleface. In 'The White Negro', published like *The Assistant* in 1957, Mailer offered an alternative account of the hold-up in a store, the young hoodlums murdering a weak fifty-year-old candy-store keeper. In Mailer's version of *Crime and Punishment*, there is, says Roth, amidst all the brutality and cowardice of the attack, some courage in taking on an institution, and a genuine daring of the unknown, in contrast to Malamud's continuing ethos of suffering and imprisonment.

When he saw the piece, Malamud could not believe what he was reading. It was all too close to the anti-Semitic taunts he had already thought of in his initial depiction of Frank Alpine: Aren't the Jews really just about suffering? Frank asks Morris, Isn't that what they like doing? Malamud wrote two unsent letters to Roth (HRC 16.5): 'I wish I could say Roth is looking after his friend Malamud but I can't.'

He complains of misrepresentation, made worse by its being by a fellow-novelist. 'My father used to say in Yiddish, if someone saw something badly, "Let him take his eyes in his hands and look."' That father, says Malamud, is 'the grocer Bober was patterned on. He was a good man.' It was not an ideological stereotype: 'Whenever I write of a good man I am writing of him.'

Malamud believed that in the novel he had tested the grocer's goodness by putting him into critical relationship with Frank. Morris's example does not bind Frank, Malamud argued. 'Frank makes his own choice, and to the extent he becomes the kind of man he is moved to want to be, even through an act of service, he is thereby a free man.' 'In fact, Morris, before the illness leading to his death, orders him to leave the store. Frank returns, after the funeral, out of a need of his own, not because he has been hypnotized or made will-less by Morris.' It is not Morris's revenge any more than circumcision is an attack on the body: 'It is Frank's way of entering a tradition by means of a symbolic act which began with a childhood interest in St. Francis'. Malamud had built up the presence of St Francis for Frank, draft after draft, as the image of a human being, of whatever faith, born good from the very start. But references to a saint did not help. In Jerusalem one evening—so Malamud continued furiously in his unsent letter—'Mrs Gershon Scholem, making an error analogous to yours, called *The Assistant*, "Your Christian book!"' Malamud, the charge went, made his Jews into Christ figures, suffering for others, and thus associated being chosen with being a victim. It was a charge much repeated ever since. [13]

It hurt Malamud—it damaged his book and what his book struggled to stand for—if people did not see that what suffering meant in *The Assistant* was something neither entirely sought nor utterly passive. Later, he could put it wittily enough, assuming the Jewish shrug:

DANIEL STERN: What about suffering? It's a subject much in your early work.
MALAMUD: I'm against it, but when it occurs, why waste the experience? (TH, 19)

But in full seriousness he had written in 'Imaginative Writing and the Jewish Experience': 'The truest learning must be of suffering, because in suffering the self is contemplated as it has never before been contemplated.' In the inside cover of his *Assistant* notebook he quoted Aeschylus, 'Who acts undertakes to suffer'—the two were not separate but intervolved in the struggles of Malamud's people.

To Roth, all he finally sent was the last few words in his draft: 'It's your problem.'

But to Malamud, being too Jewish for some Americans or too Christian for some Jews was not a problem. It marked out the holding-ground in which he worked; it forged the melting pot in which he found new combinations of possibility. In the Norwegian edition of the novel Malamud took the opportunity to say: 'as for the Christian elements in Judaism, ideas flow forwards and backwards, and it is useless to define love, charity, endurance, as the particular quality or province of one religion over another' (Ibid. 87).

Assimilation was not a problem either: he loved the rich intermixtures and ambiguities, the Americanization of the Jews, the Europeanization of America. Assimilation was what Judaism did: find in the world a home for values, otherwise dispersed and fragmented. To some, in the next generation, the Jewish tradition of assimilation might seem too passive an accommodation, too cravenly the result of anxiety over economic survival, and eagerness for respectability, and the need safely to belong without trouble. To Malamud, on the contrary, assimilation for the second-generation children of the immigrants was at that historic moment a form of creative realism, of incarnation for the estranged and the serious, the lost and scattered, the spiritual and the ancient within the real and the modern; a strategy simultaneously for both survival and influence.

The Hebraic represented one ancient gene, one central resonant symbol of surviving experience, in the making and remaking of the human creature. At the same time, therefore, Malamud did not want to be labelled a Jewish writer, like Isaac Bashevis Singer writing in Yiddish. He did not wish to be made predictable or stereotypical within some narrowly defined club or group. In that grocery store the young Malamud, bursting with need and imagination, was still living claustrophobically imprisoned in a small version of the shtetl, when he yearned to be living in the America just outside. As a writer what he wanted was to be surprised at what the Hebraic still meant, and in what form and company it emerged and was transmuted. He loved that borderline across which Frank Alpine wavered: the good man who did bad, and the bad man who did good, until neither was clearly separate from the other.

In his finally unused screenplay, Malamud begins with Frank alone on Coney Island boardwalk, thinking of the past, as a Jewish newspaper slowly blows past him, showing brief photographs of the concentration camps. Then he cuts to Morris reading his Jewish newspaper. But Malamud ends with Frank reading to himself, in hope, two verses from the first psalm:

But his delight is in the Law of the LORD; and in his law doth he meditate day and night.

And he shall be like a tree planted by the rivers of water, that bringeth forth his fruit in his season; his leaf also shall not wither; and whatsoever he doeth shall prosper. (LC I 46.1)

5

⤙◆◆◆⤚

'Because I *Can*'

Corvallis and Rome

Alex Inkeles was sure, from early on, that the 1950s made a new life for the Malamuds:

> One thing I do want you to tell me about is the inner peace which I sense the two of you have made, won or captured in Corvallis. I especially sense it in Ann, but I feel it in the whole family—a kind of relaxed, pleased, almost satisfied and fulfilled feeling. I am sure that it has mainly to do with regular hours, absence of competitive pressures, a minimum of social events and such, at least as much as from Bernie's certain sense of greater meaning in his present work.   (20 November 1950, HRC 11.5)

There were always going to be anxieties, however. To Ann, Bern (she never liked the Brooklyn 'Bernie') was her 'rock of Gibraltar', but she also used to say that he was born with a baton in his hand. At least, when he fussed too much about whom he wanted to invite for dinner or what they were going to have, she was prepared to drive him out of her kitchen. But it was an old-fashioned patriarchal setup, not uncongenial to a woman whose own father had deserted the family. When Malamud was away in New York in summer 1952 and March 1954 and again in the summer of 1958, Ann was often worried about spending too much. Always wanting to be easy over money and urging her to be generous with herself and the children, Malamud nonetheless was constantly sending her his lists and reminders and reckonings.

He writes her from the family store 28 June 1952: 'Pop is a nag: "When are you going to take a shower—it's so hot." "That's not the way to shave with an electric razor. Let me show you how"—all day long. I have no doubt that I get my own nagging qualities from him.' Malamud can also become irritated by his wife's neediness for his return. She in turn worries about his weight, once even drawing him a little unkind comic sketch of his growing paunch. In a letter of 28 July 1958 Ann listed checks cashed and paid, then concludes; 'I feel more like a secretary than a wife!'

During these absences, each partner worries about not receiving letters from the other. There is also Paul's asthma and some concern about his eyesight, and there is fuss about Ann letting Paul watch television whilst at the Californian home of his grandparents: 'Please keep Paul away from the gangster movies—I insist on that. If necessary, disconnect the plug of the set if he has access to it while you're busy. I want him to see only children's programs ... he may also see a science subject if not too frightening. Please be careful about this' (24 July 1952). Malamud is worried about his son watching television reports of the recent earthquake in Los Angeles and 'compounding his anxiety'. Yet there are also comparisons with how other parents, with different and surer models from their own childhood, manage to raise their children more freely. Bernadette and Alex Inkeles don't nag or shout at their daughter 'and quite frankly, observing them,' Malamud writes, 'I felt guilty about our handling of Paul. I vowed I would improve ... and I know you feel the same. I am dead serious about that. I will make a greater effort to control anger and impatience and I only hope we can check and assist one another when we have to' (11 July 1952). Ann agrees, but, tougher in this than her husband, argues for at least a minimum of conventional discipline: 'for I don't go along with *any* philosophy that fears frustration for a child at every slight denial, nor do I feel that *any* child should be allowed to believe that she can monopolize conversation and attention at any time during the day or night regardless of others' needs' (12 July 1952).

In 1954, Janna aged two is asking 'Where's my friend, daddy?': 'I told her you took an airplane and went to see your brother, "Uncle Eugene", so now she has something to talk about and pin it on, because when we went to your office, she expected to find you there' (March 1954). Ann is careful not to leave the kids with a childminder, however competent, because 'I ain't doing any thing you might not approve of while you're out' (March 1954). Later, Paul, nearly eleven, when asked if he has a message for his father, says calmly, 'Just hi, hello, give him my best wishes' (22 July 1958). Janna he dismisses as 'that little abstraction'. When in his father's absence he is given the very first serving of cake, and that a very generously proportioned one, Paul says drily, 'I suppose when Daddy comes back we'll go back to the feudal system again' (21 May 1958).

But Malamud would also send home little illustrated stories for the children. One for Paul, aged just five, tells the story of a bunny named Weathergood who only ever likes to eat one thing, a head of lettuce, but (like his austerely comic creator) had such 'a sensitive palate' that 'he could taste many subtle flavours in the lettuce leaves' (17 July 1952). In *A New Life* Levin tells Pauline's little boy a story which gets him so pleased and excited that he urinates on Levin's lap; in real life this was Paul.

In 1955 Malamud was co-author of a published story for children, *Kim of Korea*. It was largely written by Faith Norris, his colleague at OSC, talented but fragile of ego, and easily discouraged by initial rejection. Faith helped Malamud learn how to drive. What he did for her was to take her basic story in its original draft and help her revise it, making her come to his office like a student, with a deadline for each chapter, and giving her no more than the allotted time. During his trip back to New York in 1954, he also helped find a publisher, Julian Messner, who wanted Malamud to use his own name, alongside Faith Norris's, on the title page. Not wanting to be known as a children's writer, he refused and came up with 'Peter Lumn' instead. They shared the royalties, Malamud receiving just over $950 in 1956.

Kim (named after Kipling's young hero) was a Korean orphan boy who is adopted by an American soldier towards the end of the Korean War. The Norrises had lived in both Japan and Seoul, Korea, and it was Tom Norris's idea to write the story of a poor boy who gains a new friend in Sergeant Len Minner, then loses contact, and has to travel many miles across country from Seoul to refind this second father, after the Americans have moved camp to Inchon. No one can now know how much is specifically Malamud's. But one subtle movement which surely pleased him is where, in chapter 1, Kim climbs a path with the American soldier, who has been wounded in the leg:

> Usually, in his excitement to get to the top, he skipped and ran the whole way, but this afternoon he tried to make himself go slow for Len's sake. Twice he forgot and began to run, but both times after he had gone a few yards he stopped to wait for Len to limp up to him.
>
> Len liked it when Kim ran ahead. It reminded him of how he used to run as a boy back home on his farm in Indiana, and both times he was pleased when Kim stopped to wait so sympathetically.

There is also a characteristic but larger-scale twist near the very end. Just when he is close to reaching his goal, Kim is suddenly upset by the thought of what previously, mile after mile, he has been striving for—the opportunity to leave for a second life in America. The very journey he had undertaken meant that 'he had just really begun to learn about his country. And he loved it. But if he found Len, he would soon have to leave' (chapter 9). Finally, Len assures Kim that he will have a new family and receive a good education in America, and then, if he wishes, can return to be with his people and help his country.

What interested Alex Inkeles was how, on its own journey, the Malamud family-life now began to expand upon a firmer basis, increasing the range of tastes and experiences. Malamud's own parents had come over from Russia, in search of freedom, only to go nowhere outside the store. Malamud told Eugene that so much of the brothers' anxieties about change and movement came out of their parents' terribly constricted lives. But he loved it when his own children showed more freedom or more aptitude than he had ever managed. He wrote to Eugene that Paul had got an airgun which he was to use carefully in the basement, under his father's supervision, to help improve his eyesight. Malamud remembered having such a gun of his own as a boy and shooting everything with it until one day it disappeared. Malamud suspected his anxious father. 'I'm sure Paul will control himself more than I did' (12 December 1952). But it was Janna who was proving herself the more physically free and fearless one, determined to overcome the old obstacles. 'The other day she asked me to go with her to the school yard,' he wrote Eugene 1 December 1957, 'so she could practise tumbling over a bar, because the other kids in her class could do it and she was timid about it; it didn't take her long to master the trick, but I expect to be called soon to oversee her tackle something else' (HRC 36.5).

> Yesterday, while Ann was preparing dinner, I took Janna to the bank of a river she likes. She waded in the cold water, scooped up minnows with a strainer and learned how to skim flat rocks across the water. She is very intense about these things and makes it a point of honor to learn when she is learning ... As I sat on a log by the river, watching her yesterday, it was as if I were reading a long poem, every line full of beauty. The lines were her movements and the changing expression of her face, even the way the wind blew her hair. Children are such aesthetic pleasures to watch.[1]

One of Malamud's favourite poems was Yeats's 'Prayer for My Daughter'. In vain he searched the Malamud genes for Janna's happy athleticism and grace. But Ann would say that if she had had twelve children, all of them would have turned out Malamuds.

Malamud reported again on the children in a letter to Rosemarie Beck, 11 September 1959, as Janna was entering third grade and Paul moving up into junior high school:

'I wish I were a kid again,' Paul said the other day, 'before I heard of the atom bomb and began to worry about my health.' He is a bit of a hypochondriac but I hope he will lose some of his anxiety about himself as he grows. His sister, though sensitive, is an outgoing type. We learned from our mistakes with him how to bring her up. And so it goes.

But Paul was taking up the cello. His teacher reported that Paul never wanted to go on to anything new until he had mastered what had gone before. That pleased Malamud; it was of course like his own discipline. Paul's cello-playing was good, he reported to Rosemarie Beck, the following year: 'He has a Bach piece now and I thought what a miraculous thing it is to have your child play Bach in your own house. My poor father should know' (1 April 1960).

Malamud was doing much better than his own parents. In 1956 Malamud gained a *Partisan Review* fiction fellowship which funded a year's writing-leave 'on the basis of literary merit and financial need and in the light of the editors' long acquaintance with contemporary American writing'. That year awards were also made to the novelist James Baldwin and the poet Elizabeth Bishop. The Malamuds decided to spend the time in Ann's beloved, romanticized Italy, along with their two young children.

There was, before tax, $4,000 of Rockefeller money from the *Partisan Review*, plus an additional half-salary only, of $2,225 from OSC for a year's sabbatical. A year earlier, the administration had rejected Malamud's request for leave with full pay as 'unusual', because he did not hold a substantial administrative position ('section 2B of the Administrative Code provisions for sabbaticals', as cited by Dean Colby). In 1954 and 1955, income from royalties had fallen back to $271.85 and $478.78, respectively: he earned just over $4,800 in 1954, $5,600 in 1955.

Nor was Malamud doing well in terms of career progress or academic satisfaction. He had been told that he would be advanced in rank when he had completed either a PhD or a novel. By the time *The Natural* was published, it was 'too late to do anything this year about a promotion', according to his Head of Department Herb Nelson, and, according to Nelson, 'in his discouragement' Malamud had 'considered handing in his resignation' (11 March 1952, OSU box 6). By 1954, as assistant professor, Malamud was pressing to teach literature classes. In response to Malamud's written request, Ralph Colby grudgingly admitted that a PhD was not necessary and that 'Bernard might do a good job', but he also wrote Herb Nelson that 'what is irritating is that the letter goes so far in trying to make a water-tight case' (20 May 1954). Promotion to associate professorship did not take place until the end of 1958, just before Malamud received the National Book Award for *The*

Magic Barrel. Up till then he was still teaching three sections of freshman comp to one section of creative writing. The promotion came because he had 'achieved distinction as a writer'; had received offers from 'other institutions' (Los Angeles State College); was 'an effective teacher'; and had provided 'the initiative and leadership in establishing the Liberal Arts Lectures and the Classic Foreign Films series'. Dean Colby also noted that on examining the budgets of the Department of English since 1955–6, 'I find that in the years since then he has not been advanced in salary as much as others of the same rank and comparable length of service' (26 May 1958). Malamud asked for a salary of $6,750 and received $6,250.

But he had just completed *The Assistant* when in early September 1956 the family sailed out of New York on the SS *America* via Genoa to Naples, then on by train to Rome. There they found and rented for nine months a two-bedroom apartment on the Via Michele di Lando, near Piazza Bologna. Paul, aged nine, was enrolled in the Overseas School, on the far side of the city, with other American and English-speaking children. Janna, four, went to a Montessori kindergarten run by Ursulan nuns in the mornings, the time when her father would do his writing. In the afternoons, husband and wife often explored the city together. 'I used to walk, walk, walk all over the city,' wrote Ann in some notes (LC II 14). They visited the parks, fountains, and piazzas, the churches, catacombs, and museums. Malamud stood at Keats's grave and in the room in which he had died. They ate with Ann's aunts and cousins and old family friends. What Janna remembered was 'a different Italy, poorer, much closer to the nineteenth century than this one, still caught in the war's aftermath. Widows and older women wore only black. Men with donkey carts swept the street' (MFB, 146). She recalled her father purchasing a grammar book and teaching himself some basic Italian: 'The melodic voweled language appealed to his ear, amused him, and forever after he invented Italian sounding words. "Ann," he'd announce at dinner "I'd like a slice"—in his mock Italian, a *"sleechay"*—"of bread, please."'

What Malamud particularly loved was what he felt united the Jews and the Italians: namely, a full emotional commitment of the personality to the events of daily living. 'This is especially important to comprehend at a time of evaporating personality, when there is such a strange movement among us for everybody to be like everyone else.' In the vivid selves of the old Jews of his childhood and the Italians now around him, Malamud found 'the image of the man and woman so deeply engaged with life that he could not fail to offer it anything less than the fullest selfhood' (TH, 189). Back in Oregon, he bemoaned to Rosemarie Beck the homogeneity of the people: 'Nobody wants

to be different. I don't mean in the Beatnik sense; I mean where uniqueness
lies. Why is it that it takes so long before the average person realizes what his
human wealth is, and how to achieve it?' (16 October 1959).

He remembered Paul in the Uffizi art gallery before the Birth of Venus,
'practically leaping and dancing round the room, and saying, I know I'm
going to be an artist' (LC II 14.10). Later, on the back of a page in a notebook
for what became *Dubin's Lives*, he wrote a little sketch-poem 'To Paul,
January 5 1974':

> When you were a little boy
> You danced before the Botticellis
> At the Uffizi.
> The 'Venus
> Risen from the waves'
> Made you cry out
> 'I know I will be an artist!'

Paul himself wrote an equivalent poem, 'Italy 1956', in the late 1980s after his
father's death:

> The old monk
> May have been surprised to see a Jewish man
> Like my father in Assisi
> so soon after the war
> but obligingly, unctuously,
> took our picture
> me huddling against his overcoat—
> and then we went out into the terrace
> where St. Francis had spoken to the birds.
> He was delighted, awestruck—I was bored
> I'm awestruck now to think that I was bored.

One hot weekend Malamud had taken Paul to see the Giotto frescoes in
Assisi, the home of Frank Alpine's favourite saint. The boy was thinking of
the things not much respected in the Malamuds' cultured home—television,
Donald Duck comic books, coke.

> In the mornings Dad walked me to the schoolbus
> doing multiplication tables
> through the smoky pastels of winter Rome
> and at night, sometimes, came to meet me.
> If I had been good
> I got an Italian comic or roast chestnuts
> from the chestnut man

> hot from the charcoal, wrapped in foil.
> 'My father didn't have much of a life,' he said
> 'and our relationship wasn't always good,
> 'but later in life you'll remember this—'

He remembered Rome after poverty and war: the colours, the flowers, the shops and rich leather smells, the fountains, the father and mother there 'like happy birds—sometimes unhappy ones'.

> yes, it's true, I remember him
> just now the way he said I would
> as my father—
> an ugly, affectionate Jew
> waiting for my schoolbus
> to put his arm on my shoulder, then,
> and take me back home in the Roman dusk
> walking in his rumpled tweed jacket
> past the elevator cage
> up the scuffed stairs
> into the lit apartment.

This is what memory did when used creatively, in writing: it held the generations together, across the changes and despite everything that had happened and was to happen. As Malamud was to put it himself, to Rosemarie Beck, 20 September 1964:

> Paul has lately been having anxieties I would like to disburden him of, but the cause is not the cure. I don't blame myself (though Ann blames herself) for his problems, but I know enough about people to understand, where families are concerned, there are no innocent bystanders. With love and the greatest good will in the world the children are affected ambivalently. Merely the nature of the parent is the cause. What I'd like to do for him I can't, but I hope I've given him a sense of what love is so that it will serve him as a source of hidden strength.   (HRC 3.7)

The father still looks forward in 1964, knowing something of what his own past may have done to his family. What had saved him as a son was that he had known love in his family, whatever else had happened. He still relied on passing that on.

In the summer of 1957, however, the Malamuds finally returned home on the *Staatendam*, via Paris. There, though Malamud was initially disappointed with the place compared to the light of Italy, they gladly met up with Alex and Bernadette Inkeles. Long after, the Inkeleses recalled at length together the change in Malamud:

AI: He became a much less restricted person. He was more relaxed, more assured of himself. A kind of naturalism had emerged which was not there before. Even with us he wasn't so guarded a person. He didn't feel to the same degree the way he did earlier—that there were a lot of things he couldn't do on his own.

BI: I think the year they went to Europe did make a big difference. He would often say later that Ann had opened up so much of the world for him, in terms of the experiences he was able to enjoy in life.[2]

The synchronization of Malamud's life was complicated. Nelson Sandgren said that Malamud never looked like a young man, even when he first came to Oregon, as though he had missed that out.[3] But Malamud himself concluded to Danny Stern: 'In sum, once I was twenty and not so young, now I'm sixty inclined on the young side' (TH, 13). Yet even Italy could not do all that Malamud wanted it to do. As he wrote to his artist friend Rosemarie Beck much later, when with mixed feelings she returned from a similar trip:

> In a sense it came to me too late, too, not too late to have and appreciate, but too late to be ravished in youth, to be changed, inspired, stricken, renovated. Underneath a very rich experience I felt regret that it was happening so late. Really that reaction is uncalled for, but those of us who for one reason or another give up our young youth, never cease to regret what we might have had, and Italy, with its beauty would have been perfection, a lesser heaven.   (23 November 1969)

Nonetheless, the Inkeleses saw in that stay in Italy a completion of what had begun with the move to Oregon.

AI: He had had to learn how to deal with the outside world. He did some of that for himself, by his walking for instance, in Oregon, in Rome, later in Bennington: that way he had the opportunity to observe the world in his own time. But in general I think that it is true that even late in his life he had a certain degree of uncertainty about whether on his own initiative he could manage certain things he nevertheless wanted the opportunity to master. He was never sure if he had mastered that outside world. But partly there were also mundane things he wanted to leave to others, which relieved him of some necessity and responsibility and freed him up for thinking about his writing.

BI: That was how he managed his life. He tended to see it as the sacrifice that had to be made to make possible his writing. But I think it was more than that. It was a personal way of approaching living, and Ann helped a great deal because she was herself a much more flamboyant, overtly expressive person but also because at the same time she helped arrange his life.

AI: If you travelled with him, you had the same set of constraints. You had to be sure to block it all out in advance so that there would not be unpleasant surprises with regard to the regularity of meals and so on. But he started from that narrow base, an impoverished background and mental illnesses, and all the time he was trying to accumulate experience. Even though the inner capacity was probably always there, it needed the material of external experience, so as to produce the writing

The Italian experience was also the new, easy background to the writing of Malamud's Italian short stories. In *The Magic Barrel* (1958), 'Behold the Key' concerned an American research student's anxious comic search for an apartment in Rome, whilst 'The Lady of the Lake' was about Henry Levin who preferred to call himself Freeman in Italy. He loses the girl of his dreams when he denies being a Jew, only to find that she is a survivor from the concentration camps. Gradually, beginning with 'The Last Mohican' which appeared in *The Magic Barrel* and then 'Still Life' and 'Naked Nude' which first came out in *Idiots First* (1963), there emerged the new comic freedom of the experimentally picaresque volume *Pictures of Fidelman* (1969). Alex Inkeles particularly admired its development:

AI: Later on—and this is why I am especially attracted to the Fidelman stories—Fidelman himself is much more open. Fidelman is out exploring the
world. The closed environment that was most extreme in *The Assistant* is broken
out of. Even though Fidelman's a disadvantaged person in some ways, and
there's very little going for him, still all kinds of wonderful things are happening
in the environment. It was Malamud's discovery of a wider world, a wider stage
that you could move on, freely, instead of being some extra, hidden away in the
corner. All the works appear smaller than they really are; but increasingly and
in impressively different ways, they are breaking out into a new life.[4]

A New Life itself was begun in December 1957 after the return from Italy. Near the beginning, it pleases the protagonist, Seymour Levin, New York city boy in Oregon, 'that he had done things today he had never before done in his life' (LC I 32.4, p. 20).

Yaddo

The writing of *A New Life* continued at Yaddo in the summer of 1958. Malamud wrote his son about this retreat and colony for artists in Saratoga Springs, donated by the philanthropist financier Spencer Trask and his poet wife, Katrina, and run from 1926 by the formidable Elizabeth Ames:

The house I am presently living in is called 'the mansion' at Yaddo. It has an
enormous number of rooms, about sixty, I'd say, although there are only about
ten guests living here at this moment. The others, particularly the musicians

and painters, have cottages on the grounds. In winter the mansion is kept closed because it takes two tonnes of coal daily to heat the place. It takes me about three or four minutes to walk across the house, from one end to the other. My bedroom is about three times the size of our living room at home. It was formerly the bedroom of Spencer Trask, the millionaire who once owned the estate. He and his wife left the place to artists, to work here and enjoy it. People put in applications and are selected by a committee. They are housed and fed without charge. I think that's a very good thing to have done for writers and other artists, don't you?   (2 August 1958)

Ann and the children were going out to California to see Ann's mother, Ira, and Gino, her second husband whom Malamud described as rigid but good-hearted. Malamud the teacher closes his letter by urging his son to try to 'master' his swimming and his tennis, and practise his music 'assiduously': 'You will derive much satisfaction from knowing how to play a musical instrument well. Someone is playing a piano somewhere in the house at this moment and it sounds beautiful.' Malamud had never learnt to play.

He was away from the family for nearly two months. At first he felt strange and unsettled. Ann was to write twice a week and to encourage the children to write once a week. His routine at Yaddo established, it went thus: rise at 7, eat at 8, start work 9 till 12.30; half an hour's reading or resting till lunch at 1; back to work until 4 or 4.30, then nap, shower, and read before dinner at 6.30; afterwards, social—croquet or ping-pong, charades, poker, listening to music—with bed at 11, reading for an hour before sleep (5 August 1958). By 8 August he was struggling with a new chapter, feeling like 'a cripple' and wanting to be lazy until the imagination filled up again with ideas. 'Since I almost always get what I ultimately need,' he wrote Ann,

> you'd think I would be content to work and wait, knowing that what I need will come, but I am not—feel uneasy, even guilty that I am not working hard or consistently. In a way that sort of feeling is a bit intensified by my being here, for what is Yaddo but a place to write

Ann replied on 11 August that his tone reminded her of his summer away writing in 1943: 'sounds subdued and monastic: the kind of letters you wrote as a bachelor from Brant Lake!' She herself was struggling—'rather low again, but not to the point of tears! ... No more long separations, please' (30 July). 'I hope I can get through the summer without sinking, and I'm sure I can, but I do miss you a lot and feel lonely. Life ain't the same without you around to ask me about the mail' (22 July). She ends her letter: 'Enjoy your freedom, for this is your last fling alone, as far as I'm concerned!'

Malamud's own mood began to ease and lighten. One of the people who came to fill up the mansion was the painter Rosemarie Beck. She was thirty-five, and 'wacky on the subject of astrology'. She wouldn't let him walk on the outside of the road, on the edge, because 'my Uranus wasn't in good shape' (to Ann, 8 August 1958). She had a struggling novelist husband Robert Phelps, whose first novel *Heroes and Orators* was concerned with homosexual love, and a nine-year-old son, Roger. She was glad to find a little time at Yaddo to be away from both, so that she could work. 'The night before last', Malamud writes Ann, 13 August, 'Rosemarie and I skipped supper here and walked to town .... Rosemarie apologized at least six times for spending my money; she has been conditioned in a terrible manner. Last night she was telling a group of us how her husband and she used to steal food in the grocery store when they were very poor.' He goes on: 'She's an absolutely genuine person, thin as a rail, coughs a lot, skin without luster, but an enormously rich personality. I love to listen to her; she sounds like a character someone has invented in a book. Her phrasing is striking. The other day I heard her say: "These ghetto Jews, carrying their wrath in their fists." She started a portrait of me.'

Her own first impression, as she wrote to her husband, 15 August, was that Malamud was 'nothing great' but 'has a good heart'.[5] But they were already 'fast friends', and in her journal for 27 August, towards the end of her stay, she reports 'Bernard will be my friend for life I suppose—or so he says'. 'I've talked everything out with Bernie,' she writes the following day, 'given away everything.' Life like art, she wrote him later, needs making and arranging, but with him she felt ashamed that she had simply been what she was. 'Raw "truth" is a messy monster who lives in the moment' (19 March 1961).

Jewish by birth, but her religion only that of a dedicated artist, Rosemarie Beck was proud and determined but innerly insecure and needy—vulnerable to being dismissed as an old-fashioned figurative painter in the age of abstract expressionism. Malamud offered her some faith: 'Emptiness is a time of filling', he would write (16 February 1962). 'Outside your talent as a painter, you have almost no self love. My wife is something like that' (26 December 1962). 'Your friendship and regard,' she replied to him, 19 March 1961, 'are the dearest things I have, and the only things I have to give. And I can give it too if you can take it.' For thirty months, she says, she has worked with a 'firmer conviction than I'd ever before possessed' because of the feeling of his support:

It was my secret support; we were conspirators in the tiresome, dangerous, obsessive, sometimes gallant, adventures of our separate crafts; we could take pride in each other. I take pride in you. I can't help it; it's not my right, but I do.

Do our rewards, though, lie in each other?

We always ask each other how we are, she says, but:

> I can never answer properly, find a simple way of telling you. Maybe it's just untellable, not in a way a finished work is, so we're together I guess for the moment in silence. But Trustingly! I'm most of the time nervous, eager, doubtful, hopeful, questioning; and I'm making an effort to be honorable too. (4 November 1965)

At least, their art thrived on what could not be said. 'O dear,' she writes him, 'I don't trust fully, or love wholly, an art that has Nothing to Hide. Secrets not-altogether-revealed are, for me, the substance of art. It keeps me aflame to think of ways of disguising my secrets. I believe it's true for you' (5 September 1962).

Looking back, both Ann and Janna thought that Malamud may well have had a brief affair with Rosemarie Beck at Yaddo, though her son insisted otherwise. Certainly a close and rich correspondence developed between the two, particularly in the late fifties and early sixties. Always Malamud's writing separated him from his family: it was a call and a demand that made him aware of himself as a man, at some essential level, always on his own. But describing its lonely difficulties connected him with a fellow-artist with equivalent struggles. It was a release of the pressure from this separate, dominant compartment in his life. Down the years, he writes to her, 'I've discovered emphatically I don't know how not to work' (25 August 1967), or as he writes in his intimate notebook, 'My fault is: I learned to live alone' (HRC 34.4). On 5 September 1962 she writes of having 'a packet of letters from Mr. B. Malamud which represent one of the truest portraits I've ever encountered of what it means to produce, or secrete, drop by drop, a work of art.'[6]

It made her feel less greedy, she told Malamud, to think that she had helped him a little too. For in turn she herself was sympathetic, increasingly both admiring and supportive in relation to the novelist. What he feared to be old-fashioned in his own writing, she called timeless. When he spoke of his own anxieties and uncertainties, it was her turn to remind him that that was how it was for the artist: 'I believe in the efficacy of doubts and fluidity of indecision—the flow of possibility therein' (9 November 1963). At various times she urged him to ignore his 'fear of failure'—because his failures would be more interesting than almost anyone else's success—and to take more rest and pleasure. 'For my money,' she had written him back in

1959, 'you're too good already and a little helpless folly would improve you. I mean, be a little more at the mercy of things, spend more, lose more, and fail more. Only you can never do this deliberately. To be truly accessible to good, one has to be a little less than one is.' When he tells her that he does not believe that the really great artists, the true geniuses, had to labour as he has to, draft after draft ('I wake up tired, I walk tired, I sit tired and write tired. I walk home tired. Put it away? I can't' (19 August 1960)), she writes back: 'Ach, your talk of genius ... I don't think it's for us to know for what we have genius' (23 August 1960). His genius, she says, lies in his ability to keep working honestly and unflinchingly, despite everything—in time, others will call *him* lucky and brave that he could be like that. But still change and rest were important: 'Maybe what you need is a little dérèglement, and then, to cure it, the discipline once again?' 'Rest from your labours,' she tells him in his exhaustion after *A New Life* has come out: 'Try to enjoy your weakness. It's out of this the next one comes. You have accomplished yourself in your work. Let it suffer for you now and become a vessel of grace all over again. You don't have to be an example for your book.'

Malamud reassured her, in her anxiety, that the relationship was truly reciprocal:

> I'd be crazy to give you up as a friend. Where do these fantastic doubts come from? Must I for the millionth time tell you your richness as a person, and my good fortune to have you as a friend? You say I've helped you; well know that you have helped me. I've never met anyone like you and I consider it a gift that I did. I do take pride in you as a woman and artist. Frame this and put it somewhere to look at when you grow doubts. (1 April 1961)

He knew what she needed from his own neediness. But what he framed, or at least wrote out and put by his desk, was a quotation she sent him, 15 June 1965, from Henry James: 'We work in the dark—we do what we can—we give what we have. Our doubt is our passion, and our passion is our task. The rest is the madness of art.' She sent it from Yaddo again where Philip Roth was also in residence, though the two did not get along. (Malamud had once told her that Roth was too often 'water-skiing when he should be diving. Or at least swimming' (11 December 1959)). Later in Roth's *The Ghost Writer* (1979) it is that quotation, from 'The Middle Years', which the young Nathan Zuckerman finds pinned on the bulletin board beside the desk of the great writer, E. I. Lonoff.

'So much labor', says Malamud of his writing, and yet on publication his readers will know little of it from the finished product: 'It is amazing that this is hidden from the outside eye':

If you think of me sitting at my desk, you can't be wrong—today, tomorrow, next month, possibly even a year from now. I sometimes wonder when there is time to live although somehow I do. (28 September 1959)

This was despite Alex Inkeles's sense that in many ways life was easier now. In his letters Malamud gave Rosemarie Beck, almost uniquely, an entrance into that holy of holies, his study, where writing was always rewriting—'drop by drop'. 'When I can't add or develop, I refine or twist. Can you see that in my work?' (25 October 1959). This writerly fixing of things is what was hidden:

> Rewriting tends to be pleasurable, in particular the enjoyment of finding new opportunities in old sentences, twisting, tying, looping structure tighter, finding pegs to tie onto that were apparently not there before, deepening meanings, strengthening logicality in order to infiltrate the apparently illogical, the apparently absurd, the absurdly believable. Sometimes, when additional material is necessary, or there must be a serious change of the old, I run into serious snags that throw me for a morning, or hold me back for a day. It's harder to combine two legs than to amputate one; or to make an old head believable on a new body. Today I had a difficult time but solved it (or think I did) in my very last hour, which accounts for my facility with this letter. (11 September 1959)

There is still the uncertainty: '(or think I did)'. Other correspondence he took less trouble over; but then other days also went less well:

> It seems to me that I've been resisting the book. I've been working on a hard chapter and the relentless effort has wound me up. I'm so tight I have very little patience with myself, though I somehow manage to do my work slowly. I'm not particularly worried, this has happened to me before, but it is uncomfortable, particularly when I come home and find I don't know what to do with myself. (6 November 1959)

At this time, Malamud had rented a room in a widow's house in Corvallis whilst the family moved into the new house. But the experience of difficulty was recurrent with *A New Life*. An unfinished novel, he said, felt like 'a sin I am afraid to be left with' (25 October 1959).

> Writing this book is like bending iron. Each day I bend the width of a toothpick ....
>
> Generally I have the fact I need from my first draft, but it is usually enclosed in nine useless sentences ....
>
> Today I worked in mosaics, sentences previously noted, and put together in many hours ....
>
> Today I invented sunlight; I invented it in the book and the sky of the dark day broke and let light fall on the white birch and green grass. (11 January 1960)

Just occasionally, at such miraculous moments of inventive language, the life on the page and the life outside did not seem quite so separate. 'I was rewriting a chapter and some of the sentences lit up as I put them down. I wish that would happen more often than it does. One of the reasons that I rewrite so often is to create the opportunity for it to happen' (19 October 1964). More usually:

> I do a good piece of writing and that same night bits of it crumble apart ... I think of each page as a wet painting. Tomorrow when it's dry, we change here and there.
>   (5 August 1960)

He needs time off in May; he takes a late-evening walk to the river with a fellow-writer at Eugene and 'dusk poured out through a hole in the sky. Dark light everywhere. I felt a little empty, a little depressed at finishing my second draft.' The next day the draft does not seem so bad, he 'wasn't sickened once in the first forty pages'. The study still feels like a prison but it is a prison of his own making:

> Art is a free man's prison. I can't imagine any life other than I am now living. I have a strong sense of the going of time but I'm not afraid of it though I regret it. I wish I knew the secret of being in art and in life at the same time. I mean of drinking life as one does in his youth.
>   (26 May 1960)

At least he can try to free up the work, asking Ann to type a clean copy so he cannot see the blotted emendations of his past mistakes. 'With a clean copy I convince myself that I'm making progress' (16 November 1959). Then he will write it out in longhand again: 'The typed page looks solid but when it is rewritten by hand it becomes fluid again and if the idea is good it bursts into flame or flower' (19 October 1964).

It is an inner drama, usually laboriously undramatic and frustrating, where everything is worked for and paid for. But just occasionally comes the unearned bonus. Bill Potts, a young instructor in the office next door to Malamud's recalled: 'One day Bern, normally quiet and solemn, burst out of his room all smiles, "A gift!" he cried, eyes flashing, and ducked immediately back into his office without explaining the revelation that had come to him' (HRC 33.9). It might have been no more than a word or a sentence that changed everything for a moment, or the invention of another twist and turn in the structure. But for Malamud as for his protagonist Levin, this was momentarily the small man's version of Dante's *Vita Nuova*.

But art was demanding and its relation to life was complicated. And there is a little living image of both these truisms in an incident that flared up between Malamud and Rosemarie Beck in 1965. In the January her paintings had been exhibited at the Peridot Gallery in New York. Malamud wrote Rosemarie a letter in praise of the smaller works but was disappointed with the form of the larger ones: 'you are not finding new ways for your iconography. You have too much affection for everything you put down' (25 January 1965). This was typical of Malamud: artists had to be hard on themselves and if she was not, he had to be for her. This was the painful primary concern. But then if she had 'too much affection' for 'everything' that she put into her paintings, then in the mixed-up levels of real life, he could only be seen as going against such affection—including some affection for her—in his criticism of her emotional ill-discipline.

Unusually receiving no reply to his letter of criticism, he wrote again on 11 February. He had known how basically unconfident she was. But he had to remember that it made a difference if the critical toughness necessary to the artist came from him, outside, rather than from her, within. It should have been an obvious second thought, but Malamud was a great writer partly because his second thoughts, his repeated mistakes, and his clumsy relearnings remained a shock to him:

> My letter was badly done. I can imagine how I would have felt to have had something of the same sort from you. Part of my difficulty was in not wanting to say what I felt I had to say .... What bothers me now is whether I am right or wrong, that I did not say it better, gently, with all the affection I feel for you.

Malamud was often an impulsive and nervy bungler, using his imagination—'how I would have felt'—too late. The 'not wanting to say' rarely stopped him saying it, especially when feeling was tensely involved both in what he had to say and in the desire not to say it. Moreover this was about art, serious matter, to which so often everything else came second, even though he was unsure it should. All this only made him say it worse, not better. And he knew this about himself:

> If I could reinvent myself, I would reinvent myself with more thought between what I say and what I think. I tend to speak very quickly and one writes the same way .... And it is only in the reflection of afterwards that you put in place and in focus and proportion those thoughts that you have that are necessary to the argument. (TH, 119)

Malamud often writes to Rosemarie Beck about form—the right time and place for the right idea. 'Here I am in my third draft and still there are too many things that are not right. When the person does not come out right, usually something is in the wrong place. When the tone is not right, it is not the tone so much as something in the wrong place' (19 August 1960). The writer cannot go on; almost humiliatingly at times, he has to go all the way back to find out where the place was that it started to go wrong. But in life you could not easily go back.

Situations at best were only mended. Janna recalled Rosemarie Beck in 1968: 'She came to Vermont and stayed several weeks painting my portrait and my brother's. I suspect she was broke and Dad wanted to help her. I disliked sitting for her, experienced her as too familiar in some way difficult to finger' (MFB, 156).

The Magic Barrel and the National Book Award

But Rosemarie Beck always insisted to Malamud that he had done well, despite all the pain on the *inside*:

> You've grown so much since I've known you. And *that's* the given fact, the lucky factor in your writer's life if not in your life as a perfectly willing a-waiter of human happiness. It seems to me that merely being able to bear it without safety valve of distractibility is a sign of strength and some honour, even if it sounds romantic.

Increasingly, after a 'long seeding period', the work was gaining rewards in ways that she herself had never experienced, yet he did not seem sufficiently to appreciate:

> At least your *outside* is fortunate. Your career advances, you're immensely respected, your fame is sure, you're read. And you have no wasteful vices (unless you want to call your nature a vice. My dear, my dear, that's the nature I dote on!), no vices of character like, say, Mailer's megalomania or Herbert Gold's hapless messiness etc., no literary enemies, no temptation to waste your talent on worthless entities.   (9 November 1963)

Even by 1958 things on the outside were going well. The reviews of *The Assistant* had been good—Herb Gold in *The Nation* called it almost perfect; Harvey Swados in *The Western Review* thought the ending rivalled anything in contemporary fiction. Though some critics such as Alfred Kazin found the moral too pointed or the whole too like a parable, it was still praised for its compressed force and religious power—albeit, said Charles Poore in the *New York Times*, in the old-fashioned European tradition of the great nineteenth-century novelists. In 1957 Malamud earned over $6,500 including $2,800 in royalties; in 1958 with promotion from OSU, nearly $9,000 with royalties over $2,200.

In 1958 moreover *The Assistant* received both the Harry and Ethel Daroff Memorial Award for Fiction from the Jewish Book Council and the Rosenthal

Award of the National Institute of Arts and Letters. Malamud attended one of the award ceremonies in May, pleased that it was broadcast 'and my brother heard it' (to Ann, 22 May 1958). Ann was at home in Oregon with the children, writing 25 May:

> Of course, I should have liked to be, but somehow I don't regret not being there. I am very happy that you are doing the kind of work you want to do and also are achieving recognition for all that you are and have done, and glad you have been honoured by an award. But as for the ceremonies of these things, it must be my age or something, but somehow they just don't seem to be very important in themselves. I share your triumph anyway, even across the continent, and the rest is unimportant.

Chester Garrison believed that such things became more important to her over the years and that, in return for her sacrifices, she enjoyed the social benefits and advantages of her husband's success—'more so than Bern'. *The Assistant* had also been entered for the hugely prestigious National Book Award but failed to win the prize.

Yet the following year, in 1959, Malamud won it for *The Magic Barrel*, with Ralph Ellison and Alfred Kazin among the judges, though Kazin himself had expressed reservations in an earlier review.[7] It was the first time a book of short stories had won the award for fiction since William Faulkner in 1951, and it defeated Nabokov's *Lolita*. It was dedicated to Malamud's struggling brother, Eugene. In his acceptance speech in 1959, Malamud himself spoke rather grandly against the modern-day devaluation of man: 'the writer dare not accept it ... the writer must imagine a better world for men while he shows us, in all its ugliness and beauty, the possibilities of this'. At the same time, praising the short-story form for containing much in little, he declared that with the award going to a short-story collection a 'small miracle has come to pass'. In fact, one of the founders of the prize had opposed the decision, arguing that to give the prize to short stories, which 'couldn't help to sell more than a few copies of Malamud's books', was against the purpose of the awards—namely, to increase major book sales.

Richard Stern remembered Malamud at this time:

> Back then, there was no moustache, just a bald, sharp-eyed, shoe salesman's face—till you watched it in action, an intensity of alert scepticism overhauling naiveté, amusement salting belief. A finicky, sharp, funny, roughly frank, partly innocent, crazily meticulous fellow, who carried lists of chores and checked them off as he did them. 'To keep myself from going crazy.' He'd been living in Oregon for a few years, teaching at Oregon State. There they gave medals each year to faculty

members who had done the most for the University and mankind. The year Malamud won the Book Award, he'd gotten the bronze prize. The gold had gone to the inventor of a better breast-cup for cows. The silver had gone to a Professor of Logging.[8]

At the National Book Award ceremony, Malamud refused to pose for newspaper and television cameras vulgarly holding up a copy of his book; forgot his winner's $1,000 cheque and left it on the podium; and delayed by a reporter in getting to the dinner in his honour, was told by a waiter, looking him up and down, that the table was full and there was no place for him. In an interview with W. G. Rogers he also reminded himself of his wife's triple commandments: 'Don't forget that at least one writer who didn't amount to much won this before. Don't let this go to your head, the whole business is aimed at man's vanity. Don't forget that you didn't win for your best writing, for that is still to come' (LC I 50.3). As Alfred Kazin later put it, it was like seeing a Malamud short story unfold.[9] Yet it also led to the award of one of the first Ford Foundation grants of $15,000 to creative writers for two years' writing, between 1959 and 1961—the other recipients including Saul Bellow, James Baldwin, Flannery O'Connor, Theodore Roethke, and e.e. cummings.

What pleased Malamud above all about *The Magic Barrel* was that the drama lay austerely in matters of principle, belief, and feeling amongst the dispossessed. It was like a Jewish Brooklyn version of Joyce's *Dubliners*—'The First Seven Years', 'The Mourners', 'The Girl of My Dreams', 'Take Pity', 'The Prison', 'A Summer's Reading', 'The Bill', 'The Loan'—interspersed with the Italian stories, 'Behold the Key', 'The Lady of the Lake', and 'The Last Mohican'. It also drew upon Sherwood Anderson's account of the writing of *Winesburg, Ohio*, when there appeared before him at night the faces of all the people he had seen and often neglected, wanting their stories told. As Arthur Foff described the world of *The Magic Barrel* in the *Northwest Review* (Fall–Winter 1958):

> Out of a world of dispossessed strangers, two characters, often an older person and a younger man, meet .... The physical background, in short, is as skeletal and yet as inescapable as the gutted ground of a concentration camp or the high, narrow barriers of a ghetto. Yet, once a cosmic accidentalism has crossed these two lives, the characters are transfixed in a long and agonizing moment. The irrelevant, chance meeting becomes the necessary relationship. The impossible demand becomes the imperative debt.   (LC I 30.1)

These are unequal encounters between unlikely counterparts. They could indeed be dismissed or neglected as life's accidents—unless something happened or somebody cared. Why shouldn't a landlord kick out his long-time unsavoury tenant? Why should the baker give money to the man who never repaid the last loan, years earlier? How can a poor man not pay another? Why does a scholar forgive the refugee who stole his manuscript? How comes it that a poor young widow won't take money from a would-be benefactor? In different ways in 'The Bill', 'The Loan', 'The Mourners', 'The Last Mohican', and 'Take Pity', loans or obligations ought to be met but cannot; antagonisms suddenly fall apart in leaps of generosity or regret; guilt is imagination imprisoned or too late. A line is crossed and something morally good suddenly has the bad or sad within it, or the sad and the bad something good equivalently.

Above all, what interests Malamud is that 'impossible demand' becomes 'the imperative debt', in particular at the end of the two great stories of risky belief, 'Angel Levine' and 'The Magic Barrel' itself. Believe in this impossible man! says the first. Love this damaged woman! says the second.

In 'Angel Levine', Manischevitz the tailor prays God for the health of his wife. 'When she died,' writes Malamud in a typical compression of wit in pain, 'he would live dead.' But God has absented Himself, and the tailor is no Job: 'Upon him suffering was largely wasted. It went into nowhere, into nothing'—Malamud adding, again characteristically—'into more suffering'. What is asked of the tailor is to believe that a seedy-looking, unreliable black man from Harlem is really a Jewish angel on probation. If in this strange form and unlikely place he does not bring salvation, he will deteriorate for lack of recognition and trust. Amidst scenes of zany comedy, it is asked of the tailor that he should say to Levine: I believe you are an angel from God. As often in Malamud tales, it is a fantastic setting with realistic people nonetheless set inside it. What is more, it is a fantasy that, in a moment of crucial reversal, can only finally sustain itself if it is made real by the difficult, creative belief of those living inside it. Manischevitz has to take the tale's chance: 'believe, do not, yes, no, yes, no. The pointer pointed to yes, to between yes and no, to no, no it was yes'—

'I think you are an angel from God.' He said it in a broken voice, thinking, If you said it it was said. If you believed it you must say it. If you believed, you believed.

Malamud must have loved that double 'it' set at the centre of 'If you said *it it* was said,' marking the very process of creative commitment. This is what Malamud meant by a notebook entry made when writing *Dubin's Lives*: 'The sentence as object—treat it like a piece of sculpture', carving out the possibility of belief (LC II 1.5). It was as though being able to say it made it true. For this also is what Malamud meant when he wrote to Rosemarie Beck of 'strengthening logicality in order to infiltrate the apparently illogical, the apparently absurd, the absurdly believable'. Irving Howe had it right when in a review in *Midstream* (summer 1958), he wrote of Malamud driving up at double-speed to a climax in which a synoptic gesture 'compresses and releases' an essential meaning: 'gambling everything on one or two paragraphs'.[10] Or even one or two sentences. 'There are Jews everywhere,' the tailor tells his recovered wife.

There is the same sudden commitment near the end of 'The Magic Barrel' itself, when Leo, the young rabbinical student, sees a photograph that the marriage broker has never before shown him and suddenly, painfully pledges himself to this one, however unlikely. It is turns out to be the lost, wild daughter of the marriage broker himself:

> Her face deeply moved him. Why, he could at first not say.... It was not, he affirmed, that she had an extraordinary beauty—no, though her face was attractive enough; it was that *something* about her moved him. Feature for feature, even some of the ladies of the photographs could do better; but she leaped forth to his heart—had *lived*, or wanted to—more than just wanted, perhaps regretted how she had lived—had somehow deeply suffered: it could be seen in the depths of those reluctant eyes, and from the way the light enclosed and shone from her, and within her, opening realms of possibility: this was her own.

In November 1954, when this was still in draft and entitled 'My Love is Like a Shallow Stream', Malamud wrote simply: 'Feature for feature, even some of the ladies of the photographs could do better; but she had lived and deeply suffered'. But the sentence flowers as soon as he inserts into his draft the imaginative 'or' clause: 'she had lived, *or wanted to*'. Excited, he can turn that 'or wanted to' into '—more than just wanted'. And then he can add to that 'more' (in the final version only) the subtle backward movement of 'perhaps regretted how she had lived'; and finally '—had somehow deeply suffered'. This is what Irving Howe admired about Malamud in his review of *The Magic Barrel* in *Midstream* (summer 1958): that he combined 'literary sophistication' with 'an unruly comradeship for ordinary people'. For Malamud's gift was continually to make and remake himself a writer in the struggle of writing, fashioning his vocation out of the ordinary in making his characters also more fully realize themselves. Even his tiny alterations are to do with the man's authentically surprised awkwardness changing to beauty, the semi-articulate precision stuttering towards real thought, beyond facility.

But Rosemarie Beck believed Malamud was giving too much away of the unrevised self when he gave a public talk on how 'The Magic Barrel' developed over six months in 1954. He listed his sources.[11] But the most significant source of all lay in Malamud himself:

> I was having trouble with the story; it was not developing into the sort of thing I wanted.
>
> Then one day my wife and I were having a discussion, in the course of which she said, 'You talk a good deal about love, but you don't always love.'
>
> Later on I admitted to myself that what she had said was true

It would always be 'later on', but it took him back to the years of difficult childhood and difficult courtship, to the visit to the psychoanalyst about the relation of words and feelings, and to the continued withholding of himself in his writing-room:

> and thinking about it I concluded that the problem of not loving, of not being able to love, was one of the central problems of our existence; so I immediately tied it up with the idea for my story. Here was a man who wanted to marry for love; would it not be dramatic if he wanted to do so to prove that he could love? (TH, 84)

He also recalled a review of Whittaker Chambers's autobiography *Witness* (1952) in which the reviewer 'had questioned his love for God, because it seemed to the reviewer that the book did not give any evidence of love for man'. Thus, feeling he needed a religious element in the story, Malamud turned the young man from a teacher, as he himself had been in the late thirties, into a student rabbi. Then Malamud gave Leo this 'terrifying insight'—that he had turned to the marriage broker because he felt incapable of finding love either for himself or in himself. But now he sees he cannot settle for anything less than that:

> 'I think,' he said in a strained manner, 'that I came to God not because I loved Him but because I did not.'
>
> This confession he spoke harshly because its unexpectedness shook him.

Thought *happens* to Malamud's people, not in the form of intellectual brilliance, but because, from the midst of unsatisfactory experience, their botched lives are trying to tell them something. It comes out back-to-front, doubtfully, through double negatives and perilous joined fates:

> Though he prayed to be rid of her, his prayers went unanswered. Through days of torment he endlessly struggled not to love her; fearing success, he escaped

it. He then concluded to convert her to goodness, himself to God. The idea alternately nauseated and exalted him.

It risks everything it could be.

A New Life

In 1959 Malamud had told Richard Stern what Stern described as a 'wonderful idea' for a novel:

> It was to be about a man singularly gifted for love, able to gratify the complicated needs of many others, but himself without the ability to love. I had seen Malamud give advice and money to un- or scarcely known petitioners. He wrote them recommendations, answered letters, worked out other people's problems. His generosity was brusque, his sympathy dutiful, sceptical. When his novel, *A New Life*, appeared I found no trace of the theme (or little else for which I cared). I wrote him to that effect and he wrote back sharply. (Richard Stern, 93)

Stern could see the role of moral duty, like a form of will, in Malamud; what he wondered was how far the feelings that Malamud felt he *ought* to have were a substitute for all that he did not spontaneously feel. Malamud had tested himself once in 'The Magic Barrel' when in 1954 Ann criticized Malamud for talking about love far more than actually loving. Now he was to test himself again in the writing of *A New Life*.

Malamud had a notebook labelled 'Story Ideas—Oregon' which he used from September 1948 to October 1956 (HRC 22.2) What is remarkable is that it shows how much the ideas for the stories, for *The Assistant* and for *A New Life*—work that was to take ten years to complete—existed initially alongside each other, front and back of the same pages, almost as soon as Malamud, bursting with projects, had settled himself in Oregon. There is a possible story to be called 'The Assistant Professor', a 'forceful, strong-minded—even loud mouthed' young man in conflict with an older academic. The older man is the president of the American Association of University Professors and a liberal, but he backs away from direct action for fear of losing his job, because he remembers what it was like to be in the Depression. There are also notes about 'love for a student—a love story?'; also for a story concerning a male student who is suspected of cheating; and about Fabrikant the liberal scholar who does 'many a "good" thing' but destroys it all with 'some spontaneous "bad" thing'. They could make up a series of short stories built around the happenings on 'a small campus or a small college town'. In all these instances

Malamud later adds 'NL' in the margin, checking off his sources for what turned out to be *A New Life*. For the next thought in the notebooks is that these short stories may become 'a short novel about a teacher', centering around the drama of selecting a new departmental head.

But this novel is also now competing with another in the notebook. In 1953 there is a note dated 24 January on a 'possible novel: young man holds up a grocer ... the enormous difficulties of redemption'; another dated 25 February: 'Oregon novel must deal with problem of someone trying to be a good man'; and on 3 March a return to what becomes *The Assistant*: 'at the end the "apprentice" decides to become a Jew'.

By 1957, on publishing *The Assistant*, Malamud had written up another of his 'plans for artistic creation', describing to Robert Giroux a 'seventy-five to one hundred thousand word novel whose title may be *The Easterner* or *The Fanatic*', the adventures of 'a New Yorker of thirty, possibly Jewish, possibly an ex-Catholic, a man with a religious bent, who, after a period of unhappiness, perhaps even drunkenness, accepts a position to teach in a small college in the Northwest' (LC I 32.2). In the end, in *A New Life*, Malamud has both a Jewish protagonist from New York named Levin and an ex-catholic rebel predecessor from Chicago called Duffy. But at this point in his planning Malamud made a key structural decision: typically, he decides he will have *two* battles going on at the same time. One is in the department where two 'small men', one conservative, the other somewhat of a liberal rebel, compete for the headship. The idealistic New Yorker, switching from one to the other till disappointed in both, eventually attempts to take the leadership into his own hands. The other involves the relationship he undertakes with a young married woman with two children, even whilst he is teaching and preaching morality and responsibility. 'Realizing the contradictions of his position, he attempts to give her up, but is drawn back to her because of her unhappiness.'

What is more, in the final planning of the novel, what will tie those two battles even more firmly together, while deepening their contradiction, is that Pauline, the married woman beloved of the New Yorker, is also the wife of the conservative would-be head of department, Gerald Gilley, whom the New Yorker opposes. It is what Levin himself calls in the first draft 'a dangerous combination' (LC I 32.4, p. 181). Thus to find a new idea in the amalgamation of old thoughts—that was the sort of invention that could made Malamud cry out, as to Bill Potts, 'A gift!' When he was writing 'The Light Sleeper', Ann had told him that his liberal ideas about freedom and humanity and idealism and love were hardly new or original, but were almost clichés. Now Malamud had formal counter-moves: he could create situations in which there was no one thought but a series of overlapping, undercutting, interrelating thoughts that created a richly mixed density. This too his habit of cumulative revision allowed. As he once told his student Nina Pelikan Straus, 'There was no such thing as pure ideas.'[12] The first insight, the initial hypothesis may be absorbed, Malamud told his students, into all that follows from it. To achieve a framework for these developments, from the first draft onwards he once again locked his novel into place chapter by chapter, paragraph by paragraph, until he left himself only the sentences to work within: 'I have a kind of mind that wants to complete something. Feels an architectural form. Once I get it that way, if I have to revise, it's usually pretty much in the same architecture, but with different stresses' (TH, 122–3).[13]

It was important to Malamud that *A New Life* felt like a new start to him or he could not write it as he wished. The books before it, he wrote, came out of the world of his father: 'If *The Natural, The Assistant, The Magic Barrel* indicate the first stage, every book since then, up to *Dubin's Lives*, indicates the second stage, the attempt to grow in understanding, feeling, art' (HRC 27.5). What is more, *The Assistant*, he said, was 'in the European tradition. So am I,' but he then added in an interview with the *New York Post* in September 1958:

> My next book will be an 'American' novel. It's different from anything I've done. I've just finished a chapter working on it up at Yaddo and it's beginning to open for me. It'll be something new for my readers, and the first time for me: a romantic love story, with warmth and richness.   (CBM, 4)

The protagonist, Seymour Levin, is a man brought up among Jews, in a Jewish ambience 'which may be ethical or symbolic rather than theological'. There were few Jews in Corvallis—though Jim Groshong made an impression on Malamud when he said he wished he had been born a Jew. But when such as Levin 'walks into a strange country', then Malamud asked of this experiment in the second stage of his career: 'What stays with the Jew who is not steeped in Jewishness?' (TH, 138).

Jewish history, wrote Malamud, 'may be said, in one form or another, to prefigure the American experience' (Ibid. 187). But it was now the American experience that was to be Malamud's subject, in the democratic freedom of possible self-invention and self-renewal, in the constitutional commitment to an ideal. 'He knew he was doing something that he hadn't done before,' said Robert Giroux, 'and he was having psychological difficulties, writing difficulties. I had to convince him it was well worth going ahead with and finishing.'[14] *A New Life* was the American adventure in small, the New Yorker in Oregon, as Malamud explained to an audience in Corvallis to which he returned to give a reading in 1967, shortly after the publication of his fourth novel, *The Fixer*. Looking back, he said of Levin's journey:

This echoes American history: the West was settled by people coming from the East .... It has now become, of course, a going back and forth—a mutual influence, which it should be, and one of the paradoxical things is that Americans from one part of the country we call the United States appear as strangers, almost foreigners in another part of the country. That tells you something about the nature of man; he is frequently afraid of faces he does not recognize. But to get back to the book again, the character from the east extends into the dim past to the birth of man in the east and his westward migration leaving new cities and cultures behind him. If a writer tried to get some sense of the recurrent quality of the past into his stories—a quality that will never end, we say it has this mythological quality. All four of my novels have this quality; they are all works of imagination, invention. Roy Hobbs and Frank Alpine go from West to East to find their fate; S. Levin and Yakov Bok go from East to West to discover theirs. (OSU 3.38)

As Malamud spoke, there were before him in the audience colleagues who had been in part the models for characters in the book. Preston Henley was sitting next to his mother, the poet Elizabeth ('Bett') Henley. She had been cast as Avis Fliss who has an abortive affair with Levin and an ongoing relationship with Gerald Gilley—and this was true of Bett herself in relation to Malamud and Herb Nelson, respectively:

Malamud had quickly turned to the topic of a reader finding similarities between fictional and actual characters. It was, from my recollection, the initial stage of his lecture. And I remember feeling Bett wince as soon as the topic was addressed .... I suspected she found her former friend-and-colleague's comments hypocritical—an attempt to deny that he had offended some of his colleagues and thereby escape having to apologize.[15]

At the end she spoke briefly to Malamud in front of the stage. On the way home she said to her son that she had told Malamud, whom she had once warmly respected, that it was wrong to have hurt people who had befriended and supported him when he had been at Oregon State.

Others took a different view. Ed Smith, one of the younger men in the department, had written Malamud, safely in Bennington on publication of the novel, 'I blessed you ... for showing up the whole mechanical approach to teaching comp and worse, our mundane, materialistic attitude towards what we were supposed to be doing as academicians' (8 October 1961, HRC 9.4). He felt he could identify everyone—there were 'a thousand verifiable details': Faith Norris's garden serving for the Bullocks' party; Herb Nelson, with his fishing and hidden files and dubious photographs, skewered in satiric revenge as Gerald Gilley; Groshong as Bucket, Herb Childs as Fabrikant the scholar on the horse with the two-tone laugh; and Peterson—'Unperceptive and, I feel, without courage, he's one of the men who kept Oregon State fifty years behind the times,' Malamud wrote of him to Sylvan Karchmer, 17 January 1963 (HRC 11.9)—parodied as the ageing Professor Fairchild. Dying, Fairchild speaks haltingly of 'The mys- mystery—of the in-fin—in-fin—in-fin'. 'Infinite,' says Levin, helpfully. 'Infinitive,' Peterson corrects finally (*A New Life*, 292).

Instead of the infinite, what Malamud offered was a small man in a situation that felt too much for him. Saul Bellow's *Henderson the Rain King* had appeared in 1959 and Malamud admired and envied the scale of its African quest, the power of its imagination, and that great inner voice, boldly insisting, '*I want, I want, I want*'. But in the second draft of the *A New Life* he speaks of Levin as 'not brave in his brave life'. He was formerly a drunk; his father had been a thief; his mother committed suicide in the kitchen with a bread knife. His story was brave—overcoming addiction, fighting for liberal values in a department tainted by McCarthyism, seeking love after a loveless childhood with a married woman—but he himself was scared by it. The son of such a father, he had as a child a mortal fear of exclusion, of anything less than universal approval; an anxiety which he also associated with having been poor all his life. He was scared of being labelled a radical, even a communist, and suffering not only unpopularity but economic punishment. It had happened to the poet Duffy, his lapsed Catholic predecessor—a character modelled partly on a young professor of science Ralph Spitzer, who was fired from OSC on Malamud's arrival in 1949 for being a communist, partly on a volatile Irishman Jack Cronin, who left the department after trying to make reforms, and partly on the poet Gene Lundahl, who had led the protest on the college football field against its military training corps. Thus rawly in draft, here is Levin, the Chaplinesque little man filled with enlarging ideas:

> Radicals were relative but in New White Plains he felt like one. The word gave him gooseflesh; too many people had forgotten American history. Too many were frightened by daring, imaginative possibility—enlarging ideas so vastly different from the rocklike prejudices they had acquired ... But he argued back, don't be afraid of names, and christened himself a conservative radical; let's see what they can do with that. It means I am for what's good but I want what's better. His purpose as a self improved man, he said to himself, was to improve the common lot, however he might, at a time of peril, anxiety,

betrayal of freedom, continued aggression of men. He would work as a teacher, with others who thought as he did, to create a saving remnant: those who would go further than the teachers in the name of democracy, humanity—cheers, whistles. Then he had met Pauline. What upset him now was the realization that his love for her had made him ineffectual in dealing with her husband.   (LC I 32.6 inserts B and C)

What Malamud had created was not a hero who was braver than all the rest but only a man relatively less frightened than the others. He was an apologetic product of Malamud's own inferiority complex. Amidst the accompanying uncertainties of tone and scale, the test was what Malamud could then make of him, and what he could then make of himself: 'Who, after all, is Levin but a weak man striving, as Chekhov said, to squeeze the slave out of himself' (Ibid., insert A).

In retrospect Malamud was to think that 'my feeling about Levin is that perhaps I was a little too hard on him. I'm sorry if he comes out to some people as a schlemiel. I respect him more than that' (TH, 138). Malamud borrowed from a young member of staff, Ed McClanahan, the folly of leaving his flies open whilst idealistically addressing his class. But Malamud hated the way his work was vulnerable to readers patronizing his characters as 'schlemiels', Jewish fools, comically lovable in their safe ineffectuality. The mediocre schlemiel was like a form of the anxious, defensive sentimentality against which Alfred Kazin, for one, had warned him in his review of *The Magic Barrel*. As the critic Martin Green was to put it in a savage review of *A New Life* in the *Financial Times* (17 April 1962), speaking of 'the fault of all Jewish writing' in its downtroddenness:

> The hero is taken both seriously and non-seriously, his emotions are both exaggerated and underplayed, his style is both pompous and ironical. Everything is to be taken both seriously and comically at the same time: steeped in that sweet-and-sour Jewish humour (if you have read no Jewish fiction, think of Chaplin films). The weakness of such writing is that it is always patronising, however lovingly, its subject.

Yet Malamud found his way in the novel, when he set his man walking out of the college into a new world. One of the ways that Malamud made himself more oriented within life, Alex Inkeles had noted, was to walk. When Malamud first arrived in Corvallis, one of the small things he first appreciated on these walks was the way that like colonizers, people had bothered to plant flowers in the strips of old earth left outside their homesteads. He gives the same insight to Levin, the protagonist in *A New Life* where in a second draft it is said, 'Levin enjoyed also new combinations of the old: roses occasionally climbing telephone poles, flowers—like Pauline's—planted at curb strips, plants fertilized by sawdust' (LC I 33.1, p. 81). As the city boy walked further out into the countryside he felt, bizarrely, he was watching 'bread growing in harvested fields' (Ibid. 136). And these walks, as he describes them in his third draft, involved surprises of landscape and perspective—varieties of colours, delicate compositions with distant trees, 'the poetry of horizontal and vertical in space' (LC I 33.3, p. 60). So it was to be, also, in the walk at the beginning of the first draft of *Dubin's Lives*: 'The biographer trotted on, enjoying the sweep of space in every direction. Uccello: "What a beautiful thing, perspective." He loved the free pleasures of perspective' (LC I 1.4, p. 3). These walks made him feel as though he had a painter's eye, he felt he was walking in art. 'And when I am home,' he wrote Rosemarie Beck, 'I am still walking' (30 December 1961). It was like practising the imaginative arts of combination and perspective in another medium, the shifting languages of horizontal and vertical—terms he began to use more and more in the opening up of his writing. When writing goes well, he wrote Rosemarie Beck, it is 'like suddenly loving the country road down which you are walking' (27 May 1962). 'Today I invented sunlight' (11 January 1960): he invented it in the book, looked up, and found it suddenly shining outside. Or in a note to himself, whilst writing *Dubin's Lives*, 'I'm walking in words looking for distance' (LC II 1.5). What Malamud could hardly stand in his writing was thinness, flatness, the sheer plod along lines that were not turning into another world for him to *live* in. In the novel's second draft, near the commencement of chapter 3, Malamud pencils in a note to himself: 'A man's freedom in space' (LC I 32.5). A second life in a new world outside.

But when in this new spacious life out west Levin begins to make the same mistakes he had made before in the east, the circle closes again: 'space corrupted by time' (*A New Life*, 160). In his bachelor loneliness he is drawn to Nadalee, a student in his class. She was loosely based on a student, Kathy Kohner, better known as the Gidget, who used to babysit Paul and Janna and would tell the ever-inquisitive Malamud about her sexual escapades.[16] But the story of young teacher and girl student goes back in Malamud's imagination to the early notebooks of 1940. The hungry Levin hopelessly seeks to resist temptation. He meets Nadalee in the college bookstore, relieved to see her diminished from temptress into nice kid. He tries to think of her as his daughter—only to dream of her growing into a masked beauty to whom he makes love and then discovers his sin of incest. After a comic car journey to meet her on the coast, Levin finally makes love to Nadalee—only to find in the aftermath that he has no true affection for her. 'This reaction was an old stock-in-trade of his and did not help endear him to himself' (Ibid. 152). He has not left his past behind him.

There follows a further sequence of twists and turns. When she gets an unexpectedly poor grade C, Nadalee comes to Levin to ask him to change it or her father will be angry. He refuses on the moral grounds which they both know he has previously forsaken: 'I see there were things you could bring yourself to do,' she says angrily, 'when they suited you' (Ibid. 155). He knows he 'had got her without deserving to—fruit for teacher—a mean way to win a lay' (Ibid. 160). But he won't go further down that track, in falsifying her marks, even at the risk of her telling her father. Shaken, he then goes back to check her scores and finds, the blunderer, that he has truly miscalculated and she has genuinely earned a B, not C after all. He then officially gains permission to change the grade, however embarrassingly, for the right reasons. Yet they are so close to the wrong ones that when Gilley finds out about the affair, Levin's guilt obscures what is also his innocence. This is the roundabout way of Levin: it is not unlike Frank Alpine stealing, returning, and still stealing money in *The Assistant*.

This is what it is like for Levin, always on the verge of what from outside would look like hypocrisy. Something *like* hypocrisy—though on the inside it felt more innocent and more trapped than that—was where Malamud lodged his imagination. Thus Levin has to make himself catch a plagiarist, 'though one of his own painful memories was of cheating on a math final in college' (Ibid. 165). That was the way of the world: 'the reformed judging the unreformed. Better that than the other way round' (Ibid.). Yet when he cannot find chapter and verse to prove the case against Albert Birdless, he cannot bear to continue persecuting the boy: 'Happening to meet the boy's eyes, the instructor saw they were soiled with worry, and his face had taken on a yellowish cast .... Albert might be guilty: if so he had got to where his guilt, by some trick of human drama, rubbed off on his prosecutor' (Ibid. 170).

In his review of *The Magic Barrel* Kazin himself had admitted that no writer came 'so close to the bone of human feeling' as Malamud at his best. But Malamud characteristically managed this back-to-front, through doubts and fears of his own and of his characters. Like Roy Hobbs, like Frank Alpine, Levin is now living a second life—'Levin felt low. Once in his life he hoped to be somebody's unchallenged first choice' (Ibid. 110). But this time it becomes a second life in which primal feelings came back all the more powerfully, as if felt for the first time again, for being belated, unexpected, yet generously restored. It is a new feeling that comes out of the Eden of the landscape. Thus Levin lying with Pauline the first time in the open forest, in a paradise regained:

> 'Spread your coat.' She spread hers over his, then stepped out of her shoes. She removed a black undergarment, the mask unmasked. Lying on the coats, Pauline raised her hips and drew back her skirt, to Levin the most intimate and beautiful gesture ever made for him.   (Ibid. 194)

'*Ever*'. 'Naked she looked unmarried' (Ibid. 200). In a review in *The New Leader* for 2 October 1961, Stanley Edgar Hyman, later to be a colleague of Malamud's at Bennington, spoke well of such moments: 'Levin attains to sanctity (and I think that this represents a considerable advance for Malamud) not through denying and mortifying the flesh, like the anchorite Frank Alpine in *The Assistant*, but through indulging the flesh, and his adultery is a holy adultery.' 'Holy' may at first sound fanciful: Herb Nelson, for example, rather characteristically reported to Ed Smith that he had thought 'the last third' of the book, with the love affair, 'dull and boring' (HRC 9.4). This was the man whose heart, said Malamud, was made of corn flakes. But 'holy' was the word Levin used when, at his lowest, drunk in a cellar, he saw his rotting shoes transfixed in a shaft of light as though painted by van Gogh. 'I like the Hasidic approach to things,' he told Rosemarie Beck, 16 October 1959, 'to fill each with spirit or God, like van Gogh's chair, and my friend Ben-Zion's chandeliers, flowers, clouds, knives, forks and dishes. I love the sheer palatability of things. I sometimes would like to eat a painting and be consumed by the spirit of the things in it.'

Yet as Pauline offers herself to him in the midst of this idyllic paradise, comically, meticulously Levin hangs his trousers on the branch of a fir. A friend said to Malamud, knowing his own carefulness, that she thought that detail was something that had really happened. Malamud said nothing at all but smiled, she thought, ruefully.[17] But such notes of clumsily leftover awkwardness are an honest comic counter-point—the old cautious man adjusting to a new world almost too bold for him—that makes the whole increasingly and touchingly serious.

Thus here is Levin again, further on in the affair, in the middle of driving back home from a visit to the doctor. The doctor has just told him that a comically undignified anal pain he has recently experienced during this adulterous intercourse must be psychological—'Tinsion is all I can find'. This is how the reality principle gets to (what Malamud's calls) 'our boy' in the midst of sex—or in the midst of driving:

> [Levin] was asking himself what he was hiding from: That he too clearly saw her shortcomings and other disadvantages, and was urgently urging himself to

drop her before it was too late? That he was tired of the uneasy life, fed up with assignations with the boss's wife, sick up to here with awareness of danger and fear of consequences? Here was truth yet not enough truth. After mulling these and related thoughts, Levin tracking an idea concerning Pauline fell over one regarding himself: the dissatisfaction he had lately been hiding from, or feeling for an inadmissibly long time, was with him for withholding what he had to give. He then gave birth. Love ungiven had caused Levin's pain. To be unpained he must give what he unwillingly withheld. It was then he jumped up, stalling the car.   (*A New Life*, 208)

Love is felt as pain. That is how it comes, disguised or unrecognized, in a second life and a fallen world—late, awkward, beset with apparent difficulty and reluctance. He rehearses all the post-lapsarian objections and reservations: Pauline's lack of beauty, big feet, no breasts, her insecurity; a husband who can destroy his newly won future, and the responsibility of two young children; the old romantic temptation of his youth to turn sex into love. In the first draft it is *because* he 'lusted' that he began to doubt he 'loved' her. In the second, Levin asks himself why he should insist on 'paying' for an experience that he should simply accept as one accepts sunshine or rain: it is, he thinks, a 'masochism' which he 'secretly delighted in' while 'hating himself for it'. But finally 'who was he kidding?' These thoughts are what he calls 'truth', and may be truer still for other characters in other stories at other times; but for him, in his deeper feelings, 'not enough truth'. The greater truth, the felt law, the character he finds from within his own story, remains something surprisingly simpler, more unexpectedly innocent, even in adultery:

'The truth is I love Pauline Gilley.' His confession deeply moved him. What an extraordinary only human thing to be in love! What human-woven mystery! As Levin walked the streets under a pale moon he felt he had recovered everything he had ever lost.   (Ibid. 189)

'*Everything ... ever*' again. It is like Manischevitz hearing himself say he believes in Angel Levine. Malamud was not a writer unless or until he could be surprisingly moved by himself in the way Levin and Manischevitz were. In the first draft, it was merely 'What an *extraordinary* thing to be in love!'; in the second (Illustration 16), 'What an extraordinary *human* thing to be in love'; in the third finally, 'What an extraordinary *only* human thing to be in love'. It is an enriching, layering process, very quiet and precise verbally, making big things happen in small places, going back and back and back to the primal feel of those feelings, by the magic of a word or two, until it rings true. Malamud writes for those who are moved by the inclusion of that single word 'only' and know something of the difference it makes. In revision, he wrote to Rosemarie Beck, 'I have to sweat to remember (and I do slowly, even if one can't call it remembrance) what I should have got in but didn't. The afterthought frequently saves me' (28 March 1965). Still he does call it something like remembering because at its most powerful it feels like something he had forgotten. 'This had been passed down to me but I had somehow forgotten. More than forgetting—I had lived away from it, had let it drift out of my consciousness. I thought I must get back what belongs to me; then I thought, "This is how we invent it when it's gone."' (*A New Life*, 197). It made for a future which awakened the past. 'The thought isn't a new one,' Levin says to Pauline early on in the second draft, 'but I seem to learn the simple ... in a complicated and roundabout way' (LC I 32.5, p. 16). As Stanley Edgar Hyman saw, Pauline is Iris from *The Natural*, 'no longer scorned'.

In such ways the hard-won simple now feels primal again. There is a joy in the writing. 'How love perfects each imperfect thing! What she was was beauty. With breasts she couldn't possibly be the one he loved. I mustn't forget this' (*A New Life*, 211). 'Once she drew back a lock of hair to adjust a barrette and revealed an ear pinned like a jewel to her head ... Lord, thought Levin, how beautiful women are, and how hungry my heart is! But how short life, how soon gone!' (Ibid. 205). On his very first night in Cascadia, as he falls asleep in the Gilley household, Levin feels as though he is being covered with a second blanket—or perhaps that was what Pauline was doing 'to the children across the hall' (Ibid. 26). He was finding in a second life what had been lost in the first: 'The death of my mother, while she was still young', Malamud told Joel Salzberg in an interview, 'had an influence on my writing, and there is in my fiction a hunger for women that comes out in a conscious way' (CBM, 128).

Malamud's was the ability to create—in place of abstract thought—that anterior mass of dense and confused human feeling, which thoughts themselves came out of. 'I would love to be an experimentalist,' he wrote Rosemarie Beck, 19 February 1960, 'but I haven't it in me. My gift is to create what may be deeply felt.'

But the task was now to take that lyricism and see whether what was deeply felt in its sexual poetry could serve as a basis for austere and permanent marriage. 'He hadn't planned ... to be anyone's second husband before he was somebody's first' (*A New Life*, 320–1).

First there was the paradisal free gift. Then there was the realization of unplanned love that compromised his hard-won 'freedom'. But there now followed a *third* twist. As the relationship becomes more difficult and painful to sustain in its snatches of secret joy, Levin resolves to give up Pauline for her own sake—to give her up out of love itself. This is what Stanley Edgar Hyman might have called the return of *The Assistant*:

> Renunciation was what he was now engaged in; it was a beginning that created a beginning. What an extraordinary thing, he thought: you could be not moral, then you could be. To be good, then evil, then good was no moral way of life. But to be good after being evil was a possibility of life. You stopped doing what was wrong and you did right. It was not easy but it was a free choice you might make, and the beauty of it was in the making, in the rightness of it. You knew it was right from the form it gave your life, the moving aesthetic the act created in you.
>
> I must give her up, he thought, if I haven't. (Ibid. 249–50)

This is one of Malamud's great rediscoveries: that the aesthetic and the ethical are not separate categories, not because the aesthetically beautiful is the highest good; but because good itself is beautiful. Morality: not dull, not slavishly conventional, not merely obedient, but something—perhaps in reaction to his father's life or in sympathy with his mother's—that moves Levin as love of life, 'anybody's life' (Ibid. 249). 'The form it gave your life' means that what an artist does on page or canvas a man can do with himself off it.

But Malamud would also add: 'There's more than morality in a good man' (TH, 18). For on this occasion, in the unpredictable relativism of life, renunciation turns out to have been not simply a moral achievement but, mistimed, a mistake. There is a *fourth* movement in the love affair which gives a further deepening amalgam to the simplifications called 'love' or 'freedom'. For just *after* Levin has finally succeeded in giving her up, Pauline comes back to him—though this is what, in repeated little images, the book has always been doing: going away only to return.

> Levin warned himself, Take off, kid, and in their deep kiss saw himself in flight, bearded bird, but couldn't move. (*A New Life*, 193)

> Levin pictured himself leaving her under the tree in the rain. Later he returned to see if she were there. (Ibid. 194)

> He rose hastily, upsetting the cup on the table. Levin watched the stain spreading on the rug. He ran to the kitchen for something to mop it with.
> Why don't I keep on running?
> But he returned with a cloth and dabbed at the rug. She wanted to do it but he wouldn't let her. (Ibid. 318–19)

Rather than yield to the temptation to escape reality, the book keeps returning to itself, through recommitments made more powerful by the obstacles they have to overcome. It is like Abraham, the founding father, in Kierkegaard's *Fear and Trembling*, still faithfully, hopelessly clinging to his desire for a son, long after it had seemed it would never happen: 'For it is great to give up one's desire, but greater to stick to it after having given it up; it is great to grasp hold of the eternal but greater to stick to the temporal after having given it up.'[18] Jews, Dubin tells his Buddhist-minded daughter, live in the world and stay in it.

It is like a return of the test he had passed in the second movement, when he had so many plausible reasons to think that what he felt was not love. At the same time Levin was giving her up, Pauline had been struggling to do the very same, as though even in this, beautifully, they were still two sides of the one thing. She tells him: 'I fought against myself for your sake—to save your plans—until I no longer could':

> 'Then I thought, I must go to him, and that's what I did.'
> Levin sat like a broken statue. The destruction of love she could not commit he had accomplished. (Ibid. 318)

The paragraphing is devastating. It was only a month ago, but where now has his love gone? 'He had had and hadn't it' (Ibid. 322). It is in this second life where sometimes you seem to have to work against the natural grain of existence, that Malamud produces the test of not feeling love—not knowing what else or where else it might be if it were not simply a feeling. It makes for another of Malamud's great stuttering riffs in which, once again, Levin tries to 'escape' his 'premise', only then to 'return' to it:

> I have no cause now not to love her, granted I loved; I grant. I loved her; we loved. She loves me still, I have never been so loved. That was the premise, and the premise you chose was the one you must live with; if you chose the wrong one you were done to begin with, your whole life in jail. You cheated yourself of the short freedom you had in the world, the little of life to be alive in. He craftily told himself time alters everything, premises wear out, change produces incompatibles. He sniffed out reasons to escape, go where he pleased, unbound, unburdened, where fancy fancied and the feet followed.... Then by devious ways he returned to the premise: She was his love, changed by it only as he by hers. What was changed beyond that was badly willed, now unwilled. A man sentenced to death may regain freedom; so may love. It was possible, it surely had happened. No matter what he had suffered or renounced, to what degree misused or failed feeling, if Pauline loving him loves; Levin with no known cause not to will love her. He would without or despite feeling. He would hold on when he wanted terribly to let go. Love had led them, he would now lead love. Having reasoned thus he cursed reason. (Ibid. 324)

Never has austerity seemed so creative. It is done with a passion, a reluctant passion, in the face of what actually seems to him to be the very absence of feeling. But Malamud works hard to generate those two double negatives—I have *no* cause now *not* to love her' 'Levin with *no* known cause *not* to will love'. The reader can see them getting worked out in Illustrations 17a and 17b, first draft as typed up, and Illustrations 17c and 17d, the second. In 17b he vows, twice over, to wait for love to return: in 17d he actively makes the return—to the premise that requires him to hold fast. In the margin of 17d he adds 'or despite' so that it becomes: he would love *'without or despite feeling'*, simultaneously adding to his troubles and to his fight against them. Yet Pauline worries that the commitment is now mere will on Levin's part, and puts to him the challenge of loving her only on principle.

In a public lecture, 'Hunting for Jewishness', given around 1965, Malamud was able to say what these microscopic back-to-front, double-negative, and recommitting structures stood for at the macro level of human meaning:

> The fulfilment of love is knowing that love must become service, must become responsibility, and that love can't simply stay as love. Now if you think that is puritanical you may, but I think that love is not very well understood in American life, partly because our country is so very much moved by its young people and we are so very much concerned with young people who have romantic notions of love, incomplete notions of love. Love is, as you know, deeper and more complex, less satisfying, more satisfying, more intense, more impossible than most people even know or have contemplated. (LC II 5)

Even Pauline was far from ideal. The models for Pauline were probably Ann Decius and Pauline Huff and possibly Jane Hanson, all talented Oregon women with dissatisfactions, personal uncertainties, or struggling marriages. 'I want to know more and do more with my thirty two years,' says Pauline in the first draft, 'but I don't know how.... Often I find myself wondering how to use my mind for something more than a repository for grocery lists' (LC I.1, p. 168). Ann Decius most resembled Pauline physically—Norwegian blond, chest as flat as an ironing board, large feet; though Ann Malamud claimed there was no affair with her husband; Pauline Huff was a bohemian painter who caused a local scandal by leaving her poet-husband Robert; Jane Hanson was also an artist who took part in Malamud's extra-mural creative writing class in the evenings and some time after the Malamuds left for Bennington committed suicide.[19] There was also Rosemarie Beck. It suited Malamud to rearrange his life, secretly bringing together separately compartmentalized elements of it, in this way. For whatever their nature, Malamud used these extra-marital relationships in an extraordinary manner: he was using adultery, imaginatively, to support marriage. Levin was doing just that inside the book, but so was Malamud in creating the work. He was using the excitement generated by a woman manifestly not resembling Ann, in order to reawaken and transmute the struggle he had to save the relationship with Ann in 1945: 'Now I am on my hands and knees, trying to collect the substance I wasted.' What he had done to her feelings and to his own linked back to those feelings of depersonalization which drove him to see a psychiatrist in 1942. This again Malamud used nakedly in his first draft: 'I feel as though I were sleep-walking,' he says, 'My feelings are crippled.' 'Shouldn't you see a doctor?' asks Pauline. 'I did once, years ago. He said it would go away and eventually it did' (LC I 32.4, p. 321). Later Malamud summarized it thus:

> Levin has a period of very intense suffering when he cuts himself off from Pauline and he lives through a time of trying to purge or change his love which he is never able to do—that is to say the intense emotional experience that occurs as a result of this produces a time of stasis of feeling … a kind of half-deadness with his response to living, to life, what goes on around him, which I feel he begins to show signs of losing at the end of the book, a kind of depersonalization if you will. He has had so much that he cannot take any more and this is how he responds to it by a somewhat slow deadening of the self.   (LC II 11.5)

This depersonalization had happened to Levin before, in what in Illustrations 17a and 17c is called 'nervous reaction' following upon his vision in the cellar. But what felt like the lack of feeling was really the admittance of more than could be borne. In the same way, love, said Malamud, is not just a single emotion but a complex condition inside itself: 'there is fear in love, there is anxiety in love, there is great pleasure in love, and there are all sorts of things in love. That is what I am really saying' (Ibid.). Such complex feelings are saved by a language whose richness and beauty transcend the pain, the sorrow, the content to which it remains still loyal, giving such things a value they can hardly give themselves. It may only be the morally forging beauty of a little connective word like 'when': 'He would hold on when he wanted terribly to let go'; or 'if': 'I must give her up, he thought, if I haven't'; or 'what': 'To be unpained he must give what he unwillingly withheld'. Yet these words are sentence-making achievements.

Such achievements are hard won. This cunningly unsynchronized story is set in the time of year 'between end of winter and spring' which, Malamud said, 'is to me a very dramatic time' (TH, 85). The Oregon winter was stranger, shorter, and more beneficent than the New York one. Springs came so quickly, Malamud told Rosemarie Beck, that there was almost 'no yearning for them, the loss of a hungry emotion' (6 February 1960). Before, out east, 'I used to make all evidence of change in nature go at once to the heart. This became clear to me as I wrote it into Levin's experience this week' (3 October 1959). What Levin wants is a sustained *human* spring, created by will, out of yearning:

> Although Levin rejoiced at the unexpected weather, his pleasure was tempered by a touch of habitual sadness at the relentless rhythm of nature; change ordained by a force that produced, whether he wanted it or not, today's spring, tomorrow's frost, age, death, yet no man's accomplishment; change that wasn't change, in cycles eternal sameness   (*A New Life*, 190)

'Whether he wanted it or not' is not in the first draft but is a characteristic revision, a later parenthetical insert, barely finding space for itself. The desire frustrated within it had then to find its own room, create its own change, in its own time within the season's cycle. Yet the change cannot simply be planned either. The lovers find out only in retrospect, of course, that it was just before they gave each other up—when their sexual relationship was at its most tense and unsatisfactory—that Pauline was made pregnant. 'I didn't think of the possibility of conception those last times,' says Levin. And Pauline replies, 'You want the right feeling for every event?' (Ibid. 314). Life itself in this book is not simply conceived, or synchronized, or made convenient, like that. But that is also the very condition that makes for the necessity of human intervention and correction at the second attempt, that requires responsibility to fight for change to have its own place in time.

'Accomplishment' is the word Malamud beautifully chooses. And accomplishment is achieved in Levin when finally he has to face Gilley, listing all those disadvantages Levin had previously rehearsed to himself—Pauline's age and past and neuroticism, the two kids, the exciting illusions inherent in an illicit 'lay'.[20] Gilley won't give his family up without a fight, he says, unless in turn Levin agrees to give up his future and quit college teaching. And Gilley concludes: 'Why take that load on yourself?' In the first draft it went on:

> 'I have to,' Levin said.
> 'What do you mean "have to"?'
> 'Because I can,' he said bitterly.   (LC I 32.4, p. 343)

But the final version is what Malamud is really after—no 'have to', no 'bitterly', but Levin replying with just one shot at it, unequivocally, love-in-defiance:

> 'An older woman than yourself and not dependable, plus two adopted kids, no choice of yours, no job or promise of one, and other assorted headaches. Why take that load on yourself?
> 'Because I can, you son of a bitch.'   (*A New Life*, 344)

It hurt Malamud when people saw the end as a defeat, an imprisonment, another suffering sacrifice or masochistic compromise. Everything he had done was to carry it through all that doubt and danger into 'accomplishment' instead. It is a classic, almost ancient pledge of strength and capacity, at what has become an incongruous and ill-timed wedding ceremony. But Levin knows what his best feelings have represented and he will now *be* them, even when they themselves are no longer or not yet conveniently to hand. This is his moment, his equivalent 'I think you are an angel from God', that he thus commits himself to live with, long after the moment. Though no one would want to lose the angry zest of the last five words accompanying them, it is those first three that are the three most important words in the book and almost in the life: 'Because I can.' Let the outside world 'babble about adjustment, interpretation, adaptability,' wrote Rosemarie Beck, 7 September 1961: that was not the artist's inexorable way. For of *A New Life* she concluded: 'The struggle, the drama, is in *you* and you are *your book*.' You have done this, she was saying, because *you* can. Often when off-duty Malamud would talk of literature and life as though they were two things. Janna recalled: 'He had once had an argument with his Bennington colleague, Stanley Edgar Hyman, about whether one should sacrifice a baby's life to save a Shakespeare play, or vice versa' (MFB, 122–3): Malamud insisted he would put the baby first, but his own daughter half-doubted it. A preposterous question, she admitted, but 'I wonder if he would have traded his literary success for Eugene's health?' Her father was in every sense like a single man inside his study, precisely because of all he could borrow from being a married, family man outside it. The connections, like the conflicts, were subtle and complicated. Yet here for once at the close of *A New Life* the two called 'literature' and 'life' were one, as Rosemarie Beck urged him to recognize: the book could not have been what it was without something absolutely essential to Malamud; and Malamud could not have realized that something without writing the book.[21] He found his quality in it, it found its quality in him. It was what he was to call being able to 'live in' a book (LC I 26.1).

A New Life, Rosemarie Beck was to write years later, was the book that is 'the most intimate, the most nearly autobiographical (of course it's a fiction!), the one in which you feel most like you, to me, and the most truthful (for me). So when you say you're thinking about it again, expanding the theme, I exult. You tell me to be more me ... I turn around and tell you to be more you' (30 November 1967). The proposed sequel to *A New Life* was to become *Dubin's Lives*, but that was years away, to be published in 1979.

THE THIRD LIFE

6

The Beginning of the Middle Years

Harvard 1961

A friend told him that Malamud was going to be teaching at Harvard for that one summer, in 1961. Clark Blaise was a young man, Canadian-born, from a little college in Ohio who discovered Malamud in his senior year as an English major and felt that his was the most important American writing he had ever read. His parents were too poor to fund him at Harvard but found $100 towards it; an old girlfriend had been going to donate a similar sum to the United Nations but gave it to him instead. A friend in Boston would put him up and promised him some work teaching French. He sent in his application, together with a prize-winning story he had written at college, and hitchhiked to Harvard.

There were ten places available. Blaise did not know there were already seventy-five applicants. He went direct to Warren House, where Malamud's office was, and asked the secretary whether he had been accepted. She told him his name was not on the list and the course had been closed weeks ago. But he could go upstairs and ask Malamud himself. He had not met any author before. He walked around Harvard Yard the whole afternoon, trying to think what to say, afraid that in the meantime Malamud would have already gone home. 'Finally I said to myself, "You told yourself you are going to be a writer. Your life is over if you don't talk to him today."' So the young man went back in, climbed the stairs and found Malamud, a sort of Groucho Marx figure, sitting at a table in the back of a huge office, the bookshelves empty save for shoeboxes and stacks of manuscripts.

He was not particularly smiling or welcoming. He was sitting there, and he said, 'Yes? What?' I said, 'I applied for your class and my name isn't on the class

list.' He said, '*They* selected the class'—meaning the Harvard faculty—'when
I was still at Oregon, and it's not fair to people who submitted in good faith.
Find your story up there and give it to me. Come to the first class tomorrow,
Blaise. I can't promise you're in, only that I'll read it.'[1]

Malamud picked a further handful of applicants. That is how Clark Blaise,
the novelist, became one of the writers who were 'the sons of Bern'—the
extended literary family whom Malamud, as father and mentor, was often
able to help more than he could his own children.

William Cooper, a student who was on the list, recalls the first class:

> I remember Malamud as a man whose empathy could fill his face. I saw it
> when he had repeatedly to rebuff a rejected workshop applicant whose writing
> apparently matched his bloated, bedraggled, needy appearance. The applicant
> flung himself into the first workshop meeting banging the room's door open,
> slamming it against the hall wall. Face flushed, his eyes pleading over huge
> dark blotches below, messy black hair above, he demanded that he belonged
> in the workshop, that he must have been rejected by mistake, that he was a
> great writer just unrecognized. He ran his hands continually through his hair,
> spitting, while his demands became even louder begs. We few in the workshop
> looked back and forth between Malamud and the ranting man transfixed by
> this almost fictional scene before us—our first meeting with Malamud, this
> wonderful writer of fictional truth whose workshop we had competed to get
> into. For a moment I wondered if this was staged for some prompting reason.
> That thought disappeared when I realized Malamud might shed tears as he
> quietly and repeatedly insisted that there was no mistake and the man must
> leave the room. I happened to be sitting nearest the door. As the scene dissolved
> toward a pathetic stalemate I stood and told the man that Mr. Malamud had
> asked him to leave and that he should immediately. The man shut up, looked
> at me as if he were going to slug me, then turned and left. I don't know why I
> stood up but perhaps that was why Malamud started talking with me after the
> daily workshop sessions.[2]

Malamud knew about crazy young men. After that first class he wrote home to
Eugene, his own disturbed sibling, 2 July 1961, that he had made the students
write brief autobiographies and that they fell into two rough groups—'those
who lived through very little, and those who have lived through very
much'. Among the latter, the pattern was 'wealth, broken homes, extreme
family misery (hatred of mother or father or both), breakdown (several
attempted suicides), psychiatry, college, lack of discipline, beginning of
self-understanding, and seeking for discipline' (HRC 36.5).

But there was one other distinction to be made. For every Clark Blaise,
there was also, always, a maddened reject. And there was a version of

Malamud that went with each: respectively, the quiet formal man, disguised but fair; and the saddened, limited man behind that, sticking to the rules but sorry and vulnerable. It was like a Malamud short story where behind the achievement of every good outcome masses the impossibility of avoiding all the failed endeavours. Blaise recalled that in class one day Malamud defined the short story as 'dramatizing the multifarious adventures of the human heart'. He loved coincidence, the criss-crossing of lines, the unaccountable convergences, contrasts, and parallels whereby one life transforms some, is transformed by others, misses out on more.

'My first two sessions were lectures and they seemed to go well,' he wrote Rosemarie Beck, on the same day he wrote Eugene, but there was one student, a young man of twenty-four who 'seemed annoyed with something I had to say about "mystery" in art, possibly because I invoked other mysteries in our lives including God. Apparently he will not tolerate the mention of that kind of mystery.' 'So like you to introduce the mysteries on the first day of school,' Rosemarie Beck replied, on 5 July. She urged him not to worry about those who needed explanations and answers:

> you're not going to be the ideal impartial beholder with an all-inclusive accessibility, but your own maker with your own imperatives and biases. This limitation alone is the great good, the great privilege for your students. They'll not forget one day that they were in the presence of the mystery in the flesh.

William Cooper was one who remembered. 'We had one fairly long discussion about Stephen Crane; writing from imagination versus from experience: *The Red Badge of Courage* versus "The Open Boat".' It impressed Cooper that Malamud had minutely analyzed the works he admired for hints on methods and effects, and had catalogued in his memory selected passages, pinpointed by chapter and page, for these purposes. Teaching and reading notes testify to this. In his working copy of the novel by Saul Bellow he most admired, for example, Malamud marked the place where Wilhelm, the bunglingly emotional protagonist, hopelessly delays the moment when he will have to go before his affluent disapproving father and announce his latest failure:

> He had opened the *Tribune*; the fresh pages drooped from his hands; the cigar was smoked out and the hat did not defend him. He was wrong to suppose that he was more capable than the next fellow when it came to concealing his troubles. They were clearly written out upon his face. He wasn't even aware of it.   (*Seize the Day*, 1956)

Malamud appreciated that involuntary innocence within the self. He put in the margin 'p. of v.' (point of view) against the last three sentences, to mark the shift from character to author across the very boundary between within and without. It marked the sort of point that was useful to Malamud when in 'Idiots First' a dying father begs a servant for immediate access to the rich man who could help send his idiot son to relatives in California. ' "Look me in my face," said Mendel, "and tell me if I got time till tomorrow." ' In the first draft, 'A Long Ticket for Isaac', the father says simply: 'Look in my face'; but, finally with Malamud's Yiddish-English poetry, there in 'my face' is indeed 'me'.

Sara Witter, the only woman student in her half of the group, remembered stories and instances from Hemingway, Graham Greene, Katherine Anne Porter, Flannery O'Connor, and Isaac Babel. She kept her notes:

> He talked to us at the beginning about how in these stories a dissatisfied person looks for human contact. There was always the question of where was the drama. And there was the problem of people who fail to confront the meaning of their experiences—they drift into confusion or destruction. To say this to a bunch of fairly callow young people is interesting because we didn't know what the hell our experiences were all about, even if we had experiences in that sense. But the idea was he wanted us to push ourselves to take chances and to dare to write about things that gave us difficulty. He said that his own area concerned questions of failure of love, and characters evolving through feelings of failure to a sense of love. I thought of his story 'The Maid's Shoes' where the nervy work-obsessed professor gives his maid new shoes but does so unkindly, and the way they are given makes the difference. Malamud started by saying he wanted to find out what was the truth that people were trying to tell in their stories. He himself seemed very pared down, physically, as though he was really focused on the essential.[3]

Students would also read their own short stories out loud in class, and then there would be open discussion. Malamud was good at ensuring that criticism was courteous ('Mista Penna, get some civility into your comments'). Clark Blaise noted that Malamud would take risks, violating the unwritten rule about not looking into the writer's autobiography, whilst posing as a Jewish uncle: 'Miss Geller, have all these things *really* happened to you?', 'Who hurt you so badly that you're writing like this?' If he saw the person was in pain and the story was no more and no less than therapy, he would talk about the issue rather than the writing.

Blaise also remembered him reading a story by Howard Nemerov about a man and woman at a restaurant: all the time they were talking, the man who had taken off his shoe was rubbing his own foot underneath the table. 'Don't ever write a story like this. Freudian devices. This is not a story; this is a case study.' Malamud was suspicious of what Blaise calls 'the Delmore Schwartz syndrome, the Herzog syndrome, certainly the Portnoy syndrome—Love me! Need me! Redeem me!—the whole notion that to be a Jewish writer was to be somehow exploitative of your neuroses and your passions.' He told Blaise: 'Have the insight to recognise the neurotic patterns and the integrity to break them.'

As a teacher he was quietly authoritative, tolerant, almost withdrawn. But if even momentarily a student could break the patterns and produce something not formulaic but surprisingly beyond the idea of the constructed self, then, said Blaise, you could see Malamud's eyes, mouth, brow 'suddenly dance over a sentence, a word, an idea. Oh, it is possible to enrage a teacher, to infuriate or embitter him or her, but only the rarest, I think, instruct by an almost private show of delight' (*Resident Alien*, 23).

This was the Malamud who, whilst he was writing *Dubin's Lives*, his novel about a biographer, was to say to one of his favourite former students:

> I've often thought of giving a course in the human sentence. It would include grammar and logic and educate young people to love the written word and eventually themselves. Now that I'm on this book I think the course should be called 'Lives'. Students would read, say, Nadezhda Mandelstam, and at the same time write an autobiography which will be discussed in a seminar by the class.[4]

What he would notice in such a course was precisely why in any specific instance it was a '*human* sentence'—what turn or nuance made it so.

That Harvard summer course came to an end all too soon for Clark Blaise. But Malamud kept in contact:

> He had said, as I was leaving after that first summer we met, 'You can ask for any favour.' He said it so forcefully that I never hesitated; so long as I wrote, and wrote as well as I knew how, he would stand behind me. In 1980, when I was forty, he advanced us the down payment for our first American house. But back in the fall of 1961, I was working in a book store in that same university community, when he showed up in the store, quickly inscribed a prominent stack of his new novel, *A New Life*, and when the owner came running over, suspecting vandalism, he said, 'I've signed your stock as a deposit on Blaise's freedom for the afternoon. Let's beat it.'

In the store Blaise was working twelve hours a day without much time to write a book of his own, though he did manage one story in tribute to Malamud and *The Assistant*—'How I Became a Jew'. But there he was that afternoon 'walking with the writer I most admired, answering as best I could *his* questions about me: what did I intend to do with my life? Was I working? Was I happy? What could he do to help?' (*Resident Alien*, 23) That was the afternoon Malamud offered to write the letter that got Blaise into the Iowa

Writers Workshop with a scholarship, the only creative writing programme there was at the time. Malamud was somewhat sceptical about it and about university institutionalization, but because of his new-found fame he could get him in: 'If you want it, I will do it.' In his new prestigious life Malamud liked being able to help strugglers: he had been one such himself, and his success now enabled him to offer others the help that he had needed.

By the close of the year Clark Blaise was thus moving on to Iowa, to be taught by Philip Roth, while Malamud himself was en route to a post at Bennington College. Malamud had been invited to teach at Harvard in 1959 but the Ford Foundation grant would not allow it within its terms. He was to return to Harvard in 1966 and 1967. But on 25 March 1961, he wrote Herb Nelson: 'I have accepted a position at Bennington College, Vermont 1961–2 and therefore request leave of absence from Oregon State University for that period' (OSU box 3). He never went back, save to revisit. He told Rosemarie Beck he had 'no complicated emotions' on leaving the West—all places had simply become 'places to work' (1 June 1961).

The Bennington Move

It was the poet Howard Nemerov who had been mainly instrumental in inviting Malamud to Bennington, at a salary of around $8,000, requiring the teaching of two courses—freshman language and literature, and advanced prose fiction. Gone were the Oregon days of freshman comp. 'Altogether I teach about five hours a week, two on Tuesdays nights,' Malamud wrote Sylvan Karchmer, back in Eugene, Oregon, 'And I have about seven hours of counselling, which is where one's time goes mostly, at Bennington. But the girls are very sensitive to art and literature and it is a pleasure to teach them. Their comprehension is amazing. I'm often surprised at all they see in a piece of fiction; and how quickly they unearth the meaning of it. That they are imaginative and pretty adds to the pleasure' (HRC 11.9).

Bennington had been established in 1932, as a progressive college for young women. Its founders wanted a college community for a town too often deserted for the rest of the year by its summer residents. On the educational model established by the philosopher John Dewey, they sought to create a school that would emphasize the individual student devising her own programme across the disciplines, in consultation with an individual adviser and in the light of her needs. Education was not a regimented preparation for life by means of qualifications, grades, and examinations, but an exploration which never ceased—what Dewey in *Democracy and Education* had called 'an experiment with the world to find out what it is like'. It was to be learning by active and living practice, breaking down the artificial barriers between blocked-out subject areas, between teacher and taught, between the curriculum and the extracurricular, within a community that valued freedom and discovery. In the winter term, students went off to work-experience to connect them with the wider world. The traditional commencement statement, read at every graduation from 1936, expressed its then almost unique ideal:

> Bennington regards education as a sensual and ethical, no less than an intellectual, process. It seeks to liberate and nurture the individuality, the creative intelligence, and the ethical and aesthetic sensibility of its students, to the end that their richly varied natural endowments will be directed toward self-fulfillment and toward constructive social purposes. We believe that these educational goals are best served by demanding of our students active participation in the planning of their own programs, and in the regulation of their own lives on campus. Student freedom is not the absence of restraint, however; it is rather the fullest possible substitution of habits of self-restraint for restraint imposed by others.

When Malamud arrived, there were up to 350 students, all female, sometimes described as 'well-bred, well-read and well-fed'. Ann Malamud found it hard to settle with the reality behind Bennington's boundary-crossing ideals:

> Bennington is small and was kind of navel-contemplating. The college sits on a hill and is isolated. It did not have the communal life I had been used to in Oregon, a big Western open place where we had so many friends. I remember Alex Inkeles, our good friend, saying 'Ann, you're grieving for a lost home.' I don't think wives in general ever had a very happy time there because there were a lot of young, nubile, bright and sometimes quite aggressive young women and a lot of permissiveness as a result. There were too many lines that were crossed. [5]

This was a place so 'sensual', indeed so permissive, that—it was said in unkind jest—faculty were positively required to have allegorical names like Goosen and Feeley. In fact the college's creative idealism was genuine. But it was a virtually all-male faculty, with an all-female student community until 1969, in an intense, remote location. The weekly advisory sessions between individual faculty members and individual students were a form of 'counselling' that ranged from the strictly academic to the personally confessional. They could be good for students in need of confidence-building, but also dangerously tempting in the potential for student crushes and staff exploitation. Some young women thrived and matured in such intervolved relationships, some were expected to become adoring young wives, others were hurt and damaged. Malamud said he was always willing to listen to whatever his students wanted to say, and sometimes indeed he was eager. Though there was gossip—and Malamud loved the gossip—the insular community was discreet and even secretive about the freedom of its sexual liaisons.

But for Malamud it was a world of artists with its own created culture. Bennington had a tradition of taking interesting, creative people, regardless of qualifications—and this included staff as well as students, free to teach whatever was uppermost in their minds: the poets W. H. Auden and Theodore Roethke, the psychologist Erich Fromm, the literary theorist Kenneth Burke, the dancer and choreographer Martha Graham. In the fifties and sixties Clement Greenberg was establishing there a whole school of abstract expressionism, and at various times there were the painters Jules Olitski, Paul Feeley, Pat Longo, and Kenneth Noland, the architect Anthony Caro, the sculptors David Smith, Tony Smith, and Isaac Witkin, the composers Henry Brandt, Lionel Novak, Louis Calabro, and Marc Blitzstein, the cellist George Finckel. Essentially, though they were in academe, they were not academics: they would not become institutionalized teachers, but rather offered themselves, for both good and bad, as human beings in the midst of their own work. Students such as Anne Waldman, the poet, could openly see that 'they were sensitive, troubled humans—often alcoholic—struggling with their work, not resting on their laurels.'[6] In comparison Malamud himself was private, careful and well-prepared, soberly reserved to the point of shyness, and always, as Anne Waldman puts it, 'a master'. But at the point at which Malamud arrived, the dominant and charismatic literary figures were Nemerov and Stanley Edgar Hyman along with the poet Ben Belitt.[7] When he gave the commencement address in Bennington, 12 June 1981, Malamud recalled: 'The best thing about the college has been some of the extraordinary people on its faculty and, of course, a good many of its gifted students. Richness comes from richness; people are the gift—those who give and those who give more. I might also shake a stick at the college and say that given its freedom, its uniqueness, it ought to be better than it is' (LC II 8.15).[8]

Though Hyman, like himself, was a product of Erasmus High, the personal relationship between Malamud and Hyman never prospered. But at the intellectual level, Clark Blaise said that one of the reasons Malamud admired the (in every way) heavyweight Hyman was because Hyman was a critic who did not reduce a work to certain identifiable component parts but tried to swallow it whole: 'I think Bernard felt that Hyman was in his own criticism trying to write a great novel. *The Tangled Branch* about Darwin, Marx, Frazer and Freud as imaginative artists in their own right was a great epic work in which everything he had ever read went in.' It was large-minded thinking in the Bennington tradition—in the sense in which Nemerov in *Reflexions on Poetry and Poetics* (1972) spoke of Kenneth Burke's as a mind explosively wanting 'everything, preferably all at once'. Hyman's famous course, 'Myth, Ritual and Literature', traced literature from its very beginnings: brilliantly harnessing the kind of intellectual destructiveness he found exhilarating in Freud, he sceptically probed the way that texts rationalized themselves, in the effort to justify beliefs and actions. To a young instructor such as Alan Cheuse the scepticism went further: 'Hyman would give you every chance to fail. Malamud would give you every chance to succeed. Malamud was more like the hero in his own *God's Grace*: he gave the animals every chance to be human.'[9] Hyman was married to Shirley Jackson, whose classic short story 'The Lottery' imagined a parochial town like Old Bennington where every year one victim was ritually stoned to death by lot, in the name of unthinking tradition. It was a veiled allegory of what had happened to the Jews in Germany. When she died, it was said that Bennington girls were almost queueing up to be interviewed for the post of her successor as wife.

But above all they adored Howard Nemerov, who was proud, sensitive, hard-drinking, and aristocratically glamorous. Nemerov, Malamud wrote Sylvan Karchmer, 18 November 1961, 'is tall, handsome grayhaired, almost formal, somewhat withdrawn, a man of the highest ideals, some so high for himself that they must bend his back' (HRC 11.9). His major class was called 'Language and Literature' but was mainly about the poems of Donne and of Blake: 'He would talk about the poems and free associate,' Nina Pelikan recalled, 'and he would smoke, and we would smoke and every time he took one of his long Parliaments, everyone would lean forward with a match. And he would shake because he had been a pilot in the war, and we had all sorts of romantic ideas about what he had been through, this heroic man.'[10] Janna recalled Nemerov and her father walking miles together in the snowy woods, in a way that was to serve as a model for the biographer's melancholy walks in *Dubin's Lives*: 'The two men would go out for a couple of hours at a time; Howard, tall, crew-cut, bareheaded, a wool scarf around his neck. Dad shorter, solid in his winter jacket, balding head under a tweed cap' (MFB, 173). Nemerov would say little, except to speak of literature or to point to a bird with his stick and give it a name, and his frequent depression depressed Malamud, who would often come home groaning to his wife, 'Oh, no.' When Janna 'oblivious to [her] own aggression' once told Malamud how much smarter Nemerov was than anyone, including him, he was hurt, as usual, by comparison with a handsome charismatic intellectual (Ibid. 175–6). Yet

Malamud admired Nemerov's intelligence, and knew the pain it cost him: as he put it in a poem on Nemerov which he sent the poet 19 August 1975: [11]

> He sees two 'spects of every thought
> And makes three of two dimensions;
> If there are six
> Like the old monk in the Noh
> He casts a net of metaphor
> And reduces all
> To one speculation.

Malamud loved the artists who added a sense of the extra dimensions of the world, by means of expansive intellect contained within verbal contraction. But in 1963 Nemerov sent Malamud a manuscript-work of self-analysis in which he concluded that all this famed intelligence of his existed only to find what he expected to find: he was a plausible fraud, and there was no self 'only an echoing emptiness within'. Malamud found it dazzlingly brilliant but advised against publication because it was a work of suspect explanation rather than real discovery: 'I miss passion, thunder, protest, and I feel, as you suspect, that ultimately the work camouflages. You do not reveal the true self though you point at it' (HRC 14.9). Nemerov replied laconically that what Malamud 'missed' was what Nemerov simply had not got: self, passion. It was Malamud who believed in such things. And though Malamud did not think Nemerov cold, it was certainly warmth that Malamud believed in. Without it thoughts were not really felt. For all Malamud's anxieties about his own intellect and educational background, for all his defensiveness about sentimentality, it was coldness that remained Malamud's most damning criticism of writers whom otherwise he admired as more formally intelligent than himself.

From Bennington he wrote Rosemarie Beck that he was surprised that for all its creativity and prestige, the place was lonely to him: 'People keep to themselves more than they do in the West' (30 December 1961). When one of his students, Karen Jackel, first encountered him carefully locking up his office in his flat cabby's cap, she took him for the night watchman and asked him to kill a wasp for her (HRC 18.17). This underrated and hidden man, fronting the world with a rather quiet and sad dignity, had worked hard for his success, but sometimes those outside seemed hardly to recognize it in him. And, worse, inside he doubted it himself, finding his triumph a lesser blessing than he had hoped, and fearful of celebrating it for the sake of what might follow. The students were often glamorous but Malamud himself had no glamour. He was also aware of his own limited academic background.

Once, when he was able to put some canny question to a visiting lecturer from Yale, he delightedly told his student Danny Myerson, 'I know some tricks from teaching at high school.'[12] Jay Cantor remembered his own initial impressions as a student in Malamud's writing class when he returned to teach at Harvard in 1966–7: 'Malamud was a short man, with a close-clipped greying mustache, wearing often a grey cloth cap and a somewhat grey and restrained manner. He was surrounded then, and always, by an air that was both melancholy and decisive, as if he were weighed down by the guidance of a special Talmud only he knew about that said he must move, speak, act, in a certain way, whether it gave him pleasure or not.'[13] He carried something apparently as fragile as it was valuable within him, whether it was his gift, his law, or some time bomb from his past. But he was Malamud in its Hebrew meaning, the teacher—elevated and protected in his favoured role of sage, father-figure, helper, master.

But never quite securely. As a little girl in Oregon, Janna remembered listening as he willed himself on: 'I'd hear him shaving in the bathroom, on the bad days cursing quietly to himself, on the good ones announcing to all within range, firmly, audibly, "Someday I'm going to win"' (MFB, 19–20). Yet in a sense that day never came, despite all the awards. Or when it did come, all the suppressed needs and insecurities from the first life came back into the life which had strugglingly redeemed it, and made for a third life, a middle age, that threatened to lose or spoil the gains of the second. 'No matter how much happiness or success you collect,' he was to tell Michiko Kakutani in the *New York Times*, 15 July 1980, 'you cannot obliterate your early experience—diminished perhaps, it stays with you' (HRC 33.9). At the same time, that first life also seemed no good to Malamud, was exhausted, as a source for further writing, in his casting about for new subject-matter and further development. And at yet another level, historically in the acceleration of American development, a man who was emphatically a product of the depressed thirties of Brooklyn found himself suddenly in the liberated sixties of Bennington.

There was a project for this third life—one that was to balance him more equitably between writing and living. He wrote Rosemarie Beck, 3 April 1959, 'The more I see of artists the more I think of the great talent in the frail self.' How many 'nebbishes'—weak, spineless people—look good, he said to her, because of 'this marvellous book of magic in them'. What Malamud wanted, he told her, was to 'look good as a man', to use some of his magical talent as an artist to 'improve as a person'. It 'goes with the theory I have of the person as "stuff"': 'stuff' was the raw material of one's life, and self-will could be deployed to reshape that stuff and form it creatively not just in writing but in living. In turn, it was this creativity in life that might most improve the writing: 'I think that art would be richer if the self were.' That is what, for all his own troubles, D. H. Lawrence was to stand for in the writing of *Dubin's Lives*: the challenge to the writer not to use writing in place of living. But on 6 November 1959 Malamud wrote Rosemarie Beck that he was moved to read in Richard Ellmann's biography that Joyce called himself, 'the foolish writer of a wise book': 'It's true—one garners his strengths for his books and remains a weakling ... But what of his insane daughter Lucia, who might with more love and care on his part have lived a useful life, at least fulfilled herself a bit as a woman?' It was not that Joyce did not love his daughter in his way, but 'he could not help but come first with himself.' What—or who in the family that remained—could Malamud help?

He needed to help himself also, to live more. Malamud had long since limited his life for the sake of his work—or at least rationalized his ingrown limitations by that means. Yet at the same time, he feared increasingly that his work would be damaged by that very limitation of his experience, especially when he had used up his childhood experience. He wanted, as ever, to break the circle. One of the epigraphs to *Pictures of Fidelman* (1969) was taken from Yeats: 'The intellect of man is forced to choose | Perfection of the life, or of the work'. Fidelman cried: Both; Malamud still feared: Neither. Yet he invented worlds, characters, stories. How many lives could he himself have, and have now, hungrily, at once and all together?

As Doris Milman, a friend of his youth, had said: Malamud was not simply a dissembler but 'it was characteristic of him that he presented himself differently to different people' (10 March 1988, HRC 15.7). Thus the young writers and would-be writers who now began to surround Malamud in his fame, the students and young colleagues who became the sons and the daughters of Bern—together they provide between them a varied multiple picture at the commencement of those difficult years.

'Some Have to Wait to Be Seen'

It was a second family for Malamud. As his Bennington colleague Claude Fredericks was to remark in his journal for 30 July 1980, Malamud was at his fondest 'when he is doing a favor, when he is needed and helping, when he feels his own necessary sense of virtue in active play.'

The young men brought their future wives to him. In December 1963 Clark Blaise brought a fellow-writer, Bharati Mukherjee, whom he had married in September. At first the idea of a marriage between two writers worried Malamud, but gradually Bharati became a figure recognized in her own right and a daughter. Later she dedicated her first collection of short stories to Malamud because she had seen in a selection of his stories, quite suddenly, a version of her own predicament as an Indian amidst the racism of Canada, where the couple lived in the 1970s. 'His Jewish characters, trying to accommodate, assimilate, negotiating division: I thought, my God, that is what we're doing, trying to walk the tightrope of wanting to belong and at the same time not be inundated by the demands of the mainstream.'[14] Literature offered the alternative belonging, and Malamud read the manuscripts, offered the loans, wrote the references which his people needed

Sometimes these sons and daughters felt like replacements for the first family. 'But I think,' said Clark, 'that what he wanted for all of us, including his son, was to find some way in which we could be happy and productive.' To Clark Blaise's mind, if it was he who was Malamud's good son, the steady one, then it was Philip Roth of course—nineteen years Malamud's junior—who was, as ever, cast as the bad one. Roth and Malamud had already met in Oregon in 1960. According to Malamud, Roth had given a lecture including an account of Malamud's fiction which made Roth in turn uneasy and later apologetic, with Malamud there in front of him, and left Malamud himself irritated but finally appeased by a high rating. According to their host later that evening, the two had talked about how, amidst a heavy teaching schedule and family responsibilities, Malamud had been able to produce world-class fiction. Malamud explained his routine and then proceeded to leave for bed:

> Heading out, jaw set, he delivered his curtain line with quiet fervor: 'I am a *very* disciplined man.' And then he jerked open the door of—and stepped into—the closet.
>
> It was an easy error; the doors were adjacent and nearly identical. In the midst of our laughter, Malamud stood silent but with his stolid face eloquently saying something about, no, it wasn't done for dramatic effect, nor would he pretend so after the fact, and no, his final sentence was still true, and a mistaken door was simply a part of the surtax to be paid by everyone on the planet, and if we could understand that, then (small lip twitch), well, perhaps it was a tiny bit comic.[15]

Roth was always comically annoyed to think that whenever he eventually settled down to his morning's writing, Malamud somewhere had already been hard at it for two hours. In turn, Malamud half-envied Roth, like Bellow, for being so exuberantly prolific: 'I met Philip Roth. He has a novel coming out and another done. I looked at him. "Psychoanalysis and laxatives," he said' (HRC 21.7). It was Saul Bellow who was ruefully to describe himself,

Malamud, and Roth as the Jewish literary equivalent of the first-generation rag trade gone upmarket—the Hart, Schaffner, and Marx of literature.

It was Roth's *The Ghost Writer* (1979) that was written partly in memory of Malamud in Bennington. E. I. Lonoff was the austere older writer in the book, a city Jew strangely secluded in the New England countryside, who looked like nothing more than an insurance agent or the local inspector of schools. Malamud always claimed that Lonoff was modelled on Bashevis Singer and on the *Partisan Review* editor and critic Philip Rahv as well as himself. Hope, the unhappy neurotic stifled by her husband's vocation, was closer, he said, to Tolstoy's wife than to his own. But the room that the young aspirant Nathan Zuckerman sleeps in, with the wall of books, was the one in the house that the Malamuds bought in 1968 at Catamount Lane, in which Roth himself slept. 'He was saying to me, "I turn sentences around. That's my life. I write a sentence and then I turn it round. Then I look at it and turn it around again." '[16] Zuckerman reminds Lonoff that Babel said that if ever he wrote an autobiography he would call it *The Story of an Adjective*: in the inconceivable event of his writing it, says Zuckerman, that is what Lonoff's own life-story would have to be called. When at day's end Lonoff finically describes to his young devotee how to work his temperamental record player should he want to use it, Zuckerman realizes that this 'is the excruciating scrupulosity, the same maddening, meticulous attention to every last detail that makes you great' (*The Ghost Writer*, 66). 'Oh, the fussiness, the fastidiousness! The floorwalker incarnate! To wrestle the blessing of his fiction out of that misfortune—"triumph" didn't begin to describe it' (Ibid. 67).

'Where I said I had become more *flexible*,' Malamud told an interviewer, editing as he went along, 'Could you change this to more *relaxed*?' (HRC 31.6).

In Roth's comic exaggeration of exaggeration's own opposite, the really wild part of Lonoff's week consists of going to teach in the college. On Sundays for a change and as a concession, he breakfasts late, reads the papers with Hope, and they go for a walk in the hills—until his evident desire to get back to work makes her turn round. 'I am haunted by the loss of all that good time. I wake up Sunday mornings and I'm nearly crazy at the prospect of all those unusable hours' (*The Ghost Writer*, 19). He asks himself, 'Why is there no way but this for me to fill my hours?' (Ibid. 20). Nothing else happened (Nothing? thinks Zuckerman: Genius happened! Art happened!): only reading and writing, drafting and re-drafting. He wouldn't try to write after early afternoon when he is tired if he could think of anything else to do. This man isn't Saul Bellow, who becomes Felix Abravanel in Roth's novel—a handsome, charismatic man of electric intellect who needs the large human types he portrays in his fiction in order to match and challenge himself. Abravanel dismisses Lonoff as 'the complete man'—so self-sufficiently pared down as to be as unimpressive as he was unimpressed.

And this had its Chaplinesque comic side. On one of his London stays in the early sixties, Malamud, preparing to visit the beautiful Irish novelist Edna O'Brien at her home, gallantly sent on ahead of himself a full dozen red roses. When he arrived, however, he carefully counted only nine—the rest, it turned out, were given away to the girl next door. Disappointed, he went away again, three roses down. One slushy winter's evening in New York some time in the seventies, according to Janna Malamud Smith, the artist Helen Frankenthaler laughed at a Malamud calling to take her to dinner, wearing rubber galoshes over his shoes (MFB, 211). 'I may be comic and even silly,' Malamud said to Claude Fredericks over the telephone, towards the end of his life, 'but I am one of those strange creatures, a *good* man.'[17]

Then again, back in Bennington there was Malamud the host. If Malamud held a dinner party, people didn't arrive late, but nor should they arrive early. Minutes before the prescribed time, there would often be an orderly queue forming in the Malamud driveway. When Alan Cheuse arrived late for a Malamud birthday party, he was lucky to be able to produce a speeding ticket. Malamud abruptly took it off him, saying 'Let me see that,' and then, sweetly, 'It's my birthday,' and paid it promptly the following day. 'Bern is always early,' noted Claude Fredericks, 31 July 1980, 'imagining everyone who isn't already there late or never coming at all.' Earlier that June Fredericks forgot to announce a class Malamud was due to hold, and Malamud arrived to find no students were awaiting him and he had come in vain: the result was first disappointment, then anger.

But beneath the obsessive orderliness, that anxious and fussy need for precision which he somehow channelled into creativity, Clark Blaise knew of something serious that Malamud had never even told his own wife. Blaise recalled:

In the seventies and eighties my mother was dying of Alzheimer's, and I was seeing myself in that light, as someone who would be prone to it. In the early eighties I had a strong sense in fact that I was losing the kind of fluency that I had had at one time. I knew that Bern had always been the type that carried around that little yellow notebook with him, and he would always make notes to himself, and if there was a phone call he would jot down the things he wanted to say, and if he was in a conversation sometimes he would still be jotting things down in front of people. He said he felt very early in his life, in his twenties, that he had had some kind of stroke or debilitating blow that had made him become this note-taking premeditated kind of person.

Whether this was a physical or psychological event, or indeed true at all, it helps explain why he seemed to his son Paul to have a 'slow, deliberate, cautious manner':

> He made notes about everything—reading, writing, teaching, personal mat-
> ters—in a peculiar crabbed hand that was difficult to read. Sometimes in the
> morning when he was shaving, he could call out to me or to Mother and ask
> us to note a word or phrase on a writing pad, so that he would not lose it. I'm
> sure whatever he was working on was on his mind most of the time. He tended
> to read the way he wrote—slowly but thoroughly, underlining all kinds of key
> words, phrases, or thoughts he considered important.   (MWB, 6)

All that which seemed so schoolmasterly slow—always doing in at least two goes what occasionally at least might have been done well enough in one—was the work of a second self guarding and checking a first one which, wrapped up in concentrated attention, had to be nursed into its sporadic gifts of insight. The fearsome difficulty might be physiological in origin, but it was also plausibly the result of overconsciousness of educational deficiency, or the felt want of a greater, easier sort of talent, or an impoverishment in self-confidence. But inside that slow old-fashioned machine, that knew no short cuts and could function only as a cumbersome whole, was the hidden intensity of a massive pressure cooker.

Roth's Lonoff just looks at the blank snow. And looking at Bennington snow was indeed what Malamud did. From a college-rented house in the Orchard, early on in his Bennington years, he wrote more powerfully to one of his students than he usually bothered to do in a letter, 'Winter has surprised me,' he says to Arlene Heyman, 6 January 1962:

> But the true beauty of winter is visual. We live on the campus now—moved on
> the first of January, and from my window in the morning my first sight is the
> vast white sweep of the hills and trees, and in the background the mountains. I
> walk to my office along the path by the pond, enjoying the sensation of being
> alone on the landscape, and remembering what it was like as a child to walk in
> snow to school; only then, in the city streets, there was an ambitious stamping
> of one's footmarks on the clean white snow, a symbolic conquering of space,
> and destruction of white experience. Now the emotion is in looking, in the
> poetry of white, with hills, and the white rhythms that feed the hungry eye.[18]

Yet this was not merely looking at snow: something else was also going on inside those terms, connected with being a mature writer, that shifted the emphasis from first-person stamping to the third-person register of other rhythms—though the 'ambition' was still contained in the 'hunger'. It has to do with what Roth's Lonoff says, in reply to Hope's complaint that he shows concern for everyone in need—except for himself and his own needs: 'Only my "self", as you like to call it, happens not to exist in the ordinary sense of the word' (*The Ghost Writer*, 39).

Others sensed this about Malamud. The self, he had told Rosemarie Beck, was 'stuff' and the writer was an 'instrument' to work upon it. More simply, Malamud's own publisher, Roger Straus, did not even believe that his author had a life as such. Malamud did not seek publicity; he would not be tied down by advances; he did not haggle much over terms, noted Straus, 'and I don't think there were affairs. Everything was up here, in the head, nothing down there.' When he was asked what he thought of a biography of Malamud, Straus laughed: 'I think it's ridiculous. There was nothing there; as a life it was unexciting. Saul Bellow was filet mignon, Malamud was hamburger.'[19] The glamorously rich and loudly exuberant Straus possessed that 'animal magnetism' which Malamud also associated with Bellow: Malamud knew that Straus thought him to be his dull social inferior, in origin the poor Eastern European Jew as compared to the rich German version. Malamud said once to Giroux, 'Bob, did you think Roger was rude to me?' Giroux admitted it of his partner and was sorry.[20] For all Straus' entrepreneurial flamboyance, it was Giroux, Malamud believed, who 'sets the feeling of the house' (HRC 10.5).

Letty Cottin Pogrebin was a friend who repeated the Bellow–Malamud comparison: 'Bellow had a personality that was big and public and readily described. The thing about Bern that was so interesting was that he seemed to want a personality. They were like Mozart and Salieri and Bern, I think, saw himself as Salieri. If he had been born at another time, without Bellow there before him and Roth a little after him, he would have stood alone and been great. Perhaps if any one of them had been alone in that age, they would have been the age's Shakespeare. But it always seemed as though they were ranking and being ranked. And I wonder if Bern ranked himself low.'[21] When Bellow won the Nobel Prize in 1976 and virtually ended Malamud's own chances, Malamud tried hard not to seem envious, but he wrote ruefully in his notebook for *Dubin's Lives*: '21 October Bellow gets Nobel Prize. I win $24.25 in poker' (HRC 19.5). The minor gain was at the notorious Bennington poker school where Malamud alone went home early after making one or two drinks last the night. When he went to the horse races at Saratoga Springs with Howard Nemerov, Malamud lost seven dollars and Nemerov twenty-one—'which means he was three times more adventurous than I' (MFB, 174).

Even his good friend, the novelist Daniel Stern, recognized that he knew only a very little of the man's inner life: 'There was much given and much held in reserve. He was available, helpful, richly involved in a friend's life. And yet there was always some held back, private—something perhaps he was not even aware of. I think he felt, with his somewhat austere vision of life that friends had somehow to earn each other. I think, except as an artist, he was not entirely available to himself' (MWB, 29). Inhibition overlapped with safe keeping.

But it was a student from the early days at Bennington, a sophomore on Malamud's arrival there, who came to understand him in terms of those flowing 'rhythms' he felt in the snow—Nina Pelikan Straus:

> He was too emotional a man for there to be rigid separations finally. I think he appeared compartmentalized because it was so necessary. He needed to be a respectable husband, and he needed to be a writer, and he needed his discipline, and he had to be a father. But emotionally this man flowed like a river, and the people who didn't see it, they found him stiff. I think of him as a canal: the river flows but then there's this lock, and you have to wait. If you see the outside of the man, it seemed locked up. But I felt this current.

When, later in their continuing relationship, they sat together at a Bach concert—and Malamud loved Casals' comment that Bach should be played as though he were a gypsy or a Jew[22]—they began to feel themselves in unison and Malamud was happy in the physical comfort. The undoubtedly sensual element in the relationship was not consummated but transformed. On the whole, Nina found Malamud could be more open in his letters than he could personally, and she herself had a voice that came across in that medium. Where Ann and he could be so abrupt and nervy with each other, Malamud liked the mellifluous in others. Nina, for one, did not rattle him and could manage the flow between them without it becoming sexual as such. Kate Hickler, a Harvard student of his in 1966, thought that the lonely Malamud was a more nuanced sort of person than the rest of his immediate family and that too often the responses he got were either too cold or over-bald and literal.[23]

Rhythm was important to Malamud in his working conditions. He kept his routine going, as a rhythm in search of the beat and the breakthrough. As he wrote to Arlene Heyman, 18 January 1963, in her own writer's apprenticeship:

> One thing about writing, you have to create rhythm for it. It's rough if you work and quit, work and quit; you have to stay at it almost everyday if only for a little. The quitting seems to check the flow of ideas, associations and images. Then you have to break through again into the rhythm. Having a bad time at the beginning is almost necessary, it's nothing more than the struggle to create and it's continually a struggle except that if you keep at

it right the struggle can become a dance. This week I'm dancing; I hope you are.

He remembered reading Hemingway in his youth—the rhythmic effects of the clean simple sentences, the incantatory and repetitive qualities close to the English of the King James Bible—and he told Nina, 'I was like the body of a cello which Hemingway drew his bow across. Hemingway was vibrating with the thing unsaid, which ultimately became death.'

The rhythm between Malamud and Nina Pelikan gave her access to something hidden underneath that ordinary fixed and formal self of his—something emotionally beneath it which, as Daniel Stern indicated, Malamud himself could rarely get to except through his writing. As for Nina:

> I wanted him to be my friend and my ethical father. He would talk about wanting to be *used*, which was a new concept to me and a very unusual thing for a man to say. What he had to give, he wanted to give. He said to me that he could love himself because he was a writer, because in that way he could give and could use *himself.*

He would give money anonymously through a third party; at his best, he would help someone who didn't like him or whom he didn't like: it did not matter—somebody should do it, and when not oppressed by his own poor needs he could be that somebody.[24] There was a tone in him that Nina recognized: 'I didn't know Jews. But there was something very familiar and moving in his voice, as well as the voice of his fiction, which came to me from my Russian background. The Russian Jews preserved a nineteenth-century sensibility in the depth of soul and a real sense of suffering and of compassion with it.' Malamud loved to fantasize that Nina's mother was a Russian aristocrat, a queen to Nina's princess. But Nina could hear his deeper note at key moments both in his letters to her and in conversations from which she wrote notes. Thus when he spoke of Thoreau's dictum about the mass of men living lives of quiet desperation, of silent misery: 'Some men are so low they have no song. One must allow people to have their share before they go. Even to let them get in your way, allow people their faults.' Or again, when he spoke to her of the temptation that came with beauty, and how beauty excited: 'I did not excite this kind of beauty. I had beauty of self, of soul. Some have to wait to be seen.' That is why Roth's Zuckerman wants truly to *see* Lonoff: 'When you admire a writer you become curious. You look for his secret. The clues to his puzzle' (*The Ghost Writer*, 46). For always in Malamud there was 'the thing unsaid', as he had put it of Hemingway, which got said finally only within the work. Danny Stern knew that reserve.

And so did Nina Straus—as she had become on marrying Roger Straus III after doing her work experience at the father's publishing firm. In 1974 she was tentatively planning to write her PhD on Malamud's fiction. 'I have been getting deeper into your fiction,' she wrote Malamud in May 1975, 'and it seems suddenly odd that there is YOU and then, there is YOURS. The relation between the artist and his work is insanely complex' (HRC 18.5). But it was that relationship, together with her own knowledge of the man and the teacher, which she was seeking to investigate. 'Use me,' he had said to her.

The PhD was abandoned when the wife of the dean at Nina's college set herself up in irresistible competition. But amongst the clues to the puzzle of Malamud one story particularly fascinated her in her preliminary researches. In 'Still Life', a Fidelman love-story originally published in *Idiots First* in 1963, the protagonist is a failing, would-be artist, the name taken of course from the family of Malamud's mother. Letting go of Malamud's own discipline and leaving America and Judaism behind, Fidelman humbly desires Annamaria, whom he mistakenly thinks a better painter than he, and wants her to use him absolutely—to let him love her, and shop and cook and clean for her. But because he is non-existent to her, he does not exist for himself, cannot respect himself, and can hardly paint. It is Malamud's fantasy of a slavish sexuality, wildly close to masochism. With her little religious crosses hidden under every painting she does, Annamaria keeps on tormenting him, denying him, creating the sexuality of longing and pain by daily crucifying him a little. Then one day as Fidelman desperately tries to recover his art by painting himself in Catholic vestments, cassock and biretta, in imitation of Rembrandt's 'Portrait of the Artist as Priest', he suddenly finds her seeking from him in this guise confession, penance, punishment—and finally sexual violation itself as some aroused expression of all three, as though in some strange dream of Frank Alpine's. Fidelman ends the story thus, suddenly, recovering manhood: 'Pumping slowly he nailed her to her cross.'

She knew from her own experience how tangled up Malamud could be, how the idea of service to others could veer off to extremes of masochism or narcissism, or abruptly provoke an angry counter-reaction in himself. 'He warned against the sexuality of my generation, and yet at the same time there was a great longing for that very thing which the rabbi in him preached against.' The tension could produce a frighteningly sudden inconsistency in his behaviour, without a rhythm. She was nineteen when she would tell him stories about her boyfriends, and he would enjoy them, analyse them, and give her advice. But then one day 'Malamud obviously felt some complicated thing: that I wasn't paying attention to him, as to how he was feeling. One of his feelings was, I knew, "How dare she go on, she who has so many boyfriends" ':

> And then he thrust out his shoe at me and he said, 'Tie my shoe'. I was so shocked. I tied his shoe and we went on. I thought, 'He's humiliating me because I don't appreciate the love that I'm getting.' But it wasn't, 'Take my shoe off'; it was 'Tie my shoe.' Now I think there were a lot of complex layers: humiliation of the person, aggression, envy, irritation; the master teaching a lesson in humility; tying the shoe tight that would rather be untied.[25]

More than ten years later she wrote him, 11 September 1974, 'Do you remember my tying your shoe one time. I asked you why, and you said: "To teach you humility" ' (HRC 18.5). He replied with rather appalled contrition on September 16: 'Next time *I* tie *your* shoes. My God, the hubris. It's all right to teach someone but not unlearn the lesson in the process.' At the time, in his partiality, the man could not see the two things simultaneously together: the pride involved in teaching the humility. But in the act of retrospection, he could see with the third eye of a man, beyond himself, who knew how often his characteristic inadequacy had been to half *un*do even in the act of doing. It was through this 'stuff' of memory-work that the man became the novelist, and it was the novelist in Malamud who could look through the written and unwritten pages of his mistakes and indignities and see the underlying story, the causes beforehand and the regrets thereafter.

But still it was the novelist in *The Ghost Writer* who saw deepest. It was not only that Philip Roth imaginatively guessed at the possibility of an affair with a younger woman. He also registered that shrewd truth with the naïve shock also appropriate to it, for the sons of Bern:

> They have been lovers! Yet when I tried to imagine E. I. Lonoff stripped of his suit and on his back, Amy naked and astride his belly, I couldn't, no more than any son can.
>   *I don't think I could keep my wits about me, teaching such beautiful and gifted and fetching girls.*
>   *Then you shouldn't do it.*
>   Oh, Father, is this so, were you the lover of this love-sick, worshipful, displaced daughter half your age? Knowing full well you'd never leave Hope? You succumbed too? Can that be? *You?*   (*The Ghost Writer*, 152)

No surprise perhaps were it Bellow or Mailer or Roth himself, but that it was Malamud—and that *that*, and not just life in the study, was his private life. The novelist Roxana Robinson, who was at Bennington from 1964 to 1966, remembered the anecdote Malamud told against himself concerning Norman Mailer's apartment situated high on the roof-top. Mailer prided himself on entering without putting a hand on the railings; Malamud, he reported of himself, typically used both.

Malamud—the man who knew he was without animal magnetism; the compulsive creator of routine and order; the writer whose work fought hard for the rescue of the moral life—now the lover! He was 47 and the young woman in question was 19.

'A Right Theme in Bennington'

Arlene Heyman, a beautiful Jewish would-be writer who had been at Bennington since 1959, became Malamud's student in that first winter term of his. Their affair began over the Christmas break in 1961—'I remember being in his office when he asked me whether I would meet him in New York. It made me quite nervous but excited.' [26] Technically off-campus, it continued in New York where, during the non-resident term of work experience, he had got her a placement at Farrar Straus Giroux. Malamud was besotted, recapturing a youth he had hardly had in the first place. Over the months and throughout 1962, there are a series of undated little notes he dropped into her mail box on campus: 'I hope you are yourself today, your lovely best self: you deserve to be. If you're not away come up for a while bet[ween] 2–3.' 'How much I appreciate you'; 'What a lovely smile for the world at large'; 'I love you. B.'; 'Keep the notes coming; I love 'em'; 'You are always kind, your soul glows in you'; 'You're one of the most beautiful people I've met in my life. I want your life to be as beautiful, as lovely as you are.' When she talks of changing her hair and eyebrows, she is answered lyrically: 'My guess is I'd find you pretty either way, cymbals or cello' (29 June 1962).

The thought of her got in amidst his work: 'Funny—I knew I had something to say and was racking my brains for something I had left out of my writing, but it was just to wish you the nice world always.' Even the normally time-obsessed man is somewhat modified: 'I notice I've been finishing work by 4.15. Please come up whenever you feel like it, at that time.' Arlene recalled: 'He waited for me here, there and everywhere, and when I think about it, it was awful. I was young and not fully aware of the impact of myself on somebody else.'

Lovers and Ghosts was an unpublished novel she wrote many years later.[27] In the beginning the young woman is oddly shy of being seen naked. 'I'll cover you with my body,' her artist mentor said, the first time. Yet gradually in the dark beneath the covers:

she was daring, touching him in places only his mother had touched before. He wanted to reciprocate but was unpractised, had come of age, he told her, in a sexually unadventurous time ....

Despite the twenty-eight years difference, she turned out to be more sexually experienced ... He was curious and impassioned and grateful to her in his shyly arrogant way, claiming that in his late forties, she'd restored his youth to him. He spent his early years painting, and working to earn money, a necessary waste. 'I deserve you,' he said. 'At least I hope I do'

He had said 'I deserve you' to Arlene in real life, in pride and gratitude; he had written it, earlier, as what Levin had said to Pauline in *A New Life*, published the year he first arrived. Pauline had said apologetically, 'I'm sorry, you deserve better' and 'You don't deserve this,' and both times Levin had replied, defiantly, 'I deserve you.' Malamud had also told Arlene of his unhappy childhood—and indeed that is what makes the passing reference to the mother, in the passage above, itself a 'daring' touch: 'touching him in places only his mother had touched before'. It was to be in Arlene's voice that the beautiful young Fanny calls upon the ageing Dubin in *Dubin's Lives*: ' "Lover, father, friend—love me, I love you." The self-conceived defensive ice had broken; the river of feeling flowed' (*Dubin's Lives*, 262).

Father, mother, lover, daughter, student, teacher: Malamud relished the unexpected combinations of a freer life and the rich defiance of order in the sudden shift or overflow of apparently fixed roles and years and relationships. He loved too the fantasy of the all-healing woman, taking away the scars left by the mother. And Thomas Mann's *The Holy Sinner* became a key text for him at Bennington: 'he was a man and she a woman ... that is all Nature cares about' ('The Wedding'). Unaware of incest, the young man innocently in the arms of an older woman, so curiously near to his own nature, finds 'childlike reverence mingled strangely with male ecstasy': 'In her arms, on her gentle breast he enjoyed profound blessedness, the sweet security of the nursing babe, and no less mighty male delight' ('Jeschute').

Arlene Heyman was youthfully earnest, eager to learn and improve. Away from him in the summer of 1962, she writes about changing oneself: 'It is a problem of attacking warped unconscious patterns by straight thinking, by conscious effort. And the unconscious is the stronger of the two. The pattern has been there for so long'. She had identified in herself what she called the 'Please love me' syndrome, which in her case, she thought, took the form of 'Love me so I know I'm good'. He offered his belief in her, what he called a vote of confidence. In her own creative writing as a result, she urged upon herself her own demanding version of Malamud's habits, though he urged her against over-extreme discipline. Not eating properly, not seeing people, not smoking—he urged her not to tie all these up with writing, for that was to press too hard upon the writing, and 'don't tie that up with me' (6 July 1963).

Yet in the intoxicating mixture of the intellectual and the sexual, he took her education upon himself. They went together to museums and art galleries. 'He felt for the lives of the painters as if he knew them,' she recalled. He was good at making her almost literally *see* the place of a painting in an artist's life, its relation to his triumphs or his difficulties. He seemed to have *learned* how to love these things and made her feel she could learn that too. He advised her also on her reading and its role in a writer's life:

> The best time to read is between writing your stories, and the best effect would be—it seemed so in my case—that a story will so light you that you will have a deeper vision of what you ought to be doing yourself. I had that vision when I read Sherword Anderson, and the curious thing is that he is not so good, on the whole, as some short story writers ... The point is that when you feel a sudden shaft of light in yourself after reading a story, you must ask yourself what did it and then you can do it.   (29 June 1963)

'What did it': this is what literature could do for the reader-writer by the trigger of example. It could light up for you what you had not known you cared about, what excited and moved you, from outside-in.

'The Priest' was the first story she submitted to him, concerning a defrocked Spanish Jesuit priest who became involved with a prostitute. Malamud wrote her in December 1962, 'I've not read anything by a student that has this force'. It won a prize in a national contest for stories from college magazines which he had encouraged her to enter. At the end of spring term 1963, Malamud submitted his instructor's final report on her three-story creative thesis: 'All in all the work is mature, solid, disciplined, praiseworthy. The stories are related in theme (in essence the search for freedom from the neurotic self through sex to love) and characterization: the burdened (man) and insufficient (woman) self.'

By letter they argued over Yeats and his long frustrated love for Maud Gonne. She thought no artistic truth could come out of a love so distortingly unhappy and so obsessively fixated. Malamud half-thought of himself in reply: 'He created a magnificent beauty out of his frustration ... As for frustration, his, I can see nothing wrong in being "fixed" so that you want love all of your life' (27 July 1962). What shines through his poetry, he went on:

> is not distortion or poison but suffering, beauty, discipline, art. I am not arguing for his experience, would not want it for myself, even to be as great as he was, but you misinterpret what he made of it. It racked but enlarged his

emotions; it filled him with longing, dreams, ambition, lust; with the vision of the most profound, most beautiful love. (10 August 1962)

Maud Gonne was to Yeats, he argued, 'the equivalent of Dostoyevsky's prison experiences': years later she herself said that if she had married Yeats Ireland would have lost a great poet. It was 'good for an artist to possess another self'. In turn, whether he glimpsed its future use to him or not, *Dubin's Lives* was to come out of the power of this relationship.

One day, whilst she was still his student, he read to Arlene, Chekhov's short story 'The Lady with the Dog', alone in his office. There were all the elements: the older man, his secret relationship with a younger woman, and his own wife and children. His young daughter asks him, 'Why doesn't it ever thunder in winter, Papa?' and he tries to explain:

> As he was speaking, he kept reminding himself that he was going to a rendezvous and that not a living soul knew about it, or, probably, ever would. He led a double life—one in public, in the sight of all whom it concerned, full of conventional truth and conventional deception, exactly like the lives of his friends and acquaintances, and another which flowed in secret. And owing to some strange, possibly quite accidental chain of circumstances, everything that was important, interesting, essential, everything about which he was sincere and never deceived himself, everything that composed the kernel of his life, went on in secret ...

'He was very moved,' Arlene Heyman recalled, 'I remember him reading and his eyes were wet. By then we were having an affair and I am sure he identified with what was going on in that story.' The story goes on:

> Suddenly he caught sight of himself in the looking-glass. His hair was already beginning to turn gray .... Time had passed, he had met one woman after another, become intimate with each, parted with each, but had never loved .... And only now, when he was gray-haired, had he fallen in love properly, thoroughly, for the first time in his life.

What had given him back his youth now accelerated the feeling of age, like a sudden internal blow. As Malamud was to write in *Dubin's Lives*, 'One paid for the pursuit of youth ... Wanting that much to be young was a way of hurrying time. The years ran forward backward' (*Dubin's Lives* 285).

In their real-life relationship there had been inevitable tense imbalances from the first. Malamud apologized for his own over-sensitivity and 'certain ineptnesses':

> You haven't said so but at this stage I'm convinced I owe you an apology for several unjust remarks and for involving you in some unpleasant emotions. My only excuse is the confusion of being myself involved.

At first I felt bad; regretting the asymmetry of the one-sided. But then I thought
if it was one-sided I can depend on her generosity somehow to redress the
balance. She will make it not bad.

'I can depend on her generosity': the writer in him knew the imaginative
difference it might make to address her for once in the third person rather
than demandingly or apologetically in the second. Yet still there was the
fear of emotional blundering or painful dependency, in a relationship of
potentially foolish imbalance. There were also the characteristic signs of this
not-so-young lover. Soberly kind and chivalrous, but fatherly and fussy, he
asks her for a walk, warning her to be 'warmly dressed, the country roads can
be cold at twilight'; he promises to teach her how to keep her 'checkbook
balanced'. And once in apparent apology for some shortness of manner, there
is this, poignantly, from the old life: 'My brother is sick; it upset me. I was
waiting for that phone call.'

   In the novel Arlene wrote after his death, Malamud is made into Murray
Blumgarten, a distinguished painter with the face of a Jewish businessman.
Leda is a young art student, intense and inchoate: she finds herself gaining
ten pounds, then losing fifteen, changing her hair colour every few months
and plucking her eyebrows now this way, now that: 'he said he didn't
understand why she was dissatisfied with her natural beauty, but he loved
her, cymbals or cello'. Her youthfulness becomes vitality again when she
teases him 'by throwing his clothes to the not-so-far corners of her studio
apartment. (Sometimes he chased after each article of clothing to lay it down
neatly on the arm of her couch, which made her smile.)' He for his part
teaches her as part of their love: 'Going to a gallery with him was like seeing
with five eyes, her two and his three' (which was what Malamud said he
felt like going to a show with his painter-friend Karl Schrag). He tries to
help her get more integrated, shows her how to give a routine 'rhythm' to
her disorganized work. She herself paints, often without hope. He sends
her Malamudian postcards: 'Believe in your wonderful self', 'At least believe
in my belief'. When she models for him, he tells her, 'Your soul glows
in you.' She leaves by the bedside a pitcher of ice water for her lover to
drink. In one of Malamud's drafts for *Dubin's Lives*, Fanny, pouring water,
is all that his wife Kitty is not: 'He saw it as a wifely act. Kitty had never
brought him a glass of water after sex, nor had he got her one. He got
her a tissue. Fanny seemed to need none. What happened in or around sex
never bothered her. Kitty took a hot shower; Fanny drank a glass of water'
(LC I 5.2).

   In Arlene's story, Leda remains on her side almost unconsciously
self-absorbed and inchoate. She does not quite put to herself the questions

that hang around her—what was she doing? Should she feel guilty towards Murray's wife 'old enough to be her mother'? Was she really thinking of marriage to a man so much older? These are thoughts projected instead through him:

> How a man who never changed a stroke of his painting to please anyone managed to live a double life she didn't know. He seldom spoke about his wife—to protect her? Which *her*? Almost the only remarks Leda remembered him making were that if his wife received a gift, she gave something away ...
>
> Leda believed he rarely slept with Sigrid (once he let slip that she complained about his bad breath—Leda sniffed prodigiously, but detected nothing) although Leda imagined she accepted him dutifully when he (dutifully?) offered himself. Unasked, he told Leda twice that he would never leave his wife—her mother had died when she was four, and Murray did not think she could survive another abandonment.

In Roth's version, Lonoff says, 'You don't chuck a woman out after thirty-five years because you'd prefer to see a new face over your orange juice' (*The Ghost Writer*, 64).

The affair came to an end in the summer of 1963, with painful memories on both sides for the bad parting. He had warned her about getting vaguely and transiently involved with several young men. Logically she felt she could have argued back, 'Look you're married, how can you possibly ...? '; but she also knew that she would not have been behaving that way if she had been in a better state:

> I felt the age difference and felt I should be with younger men—not anybody in particular, but I said to him that I had to be with somebody I could marry and he valued that. I think he said to me at some point that just when he would be ready to come for me, I might be involved with somebody else, and that would be very hard for him. He tried not to talk too much about his wife and did not wish to visit harm upon her, but I know he said that if I couldn't get myself to be faithful, then it wasn't going to work out. It would murder him.

They were together in Italy that summer of 1963, whilst she was on her way to a Fulbright scholarship in Spain after graduation from Bennington. But their time together was cut short. Upset by her flirtations, Malamud sensed that he was the one who had to make the deduction from her behaviour and the decision that followed from it. As a result he abruptly left Genoa on his own, deeply upset, though trying still to be kind and making sure she made her plane. He mailed her a *New Yorker* cartoon of a scuba driver retreating from a beseeching mermaid at the bottom of the ocean: 'Of course I love you,' read the caption, 'But I'm running out of air.' On 23 September 1963, she received his brief note: 'I shan't be writing. Have a good year. If you need help of any sort, please let me know.'

On his side, alone now again in his private world, he was plunged into a year of depression, whilst the family only saw him struggling over the writing of *The Fixer*. Rosemarie Beck sensed something in her letter of 19 October 1963: 'Your questions about love between the young and the old have set my mind spinning.' Might the younger one know more sometimes? Could the older one think that the affair had done the younger some good? The older one knows better, she thought, 'how to permit suffering to yield a profit, but suffering is nonetheless inherent.' It was the stuff of drama and a right theme in Bennington, but she added in a quiet bracket: '(If it hurts, let me help!)'

And yet it was not all over, though never again, says Arlene Heyman, was it a sexual relationship. Gradually it resumed on different terms. Arlene began visiting him in Bennington in November 1964, and in December 1965 Malamud read her the opening chapter of *The Fixer*. He in turn looked at her writing, probing for new themes in order to break old patterns: 'What do you stand for as a human being? Do you have a philosophy that goes beyond the need for emotional fulfilment? How do you see the world? What do you believe in other than the efficacy, or lack of it, of love?' (26 March 1966). On 6 August 1968 he writes: 'You remind me so much of myself: uneasy, when visitors are around, at not getting work done; seeking order through reading, and in the process feeling lonely.' He still could not get writing and living into relation. But she in turn states her sense of their identification: 'Whenever I hear from you,' she writes in 1971, 'I remember who I am.' As she put it, 30 October 1968: 'In my mind you have always been mixed up with all parts of my life, but especially with a state of productivity, of self-use, a way of living where work is central.'

By now Malamud knew very well he must not hurt himself again. He wrote to Howard Nemerov, in whom he must have confided, 27 November 1968: 'Thank you for conveying Arlene's message. She said much the same thing the last time she stopped by—I think in September. It would be lovely, I suppose, to be once more in love, but I can't let life grab me by the balls. I have that much wisdom.'[28]

There were still tensions. On 1 September 1968 she complains about the brevity of his letters and wonders if '(1) you're angry at me, or (2) you're incredibly short on time, or (3) you're worried about saying anything posterity might take the wrong way.' 'Let me hear from you,' she writes, 30 March 1970, 'if not a note then, better, a phone call. I care very much for you and feel that you do for me also, no matter what misunderstandings there are sometimes between us.' On 16 June 1970, he writes wryly in response to her seeking to define the relationship, 'If you were my daughter I'd be close to sixty; spare me my youth.' He was 56:

> You can be former student and present friend. Consider yourself legitimized and stop worrying, after all the talking we did on the subject, about a definition of status. If you relax about it a comfortable relationship will ensue.

Something of that nature did ensue. She would report in to him on her work and her life. In a letter of 6 October 1972 Malamud wrote that he was glad she had 'become much more frank about yourself than you used to be, at least in your letters':

> 'Me I have trouble.' You rarely said that in the past. You hid it, were afraid of the confessional. Perhaps I was, too, though I justified it by what I 'confessed' in my writing. I remember the way you asked questions to keep from being questioned. The last two or three times we were together I had little idea who you had become. Now you are telling me more.

'The curious thing', he concludes, 'is that I never really got to know you well. There was an exchange but you hid a lot. You're a generous giver of not all.' That is what had baffled and eluded him in her during the early relationship: the paradoxical relation of 'generous' at one level and 'not all' at another. Now that, in the latter years, she gave less in one sense, she could give more in another. The letters she sent him as he aged are full of warm constancy, matching her sense that he, loyally, had given 'continuity to my life' (8 June 1982).

'Isn't it good to have a history together?' he writes, 25 August 1975. He has asked her to copy his letters to her and send them to him, for the writing of *Dubin's Lives*. She tells him (17 August 1975), 'I'll bet I saved everything you ever wrote me.' The joint memories move her too: 'Do you remember, Bern, when we went into the bookstore in NY and asked if they had anything by Malamud? and then we put your books out in front where they'd be seen?' When he read her a chapter from *Dubin*, it moved her doubly—by the juxtaposition of its content, made out of their past together, and the fact of his sitting there reading it to her.

Back in 1962, he had written her about his difficulties in trying to write a play—that he had lost 'the thickness of time' which he could create only in the narration of a novel (6 January). In London, 26 July 1963, en route to meeting her in Italy, he had lamented that for him as a tourist too many experiences felt evanescent, 'as though one were taking pictures instead of taking part'. What in contrast both of them increasingly felt in the 1970s was a shared sense of the *denseness* of their history together, the sheer length and quantity of unplanned, unforeseen, but continued experience together. Thus he writes to her, 28 August 1976:

> I'm very happy about our friendship. It asks little and gives much. It is in its way a minor miracle—through the years the growth of respect and love out of the shoals of ignorance—of self and each other. What a warm, generous and lovely thing it is. I want it to be forever.

In a notebook for *Dubin's Lives* he made an entry, 19 January 1972, about 'the whole business of working backwards in love' (HRC 19.4, p. 18). With Arlene, it was as though the friendship—which had it come first might have been spoiled by sex—had come after all in the third place, after the sex, after the failure of the love that went with it, as an accomplishment. It was an equivalent to what he found in the revision of his writing: 'the flowers of afterthought': 'If we could, after the fact, only revise our lives' (10 October 1974). But by now Arlene, after taking a medical degree, was a qualified analyst, and if we could revise our lives, Malamud added, it would put you out of business.

One day in November 1973 Malamud phoned Arlene whilst he was writing a memorial piece to be delivered at his brother's funeral. 'His brother had died two days before and Bern told me that he was having chest pains while writing the eulogy. He said he was sure they were psychosomatic. So he was calling me, by now the psychiatrist. And I said, "No, no, stop doing push-ups!" because Bern would try to take care of himself by doing these exercises. "You have to see a doctor right away." He was put into hospital: he was having a heart attack.'

In the last months of his life, she was in his apartment, taking his blood pressure with the assistance of her husband, and Malamud said to her, 'Did you ever really think it would come to this?' and she replied, 'I am delighted to be able to do anything for you.'

She had married Shepard Kantor in April 1979. Malamud was asked to hold one of the four poles of the chuppa (the canopy at a Jewish wedding) and be her witness: 'I felt I was giving you away,' he wrote 21 May 1979, 'but not parting with you.'

Ann Malamud felt very differently of course. She disliked the wedding ceremony at which, rightly or wrongly, she felt Arlene was showing off over Malamud, holding his hand and kissing him repeatedly. 'It annoyed him when I criticised her. He wanted her to be married and he wished it for her, but I also feel he suffered. Because if you've really been attached to someone in that way, there is a sense of possessiveness. I said, "Oh, you know, Bern, you're jealous," and he would deny it. But there was a little sense of loss, involved with the loss of stronger, younger years.' Ann had found out about the affair in due course—suspicious of some of their meetings in college; of Malamud absenting himself embarrassingly early from a small dinner party she gave in order to go on to a student party; of the long break in London and Italy in 1963 and what he was like on his return; of an airline ticket bill she found showing he had flown for the day to Pennsylvania to see Arlene graduate with a degree in medicine. He admitted the affair, finally, though he would never talk about it much. She knew that long after the ending of the erotic involvement, they had kept up a correspondence by letter and telephone, and, despite her husband's requests, she was not always keen to be overly welcoming at social meetings. Later, after his death, she found evidence of a loan to help Arlene through graduate school and discovered that most Sundays he had gone off to make his regular phone call to her. There is a letter from Arlene, 2 January 1976, that describes one of those calls and the clandestine context still surrounding them:

> I want to apologize about telling you not to lie to me. I don't want that to hurt you, and I would have called you right back except you got off in such a hurry—I had the feeling something was the matter or maybe your wife had heard you, or maybe she was wondering what I've been doing calling you so much, and since you'd just told me you'd call in the A.M. I felt I'd have to wait. I hate all this surreptitious stuff. Why can't I call you twice in a day if I need to? Maybe I can and I've just decided I can't: 'she'll know' …
>
> I guess in general I would like for you always to tell me the truth—but honestly, it's more important that you love me.

'It touches me', Arlene wrote, 'that we have the power to make each other jealous after more than 10 years' (May 1973). Arlene herself was put out when the painter Helen Frankenthaler asked her to 'give him my love and tell him I miss him—if he's strong enough to stand it': Arlene went on, 'I have mixed feelings delivering other women's sexual challenges to you. Maybe you can use it in your novel (I tell myself). Time changes all the realities, but not the feelings' (24/25 July 1975). 'Why do you have so many women?' she had asked him, 17 February 1973, 'I don't like it.' Towards the end of his life, she wrote him of a dream she had—of Malamud as a poet, painfully reading to her before their respective spouses a poem he had written for her sake, beginning 'Where are my wife and child?' The wife here was Arlene and either her first son or the child she was currently carrying: 'And what was so poignant was that it was evident to both of us that you were writing about the wife and child that we had never been to you, but were meant to have been' (13–14 June 1984).

On her side, Ann Malamud remembered how whilst she was out one morning, their kitten had escaped the house and been run over. Malamud had been on the telephone and not looking out for the creature. She always thought that it was Arlene to whom he was speaking, he seemed so guilty. For once, she wrote a short story, 'Death of a Cat', sometime in the early 1970s, as though this time she were the writer. Over the course of the day, the wife finds herself becoming more and more furious over the cat's death—'Millie had died because of inconvenience; it had been an avoidable accident':

> Anger sent her into random reminiscences ... She thought of the years of efforts to keep house and children quiet while her husband worked in his study, read, ruminated, slept. During his afternoon naps while she had her pre-dinner drink, she'd formed the habit, at his bidding, of running out to prevent the vegetable man from taking his delivery truck into their driveway because the rumble awakened him. She remembered how he, only partly in jest, used to grab her expressive hands as they waved in the air when she talked; she had a photograph of him caught in this ongoing act of trying to mitigate her intensity. He had in part succeeded, but not until after a long struggle had tossed shards around their nuclear family.

'My Italian wife,' he would call, in explanation of the volatility.

> She recalled the air of an embarrassed household when talkative friends dropped in uninvited. Casual visits were not welcome. He worked long hours, parcelling out moments of leisure for his family and for their carefully planned evenings when the guests, in the past, had usually been of his choosing; that had changed, she had insisted on her rights of choice and he had gradually yielded, as he had tried to do in other areas. Camaraderie was something he yearned for but found hard to come to; not for him a beer with the boys in a local bar.
>
> As time went, he had learned to ease up, to accept with some grace unexpected visitors, to make room for the twists and turns of events beyond his control. He had come to enjoy playing poker with his colleagues, and was proud of his adeptness at cards after inexperience and awkwardness. And he had also come a long way in understanding her volatility.

But still when this woman needed to vent her grievances in quarrels, the two nervy people would bring out the worst in each other. 'For God sakes, leave it alone,' he would cry, baffled and thrown by her capacity to turn in a moment from hot to cold and back again, over apparently small matters. When he lost his temper, it felt as though you could hear him streets away.

His face turned purple, he'd shout. 'Why do you pick fights when I'm eating and spoil my lunch? I can feel my head pounding.' Concerned about his health, stifling resentments, she would withdraw.

And she knew and cared about his basic goodness, his strength and warmth. So they stayed together because and in spite of her nature and him.

Yet on this day she continued to struggle with the idea of the cat dying, for the sake of his distracted convenience—as though for both of them the dead creature might be a little, real image of the damage:

> Her husband embraced her quietly, warmly, compassionately, and they grieved together. After two days, her fits of tears were termed 'self-indulgent'. She had always found the reality of loss the worst of all realities to deal with. She worried how she could survive bigger losses.

Ann Malamud had had an extended affair of her own, after her husband's, in the 1960s. It helped her adjust to the loss of Oregon, to some loss in the marriage, even as it also chimed in with the times and with the permissiveness of Bennington. She had always been flirtatious, too flirtatious she had sometimes thought, though often her husband had enjoyed seeing her act so; but this was more serious and lasting.

She had met the man through the literary critic Granville Hicks and his wife Dorothy. The Hickses had a sexually 'open' marriage which Dorothy told Ann worked only if both partners understood it and accepted it, without reservations. It could not be like that for the Malamuds, though eventually they confessed their infidelities to each other. Perhaps her affair offered him more licence. Certainly Robert Giroux was surprised by Malamud's interest in having affairs, thinking the boldness was reserved for the fiction:

> I thought he'd be afraid: on the surface he seemed timid. He never told me—never confided in me—and I didn't want him to. But I did once say, 'You know Bern, every poet is an idol for young girl students, they always fall in love with poets.' And he said, 'It's happened to me, and I'm not a poet.' He did tell me one story which sounds like it was Bennington: this very attractive girl came to see him. They were alone and she just dropped her clothes. And he said, 'What do you think of that, Bob?' and I said, 'I think it's a short story'. And he did write that story about an older man, in *Dubin*, and then again in changed form in 'The Model' where an old man hires a girl and makes her expose herself by pretending he wants to paint her.

'What I regret during that period', Ann Malamud concluded in painful retrospect, 'is probably that I was not as helpful, that is as sympathetic to Bern, as I ought to have been. It certainly shook the marriage':

What I have thought about is that if I had had an intellectual or an artistic pursuit in my life—it doesn't mean that I might not have had an affair, but it certainly means I would not have spent years on and off fantasizing about this man and finding it as compelling as I did. This was especially true of women for most of our history, without a disciplined pursuit that absorbs them as it does their husbands. If I had been a lawyer or a doctor or a musician—Bern used to kid me and say, 'I wish you were a pianist, and you could play piano for me', that would have delighted him—if I had had a compelling vocation and other interests in addition to my family, I wouldn't have spent so much time in this kind of Madame Bovary illusion.

Arlene Heyman recalled Malamud saying even to her that he regretted he had not helped Ann to have a career, above and beyond some voluntary courses and part-time administrative work in the college.

There are in the archive in Texas curious letters from Pat Lee, wife of the man with whom Ann was conducting an affair, which survive from Malamud's file. One, written to Ann, is dated 31 December 1967 and asks her forgiveness for a 'jealous impulsive act' which has inflicted anguish and embarrassment. She had sent to Malamud some of the love-letters Ann had written to her husband, Harry. The other, 23 September 1967, is to Malamud himself and says 'I love you for all the right reasons but don't be alarmed ... I am mute to all now and appreciate you more each day'. She was now separated. Malamud replies formally on 26 September that 'the press of my work makes it difficult for me to carry on a correspondence' (HRC 9.1).

Claude Fredericks was a Bennington colleague who kept a journal for almost every day of his life since childhood. It was a Proustian life-project that Malamud admired for being at once so sustained and unrewarded. In 1979 Malamud read the whole of the journal for 1967 as a kind of novel, enthusiastically recommending the work to Robert Giroux for publication despite the contentious difficulties of editing—and even though he also made careful notes of some of the less complimentary adjectives occasionally used to describe his wife and himself. He was impressed also by Claude Frederick's taste, a world away from his own functionalism—the impeccable minimalist Japanese house which Ann called a temple, the beautifully detailed dinner parties. Fredericks did not seem to compromise in his ideas on how to live—his devotion to Greek and Eastern philosophy, his writing, his sexuality—and this was something in others which always impressed Malamud, not least because of his own uncertainties. But Claude Fredericks himself watched the Malamud marriage with unease:

I watch the complicated nightmare Ann Malamud endures with Bernard, I listen to the complaints of lovely Karen Jackel over Malamud's lechery ... He is,

> I gather, suffering from blocks now, and I think it is because he is undergoing,
> in his strange promiscuities, the same kind of crisis I am undergoing. Blocks
> come when one can't face the truth about one's life, where there are clusters
> of thoughts one must repress. But out of such repression, out of such lies &
> deceits, often explode—masterpieces. (14 October 1962)

He found Ann bitter: '"How about *my* problems for a change?' she says
with that rude, selfish, blunt voice she has, desperate in her solitude' (19
September 1963). He writes 3 November 1963: 'I found myself saying to Ann
Malamud almost fiercely—You never like anything. I suddenly was sick of
her destructiveness, forgetting for a moment the deep causes for it.'[29]

The marriage recovered in the 1970s, as a more social marriage with life
spent half the year in New York. 'But that doesn't mean that it was a smooth
marriage after that,' Ann Malamud herself reported, 'It was not, because I had
become more assertive and less tolerant. And there were always things that
we could quarrel about.' Friends remembered the embarrassment of some of
those mutual minor unkindnesses carried out in public. Ann would abruptly
deliver the punchline to one of his much-rehearsed, slowly delivered funny
stories; Malamud might tell her to stop following him around at a party, or
not to interrupt him, or not to sit on his knee because she was too heavy;
she would introduce herself sourly as the woman who ironed Malamud's
underpants; he once said in her hearing that he could not stand the idea
of divorce—because of the sheer disruption it would cause his work. In his
journal for 20 August 1975 Claude Fredericks wrote of a dinner party at the
home of Reinhard Mayer where Malamud began talking at length of the
pains and difficulties of marriage in front of his angry wife: 'Why would a
man give up his freedom? Why would anyone? ... To raise children and keep
a house.' It is no wonder that Malamud did not wholly relish the biographies
of Robert Frost or Thomas Hardy, with the stories of the petty meannesses
in their marriages set against the accomplishments of the poetry that came
out of them. 'I don't know what any future biographer will do with me—I
imagine little,' he wrote to Chester Garrison, 20 September 1978, 'but I think
it was fair for Lawrence Thompson and Robert Gittings to say who Robert
Frost and Thomas Hardy were':

> They were complex, inverted, almost totally self-centered, difficult men. They
> were bound to be difficult husbands ... I can't see how the biographers, doing
> their job, could have failed to portray them as they presented themselves.
> After reading the biographies I was somewhat disgusted with each of them,
> but as time went by, perhaps drawing from my knowledge of myself—faults,
> insufficiencies, self-centeredness—I made my peace with both of them and
> have vowed to continue to love their work. I'm sure that's what they would

have wanted: 'judge our lives as you please but don't let it interfere with the pleasure of our work. Keep that clean, pure. Love it for what it tells you of yourself as well as us' (OSU box 2).

'He Has to Make his Children's World As Well As his Own'

Malamud once said to Gloria Stern, 'Why don't you let Danny have an affair? It would be good for his work.'[30] It was a cliché for the writers of the sixties—doubtful as a form of genuine experience, good as a rationalization for the perks of bad behaviour and the reassurance of a yearning ego. But what Malamud had said for Danny Stern, he also meant for himself. Or at least for the part of himself which was used to being separate from his family; which in the study lived both in free fantasy and under high pressure; a part of him which, never wholly faithful, had long needed the affirmation of women, hungering from the past for experience for a future. A writer needs beauty, he told the Bennington girls. He had worked so hard when young, been so deprived of the experience of love, he would say. 'I am,' he told Nina Straus in a later conversation, 'a woman-centered man, possibly because my mother died young. The lyrical quality of myself is attached to women. The sheer beauty of women and children is one reason for having a family.'

But having a family also became a strain. Ann's needs, his needs, the claims of the family, the writing, the alternative life: so many secrets and compartments and conflicts lived with, even toughly tolerated, but unreconciled. On 10 August 1962 Malamud wrote to Rosemarie Beck, 'I know just how you feel about being home again and facing one's *other* problems, the family ones, the practical, with the desire to go at one's art.' Though Ann bore the brunt of household management, it was still the interruptions that bothered him: 'I try to make believe the interruption benefits the art; at least I have time, no matter what I'm doing, to think.' Sometimes he comes back with better ideas but often 'with nothing more than fury at the interruption.' So it was with obsessives: art was his religion. Roth's Lonoff set himself three hours' careful reading each evening: if he missed a session in the middle of a book, he lost touch with its inner life and had to start again from the beginning. The only interruptions Malamud welcomed were his own: 'My reading has slowed down,' he wrote Arlene Heyman, 14 February 1962, 'because I revery so much between sentences—sometimes between words'. Really he was working all the time.

Janna would learn poems by heart to win her father's attention. At the age of sixteen, she borrowed books for their own sake but also in order to get into his study:

> I'd interrupt him in his study to replace one and take another, or to tell him about something I was learning, recite a poem I had lately memorized, or simply get him to explain some idea. He delighted in my intellectual awakening. I enjoyed holding his attention. But more than that, I found *him* then, at his quiet best.   (MFB, 259)

But there other times when he was not at his best. 'Anytime I brought a boyfriend home,' said Janna, 'he would instantly light on some word the poor guy misused and set up a formal public exam, a show trial for whoever happened to be in the room. "Which is the correct pronunciation of *exquisite*? How do you spell *cemetery*?"' (Ibid, 56–7).

One lunchtime, just out of college, Janna showed her father a short story called 'The Day No Pigs Would Die', which she had been using in a summer-school teaching programme. It was, rather sentimentally, about a father who could not bring himself to force the slaughter of a pig his son had raised. She loved it, was proud of her first efforts at teaching, and gave the story to her father to share. Immediately he pronounced it second-rate: 'Let me show you how it ought to be done', he said, fetching a copy of *Jude the Obscure* from his study. 'This', he said pointing to the passage, 'is how a first-rate artist talks about killing a pig.' Jude had appealed to Arabella to have pity on the creature but she forced him to continue and, because he did it reluctantly, he did it badly as a result. It was a little parable about pity and sensitiveness, even to the point of clumsy and ineffectual weakness. But here, ironically, was sensitive Malamud, immediately the teacher again, impulsive upholder of writerly standards, stinging the feelings of the new young teacher, his now prickily rebuffed daughter. It is a little image of how difficult it was to get it right in the tangle of interrelationships between literature and life, books and family.[31]

Alex Inkeles had another image of Janna, one holiday in Spain in 1965, bearing the family strain. 'In this family Janna played a special role. She was a bedrock of support if at any time things were dissolving. She was the steady, sensible, secure, capable one who could help pull everything together and keep everything going.' The two families were holidaying together in Spain and the water stopped running. There was the ocean facing them, but the toilets did not work, and the dishes could not be washed. Malamud would venture into the sea occasionally but most usually it was to continue some sort of discussion waist-high in water. Now there was no water in the house: 'With someone so sensitive to his environment as Malamud, you'd think the world was going to blow apart.' But Alex and Janna, aged thirteen, found a source of water somewhere and formed a bucket brigade: 'The two of us became very good friends because we were together all of the time, taking the buckets of water to the house. That's my image of Janna in the constellation of this family.' [32]

Equally, Chester Garrison had early noticed the needs of the son in Corvallis. As a little boy, Paul, he felt, learned that he could best get Malamud's attention via his teacherly side. He would constantly ask questions in the midst of other conversations. When Malamud was writing at home, Paul would simply say to inquirers what in a sense he believed, as well as what Malamud required—that Dad was not here. It was a pattern that continued, Garrison thought. He recalled one of those occasional reunions of the two families in Vermont, years later, the children grown up. The Garrisons were just back from Istanbul, and Paul had returned a little time earlier from a difficult government posting in India where he had become ill: 'He decided to say what he thought was interesting in India, but the company was more or less interested in Istanbul. And then he got mad. He said, "Nobody listens to me," and he took off for the bathroom.'[33] Paul wanted to be a writer, but it was impossible to follow his father and impossible to take even his well-meant criticisms, not least when they hinted at a lack of warmth. Arlene Heyman said that Malamud told her that, at its worst, he felt like a man locked in a suit of armour as far as Paul was concerned.

Paul himself remembered bringing three or four friends from the Cambridge School to the house in Bennington to stay for a week one summer:

> I remember how uncomfortable Dad was with them. He called them 'gents'; 'Okay gents, if you want to take the car, you can have it.' Maybe he was intimidated by the fact that these boys had gone to a prep school. He had some caricature in his mind about what that meant in terms of social attitudes. Then after my friends had gone away, Dad called me into his study and mentally ticked off a list of ten things he thought had gone wrong or right with their visit to me. [34]

Malamud was worried about him, but not jealous in the way he could be over Janna. Some family friends thought that in his formative years Paul, so often silently withdrawn, did not always get the emotional support he needed—as compared with Janna, the sunny child, later the practical managing type, who seemed so easy to love and admire. Nina Pelikan Straus was not as nervous as most in trying to find the right tone in which to broach sensitive subjects:

> Forgive me, Bern, but I see how much [Paul] needs your love and approval—not your wisdom and good advice, but your tolerance of who he is. He does not believe you like who he is and this—I think—stops him from reaching out. It does not matter to whom, does it? Man, woman, he must begin .... I hope I do not overstep our friendship in speaking out. Paul seems to keep coming home, not because he cannot make way in this absurd teaching profession of ours, but because he wants something from you. An embrace, perhaps. It seems simple-minded, but it is everything sometimes.   (17 June 1979, HRC 18.5)

Karen Jackel, now Wunsch, recalled that Malamud, arguably thinking back to himself and his own youthful fantasies, had once wished for an older woman to initiate his son into the ways of the world.[35]

At a dinner party when Paul was a young man, he and his father said something to each other 'that was funny and pleasurable and a woman at the table said to Malamud, "Oh, you seem to have a good relationship with your son," and he said, "Well, you should see the relationship I have with my daughter." Pouff! You should have seen Paul's face.' The Inkeleses were among those present:

A1: Obviously it was a kind of insensitivity—but it was an unthinking affirmation of what was immediately uppermost in his mind and foremost in his feelings, which was the strength of his attachment to Janna. It wasn't an effort to do anything to Paul but was like pushing the 'Janna button', so that the 'Janna response' just came out, without a realisation of it.

B1: I remember something that our daughter had with Bernard when he was in Stanford hospital with his heart problems, and she went to see him and he said to her, 'Ann, can you tell me why Paul thinks I prefer Janna?' She was absolutely amazed. There was a certain lack—we all have a certain lack—of self-knowledge.

Yet Janna knew this ostensible insensitivity too—though it was actually something far more thin-skinned than that. In 1976 on the eve of Janna's marriage to David Smith, when everyone else had gone to bed, Malamud sat alone with his daughter in the living room, reading: 'He appeared to be concentrating on text but was ruminating. Perhaps the meeting with David's family, the rich food, the wine, carried him somewhere unhappy. He liked David, but ... He put aside his book, cleared his throat, fumbled. He had my attention. "You know," he said, "I wish you were marrying someone Jewish"' (MFB, 212). Nothing could have been worse timed, though it was precisely what the time made him feel and impulsively need to say. The thought that he himself had not married someone Jewish, and determinedly so, was both a potential riposte but also a potential cause. He could not revise what had blunderingly been said in life, and he himself had admitted, 'If I could reinvent myself, I would reinvent myself with more thought between what I say and what I think' (TH, 119). But in one of the early drafts of *Dubin's Lives* when Dubin hopes his daughter might marry a Jew, Malamud wrote: 'He was moved by the thought for his father's sake' (LC I 5.5).

Yet looking back, Paul Malamud thought this finally, for *his* father's sake, in defiance of the modern fashion of claiming filial victimization:

> Dad gave me as much emotional support as he could, given the odd nature of his work, which constantly involved imagining different worlds and being absorbed in them. If he were taking part in this discussion, he would remember himself loyally walking up to my room to sit on my bed and chat with me before I fell asleep as a child. He would remember holding pots and pans for me to get sick into when I had a stomach ache as a child. He would remember reading Beowulf to me that year in Italy. He would remember doing my eye exercises with me for years to strengthen my wandering eye and driving me to Eugene, Oregon, for the opthamologist. He would remember taking me to the Corvallis clinic for my allergy shots. He would remember teaching me to drive. He would remember reading every report card and discussing the grades with me (good except wood and metal shop). He would remember that he was the one who wanted his children to eat dinner with him every night they were at home. He would remember that one of his reasons for going to Italy was to give his children the then-remarkable experience. He would remember coaching me with relish about how to get attention in class—stick your hand in the air and wave it around. He would remember our weekend phone conversations—beginning with collect calls from me to Mom and Dad from the school pay phone almost every weekend when I went away to a prep school in New England and continuing throughout college and various circumstances for the rest of his life. He would remember trying to share what he saw as fun and amusing in the world around him with me throughout his life (he was a delightful storyteller). He would remember giving me a lot of money in my teens and twenties, though he had some reason to be anxious about his income. And, quite frankly, he would remember himself giving measured responses when I was an irritable adolescent.

He concluded with a sense of specific inner connections that eschewed the notional standards of the so-called norms:

> I wouldn't know what standard to measure him against. Clearly, he tried to be nice to me because he had not been able to do anything for Eugene. Among the mostly academic group of people my parents knew, I'm not aware of

who among the group of their children now grown up has had a nicer life than I have. [36]

Malamud told Clark Blaise that he feared his writing had damaged family life—'it was always writing, writing, writing'—and that the sacrifice in family feeling had told most of all upon Paul. That too was a worry he took—where else?—but into his writing:

> I was going to write a story about a father and a son, but I discarded it. The reason I discarded it is that it seemed too simple a tale, like stories I had done in the past. I wanted something new and perhaps I would have written it if I could think of presenting it via a technique I had not used up to now, possibly a new point of view—for me.   (LC II 6.3)

It was 'a story I thought I would write about 30 years ago about a father and a son who could not get a job during the depression' (LC II 6.3). He wrote it, finally, in 1967 and called it 'My Son the Murderer'. 'It brought home to me that a writer should go where the trouble is,' Arlene Heyman wrote him near the end of May 1973, when she read it in his collection, *Rembrandt's Hat*.

In 1966 and 1967 Malamud was again teaching creative writing at Harvard. 'Malamud named Visiting Professor' was the local newspaper headline reported to him by one friend, followed by 'English Department Will Lose 12 members'. 'Seems like a fair exchange,' commented Felicia Kaplan. By the end of their time there Ann had wanted to buy a house in Cambridge, Massachusetts; but for Malamud 'there are just too many "successful" people around, and my fiction seeks their opposites' (to Chester Garrison, 31 May 1968, OSU box 2). Initially the Malamuds had moved to Cambridge mainly because they were not satisfied with the schooling at Bennington and wanted Janna to follow Paul to the Cambridge School at Weston. They went with her because they were not ready to let her leave home, like Paul, to go it alone as a boarder. Malamud had not really wanted to lose Paul either: 'I enjoy him too much,' he wrote to Rosemarie Beck (16 December 1961). He had written her before on how much he enjoyed the earlier childhood times in Corvallis: 'The kid's sense of humor is superb. It is one of the qualities I most admire in him. I'm looking forward to tonight—I love to take him to a basketball game—he is a good companion' (11 December 1959). It was harder both in Bennington and in adolescence.

Yet the story of the father and the son came back to him, he said, during a time of watching undergraduates whilst teaching at Harvard, with the Vietnam War and the draft looming larger and larger in the background of their concerns. He had always been concerned that the artist should be a citizen too: 'I don't say accept society, I say accept responsibility,' he had written Rosemarie Beck, 19 February 1960: 'an artist lives well on loneliness, but he has to make his children's world as well as his own.' Malamud was thinking about the young people's world again:

> The idea of the story—the characters and action—were in my mind since the Great Depression in the 1930s. I think of the plot, or conflict, in terms of the struggle of the young people of *my* generation; but I was unable to write it at the time, and when I finally did, it dealt with the young people of my children's generation. In a sense I had to become my father before I could write the fiction. (LC I 62.6)

It was a story that Malamud often chose for a public reading, when he would warn his audience in advance: 'You hear one voice after another and I don't always tell you whose; but you'll know from the context. This is a father and son story which many of you will know' (LC II 8.16):

> My father goes to the bedroom and after a while sneaks out in the hallway again listening.
> I hear him sometimes in his room but he don't talk to me and I don't know what's what. It's a terrible feeling for a father.

The paragraphs are continuous and yet at another level are not so: like the son and the father, they are at once so close and yet so far apart. Theirs are bare helpless voices calling out, floating in an unresolved present without sight of a future, without speech marks to distinguish speaking from thinking.

> Harry, your father loves you. When you were a little boy, every night when I came home you used to run to me. I picked you up and lifted you up to the ceiling. You liked to touch it with your small hand.

It is almost a surprise to find this was spoken out loud. But it may as well as not have been, in the answer it received:

> I don't want to hear about that anymore.

In the draft entitled 'a Discarded Tale', it goes: 'Pa, I don't want to hear about that anymore' (LC II 6.3); but then 'Pa' is lost and what is said breaks tonal contact and becomes like a dead matter of fact.

The father is named Leo, but is Max in the 1930s, is Malamud in the 1960s, anxious alike; the son, named Harry, is Paul in the 1960s, is both Eugene and Bernie in the 1930s, depressed in the Depression, but only one of them to the point of insanity. In a draft, Malamud put the story's key within a cliché: 'Harry, said Leo, some day you'll be a father and you'll understand how I feel now.' Then Malamud threw away the cliché, leaving the key still there to be deduced but invisible. This is what he called 'making the moral esthetic': 'it is not visible, it is itself the fabric. It is expectedly hidden; the artist defeats our expectations of its appearance until we realize it has long since appeared, has in a sense always been present' (TH, 101). But thus invisibly, in art, it was all coming together, even with pain: so many relationships over the years, often in conflict, brought into this complex artistic unification. To many who knew him, Malamud's was a carefully compartmentalized life, but in a short story like this he was releasing everything and holding it all powerfully together.

Harry is 'a young man of 22 or 23'. He wakes to a feeling that his father is in the hallway listening to him. 'Listening to what? Listening to him sleep. To him get up and dress. To him not going into the kitchen to eat. To him reading' (LC II 6.3). Harry hardly ever goes out of the Brooklyn apartment, and will not take a job even if he looks for one. He is without any apparent emotion and will not say, and may not know, what is happening to him.

Yet, for all its stasis, the story moves as fluidly from the son's desperate paranoia to the father's desperate anxiety as it does across the years for Malamud himself, who is both parties unable to get together. Equally, Nina Peilkan Straus 'saw in Paul a Bernard struggling to get out and unable, one of those Dostoevskian doubles that Malamud himself knew so well.' That is why the son was Paul no more than it was Eugene, than it was Malamud himself. But if Malamud is at once both the father and the son, he also knows deep within himself the very separation of the two and he stays as loyal to that painful reality as the father stays to the son, however bunglingly. 'If I worry about myself I know what the worry is ...,' says the father, 'But if the worry is about somebody else, that's the worst kind.'

When Malamud could do all this within himself, living equally amidst all the conflicting points of view, it was no wonder that he seemed to lack a single, definite personality in the world outside. Whatever his psychological difficulties, it was to do finally with his being a writer and being the sort of writer he was. He could barely help the sporadic breaking out of his tense emotional partialities—'You should see my daughter', 'I wish you were marrying a Jew'. But on second thought, where the writing took place, Malamud knew he was only arbitrarily himself—albeit inescapably so too. And he considered that half-blinded self as no more than one among many other equivalent characters, in the novel of the world.

Likewise then, the reader of 'My Son the Murderer' increasingly feels for *both* sides, not only one after another, paragraph after paragraph, but eventually in the self-same paragraph, knowing—at that almost impossible *same time* of Malamud's—both what it costs to say the thing and what it costs to hear it. Each suffers, yet even in that causes the other harm, in an endless circle: the son's claustrophobia received as rejection; the father's anxious and loving concern felt as intrusion. Harry must get away from this pressure. He leaves the house, but the father follows. Leo sees a man on the cold winter shore standing in the surf. The lonely man is his son. He stands by Harry in the water, fearing suicide. Malamud added this stark juxtaposition to the final version:

> Harry, I'm frightened. Tell me what's the matter. My son, have mercy on me.
> I'm frightened of the world, Harry thought. It fills me with fright.
> He said nothing.

If there was a silent ear listening to the bare and unprotected sounds of all human trouble in the world, spoken and unspoken, this is what it would hear—neglected cries like unspoken prayers. 'I'm frightened ... I'm frightened'—so nearly the same voice or so nearly, at least, a shareable feeling. But the delayed insertion of 'Harry thought' in that second paragraph takes what the son might have said out-loud back inside again, in resisted possibility of confession. That is what writing was like for Malamud 'when the next sentence may deny the last' (to Nina Pelikan Straus, 18 August 1973)—a word changing the story, the story changing a word, in constant interplay of figure and ground. In the draft, the father cries, 'I feel that I want to tell you everything I know.' But it makes no difference if the father has been through all that the son has, or if the son will ever go through a father's pain. They remain separate. And yet all the time the story itself is tacitly crying for that emotional simplicity which at some deep level, for all his knowledge of complexity, Malamud knew that he shared with his own father: the simplicity of crying, Why can't the father and son help each other?

The cold wind blows the father's hat off his head, and he chases it unavailingly till chill and frustration alike make him cry bitter tears, but the son does not move. Joyce Carol Oates described it well when she reviewed *Rembrandt's Hat*, the collection in which it finally appeared in 1973: 'We end with the son standing with his feet in the freezing ocean off Coney Island—just standing there, facing the wind—but enclosed, still, in his father's mind' (LC I 36.3). That too was what writing felt like for Malamud: one moment enclosing life within itself, the next moment still helplessly at the mercy of its own subject-matter. You could love the writing more than the life, but the life was in that writing and the writing was in a life. In Malamud's hands, James Joyce, 'the foolish writer of a wise book', would have wanted to have sacrificed more to his insane daughter, but at the same time would have also had to write about her.

At a deep level, Malamud remained, rightly, baffled about the relation between literature and life. And that itself, paradoxically, was crucial to his powers of creativity. That is why, in the future, he would have to write about writers in *The Tenants* and in *Dubin's Lives*.

7

⋖⋘⋙⋗

'We Need Some Sort of Poverty in Our Lives'

Teaching

Harry Mathews, the only American member of Oulipo, the experimental French writing group formed by Raymond Queneau, taught creative writing at Bennington in ways of which Malamud disapproved. One playful exercise was to take a poem, your own or somebody else's, locate each noun or verb, and then arbitrarily substitute the noun or verb seven places further down in the dictionary. Mathews believed that placing that sort of artificial grid over the feeling and meaning of the poem was a means of revealing its underlying structure, the inner syntactic gesture remaining even though the words were different. Stephen Sandy, poet and colleague, reported that Malamud did not think that was the way to teach writing at all. 'It should be done with sincerity and careful inquiry into one's own autobiography and experience.'[1] Though the students enjoyed the formal inventive exercises, to Malamud the sentences they were making were not what he called human sentences—because they involved no initial human responsibility, intention, or emotional involvement in the process of their making.

Peter Hayes was a young student-writer in Harvard in 1966. Brought up in the modernist tradition of Archibald MacLeish's dictum, 'a poem should not mean but be', he found Malamud's approach to writing iconoclastic in its insistence on the primacy of meaning and achieved purpose: 'The two questions that Bernie always asked the class after one of us had read our work was, "What is the story about?" and "Is it successful?"'[2] Beneath the flat-sounding schoolmasterly questions was the belief that what you would not say to critics, for fear of reductivism, you must admit to your fellow-would-be-writers. 'Every effective story—think of Chekhov, Joyce, Babel, Hemingway, Faulkner—is a revelation,' he told them, 'in essence a confession of what a person, in his deepest heart, is, even when he pretends he is not; and what is confessed to the reader is nothing less than a man's mystery' (TH, 117). Malamud's insistence on what he was not ashamed to call subject-matter or theme was connected with what people were *about*, and their struggle to find that out, both in their writing and in their lives. Katha Pollitt—the only one of his female students, said Malamud, who disobligingly would not kiss him on the mouth—remembers the first assignment he set at Harvard in 1967: ' "I want to know you better so I want you to write a piece about yourself—who are you?" I was so offended by this. I remember he didn't like the piece I wrote and then I told him I hadn't wanted to write it. The students he liked were those who gave back anything—even that.'³ Anything could be subject-matter: it could be what prompted a yes or a no. 'There's no necessity to say it positive if to say it positive is alien to your nature and experience' (LC II 10.8). Everything depended on how much the writer cared: 'There is no material, no matter how negative or trivial it may seem to be, which is in itself worthless. A writer may give depth and beauty to any subject matter' (Ibid.). The underlying idea did not have to be wholly original in itself—as long as it originated in the students themselves. 'Don't be afraid to attempt something new,' goes a note from one lesson-plan, 'even if what is new is old' (LC II 10.2). In art, ideas were made anew, as if for the first time again, since in art 'knowledge has drama—a concrete quality that abstract knowledge does not as a rule have' (LC II 13.10).

Jay Cantor recalled what Malamud would do in the Harvard classes to make a student *see*:

> Once or twice—O those were dark moments!—he actually drew a diagram on the green board, meant to represent the story's combination of personal and artistic failings (and always the two went together), going on with his back to the table, not noticing even (as sometimes indeed happened), when the writer wept quietly.
>
> The dread diagram was only unsheathed, I see now, when he thought fear had blinded the young author to the nature of his or her desires; that is to say, you had kept yourself from understanding the story you were writing—or you knew, and hadn't the courage to write it. In Malamud's own work, schlemiels like us are the characters who, from wilful, greedy soul-blindness, don't recognize the story they're in, the true nature of their wishes. That is to say, the father

you've gone to save by buying a magical spell (as in 'The Silver Crown') is also
really the father you want to kill. The characters haven't yet properly grasped,
like Fidelman the artist and lover manqué of *Pictures of Fidelman*, the themes
of their lives.[4]

A fellow-student, Pam Metz, defended the seriousness of the process, however
painful: 'He assumed that people would want to know whether they ever
really could become writers, and if so how they could be better, in order to
make their decisions accordingly.'[5] What distinguished the professional from
the amateur writer, said Malamud, was that the professional made definite
choices. One was to pay attention, equally and alternately, noted Pam Metz,
to both the deeper meaning and the smallest details. Karen Jackel was one of
the students sitting round the table at a late-afternoon session in the Barn at
Bennington, when Malamud called for 'honesty' in their writing by suddenly
and dramatically turning on the light.[6]

As a writer you were also to be always on the lookout for your own
afterthoughts, working even when you thought you were not. As Malamud
put it in a lecture given at the writing seminar in Harvard, 20 December 1966:

> He will sit down at night and listen to some music or read a book or read the
> newspaper and some word or some thought is associated with another word or
> another thought and before he knows it, he's beginning to rewrite in his mind
> or reread the passage that he wrote during the day ... He'll write a sentence
> down that may be the key to changing the whole work or the whole idea or the
> whole theme in an absolutely wonderful way.   (LC II 13.10)

This was his working autobiography, shared with the students as previously
he had shared it only with fellow-artists such as Rosemarie Beck:

> much of my more interesting ideas come to me when I am not writing,
> sometimes in great profusion, especially when I am reading at night or listening
> to music. A single word, a single thought, may start an association that ends
> with a sensation like water overflowing, something richer, a warm inspirational
> feeling, and the next thing I know I'm writing something surprisingly original
> to me—in the sense that I had not thought of it before—on my pad. By the
> time I come to my last chapters of a book, or even to the last pages of a short
> story, I have every bit worked out. Sometimes when I check my notes I see that
> on three or four occasions I've written the same idea.   (5 June 1959)

The unconscious repetition, though time-consuming, did not matter. For
this was thinking as a writer: every time the thought came back, it came
as original, as exciting, in the right place at the right time again. Malamud
would quote Edmund Wilson, 'I think with my right hand' (HRC 31.6).

Form itself, Malamud told his students, begins the moment you try for a preliminary outline of your work. The discipline of the bare prosaic outline-plan can itself prefigure the form you need—giving you a sense of the whole and thus the ability to make the terrifying task less formidable by tackling it steadily, daily, piece by piece. 'I tend to have an idea for a book and then do a cursory outline of it, or as large or detailed outline of it as I can. Then I put it away. After several months I come back to it.' When he comes back to look at it again, he then has to find something more in it: 'When I say something more, I mean something more in terms of possibility, in terms of form, in terms of excitement for myself.' It had to move him in that way, to feel warm, for him to have faith in it. If it had in it that sort of life, then it was indeed the starting-point for the writing—no more and no less than that: 'because an outline, please note, is not a straitjacket, it is a take-off point, it is the equivalent of a scientific hypothesis' (LC II 13.10). He urged the students to have the courage to rethink, reshape, and restructure scenes already written. The writer had to be unsure of himself, starting afresh with each painfully halting first draft, working his work up. But at least with rewriting the fear of complete failure is gone, because you have something down.

At Bennington Nina Pelikan Straus remembered writing Malamud a story straight out of her own autobiography, about her father: 'a story of disillusionment and growing up, and understanding suddenly the father was old. He loved it. If you wrote a Malamud-type story, and mine was in a sense, then he got very excited':

> His idea of the short story was very much his own short story. He tried very hard to stretch himself to accommodate the possibility of other kinds of stories, but I believe that was hard for him. He showed a lot of self-discipline, but then the restraint would break down, maybe just a gesture or giving someone short shrift. He was looking for something, and as a teacher what he was looking for was of a fairly narrow compass.[7]

The stories that most excited him were often about parents and the struggles of their grown-up children—in particular those moments of identification or alienation in the passing movement between the generations. It was not only a matter of their autobiographical resonance. For Malamud such stories had behind them the great old narratives of redemption or loss, of growing and dying:

> In a sense the short story tells us, time and again, how vulnerable human lives are to the human condition. It arranges experience so that we understand, at least for a moment, how events combine, sometimes to lengthen, too often to shorten our days, our joys, or, happily, our illusions; or to say how suddenly

we fall into error and how irrevocably we are judged, as though for all time
for a single mistake, and *that* though it takes a thousand errors to make a
moral man.   (TH, 118)

Each person who had sufficient luck to benefit from those thousand errors
was in debt to those ruined by the single great mistake. He might still be
judged and condemned for any one of them, if only by himself, but Malamud
was the man whose story here is that of the thousand errors. The short stories
were Malamud's condensed poems, fitting, he told his still young students,
for 'our short lives'; the novels were what it was like to live on in the long
haul of the short story's single event.

What he was demanding of them was his sort of almost religious vocation.
The writer, he told his classes, 'must develop his own character, because
he and his experiences are so often the subject of his art' ((LC II 10.8).
Writers had to use themselves as instruments to be viewed with an involved
detachment which both allowed self-criticism and resisted compulsion. This
is what Malamud had done: use and thereby justify in art the mess or
inadequacy of his life. Writing, he told his young people, was tied up with
the whole existence of the writer and he listed in note-form the items that
bore the demands of such a life: 'time, vacations, travel, eating, lack of varied
experience' (LC II 13.10) When years later in 1981 Katha Pollitt interviewed
Malamud for the *Saturday Review*, he told her again that writers had to stay
at their desk, not regretting that the day was beautiful and others were going
to the beach: 'Malamud first mentioned his childhood's Coney Island as his
example of the beach, then later wanted me to change it to Malibu to make
him sound more up to date.' Yet still of course he had no intention of going
to either. Malamud insisted to his students in Harvard and in Bennington,
'We need some sort of poverty in our lives, some sort of burden' (LC II
13.10). They did not always know how much they needed a tradition and
a discipline.

Katha Pollitt remembered in that interview the shock of how she had felt
when he had gone round the final class in 1967 telling each member publicly
and explicitly what he thought of his or her chances (' "Katha, I see you more
as a poet or an essayist", which was exactly what happened of course'):

MALAMUD: Many people who go into writing do so not because they have a talent
    but because they have an anguish. They think their sad burdens will fall away
    overnight if they become successful writers. To these people, without talent, I
    recommend no continuation ... Everyone has a desire to use some deep creative
    quality in the self, but sometimes they don't have the courage; sometimes they
    don't have enough talent to carry them through.   (CBM, 98–9)

Yet whether finally they became writers or not, it was that deep creative quality that Malamud austerely sought to address, wherever it then led them. Trauma or sickness was not creativity: neurotic patterns too predictably replayed only parts of the self and limited character development.

One of the courses Malamud taught from early on in his time at Bennington was 'Poetry and the Imaginative Process'. He gave the students a handout headed 'Some Opening Instances', about the experiential beginnings of poems (LC II 9.5). One example was the opening of Yeats's 'The Cold Heaven': 'Suddenly I saw the cold and rook-delighting heaven':

> And thereupon imagination and heart were driven
> So wild that every casual thought of that and this
> Vanished, and left but memories, that should be out of season
> With the hot blood of youth, of love crossed long ago

This is what Malamud meant when he wrote to one would-be writer of the need to be 'struck by lightning' (HRC 2.1). There were other examples from Hopkins, Keats' 'On Seeing a Lock of Milton's Hair', and William Carlos Williams on unlacing his shoes. There was Emily Dickinson on a chestnut tree making it seem as though 'the skies were in blossom', or on a circus passing the house '—still I feel the red in my mind'; and this from Elizabeth Bishop:

> Heaven is not like flying or swimming
> but has something to do with blackness and a strong glare
> and when it gets dark he will remember something

Yet linked to these Romantic lyrics of released inner surprise, of sudden remembering in the dark, Malamud also placed on his handout two passages of awe and revelation from the Bible, both from the New Testament. One was the conversion of Paul, the persecutor of the Christians, on the road to Damascus (Acts 9.3–4): 'and suddenly there shined round about him a light from heaven: And he fell to earth and heard a voice saying unto him, Saul, Saul, why persecutest thou me?' The other was the shining transfiguration that linked Christ to the great figures of the Old Testament, Moses and Elias (Matthew 17. 1–6): 'and behold a voice, out of the cloud, which said, This is my beloved Son, in whom I am well pleased, hear ye him. And when the disciples heard it, they fell on their face, and were sore afraid.'

The handout ends with one more juxtaposition. Malamud quotes Genesis 2.19–20 on the Lord God forming every beast of the field and fowl of the air and bringing them unto Adam: 'to see what he would call them and whatsoever Adam called every living creature, that was the name thereof'.

And he puts just after it Keats's famous dictum to Bailey, 22 November 1817, on the Imagination as comparable to Adam's dream: 'he awoke and found it truth'. Art was the recreation of a minor miracle, but its revelations arose out of the midst of formal discipline, the renunciation involved in an initial paring down. In 'The Swaying Form', an essay by Howard Nemerov which Malamud prized and used with his students, form is itself described as an act of 'faith'. Once an event has been isolated—'treated as a situation in itself, and considered apart from the flux of all things'—then 'nature, so treated, will reveal the [situation's] secret name'. [8] That secret name bursts out as art—the poets, like Adam, thus using words as though for the first time again. All this is what Malamud called 'the quality of surprise—that surprise which creates the marvelous' (LC II 10.9).

What, almost paradoxically, Malamud was thus trying to teach his students was *surprise* in its most serious forms. In prose fiction, as opposed to poetry, the surprise intrinsic to life was registered through the turns of *story*:

> Plot relates all the way back to the epistemological drama of our lives—that being constituted as we are, we cannot know all, and that being constituted as we are, we find it dramatic to find out, to know what is happening or has happened, to understand the nature of the mystery that involves us.
>
> (LC II 10.9).

'When the character starts to do things that surprise you,' he told Linda Lowell at Harvard, 'that's when you know the story's going'.[9]

The classes did not always work. What Malamud was saying meant more to him on the inside than he cared to show. Moreover, he often carefully conserved his energies for his writing. The language he used in class was residual: it was what was offered after the real work was over. As he said to his colleague Barbara Herrnstein Smith when he sensed that in conversation she found his views and use of language rather ordinary, 'You should know, Barbara: I never compete with my books'.[10] But student feedback could easily upset the thin-skinned man. Marjorie La Rowe had to explain to him that no criticism was intended by her fellow-students when they complained about the lack of student participation in Malamud's classes:

> I feel that we have slipped into an easy reliance on your opinions instead of formulating our own. Not entirely, but we are polite and passive waiting for you to 'pass judgement'. No one said that you would want a class that way. When we discussed alternatives to the way the class is run, it was not a slap in your face …. As for what was said of you personally, I did not hear any hostility in it at all. I mean that. When someone spoke of you as 'paternal' I didn't think

she was implying that you shouldn't be. She was explaining a reaction to you, a reason why she would hold back from speaking in class.   (HRC 7.8)

Paul Malamud knew his father in this mood:

> He wanted to be affectionate. I think he wasn't able to cope always with the non-ideal quality of a lot of relationships. He was always wishing people would be more for him emotionally, and he may have felt, 'Well, I'll try to be a good father, but why don't my kids love me more?' He could not be comfortable enough with his students, probably because of his sense of early injury. He could not think like a more cynical kind of person who was more marinated in America would think, 'This student is disagreeable', but 'This kid is attacking and hurting me', when he should not have perceived it that way. Mom said after he died, 'Your father was so sensitive.' One of his weak points was that it was too easy for him to feel cut to the quick, but to do him justice, that was the real him.[11]

And without that mixture of vulnerability and self-protection, what did get through to him would never have got through so powerfully.

Everyone sensed the defences, the shield of formality Malamud set up around himself to protect both the writing and the past vulnerabilities alike. Often in daily life he could not use that writer's third eye, that objectivity which in his writing included a clear view of himself, except in retrospect or contrition. The psychiatrist Arnold Cooper, teaching a class to Columbia undergraduates on Psychoanalysis and Literature, once asked Malamud to join him, the class having read several stories of his, including 'My Son the Murderer' and 'The Letter':

> During the two-hour session, Bern got into a vigorous, rather angry argument with members of the class as to how one of the stories should be understood. The students thought it clear that the son was the legitimately aggrieved party and the father was being impossible. Bern insisted that the son had failed to be adequately understanding, and the father's motives were pure. The discussion was heated. Malamud insisted that his interpretation was correct because he wrote it, he knew what he meant, and he knew what he conveyed. The class insisted that it didn't matter what he consciously intended; he had conveyed something else.
> Riding downtown later in the taxicab, he was silent for a long time, and finally said, 'You know, they're right.'[12]

On the page he knew precisely how to put more into his work than he was conscious of. But off the page, he would tighten and assert his control again—the just and generous shift of self and point of view often achievable only belatedly, on second thought. 'You know, they're right.'

For all his controlling caution and defensiveness, Malamud knew he needed his changes and his surprises everywhere, high and low, serious and comic. So—like so much in himself—he used his caution against itself, to provoke and use what broke out against it. This need to provoke could even include the family cat, as he explained to Rosemarie Beck, 11 June 1960. 'Cokey found me lying on the grass and licked my head above the ear. I ran my tongue along her cheekbone—was she surprised. Everybody expects the expected.'

Writing

Idiots First had been published in September 1963. In addition to the great title story, it contained two early stories 'The Cost of Living' (written in 1949 and set in the grocery store) and The Death of Me' (1950, concerning terrible squabbles in a tailor's shop); two stories that were about Fidelman ('Still Life' and 'Naked Nude') plus two other Italian stories ('The Maid's Shoes' and 'Life is Better Than Death'); a college story of unkindness, referring back to the years out west ('A Choice of Profession'); and a scene from the play he had failed to complete in 1961 ('Suppose a Wedding'). There was also 'The Jewbird', a reworking of Howard Nemerov's short story 'Digression Around a Crow', which belongs with 'Taking Horse' and *God's Grace* amongst Malamud's animal fables; 'Black Is My Favorite Color', which is in part a precursor for *The Tenants*; and 'The German Refugee', which links the early Jewish stories with the writing of *The Fixer*.

'The German Refugee' had been singled out by Stanley Edgar Hyman in a review in *The New Leader*, 28 October 1963. Going back to Malamud's tutoring of Jewish immigrants, it is the story of the Jewish intellectual who gassed himself because the wife he had left behind in Germany, suspecting her to be like her mother an anti-Semite, had converted to Judaism in his absence and found herself 'transported to a small border town in conquered Poland'. Hyman had praised the collection as a whole for making Jewish material achieve 'universality', evolving it into the Christian theme of redemptive sacrifice and in turn making that theme 'thoroughly secularized'. Offering his end-of-year report on his Bennington colleague, Hyman stated that Malamud 'at times writes very well indeed'—Annamaria smells 'like salted flowers' to Fidelman; a man crying looks 'as though he had been sprayed with something to kill flies'; a subtle thought put through refugee English 'comes out like a piece of broken bottle'; but says the secular, rational literalist in Hyman: 'his prose is often very careless. Sentences outrage syntax ('Edie bowed her head though not Cohen') and even tense ('He would watch Rosa working, then went in and wrote'). Malamud made a one-page summary of Hyman's comments, adding a long exclamation mark against the alleged carelessness of his prose.

'After I wrote "The German Refugee" [March 1963],' he recalled, 'I was determined to do a novel using political or social experience as the basis of my fiction' (TH, 139). *The Fixer* was the result of this further attempt at change—using national and historical material as a source for the imagination, and yet containing this broadened subject-matter within a single person, Yakov Bok, himself unjustly contained within a prison in late-Czarist Russia, between the years 1911 and 1913. Malamud wrote to his brother Eugene of his difficulty in beginning, 29 October 1963: 'It's set in a country I have never visited—Russia before World War One. You can imagine it takes a lot of nerve to write about a place as though one knew it. The result is that I often approach the writing with a kind of dread' (HRC 36.6).

The title came from more parochial origins. When he was writing a *New Life* in Oregon, Malamud had sometimes taken a room in the Frontier Hotel, on Second Street, Corvallis, where he could write all day undisturbed. There from a second-floor window he could see the sign of the local hardware shop of 'Jim the Fixer'. It was to be the story not of some big-time operator who could fix everything, but an odd-job man who could mend or affect little. Yet Malamud began his thinking in 1962 with six months' reading in search of stories of social injustice. Two such stories were set in America—for the original idea was to do with a moral canker at work in American life, possibly centering on the current situation of the negroes, in the light of the writings of William Faulkner and Ralph Ellison. One of those stories was the case of Caryl Chessman who, already on parole, was charged in 1948 with being the Red-Light Bandit, and found guilty of rape and kidnapping. In the course of an unavailing twelve-year campaign to establish his innocence, he became a writer despite being prohibited from writing and held under close surveillance, and smuggled out the manuscripts of three autobiographies and one novel, *Cell 2455 Death Row*, which sold more than half a million copies. The other American cause célèbre was that of Sacco and Vanzetti, two Italian immigrant anarchists who were accused of robbery and murder at the height of America's 'Red Scare' in 1920. Their defence increasingly focused upon the evidence that the prosecution was politically motivated. Their execution on 23 August 1927 seemed to many liberals to mark the symbolic death of the utopian vision of a fundamental justice and idealism in American life. It partly fuelled the writing of John Dos Passos's *USA* trilogy in the thirties.

But increasingly Malamud's initial research became involved with the notorious Dreyfus affair, when in France in 1894 Captain Alfred Dreyfus, a Jew, was falsely tried for espionage on behalf of the German Empire. The anti-Semitism behind the verdict inspired Zola's famous open letter of protest to the President, 'J'accuse', for once again it was the relation to the act of writing that also interested Malamud. Dreyfus was only pardoned in 1899 and not exonerated until 1906. But the personality of the man himself Malamud found emotionally uncongenial. 'He was a dullish man, and though he endured well he did not suffer well' (TH, 18). As so often in Malamud, to suffer was more than externally to endure. It meant the testing commitment of the inner emotions, however reluctantly.

Finally Malamud recalled a parallel to Dreyfus in a story that his father, that mild and dreamy Socialist, had told him from the Old Country. It was the case of Mendel Beilis, a Jew arrested by the secret police in Kiev in 1911 and accused of the ritual murder of a Christian boy, using his blood, it was alleged, for the baking of matzos (the unleavened bread eaten at Passover). Beilis was jailed for two and a half years, awaiting trial, until finally declared innocent—so paltry and manifestly twisted was the evidence—in 1913. Again the case involved state anti-Semitism. On being freed, Beilis found he could no longer remain in Kiev where he continued to receive death threats, and emigrated to Palestine. In 1920 he moved to America and in 1926 published at his own cost *The Story of My Sufferings*, originally composed in Yiddish for the New York Jewish newspapers but released in an English translation by Harrison Goldberg. Maurice Samuel's non-fictional account of the affair, *Blood Accusation*, appeared in 1966 a few weeks before the publication of *The Fixer*. In the article by Granville Hicks in *The Saturday Review* Malamud is quoted as saying that he had used some of Beilis's experience but not the man himself, 'partly because his life came to less than he had paid for by his suffering and endurance, and because I had to have room to invent'. To help himself, Malamud had read in Russian and Jewish history and in the life of the shtetl, as well as drawing on the nineteenth-century Russian novel, particularly those by Dostoevsky. And there was the Old Testament—the Psalms and the Book of Job—which stood resonantly at the back of the work like the dramas that lay behind *The Natural*, *The Assistant*, and *A New Life*. He also kept in mind the plight of the black man in America, from slavery onwards, and the imprisonment of Nehru during the fight for Indian independence.

But just as Malamud insisted that his works were not autobiographical, so was he adamant that *The Fixer* was a fiction and not a work of history. He wrote to Rosemarie Beck of his mixture of strong tension and mild depression, unsure both of himself and of the project:

> The doubt centers on this new novel I have in mind. I had originally wanted to center a story (because I've never done any such thing) around people like Sacco

and Vanzetti, which I, like many people, felt was one of the great tragedies of American life in the twentieth century. However, I've decided that the reality is greater than any fiction; that is to say, I doubt a fiction could equal the effect of the incident ... so I settled for a combination of a blood ritual incident in pre-Soviet Russia, plus something like the Dreyfus incident. A man is put in prison, and there he must suffer out his existence with *what* he has and, in a sense, conceive himself again. It is, as you see, my old subject matter.

What troubles me is everything that is new, that I haven't done before. Should I be working on such a book at this stage of my career, or is the whole thing a mistake from start to finish?   (3 November 1963)

The challenging newness and the feared oldness worried him alike. The case of Sacco and Vanzetti was already like a structured fiction: 'I couldn't see any way of re-forming it' (TH, 18). The sense of a reality greater than any fiction weighed upon him, stifling confidence in his imagination. A case study could not be art: art required a mythological quality. Yet Malamud himself needed an underlying reality to give reinvention initial stimulus and continuing support.

In this struggling balancing act, there is no doubt that Malamud drew heavily upon the reassuring factuality of Beilis's autobiography, on which copyright had expired in 1954. Malamud took from Beilis more than the basic predicament. There was the idea of a fellow-prisoner acting as a spy on the one hand, and the Investigating Attorney committed to being a sympathetic liberal on the other. Malamud took from Beilis the details of foot infection and the prisoner's enforced and humiliating crawl to the hospital on his knees; the terrible entry of the winter cold and summer heat into the cell, and the persistently degrading searches of the prisoner's body by his guards; the threat of being poisoned by the authorities; the prisoner's sense of isolation from the outside world and yet of responsibility to the Jewish people for whom he was being made an example; his refusal of an amnesty in the determination to have his innocence proven at trial. It was like a flat, factual score for Malamud to perform upon.

On the other hand, while Mendel Beilis was married with five children, Malamud's protagonist, Yakov Bok, is a man whose barren wife has left him. Yakov lives illegally outside the Pale as overseer of a brickworks in Kiev, whereas Beilis, with a similar post, was formally allowed residence. Where Yakov is an angry freethinker, a reader of Spinoza opposed to religion, Beilis maintained the basic practice of his faith, even though, having lived for most of his life apart from the Jewish community, he lacked a formal religious education. Nonetheless David Beilis, one of Mendel's five sons, and subsequently David's son Jay, have made a case for plagiarism against

Malamud, quite properly and carefully detailing some close verbal parallels.[13] In November 1966 Malamud insisted that Yakov and Raisl in no way resembled Beilis and his wife, but the very differences upset David Beilis in so far as the closeness of the rest of the account meant that his parents would be dishonourably mistaken for Malamud's own version of them. Malamud decently made efforts to get his own publishers, Farrar, Straus and Giroux to republish Beilis's autobiography, with royalties to go to David and David's brother, but Roger Straus was not interested. David Beilis believed this was a cover-up, intended to show Malamud's apparently reparative goodwill yet still withholding exposure of the actual indebtedness.

Beilis 'died a bitter man—in New York', Malamud concluded: 'he thought he hadn't been adequately reimbursed for his suffering' (TH, 18). But Malamud could not win against the continuing family pain: if he admitted indebtedness, he was accused of traducing the Beilis family by his portrayal of his protagonist; if he denied it, he was guilty of unacknowledged copying. Malamud was no doubt a ruthless user of whatever in life or literature served his fiction, and also ultradefensive about the claims he needed to make for his imagination; but he was also right in pointing to the most significance difference of all—his work was art not case-history. When it mattered most, his sentences offered a different dimension and a deeper emotion.[14] In 'Malamud's Hidden Secret', Jay Beilis and Jeremy Simcha Garber offer, for example, a comparison between Beilis' account of the daily searches and Malamud's. First Beilis:

> The searches were usually performed by a squad of five under the supervision of one of the deputy wardens. Every time they would come in, the first order was for me to undress. Often they had to unbutton me for my fingers were awkward because of the cold. They were quite rude and usually tore off a number of buttons during the operation. Some exercised their rude sense of humor: 'You liked to stab the boy Andriusha, to draw his blood. We will do the same thing to you now'—that was the standing joke. They would also look into my mouth lest I might have something hidden there. They would pull my tongue out in order to see deeper and better. All these tortures and insults I had to undergo six times a day. It is hard to believe, but it is the truth. No protests were of any avail. Their intentions were to inflict the utmost inconvenience upon me.

Then Malamud's 'lurid, sensational, coarse and scatological details and language', adding 'his special artistic touch, a degrading anal search':

> And twice a day since he had been in this cell there were inspections of the fixer's body; 'searches' they were called. The bolts of the door were shot back,

and Zhitnyak and the Deputy Warden, with his smelly boots, came into the
cell and ordered the fixer to undress. Yakov had to remove his clothes—the
greatcoat, prison jacket, buttonless shirt, which were never washed though he
had asked that he be allowed to wash them; and then he dropped his trousers
and long drawers. He was allowed to keep on his threadbare undershirt, possibly
so he wouldn't freeze to death. They also made him remove the torn socks and
wooden clogs he had worn since the time the surgeon had lanced the sores on
his feet, and to spread his toes apart so that Zhitnyak could inspect between
them. ...

   Yakov had first to raise his arms and spread his legs. The Deputy Warden
probed with his four fingers in Yakov's armpits and around his testicles. The
fixer then had to open his mouth and raise his tongue; he stretched both cheeks
with his fingers as Zhitnyak peered into his mouth. At the end he had to bend
over and pull apart his buttocks.

   'Use more newspapers on your ass,' said Zhitnyak.

   'To use you have to have.'

   After his clothes were searched he was permitted to dress. It was the worst
thing that happened to him and it happened twice a day.   (Part 6.2, pp. 206–7)

It was precisely Beilis's sense that 'it is hard to believe, but it is the truth'
which was in need of Malamud's transformation. For it was not Malamud but
the prison guards who were 'coarse' and 'degrading': what he was rendering,
said Malamud in notes for an interview, was 'the quality of the humiliation
and mistreatment of the Jews under the Nazis' (HRC 31.3). The search was
the worst, he wrote, and the worst was what happened twice a day, every day:
this sort of sentence, together with the defiant Jewish wit of 'To use you have
to have,' Beilis could never offer.

Malamud began writing in late September, early October 1963, at just the
point when he sent his note to Arlene Heyman saying that he would not be
writing to her. He had two or three chapters completed by the end of 1963.
On 3 December he wrote to Rosemarie Beck:

   Almost anything I do is a willed effort; is this any more willed than something
   else—the old man young woman story which I promise myself for sometime in
   the future, for instance? ... Is the sheer backbreaking effort worth it, the doubts
   of the form and my ability to bring it to something significant?   (HRC 3.7)

Whilst struggling to write *The Fixer*, he was living the pain of what ten years
later was to become *Dubin's Lives*. By the summer of 1964 when the family
spent their holiday together back in Oregon, he had finished five chapters of
the first draft. He wrote a sixth while in Oregon and finished the whole of the
first draft by the end of 1964. The second draft was written in 1965. He visited

Russia in the summer of 1965—Kiev, Leningrad, and Moscow—to check on details for his novel, whilst Ann and Janna visited Rome, the family meeting together to spend the rest of the summer in France and then Spain with Alex and Bernadette Inkeles. Malamud wrote Clark Blaise of his Russian trip:

> I couldn't stop looking—at people, houses, streets, rivers, fields—everything interested me in much the same way Italy did when I first arrived there in 1956. I walked around Kiev a good deal to visit places I deal with in my book, and saw about 75% of what I would have liked to. However I know what the reality is now, and that makes it easier to depart from it.[15]

That last was typical of the anxieties of an imaginative realist halfway through his novel: checking on what he was reassured to find he did not need to know. Meanwhile, during their own ten days in Rome, Janna, aged thirteen, often found Ann crying, alone, for no apparent reason. The marriage and the affairs on both sides were taking their toll. Ann had seen a psychiatrist in the summer of 1963.

Malamud himself was depressed and anxious. But he lectured his own students on how to use a neurosis. Its source might be worry about money or health or work or love, but was often unconscious. It produced depression or uneasiness, 'usually in the morning not long after awakening, although the person may have gone to bed healthy' (LC II 9.5). But one must learn to write in these moods and use their force for and not just against oneself.

Thus the work went on, locked into its routine. For over two years Malamud struggled to write inside the prison of his novel, managing steadily a page or two a day in draft one, two to four pages a day in draft two. Just occasionally the family got a glimpse of his innermost thoughts—as Janna recalled:

> He once, while tucking me in at night, announced that had I been living in Germany during World War II, the Nazis would have killed me because I was the daughter of a Jew. The memorable intensity of his comment makes me think he may well have also spent time imagining his own fate in Germany, as well as in the turn-of-the-century Russian world his parents fled.   (MFB, 214)

She was only a child and the father was telling her this at bedtime. But the child of a lapsed Catholic mother and a non-practising Jewish father would not have been spared. As he later put it in his notes for an interview: 'It had happened in the past and then happened more severely in the time of the Nazis, and might indeed happen tragically again if something isn't done to make it not happen' (HRC 31.3).

The third draft of *The Fixer* was begun in Bennington in the winter term and finished in March or April 1966. As he explained to Rosemarie Beck, it had been a long ageing slog, without many moments of pure inspiration:

> I suspect that what has happened to me is that I am almost totally a professional writer. I don't mind that—in fact it's the only way I can really function now as a writer, but I do regret the loss of the romance of writing. I suppose that what I'm saying is that I am no longer young.... I'd still like to achieve the heights of happiness of a young person. At least once a year.   (28 December 1965)

What was professionally extraordinary about the writing of *The Fixer* was how Malamud laboriously elaborated upon his already exhaustive drafting process, particularly in the fifteen-month composition of the first draft. In the note he supplied to the manuscript in the Library of Congress, he describes his tortuous workings:

> For the first draft I worked somewhat as follows
>
> 1. handwritten draft, paragraph by paragraph, usually destroyed
> 2. (A in the folder) typed draft, usually made the same day of the scribbled handwritten draft
> 3. After I had done a version of the next chapter (two) I did another handwritten revision of Chapter One (B in the folder) and then typed that, as much as I had written by hand that day (C in the folder). I followed that method throughout the book, of revising the previous chapter after I had done the first version of the next. However, I didn't do that for [the final] Chapter Nine.
> 4. After completing nine chapters in this fashion I rewrote the book on lined yellow paper (D in this folder) and from that my wife typed a clean copy—the completed first draft.

Five versions of each chapter—alternately handwritten, then typed up—*before* the final typing of what was then only the *first* draft. He was thus revising in two versions (hand and type) the previous chapter, *after* completing the first version of the next—as though it were one step back again for every fresh step forward. And then he had to revise all the chapters together again, in continuous sequence, as an artistic whole. This was at least three drafts in one, as of a man building in doubt from the ground, or inching his painful way forward, maintaining his routine uncertainly in the midst of what lay ahead and behind.

As he neared the end of the first draft, Malamud wrote to Clark Blaise, 2 February 1965:

There are sections that need deepening and enriching, and I would ordinarily
be looking forward to that, but the steady grind has tired and tensed me, and
I'm somewhat on the worn out side but expect to revive when the writing
begins to look as though it can live by itself.

That was the deal, as by symbiosis: that he gave his whole life to it, until it,
coming to life as a result of the long hard labour, in turn could revitalize him
for his pains. But as he finally told Saul Maloff in an interview for *Newsweek*,
12 September 1966, 'The book nearly killed me—but I couldn't let go of it.
It wore me out, made me a nervous wreck. But I wouldn't let go of it—and
that proved to me at last that I'm a professional.'

The Fixer

To Rosemarie Beck he concluded, 12 March 1966: 'a prison is a hard thing to
give variety to. But there's a man in the book and a lot of feeling.'

Malamud had long had his fears that he could not make drama out of
the sheer monotony of solitary imprisonment. But actually this is where
he excelled—turning a *theme* such as freedom or imprisonment, which in
shorthand was an intellectual banality, into an *experience* simply by making
it go on and on, closer to real time than are most realist novels, until the
situation's densened reality was irresistible. It was the 'heavy slowdown' he
had brought about in *The Assistant* to make the store 'as purgatory' (HRC
4.11). Malamud does not just put his innocent small-time fixer into that
situation, he keeps Yakov there, keeps returning him to it when he most
needs to escape it, with a verbal variety that nonetheless insists that it is still
all the same. It is not just a situation with a fixed name, for after it has
been described, explained, and even understood, it still must continue to be
lived—that is what a novel means for Malamud.

Falsely accused of the ritual murder of a Christian child, Yakov Bok, in
shock, at first feels that what is happening is happening to someone else.
Initially he hopes that if he just *explains* what has happened—why he was
tempted to take the post at the brickworks without confessing he was a Jew;
but how he had nothing to do with the murdered child—then he will be
released. But then he gradually realizes, as through a third eye, that in this
world of unfamiliar experience no one has to believe his truth. There are no
guaranteed or even minimal rules of humane conduct or reason here. The
clear internal knowledge that he is innocent may have no objective status,
may make no difference to reality. It is a major shift of expectation. 'Behind
the world', the fixer now sees, 'is another world' (Part 5.5, p. 182)—and this

other world of lies and persecution distorts and perverts the ordinary one
until its reality is almost overwhelmed and forgotten.

In this terrible new world, prison is now a matter of time, and time, and
time again—until sheerly by the repetition of itself the notionally known
becomes almost unknown again in its intensity. Here is Yakov Bok, in solitary
confinement, with all the mental structures of ordinary sense now exposed to
the strains of an extraordinary existence:

> You wait. You wait a minute of hope and days of hopelessness. Sometimes you
> just wait, there's no greater insult. You sink into your thoughts and try to blot
> out the prison cell. If you're lucky it dissolves and you spend half an hour out
> in the open, beyond the doors and walls and the hatred of yourself .... The
> worst thing about such thoughts is when they leave you and you are back in
> your cell. The cell is your woods and sky.
>
> Yakov counted. He counted time though he tried not to. Counting presup-
> posed an end to counting, at least for a man who used only small numbers.
> How many times had he counted up to a hundred in his life? Who could count
> for ever?—it piled time on. The fixer had torn some splinters off sticks of
> firewood. The long splinters were months, the short, days.   (Part 6.7, pp. 226–7)

By this point you don't leave thoughts, they leave you. The man is left
waiting for his indictment—which he also knows may never come. But that
it *may* come is like that almost hallucinatory half an hour lost in imagination
of what it is like to live on the outside again: the thought of the better
makes life worse and, because of the involuntary hope, more like suffering
than enduring. 'The indictment was very slow. The thought that it might
sometime come made it so slow' (Part 7.1, p. 243). But if he also knows
that the indictment may never come, when does 'never' happen? Given no
time at which something does *not* happen, when would be the right time
to give up waiting, even supposing he can or should or must? There is no
right time left in a world which is turning out of Malamud's ordinary world
into Kafka's or Dostoevsky's nightmare insanity. That is why Malamud is
great—not because he is naturally as great as what Dubin calls the big ones,
but because the reader can see the process of greatness coming out of the
ordinary—the limited man of 'small numbers' (be he Bok or Malamud)
finding himself in a limitless situation and gradually forced to find in himself
what can respond to it. 'The truth is,' says Yakov, 'I'm a half-ignorant man.
The other half is half-educated' (Part 3.1, p. 84). Malamud wanted to start
that low down, with the ordinary failures, as in a human first draft, and
only then created that limitlessness, that saturation which demanded more
of himself, beyond the normal boundaries of sanity. The reader could then
see the small man forced to become as Job, and the language itself, likewise,

growing great in his trouble. The thing gets made. 'The artist will leave in
his work evidence of the original material, or the fingertips of reshapement,'
wrote Malamud:

> when the stone itself is seen in the form or through the form. Or if the work is
> created in plaster, the lines the fingers make are visible—as brush stokes are in
> painting.   (LC II 10.9)

Malamud's material is words in the act of their shaping their meanings.
For example, in the shrug of his Jewish question '*Who could count for ever?*'
'forever' ought to be the object of the verb 'to count', but there may be no
object to it at all; 'for ever' is an adverb instead—he cannot count for ever,
for he'll only be for ever counting. Robert Boyers, introducing Malamud at a
reading, said that his work 'feels at every moment like a made thing, though
at the same time it is without affectation, urgent even while moving over a
small square of turf.'[16]

The guards are forbidden even to tell the prisoner what month it is.
Yakov Bok needs his splinters for some sort of order, some sort of form.
The Malamudian concern for habit is now made vital: against the unrelieved
monotony of nonexistence, Yakov needs the human rituals of the splinters,
the daily sweeping of the cell, the passing of water. The morning dark,
he notices, is different from the night dark; it has a little more freshness,
a little natural anticipation. But actually the morning is only another part
of the repetitive cycle: there is no beginning, no end, no form any more.
He guesses: 'It would soon—soon?—be a full year of prison. He did not,
could not, think past a year. He could not foresee any future in the future'
(Part 6.7, p. 228). Malamud's human sentence is under threat here: the
human meaning of the word 'future' is dissolving in front of his eyes, just
as 'for ever' did (the two formulations—neither of which are in the first
draft—come together in a later version). *After* an event has happened, you
can realize through its relief that you were waiting for it all along, even
when you were hoping against hope. But *beforehand*, you don't even know
if it can be called waiting after a while, and there is no 'before' if nothing
comes after. Here is a man forced beyond those normal expectations of sense
and reason which are inherent in language itself. But the very sense of being
beyond that framework of normality is contained within his still being forced,
unavailingly, to employ it.

For human sanity's sake, Bok needs to set an arbitrary limit of one year of
waiting—just as, in a much lesser way, Malamud himself could only bear to
think he was writing three drafts, not three hundred. After that one year, it
can only get ever more senseless for the prisoner:

Sometimes, if he thought about it, three days went by, but the third was the same as the first. It was the first day because he could not say that three single days, counted, came to something they did not come to if they were not counted. One day crawled by. Then one day. Then one day. Never three. Nor five or seven …. If he were in Siberia serving twenty years at hard labour, a week might mean something. It would be twenty years less a week. But for a man who might be in prison for countless days, there were only first days following one another. The third was the first, the fourth was the first, the seventy-first was the first. The first day was the three thousandth.   (Part 8.1, p. 280)

Frank Alpine, in contradiction with himself, counted the money he stole. But here even while Yakov is counting, nothing counts. He paces his cell in circular entrapment. 'He walked to Siberia and back' (Part 6.4, p. 218), but was still only in the cell, without Siberia's term of imprisonment.

The only help for Yakov Bok has been in the liberal investigating magistrate, Bibikov, who wants him to know he does have a friend in the world. 'You are not alone,' he tells the fixer (Part 5.5, p. 187). In manuscript B, the second, handwritten version of the first draft, Yakov replies painedly, 'In my cell I'm alone' (LC I 17.3, p. 38); then in the second draft he adds, 'In my thoughts I'm alone.' That is what the re-draftings are doing, adding to that inner dimension, creating Malamud's experiment in what 'thoughts' can and cannot do for such a man.

That thought of another human being supporting him does make a difference. In the very next scene, Yakov hears the sounds of another anguished prisoner, newly entered the next cell, and seeks closer human contact. They try shouting to each other but Yakov cannot hear words of civilized human sense, only raw heartbreaking noises seeking a language and a listener. The prisoner in the next cell then bangs repeatedly on the wall, as though to find a way through by code. Yakov bangs back, hopefully. But then comes this terrible sentence: 'Sometimes they uselessly banged on the wall at the same time.' Malamud had worked to get to it: he added 'uselessly'; he substituted 'at the same time' (one of his trademarks) for the almost equally ironic 'together'—all to make a little symbol of the human attempt at fellow-feeling foiling itself precisely through the equal needs on each side of the wall.

Then the banging and the shouting stop. Soon after, the drunken guard forgets to lock Yakov's cell. He does not know if it is a trick or trap, but eventually goes so far as to peep into the next cell. There a man is hanging by his belt. 'It took the fixer an age to admit it was Bibikov' (Part 5.6, p. 163).

As so often in Malamud, something is given only to be taken away. With the death of Bibikov, the worst for Yakov is the almost paradoxical thought that nowhere, by anyone, is he being *thought of*. He has disappeared from the world. That is why Yakov thinks of *writing*—the primal act for so many of the victims of injustice in Malamud's reading for *The Fixer*, the one thing that had saved Malamud himself—to try to give what was invisibly reduced to the vulnerable and subjective a more solid and undeniable existence in this world:

> If only his innocence were written on a sheet of paper, he could pull it out and say, 'Read, it's all here,' but since it was hidden in himself they would know it only if they sought it, and they were not seeking. (Part 5.4, p. 165)

'The more he thought about it, the more he wanted to write. He had a desperate desire to make known his fate' (Ibid. 171). 'Oh that my words were written,' cried Job, 'that mine adversary had written a book'. But in life there was no visible text of how it truly was. All Yakov has is that written travesty called the indictment, when finally it arrives. He almost thinks that if he looks at it hard enough he will be able so to rearrange the distorting lies as to make the truth shine through them.

But without Bibikov he has now only himself—whatever that is. Everyone supposed Malamud to be intellectually inferior to Saul Bellow, but what he is here conducting is a primal experiment in the drama of thinking: to see if *thoughts* can help, can transcend or remake, their own *thinker*. For in Malamud's world of the oddly chosen, those who don't have the sheer intellectual facility for a thousand ideas may be precisely the ones to know how important a single thought might be in a life.

This is why increasingly in his second draft Malamud brings in Spinoza in dramatic opposition to Job, between the two of whom the fixer is left stranded, a small man unable to emulate either. It is from his previous reading of Spinoza, long before his imprisonment, that Yakov gets the idea that the mind may be freed by the thoughts within itself. The finite may think of the infinite and in thinking of it, partly become it. As Yakov struggles to explain it: 'If you understand that a man's mind is part of God, then you understand it as well as I. In that way you're free, if you're in the mind of God ... It's as though a man flies over his own head on the wings of reason, or some such thing. You join the universe and forget your worries' (Part 3.1, p. 85).

This God of Spinoza's is very different from the traditional, personal God of the Jews. 'In the shtetl God goes running around with the Law in both hands, but this other God, though he fills up more space, has less to do altogether' (Ibid.). More like an *It* than a *He*, Spinoza's God is 'the eternal infinite idea of God as discovered in all of Nature. This one says nothing;

either he can't talk or has no need to. If you're an idea what can you say? One has to find him in the machinations of his own mind' (Part 7.3, p. 255). But what the fixer now finds is that he cannot get beyond his worries, his body, or that physical imprisonment that affects his mind too.

And yet something of what Spinoza stands for stays with him. When he is conveyed from the prison to the courthouse for a brief arraignment, he has a visionary sense of the world as one interrelated whole: 'It seemed to him he was seeing for the first time how the world was knit together' (Part 6.8, p. 230). And later back in his hallucinations, chained to the wall, he still innerly struggles after something to liberate him:

> Maybe a wall will collapse, or sunrise burn through it and make an opening as large as a man's body. Or he will remember where he has hidden a book that will tell him how to walk with ease through a locked-and-twelve-times-bolted door   (Part 8.2, p. 289)

But if you cannot find the book with the freeing thought, if you cannot for long join the universe and forget the self, if seeing your own dilemma only increases it, and your own body is the instrument that tortures you—*then* all this becomes more like the terrible vision of Job: 'Wherefore is light given to him that is in misery?' Better not to see, to feel, or to be conscious, if these gifts only serve further to take away. 'Spinoza thought himself into the universe but Yakov's poor thoughts were enclosed in a cell. Who am I to compare myself?' (Part 6.5, p. 220).

In this worst of both worlds, Spinoza had helped destroy his belief in the old God without giving him belief in the new one. Equally, on the other side, it means that Yakov still feels the lack of the personal God in whom still he cannot believe.

What is more, the fixer is persecuted precisely because he is a Jew—though in himself he does not believe in Judaism or the Jewish God. Nothing adds up or makes sense, and yet Malamud maintains a strong language precisely for that reason. Ironically Job-like, the fixer angrily maintains his ways of protest against God's injustice, in the very tradition of that great Jewish argument with God, which was to fascinate Malamud again in the writing of *God's Grace*. 'Whatever I said he never answered me,' the fixer complains of God, 'Silence I now give back' (Part 7.6, 272). As Malamud put it of Yakov in an interview after publication of *The Fixer*: 'He is not without religion. He is concerned with God .... I am always interested in the irreligious man's unrelenting concern with God' (LC I 16.2).[17]

Thus in his desperation for any word, thought, or feeling, the fixer puts together the broken fragments of what he can remember from the

Psalms, saying them out loud to no one it seems but the overhearing guards, yet finding himself in the voicing of them. 'I am weary with my groaning … Unrighteous witnesses rise up; They ask me things that I know not … Arise, O Lord; O God lift up Thy Hand' (Part 6.5, p. 221). When Malamud won the National Book Award for *The Magic Barrel*, he complained about the words of disinheritance—'fragmented, abbreviated, other-directed, organizational'—that man had invented to describe himself in the modern world: 'The devaluation exists because he accepts it without protest' (CBM, 14). But Malamud's real protest against the 'fragmented' was within his novels—as here, in Yakov's fight to make something for himself out of those still inheritable fragments of ancient words. But then, bitterly, Yakov laughs at himself for what he is doing.

The guards give him the New Testament instead, mockingly to show him the light of conversion. Reluctantly at first, he reads the story of Jesus, 'a strange Jew'. Though it is by nominally Christian believers that he is persecuted, Yakov Bok is now a man glad of anything that maintains the human spirit. 'That Yakov reads the New Testament has no "hidden meaning",' Malamud insisted, 'He uses anything he can get his hands on in his own self defence' (HRC 5.11). Above all the Crucifixion moved him, with God giving no help. Yet how can a Jew, a Christ-killer, memorize and recite this? thinks the guard named Kogin. And how can Christians originate in this and then carry out what they are doing to me? thinks Yakov. 'I know that some say Bok is a Christ figure,' Malamud said later, 'but anyone who is unjustly tormented becomes Jesus' (CBM, 28).

The whole novel is rooted in such paradoxical structures of the religious-in-the-unreligious, of belief and unbelief struggling together. Early in the novel, Shmuel, Yakov's father-in-law, quotes Job before God: 'Though he slay me, yet I will trust in him'—but omits the third clause that suits the fixer best: 'but I will maintain mine own ways before him'. In Job it is more religious, not less so, for the final 'but' of that saying, still loyal to the sincerity of its human truth. Shmuel is in the same tradition when beautifully he says of his daughter, the wife who deserted Yakov, 'I've cursed her more than once but I ask God not to listen' (Part 1.2, p. 16). And so is Yakov himself when he says of that God, 'I blame him for not existing' (Part 7.6, p. 271). For Yakov, the blame has more belief in it than has the mere belief in God's nonexistence. The good secular humanist, Bibikov, had said that though he was sceptical of civilization, 'I act as an optimist because I find I cannot act as a pessimist' (Part 5.5, pp. 184–5). But for Yakov Bok 'the thing is not to believe or the waiting becomes unbearable' (Part 7.6, pp. 271). Yet on the eve of his trial when Kogin the guard offers the prisoner his food, Yakov refuses, saying he wishes to fast:

> 'What the hell for?' said Kogin
> 'For God's world.'
> 'I thought you didn't believe in God.'
> 'I don't.'   (Part 9.5, p. 288)

There is a loyalty to *something* there, as though it did not matter even to himself what Yakov Bok actually believed or disbelieved—or thought he did. And in that loyalty he can make that something *be*, in him, even if paradoxically he does not believe in it elsewhere. As Levin said in *A New Life*, 'This is how we invent it when it is gone.'

It is a loyalty that spreads even to the guard who could have remained safely on the opposing side. Towards the very end, it is Kogin, like the lowly servant at the blinding of Gloucester in *King Lear*, who intervenes to prevent the Deputy Warden shooting Yakov on the morning of his trial, and is himself killed for it: 'His deep voice broke. "I've listened to this man night after night, I know his sorrows. Enough is enough, and anyway it's time for his trial"' (Part 9.5, p. 343). It is like being surprised by humanity.

It is the same surprise as when Raisl, the fixer's estranged wife, comes to see Yakov in prison. She did not give him a child and she deserted him for another man. He is shocked 'that the feelings of the past could still be alive after so long and terrible an imprisonment' (Part 8.4, p. 299): he had been nearly insane, chained, and reduced to a beast, but this small, domestic piece of wrecked human feeling still survived and revived even in its pain. Why has she come? She cries before him—or rather as Malamud puts it: 'Tears flowed through her fingers as she pressed them to her eyes'. Then he writes (Illustration 23): 'He watched. What else could he do? He felt the weight of the blood in his heart.' Then Malamud crosses out those first two sentences—the 'what else could he do?' should be felt anyway, without explicitness. 'As he watched, he felt the weight of the blood in his heart.' But it is still not quite right enough for Malamud, though he knows that almost psalm-like 'the blood in his heart' *is* right. Then it is that Malamud finds the sentence that by its sheer cadence creates a real imaginative feeling of the living 'weight' of it all: 'He felt, as he watched her, the weight of the blood in his heart' (Ibid. 303).

Yet at the same time Yakov also says to Raisl, 'What are you crying for?' 'For you, for me, for the world,' she replies (Ibid.). She is new to him, different from their old bitter life together. And in a characteristic double

movement it then goes, simply: 'As she wept she moved him': the first clause
unknowingly creating the second. The second draft is still residually rueful
and bitter, though: 'This was his talent, to make her cry.' But Malamud's
own heart is better, has won more from his own story, when in the final
draft he writes instead: 'As she wept she moved him. He had learned about
tears.'

Then she tells him she has had a child, after all, but the father has
abandoned them. This boy now needs a father in order not to be ostracized.
'There is no bottom to my bitterness, he thought.' Yet pretending to borrow
a pencil to write his confession, Yakov writes down instead that the son is his
own. It is all he has to give; there is nothing more he can lose. 'Whoever acts
the father is the father' (Ibid. 305). Whoever in any situation most feels the
want of pity must become that pity. In Malamud, judgment is always waiting
to be overturned by pity, the self to be turned by its own feelings. 'God will
bless you,' she says. 'Never mind God,' he replies (Ibid. 306).

Yet even in its quarrel with God, *The Fixer* is as implicitly religious a work
as is *The Assistant*. It does not matter greatly if the theology remains implicit
or half-broken, goes unrecognized or is not wholly understood. Its memory is
there, and whatsoever it really means is there, in the sudden decisive emotions
that surprise like forgotten messages reclaiming the man and making him do
something beyond himself.

Man corrects God. Perhaps that too would be part of God's plan if the fixer
could believe in Him. In fact the fixer makes his corrections out of unbelief.
'You could not pity anything if you weren't a man; pity was a surprise to
God' (Part 6.5, p. 220). And that is what Malamud's man does: surprise his
inferred or nonexistent God by offering or finding pity, when otherwise it
would seem lost to the world. 'If God's not a man,' he had said earlier to
himself, 'he has to be' (Part 8.2, p. 288)—he, Yakov, has to take that place.
This is the creature's incarnate argument against a God who, like the coming
of the day of trial or release, may be nonexistent, but should be what the man
replacing Him must be instead.

It was a thought Malamud had had in writing 'Idiots First'. There a
character called Ginzburg is pursuing the dying father and his idiot son,
like some devil or god of evil or angel of death. Finally after Mendel has
got the money and the ticket to send the son out west, Malamud adds one
more obstacle at the ticket barrier. For there is Ginzburg alongside the ticket
collector barring the way, claiming as ever that the law is the law: 'You
bastard,' cries Mendel, grabbing him by the throat, to let his son pass, 'don't
you understand what it means human?' Then there is a strange, intense,
floating moment in the midst of the mutual struggle:

Clinging to Ginzburg in his last agony, Mendel saw reflected in the ticket collector's eyes the depth of his terror. But he saw that Ginzburg, staring at himself in Mendel's eyes, saw mirrored in them the extent of his own awful wrath. He beheld a shimmering, starry, blinding light that produced darkness.

Ginzburg looked astonished. 'Who me?'

His grip on the squirming old man slowly loosened, and Mendel, his heart barely beating, slumped to the ground.

'Go,' Ginzburg muttered, 'take him to the train.'

The messages, cultural and personal, are fully absorbed in the medium. Let my people go. Look after Eugene. But it is Ginzburg seeing himself in the eyes of Mendel that marks a crucial reversal: the supernatural agent, for all its power to annihilate, is challenged by the natural passion in a grieving human and moved by it. 'This', said Clark Blaise, 'is Malamud's religious belief—that it is man's struggle that makes God take pity. It is when God—or something like God—looks into man's eyes and sees his own fury reflected in its effect on the human condition, his own cold reflection in man, that he then lets go. That's the writing act too. The novelist looking on the characters he has created, and wanting to have those characters look out from the page with that kind of need for salvation that redeems the novelist himself, claims his real feeling out of flat coldness.'

In this experiment in thinking, the fixer first thought 'Why me?' But soon he realized it could have been anyone, or at least any Jew accidentally caught in the wrong place at the wrong time and thus suddenly entangled in history. 'The involvement was, in a way of speaking, impersonal, but the effect, his misery and suffering, were not. The suffering was personal, painful, and possibly endless' (Part 5.4, pp. 165–6). At that point such double consciousness does not seem useful, the impersonal thought making little difference to the suffering itself. But crucially Yakov continues to have more of these oddly double thoughts, these thoughts that, as Spinoza might say, make their own thinker exist at different levels, extending the mind in its relation to the universe.

Another is about the strange relation of Israel and its God. From his reading of a few torn off pages of the Hebrew Bible, Yakov concludes that Israel accepts the covenant from God only in order to break it:

That's the mysterious purpose: they need the experience. So they worship false Gods ... Having betrayed the covenant with God they have to pay: war, destruction, death, exile—and they take what goes with it. Suffering, they say, awakens repentance, at least in those who can repent. Thus the people of the

> covenant wear out their sins against the Lord. He then forgives them and offers
> a new covenant.   (Part 7.3, p. 254)

God is Law, but the children of Israel have experience in which that law
comes and goes. And so the cycle begins again and again:

> Israel, changed yet unchanged, accepts the new covenant in order to break it
> by worshipping false gods so that they will ultimately suffer and repent, which
> they do endlessly. The purpose of the covenant, Yakov thinks, is to create
> human experience, although human experience baffles God.   (Ibid.)

It is like the paradoxical thought in St Paul that the law creates, back to front,
the hunger for a life beyond its prohibitions—the strict law and the yearning
hunger being two sides of Malamud himself. Out of such self-contradictory
richness comes the novel form itself, where bafflement is king. 'God envies
the Jews: it's a rich life. Maybe he would like to be human' (ibid.).

So it was Yakov Bok this time but it could have been anyone. Yet the
thought of it being 'anyone' will not finally do either, if it does not make
for experience. Yakov is at his deepest when his ordeal becomes something
which is not just *happening* to happen to him: 'He had learned, it wasn't
easy: the experience was his; it was worse than that, it was he. He was the
experience. It also meant that now he was somebody else than he had been'
(Part 9.4, p. 332). Typically, as Malamud learns through his protagonist, the
corrective addition that the experience was not only '*his*' but '*he*' belongs to
the second draft. 'You suffer for us all,' says his lawyer near the end. But
it was, says Yakov Bok, no glorious triumph, no voluntary martyrdom, just
'dirty suffering' (Part 9.3, p. 321). Yet within his experience he has found that
there is a story and that that story is *he*.[18]

Only then it is that you can make Ginzburg see himself through your
eyes. For if all those around you see you as an enemy, then at some point
you cannot remain anonymous, accidental, and merely frightened any more.
You have to be a self, you have to fit the situation you are in—or you
collapse and die. In this finally *un*assimilated novel, the Jew's second culture
makes Yakov something else, something different—inside the persecuting
world, yet not of it. Yakov's greatest mental move is then from the thought
of defiant suicide—'If I die I die to fuck them and end my suffering'—to
the thought of a defiant refusal of suicide: 'Why should I take from myself
what they are destroying me to take? Why should I help them kill me?'
(Part 8.2, p. 287). *That* is the freedom within necessity which Malamud
struggles to find in his first draft (Illustration 24). He wrote to Robert
Heilman, March 25 1960, of the possibility of creating such freedom in *The
Assistant*:

The human being is stuff, material, if he teaches himself what art can teach him, he will dare to enhance what he is. Of course to a degree. Granted the net of necessity we live in, those who think of it as net, or web, and not a brick wall, will remember the spaces among the reticulations. And if one thinks of it as a brick wall, because that is his premise, he ought to keep in mind how the scientists sometimes explain the quantum theory to those of our poor 'culture' - the balls bounce against the wall, but don't be surprised if one goes through the wall. I'm all for that. If a man thinks he is free, that is, if he knows what freedom means, he has a greater chance to be free. Knowing that is very helpful in writing stories.[19]

Like Yakov Bok within stone walls, Malamud in his revisions constantly sought to find and to make those tiny loopholes and fill them with the bursting sense of a life.

The Fixer is thus about the making of a *representative*. Granville Hicks wrote of *The Fixer* in the *Saturday Review*, 10 September 1966, under the headline: 'One man to stand for six million'. When Yakov looked to the world immediately outside him, everything seemed hopeless, and that hopelessness itself diminished his belief in whatever he had, inside him, to add to that world or fight against it. But when he thinks of himself as having to represent the Jews, then that is what enables him to give *himself* the help he had previously found wanting outside him. That means that ultimately even while he is suffering, Yakov Bok detects in that suffering the possibility of a transformative resistance—an exemplary appeal and a memory that turns the personal into the representative. The fixer achieves this, like Levin in recommitting himself to Pauline, only through double negatives, back to front. He will *not* kill himself; he will await and thus even enforce his own trial. What without Bibikov he cannot do for himself, as a sole person, he can do for himself as a representative of those Jewish memories still within him, reversing the stigma:

> All he can do is not make things worse. He's half a Jew himself, yet enough of one to protect them. After all, he knows the people; and he believes in their right to be Jews and live in the world like men. He is against those who are against them. He will protect them to the extent that he can. This is his covenant with himself. If God's not a man, he has to be.   (Part 8.2, p. 288)

Again, it is in the second draft that Malamud can find the meaning of what he has done in the first in Illustration 24. In the second he brings out those vital turns of mind: 'He is *against* those who are *against* them,' 'This is his covenant with *himself*,' '*If God is not ... he has to be.*'

Levin, likewise, in his smaller way, could only get to simple things, could only find 'the right thought', through the obstacles of complicated routes. But this time the small protagonist must accept the largeness of what he has done. When *The Fixer* won the National Book Award, Malamud quoted Melville in defence of the importance of literature's subject-matter: 'To produce a mighty book you must produce a mighty theme' (LC I 16.2). It is not, as one critic thought, that *The Fixer* is like Malamud boasting, trying to force his novel into mightiness. At what he took to be a bad time for sheer small-scale skill, Charles Samuels said that the book came out of Malamud's need to counter doubts about the narrowness of his range by working on a wider social and political canvas.[20] But in fact it is Yakov's *burden* that his story should be that great. As the realization comes through the second draft, again it is characteristically achieved through double negatives: 'One thing I've learned, he thought, there's no such thing as an unpolitical man, especially a Jew' (Part 9.6, p. 352). This is the wider, ancient meaning of political: that there is nothing human that can be sure of being wholly separate, safely unaffected, or utterly unimportant.

And even on the larger canvas, it is still the small subtle brush strokes of Malamud that matter. On the face of it, the extra stages of revision that Malamud added to the extensive process of rewriting already involved in *The Assistant* or *A New Life* contributed little in proportion to the amount of almost crazily repetitive labour involved. But however theoretically inefficient, however psychologically driven by uncertainty or depression—and whether the laborious process increased the power of immersed concentration or half-deliberately impaired facility—finally no one knows what would have happened or what might have been lost had it not been done that way. At any rate, at the end of the book there is one great image of what the second draft, in particular, gave to the novel.

The Fixer closes with Yakov Bok on his way to his trial, suddenly engulfed in a fantasy dream of confronting Tsar Nicholas the Second himself. As he raises his revolver on behalf of his people, the fixer cries, 'This is also for the prison, the poison, the six daily searches. It's for Bibikov and Kogin and for a lot more that I won't even mention.' Between his pointing the gun and pulling the trigger, what follows is inserted merely in brackets in the second draft: '(though Bibikov, flailing his white arms, cried no no no no)' (Part 9.6, p. 351). It is to be done for Bibikov—and then suddenly Bibikov himself would not have it done. It is the extra, little paradoxical thought from a separate angle, and another person, in a different dimension: not, after all, the justice of the missing God but His own mercy arguing against it. For Malamud it could only come on second thought, through another person, when the writer had a chance to raise another mind upon the basis of the first, and evolve shapes and movements beyond those offered by the predictably single-minded. That there was room for such surprise, and change, and small richness was what to Malamud made the novel form beautiful. Done even through the word 'no' rather than 'yes', this is mercy from the victimized in the name of something they better represent than either victimization or revenge. It could be straightened out and rationalized or thematized—and Malamud himself, summarizing in his customary stance of secular humanism, might speak of the defence of the 'human' or even of the 'mysterious'. But actually *The Fixer* works through a language of *paradox*, beyond logic, where patterns are created instinctively by sudden feeling or implicit memory. The shapes and their sudden changes hold the meaning, while the law, not fully revealed, works within them.

'A Rich and Famous Man'

Ruth Morris, the woman who had first introduced the Malamuds to each other, wrote on 27 August 1966 to congratulate the novelist on what he had achieved with *The Fixer*—and what it must have cost him to write the novel, whilst he maintained an outward normality: 'Bern, what completely awes me is that I saw you many times during the writing of *The Fixer*—you were calmly going about the business of being husband, father, friend, teacher—and all the while you were *draining* yourself of this!' (HRC 9.2). But Kenneth Burke sensed something extraordinary within the punishment that the book so powerfully represented: 'And as for what the heck may be eating at you with regard to Personal Complication ... please in Gottes Namen don't take me to be suggesting that I have the slightest inside idea as to what that might be, beyond the obvious fact that we all are necessarily being beaten down somewhat by something or other' (HRC 4.8).

On 13 September 1966 Rosemarie Beck had written urging Malamud, after all his pain, to enjoy his glory: 'You have paid well in advance so *that* anxiety must not constrain you.' Remarkably in 1967 *The Fixer* won both a National Book Award and a Pulitzer Prize and Malamud found himself at the height of his success. Yet on winning the Pulitzer, he was already anticipating in the *Bennington Banner* what the prize might cost him in terms of the future struggle to live up to it: 'I'm glad to have this attention focused on the book. I'm afraid, though, it won't make me a better writer' (LC I 16.2). 'Rocks on my head' was how increasingly he described his prizes to Danny Stern.

The adverse criticisms, the setbacks still counted for more, even in the midst of success. Malamud complained to Ann that even in the good reviews the reviewer too often did not understand what his work was really about. There was also a sad postscript in the history of the reception of *The Fixer*. In 1976 it was accused of being anti-Semitic, of all things, by some members of the Island Trees School Board and was removed from its school libraries. This was because it included anti-Semitic comments that were of course evidence of the outrage committed upon Yakov Bok. Here was a book on behalf of freedom and against prejudice, banned for what it opposed, in ignorance of what it stood for. The ban was later lifted as a result of court action, but there remained a stipulation that the librarian should send written notice to parents that the student had checked out a book that contained material the parents might find objectionable. When Malamud was told of the stipulation, he commented on 'a very sad situation' with a defence of what was truly *reading*: 'It confirms me more and more in the necessity of teaching students how to read fiction. The reason that the board has been in trouble is that the school board can't read fiction. Fiction is an enricher, a giver, a producer of its own kind of knowledge. There are people who are frightened by the imaginative, rather than excited by it' (LC I 16.1).

'Why kid myself,' he wrote to Rosemarie Beck, 23 September 1968, 'I work best in small rooms; otherwise one gets lost and away from the work.' Malamud was never going to break out. Yet money also came with the acclaim. In the early sixties, Malamud was earning around $20,000 a year. In 1967 his gross income was over $230,000. On 24 February, Roger Straus, who had called *The Fixer* one of the most important works he had published, wrote to him complaining of his resistance to the publication of an omnibus edition of three novels in one volume: 'It is difficult to go on thinking of ways to increase your sales, to give you wider visibility, to present you with enthusiasm and the quality your work deserves, when all of our ideas sifted through to you come back negative .... Bern, we tied up an enormous sum of money in *The Fixer* beyond—way beyond—the original contract terms, and we did it in order to put you into your present state of affluence and to put you in the position to have a capital problem rather than to have an income problem' (LC I 52.7). Payments had to be staggered over different financial years in order to reduce income tax. Malamud's gross income in 1968 was in excess of $88,000, and over $137,000 in 1969 when Malamud began donating his manuscripts and papers to the Library of Congress for tax relief of over $40,000.

'After all the years of work and emptiness,' wrote Claude Fredericks, Malamud's Bennington colleague, in his journal for 23 March 1970, the novelist was now 'famous and lionized', particularly in New York where Ann and he spent half the year. Malamud would only teach one term in Bennington, later only one class. 'I forget that Bernard is now a rich and famous man,' noted Claude Fredericks, 'and that being rich and famous, even in the most virtuous, alters something.'[21] What he saw was something that resulted from the mixture of new fame but continuing rigidity.

Fredericks has a journal entry for 5 September 1967 that recalls a scene from the evening before in the Malamud home:

> When I walked in the living room at six, Bernard and Ann were sitting in chairs opposite each other, Bernard singing Claudio, Claudio, as I walked in—but Ann, slovenly and slatternly, saying, I've just been sitting here telling Bern I must divorce him—that he is a wonderful man and has everything, that he can have any woman he wants now, that I've had him for 22 years and really ought to share him with someone else now.

It is like a scene straight out of Philip Roth's *The Ghost Writer*. Malamud, wrote Claude Fredericks, simply sat there, apparently contained and detached, 'his hands folded in his lap, smiling, quiet, impassive':

> I feel the deepest affection for Ann, but I am always amazed by what Bernard last night called her—tactlessness, her saying what she is feeling at the given moment; amazed at her own nakedness. But I am also always saddened by what seems her own desperation. I'm almost fifty, I'm not intelligent—who'd want me? she asked. Later she said: I'm pedestrian really. The truth is that for whatever reason she is painfully self-centered and like so many women strangely—lazy. The laziness is a kind of stubbornness.

Perhaps this is what comes from 'unequal marriages':

> And yet I think Bernard loves her deeply. He is too wise to look for fulfilment in love now, even if I am sure he yearns for it almost too much at times—and he is too good ever to destroy the woman by leaving her. But it must be a burden for him to live with her at times.

Malamud then took Claude Fredericks away to his study, to report on his critical reactions to an unpublished novel Claude had written ten years earlier: 'He is infinitely sweet but somehow not spontaneously warm, he is always exact and schoolmasterly in speaking of things, most of all literature, and I must ease my pain a little by remembering that.' It was too late for anything radically different.

In the complex Malamud economy, it was impossible to know how far he needed to stay impoverished, at some level, for the sake of his writing. 'Every day from nine to five for thirty years he has worked,' Claude Fredericks noted, 27 August 1967, 'He does nothing else. He really has no other interests or skills.' And in a kind of vicious circle this limited the writer he could be:

> He must 'live' more he was saying. He writes all day, he reads evenings, he allows himself to go out only two nights a week—but he senses that lack more and more, and he has, he thought, made some curiously wrong arrangement of his life. I couldn't say how much I agree with him—it is the very failing of his own writing, and if he wishes truly to be a great writer, he must indeed change.
>
> (23 September 1968)

But Fredericks was also thinking of himself, in hope that his own lesser discipline might make for greater art.

In a draft for his Malamud-based story, 'A Hunger Artist', Daniel Stern swiftly outlined in two sentences what he called Malamud's Law of Parsimony, a sort of reverse-greediness: 'That matters most which is created with the least possible means. Saying no to the feast of the world was his way of saying "yes".' For art meant that you could *see* the maximum arising out of the minimal, the extraordinary emerging within the bare ordinary, the ugly made beautiful by the single shift of a line. That was why one of Malamud's favourite moments was Lily Briscoe's final, minimalist move in Viriginia Woolf's *To The Lighthouse*—'She looked at her canvas; it was blurred. With a sudden intensity, as if she saw it clear for a second, she drew a line there in the centre. It was done; it was finished … I have had my vision.' In Malamud's vision, the almost dialectical relation between poverty and richness, need and asceticism was subtle and nuanced to imperceptible degrees which only art itself could register.

And Malamud himself did not dare tamper with its perilous equilibrium. Some time in the 1970s, Maggie Scarf advised him to seek help. She felt that the search for perfect love was damaging his health and holding back the development of his writing, 'I remember once when he was very upset—I can't remember what it was—and I was talking to him about it. I said to him, "Bern, why don't you see a therapist?" and he said "I'm really afraid of disturbing my gift." '22

Writing *The Fixer* had cost Malamud dearly. After the initial excitement of the prizes and the sales, there was finally only one thing that reconciled him to a novel that he found almost too painful to look back at. 'For a long time I could not face the book, then made peace with it particularly after my experience in Hungary' (LC II 12.3). He had refused to go to Hungary during the making of the film of *The Fixer*, which appeared in 1968 and made him an affluent man. Partly, as ever, he wanted to get on with his work, partly he was offended when the filmmakers told him that they did not want to make the film too Jewish, and had dissociated himself from the whole production. But 'my experience in Hungary' refers to a belated visit made with Ann in 1978. It was arranged through the scholar and translator Tamas Ungvari who had met Malamud at the home of C. P. Snow and Pamela Hansford-Johnson in London in 1964. In Hungary, surrounded by the country's literary Jews, Malamud patiently signed 500 copies of *The Fixer*, getting the people to spell out their names. It was not just that it appealed to Malamud's narcissism. What he saw was the remains of an East European culture which had survived the Soviet attacks on its writers, to value literature at a level deeper than any that modern consumerist America could recognize. And what they valued above all was *The Fixer* with its story of imprisonment. The experience offered Malamud what he had most wanted—a sense, beyond the merely personal and psychological, of the writer as serving a formal and impersonal mission: the ancient function of storyteller carrying news out of the isolation of the prison from town to town and country to country. It did not matter who he was or what else he had done. It was this revived sense of the vocation that, as Tamas Ungvari put it, 'gave Malamud back his belief in his book'.[23]

8

From *The Fixer* towards *Dubin*

'A Starvation Period'

Writing in 1982, the literary scholar Robert Alter argued that the vogue for American Jewish writing had reached its peak in the mid-1960s. It had been a brief and passing ten-year moment of emancipation, marking the emergence of a talented generation moving into mainstream literary assimilation. It brought with it a secular nostalgia for those origins in the old East Side and the world of the East European shtetl which it was already leaving behind. But for Alter this American-Jewish renaissance, the product of the sudden dynamic intersection of two cultures was too ambiguous, too incoherent an amalgam to survive as a genuine lasting culture. Malamud, in particular, was 'a gifted eccentric who, early on, invented a narrow but brilliant mode of short fiction peculiar to himself, connected only in the most tenuous way either with Jewish experience or with European literature; and having exhausted that limited vein, he has been floundering for nearly two decades.'[1]

In *Gates of Eden* (1977) Morris Dickstein charted a related historical phenomenon—the shift in American culture from the 1950s into the 1960s, towards the new counter-culture with all its liberationist challenges. In society, these forces included black power, radical feminism and gay militancy, the sexual revolution, experimentation in mind-altering drugs, the violent protest against Vietnam. In art, a reaction against humanist realism launched the development of avant-garde abstractionism and post-modernist experimentation in non-linear and self-reflexive forms. To Dickstein, Malamud's was the work of the old 1950s in its characteristic stoicism, endurance, and renunciation—'anguish hemmed in by form'.[2] A man such as Malamud might see the rise of John F. Kennedy as the culmination of the liberal New

Deal, but the replacement of Martin Luther King by Malcom X was precisely the sort of revolutionary change that the imagination of an older generation could hardly encompass. Malamud's old school friend Herb Wittkin certainly remembered what it was like for the two of them talking together in New York in the early 1970s, stereotypical older men wondering 'what the hell was going on' in the new society.[3]

In his review of *The Fixer* Charles Samuels had complained that the cultural commentaries which thus heralded this new era were themselves part of a pressurizing distraction. In this, Samuels was representative of all those who believed that the fashions and forces of a modern world were pushing Malamud in directions adverse to his craft. One way or another, whether in remaining old-fashioned or in trying to update himself, there was the prospect of a terrible fate for Malamud: a writer doomed to continue writing long after his moment had passed.

Yet in 1968 Malamud published *Pictures of Fidelman: An Exhibition*; in 1971 *The Tenants*; and in 1973 his third short story collection, *Rembrandt's Hat*. In 1969 he also turned back to *The Assistant*, in an attempt to convert the novel into a screenplay. Yet for all this activity, forwards and back, it was what Robert Giroux described as 'a starvation period—a sparse period when the juices weren't working.'[4] 'I'm trying to convince myself it is possible to extend the imagination,' Malamud wrote Howard Nemerov, 19 February 1969—even when 'one is approaching fifty-five, feels tired, has memory difficulties and is as much subject to the second law of thermodynamics as the holy flaming sun. Ich kann nicht anders.'[5]

The first three of the six stories in *Fidelman* had been published previously: 'The Last Mohican' in *The Magic Barrel*, and 'Still Life' and 'Naked Nude' in *Idiots First*. Malamud insisted nonetheless that from the second story onwards he had intended it to be a separate book—but a looser work, written occasionally, to make a picaresque comedy freed of the pressures of a continuous life or single-minded career. Malamud particularly liked Robert Scholes' piece in *The Saturday Review*, 10 May 1969, where the stories were described as 'six comic Stations of the Cross'. As Malamud told his audience in some notes for a reading: 'At first I thought they could be unrelated stories, each vertical, no horizontal bonds, but soon I conceived the content of the last story of the series and before long the thrust was diagonal as well as vertical' (LC II 6.3). They were portraits of a pseudo-artist, experiments in art and life, in both hetero-and homosexuality, in all the changing shapes of vocation, of betrayal, of chance itself, on a kind of Italian holiday. Fidelman begins as an art critic, tries to become

266 The Third Life

an artist, but ends without the pretensions of art as an honest craftsman, a
glass-blower:

> 'Don't waste your life doing what you can't do.'
> 'Why shouldn't I keep trying?'
> 'After twenty years if the rooster hasn't crowed she should know she's
> a hen.'
> ('Glass Blower of Venice', 167)

Malamud was changing his creature. This, as his friends realized, was his way
of letting go: Alex Inkeles loved the new freedom of exploration, Nina Pelikan
Straus the strange passive sexuality, Danny Myerson the outrageous illogicality
of sudden, generous refusals to insist on one's practical rights, and Rosemarie
Beck a writing in swift painterly strokes which created form in an instant.

   Fidelman provided a sense of possibility that could make for shamelessly
strange, wonderful, and exuberant moments. There is the avant-garde sculptor
who makes holes in the ground as an exercise in form. When he won't refund
a poor young man, dissatisfied with his exhibition, a stranger throws the
artist into one of his own holes, making it his grave: 'So now we got form
but we also got content.' There is the painter who cannot paint 'Mother and
Son'—a sort of kaddish for a mother who died young—but has to turn it
instead into 'Prostitute and Procurer'. Then he is tricked by the prostitute's
former pimp into one final revision: 'F. put down his brush, washed up, and
returned for a look at the painting. Sickened to his gut, he saw what he felt:
He had ruined it. It slowly drowned in his eyes' (*Fidelman*, 127). There is
the sensual beauty of the glass blowing: 'it made no difference if the blower
had eaten garlic or flowers—a small inside hole, without spittle or seeds, a
teardrop, gut, uterus, which itself became its object of birth' (*Fidelman*, 170).
There was the homosexual rape when a husband catches Fidelman on top of
his wife and takes him from behind. There was even a planned but discarded
scene in which Fidelman appeared in attendance at Keats's deathbed. It was
a strange liberation, achieved by a sort of self-parody, Malamud's beliefs and
Malamud's past put into the failed artist who is a lesser copy of himself.[6] It
was what Philip Roth was to call in another context 'a weirdly exhilarating
sort of masochistic relief from the weight of sobriety and dignified inhibition
that was plainly the cornerstone of [Malamud's] staid comportment'.[7]

   But Philip Roth knew his man: *Fidelman* was the fantasy of 'a libidinous
and disordered life' achieved without 'struggle', without the necessary 'coun-
terforce' of narrative tension and tested development. This was from the
essay 'Imagining Jews' (*New York Review of Books*, 3 October 1974) in which
Roth argued that *The Assistant* and *The Fixer* were novels of masochistic

Jewish suffering, adrift from contemporary reality.[8] But simply take away that suffering, in unearned fashion, and Malamud, said Roth, was not truly Malamud.

The Tenants was written to make a social difference in the contemporary world—to bring about a greater understanding of the black and white races such as Malamud believed had only previously been achieved by William Faulkner. It began in outline with the title 'Two Writers', one a Jew significantly named Harry Lesser, the other a black man called Willie Spearmint (no Shakespeare), left together in a decaying tenement that was to stand as a modern version of Robinson Crusoe's castaway island. The click-click of Willie's typewriter heard by Lesser is an echo of Crusoe's discovery of footprints in the sand, on an isle he had thought to be deserted.

For nearly ten years Lesser has been writing his third novel: now he is nearing the end, he can't move from the building where it was begun, until it is complete. Yet in a dying building made a squat, he is suddenly joined by Willie, a raw young black writer with a capacity greater than Lesser's to escape his writing self and live in the love of women.

When Willie asks a reluctant Lesser to read his manuscript for him, the more experienced writer makes traditionalist remarks about form and order and craft and technique which only cause the other bitter hurt and violent anger. Lesser was moved by the struggling black self-expression in the book, 'but it takes a unique writer to write it uniquely, as literature. To make black more than color or culture, and outrage larger than protest or ideology' (*The Tenants*, 66–7). Willie hits back: what Lesser took to be autobiography in his writing was really fiction, and what he took to be fiction was autobiography. *He*, Willie Spearmint, in his individualism was the art; form and genre were Jewish coercion. In the battle between content and form, ideology and art, this is an extreme and transmuted version of the muddled controversy between Ralph Ellison, the author of *Invisible Man*, and the Jewish critic Irving Howe that simmered on throughout the 1960s.

In a journal entry for 22 October 1971 Claude Fredericks was initially surprised by the risk of the endeavour—the attempt at a black language, the magical sense of the building as the ruins of a society, the fight of order and disorder within different versions of writing: 'Bernard increasingly questions in himself the validity of the kind of order his own writings, he thought, demanded: the sacrifice of a life—like Flaubert. And the animal energy of the black is the image of that very life he hungers for now too late.' Malamud's imagination had been set going initially by a series of newspaper reports in January 1969 on New York slum landlords, seeking to get lingering tenants out of apartment properties which the landlords wished to sell off or tear down and convert into new office buildings. Essential water, heating, and elevator services were shut off; telephone threats were made. But in an 'Afterword' to a reissue of the novel in 1997, Paul Malamud sketched out his father's sense of the broader background:

> The son of a Jewish grocer in Brooklyn, New York, who had emigrated from Russia around the turn of the twentieth century, Malamud used *The Tenants* as an opportunity to re-visit the past and to imagine the future.

The Jewish experience of the thirties was turned into the black experience in the sixties. In literary terms, the fifties and sixties had produced an explosion of black writing—Richard Wright, Ralph Ellison, and (particularly admired by Malamud) James Baldwin—including also lesser-known writers such as LeRoi Jones, Malcolm X, and Eldridge Cleaver. Jones, noted Paul Malamud, was an example of 'black rage':

> Some of Jones' work was considered by critics to be violent and anti-semitic, but this was often treated as an 'authentic' and necessary expression of an oppressed people. Willie Spearmint, the black writer in *The Tenants*, exemplifies this kind of personality. In the sixties, it was thought by some that it would be easy to integrate American blacks into white, middle-class culture if legal segregation and vestigial white racism were surgically removed from the American body politic, but Malamud's pessimistic treatment of Willie's rage is perhaps more prophetic.

In social terms too, the tradition of Jewish assimilation that Malamud had known amongst his own community in the thirites was under both question and threat:

> The influx of blacks into Northern cities had also brought American blacks and Jews together. Black anti-semitism was fuelled by the fact that the people who owned the shops and the buildings in cities where they lived or migrated were sometimes Jewish. Blacks accused Jews of gouging them for unjust rents and making them pay high prices for food.

Some Jews had played a particularly prominent part in the black civil rights movement of the fifties. But, Paul Malamud concluded, 'some elements of the black community came to downplay racial integration for a kind of separatist ethno-centrism.' Thus, when he wrote *The Tenants*, Malamud 'was addressing a subject that was central to his place and time while attempting to employ it for his own fictional purposes. One of his purposes was to find new fictional challenges—Malamud prided himself on seeking new forms and story situations; he didn't like to rework previously successful material again and again.' But the new in his art was now meant to meet the new in society.

The question was whether Malamud was adequate to this socio-historical challenge. The artist Jules Olitski remembered Malamud at an event in Bennington when a black activist spoke heatedly, and Malamud seemed amazed and upset by the man's vehemence against whites. Olitski was himself surprised by Malamud's surprised reaction, noting what seemed to be a sort of hurt innocence in the novelist. It was always there in his eyes, the earnestness of the child.[9]

Ann Malamud said that Malamud had had a young black friend in his boyhood whom he had met at the Flatbush Boys' Club. They had gone together to the old Parkside moviehouse on Saturday mornings, but at some point the friendship had gone badly wrong, something to do with money that Malamud had provided for both of them and a subsequent proud rebuff. Later Malamud had taught black students in a night school in Harlem. Moreover, *The Tenants* was building on work he had already done in 'Angel Levine'; and in 'Black is My Favorite Color', a story from *Idiots First* on the unavailing love of a weak, well-meaning Jewish man for a beautiful black woman. In an interview he gave after completing the novel, Malamud told Alan Forrest: 'It is a great pity that two groups of people, each with an identical history of persecution, are living together with that amount of antagonism. One can only hope that eventually they will recognise each other's history and come together' (LC I 40.2).[10] What fascinated him and made him think of a novel was what he called 'the mix-up of cause and effect' (TH, 22), the mutually exacerbating reactions of white upon black and black upon white arising out of the original injustice of inequality.

'A great pity…one can only hope.' But a review in the *Economist* (13 May 1972) was to speak of *The Tenants* as demonstrating the sheer humane 'impotence' of 'the liberal ethic'. Willie was in danger of being a white man's stereotype. Melvin Maddocks in *The Atlantic* (November 1971) was kinder in suggesting that the impotence was precisely the result of all that Malamud had courageously forced upon himself in the novel:

> Willie stands for all in life that can't be charmed by Malamud … One measure of a writer is the obstacles with which he chooses to confront himself. *The Tenants* is almost certainly Malamud's make or break novel. He has placed everything he has lived by—including, of course, writing itself, on the line. He has backed himself into a corner from which his customary strategems—all the ingenious paradoxes of sardonic piety, all the wry aesthetic manifestoes—cannot extract him.   (LC I 40.2)

But writing does not bring the two men together. Competition over a white woman, Irene, drives them apart.

The Tenants becomes a novel about a man trying to write a novel. Lesser's fiction is about someone he imagines to be 'not he' and 'yet himself':

> What it may come to in the end, despite the writer's doubts, is that he invents this character in his book who will in a sense love for him; and in a sense love him. (*The Tenants*, 192–3)

If Lesser can create that character, then perhaps in the world outside his book 'he may love his real girl as he would like to love her'. If he cannot do it, he has lost nearly ten years. But if he can, then all the time past and seemingly lost is turned round into a redeemed future. As Malamud puts it in his first draft, each chapter benefits from 'hindsight'—which 'was the same as foreknowledge in writing' (LC I 41.1, p. 97). That is always for Malamud the alternative story, the alternative time-path which literature offers to life. And it is why it was impossible to know what was happening to Malamud at any specific point in time, historical or personal, because of his capacity later to rework its passage. 'An invention of choices to outwit tragedy,' he called his book (CBM, 33). For give me just a few more months, Lesser says to his landlord, and years will change within them: 'When you read it, Levenspiel, even you will love me. It will help you understand and endure your life as the writing of it has helped me sustain mine.' To which Malamud ruefully replies to himself, via Levenspiel: 'For Christ's sake, what are you writing, the Holy Bible?' (*The Tenants*, 22).

But if the novel goes unfinished, then it is not even like the painting that Lesser describes earlier, by Lazar Kohn, a former friend who died young. Kohn's was a green-and-orange portrait of a woman who seemed to have eluded the painter, a face trying to make it through the brushstrokes of endeavour. Yet the painting remains there, paradoxically successful as the uncompleted woman of an incomplete man—still an object in the way an incomplete novel can never be.

But it gets worse for the novelist. Willie pitilessly burns Lesser's manuscript for stealing his girl. Irene leaves Lesser because she is finally able to say to him (and indeed to Malamud himself) that she is more important than a book.[11] Without either book or woman, Lesser finally struggles to rewrite the same work better than before. But he forgets that some passages from before, which he had meant to write down again, are only in his memory of the previous draft and not on the page of this one. It feels like trying to force his way back into yesterday: 'Much that was difficult to reconstruct in the present rewriting, sometimes impossible, he had written well in the destroyed draft—words, transitions, whole scenes he could no longer recall, squeeze his brain as he would' (Ibid. 184).

It is thus a novel that constantly reveals what before had been the hidden under-story in the making of its predecessors. One reviewer in the *Chicago Sunday Times* told his readers that the next time their friends wanted to know what it was like to be a novelist, they should direct them to *The Tenants* (LC I 40.2). On one page the novelist describes his dilemma: 'One drizzling morning, Harry, stuck for a transition between scenes, was standing at the window, trying to draw up an idea out of the street, the city, the human race' (*The Tenants*, 38). Then within a page, the book itself brilliantly solves just that sort of problem. As the desperate landlord shouts through the door to Lesser to open up so that they can talk man to man, Lesser replies that he is busy, there is nothing new to report on the work's progress. Then this transition and return:

> A moment of listening silence. When he spoke, Levenspiel's rumble was throaty, low, closer to the self, as though he had gone for a walk in the park, thought things over, and was trying for a better effect.
>
> 'You remember,' he said, 'I told you about my daughter, Lesser? ... I'm on my way to the hospital to see my baby in intensive care.' (Ibid. 40)

The 'as though' is a brilliant move, realism turned into metaphor.

But if it does not succeed at some *other* level of theme and story, the writing of *The Tenants* can only become its own subject-matter—with all the risks of collapsing into a circle of trickery. Actually, it was not trickery—in fact it was the other way round. Anxiety about writing *The Tenants* was worsened, because anxiety about writing was also what the novel was about: 'The novel was tied up with this, which did not help' (LC II 13.10). But there are three different and near-surreal endings to *The Tenants*: Lesser returning Irene to Willie in a fantasy wedding which Lesser tells her he is himself imagining within his book; the Jew smashing the head of the black, as the black castrates the Jew, each uselessly feeling the anguish of the other; and finally the landlord left crying repeatedly for mercy. And in each it is as though through Lesser's failure, Malamud is also failing to resolve his own book.

Getting his friends to read it, Malamud anxiously consulted them through a series of set questions—'How do you like the book (strengths, weaknesses)? What do you think it means? Would you call it a cerebral or willed work? What sort of reception do you think it will get?' He wrote down his usual careful memoranda from telephone conversations, noting the book's vulnerability to a wide range of interpretations and accusations. Ben Belitt

called it 'a plea in art', 'a prayer, an appeal for mutual compassion' (LC II
7.3). Robert Giroux never told of his own reservations.

But Malamud had always been more than usually uncertain about it. He
had been divided in some notes dating back to 5 May 1969 as to what book
he should be writing. The book that was really worrying at him was the story
of the love affair between the ageing man and the young woman: 'I am closer
than I have ever been to the confessional. For the kind of man I am, this
sort of thing isn't easy. There is still the real problem of whether this is the
book I should be doing now' (LC II 5.5) Instead there was either 'the Tribe
story'—which was to become *God's Grace* begun finally in 1980—or 'the
Tenement (Island) book'. He went of course for the Tenement story, and
he told Israel Shenker in an interview that *The Tenants* was a 'tight, tense
book, closer to the quality of short fiction' (CBM, 34). But everything was
still pushing towards the far lengthier commitment of *Dubin's Lives*—and
also, in reparation of the failed experimentalism of *The Tenants*, to making
its ageing protagonist a writer.

However much the individually outstanding stories might transcend the
process, the writing of short stories was what went on in between the
novels. 'I get so impatient waiting for ideas to jell,' Malamud had written Rosemarie Beck, 6 December 1962, 'but the simple fact is that they
can't be rushed so I am trying to work patiently on simple short stories. Better that than to moon about waiting for the big ones to come.'
For the time being, there were no such big ones it seemed. *Fidelman* was
short stories turned into scenes from a novel celebrating discontinuity. *The
Tenants* was closer to a short fiction. *Rembrandt's Hat* (1973) was Malamud's third collection of short stories, after *The Magic Barrel* and *Idiots
First*.

Two of the eight stories came from the late sixties—one was 'My Son
the Murderer'; the other was 'Man in the Drawer', an account of a half-
Jewish Russian writer and his effort to get an anxious American journalist to
smuggle out his stories, which won the O. Henry Prize in 1969. Derived from
Malamud's trip to Russia during the writing of *The Fixer*, it ends with three
brilliant sketch-summaries of short stories—any one of which would have
made a fine story by itself—but presented as written by the banned writer as
though he were a Soviet Malamud in the tradition of Chekhov, Gorky, and
Babel, writing the Russian *Magic Barrel* of 1958. 'When I write about Jews
comes out stories, so I write about Jews.' The last of the three outlines is the
story of the Russian writer despairingly burning his manuscript in front of
his young son.

The rest were written after the completion of *The Tenants*. The title story is about a misunderstanding concerning a vulnerably touchy artist and the critical neglect that he feels has been caused him by a scholarly colleague in their college. Two are again on father–son themes ('The Silver Crown' on a son's equivocal resort to Jewish magic to save his dying father, and 'The Letter', concerning a father and son in a mental hospital). Two more are unconsummated love stories—'Notes from a Lady at a Dinner Party' on an illicit flirtation, and 'In Retirement' concerning an ageing lonely widower who tries to squeeze love out of nothing. He picks up a letter by mistake, through which he can imagine the life of a young woman in his apartment block, only to be humiliated as a sort of pervert when he tries to contact her.

In his files Malamud kept a short essay on *Rembrandt's Hat* written by one of his students. Mary Busch identified throughout the volume's variety a constant underlying sense of characters who are alone and entrapped, who 'cannot confide engulfing feeling until it is beyond sharing' (LC II 10.6). The America traveller is frightened of taking responsibility for the Russian writer. The incipient affair at the dinner party never takes off. The son in 'The Silver Crown' cannot trust the irrational. The elderly man of 'In Retirement', says Mary Busch, 'emerges from hiding in imaginings into real acts' but then 'he is shamed into his age, which holds his youth prisoner'. A common theme, as in 'My Son the Murderer', reveals 'one who longs to touch another who cannot feel it'. 'In moments of passionate freedom,' she writes, 'these characters strive to break out of the monotonous order of their lives to realize the yearnings of their passions.' But too often they revert back to order. 'The tone of these stories multiplies voices from varying altitudes, latitudes, and zones. It shifts from evasion in objectivity to hurt disguised in irony, to show the mistrust, malaise, and displacement of the characters from different levels of awareness.' Malamud had taught her to read him well even in his disguises. He underlined these sentences in particular: 'The stories revolve around those who reject to live the newness of future time by clinging to habit, order and despair, except for those who allow the violence of feeling to free them, however momentarily, as it surges through to transform these characters into ideal forms.'

Mary Busch was thinking finally of 'Talking Horse', where a man erupts through a horse's body to free his true spirit. Something in Malamud loved animal stories. When he was once asked if he knew there was a racehorse called Malamud, he told his informant it was his uncle. When he himself inquired of a passer-by in New York what was the breed of dog he was walking, the man delighted him, he said, by replying that it was a malamute—and he called him Bernard. He loved the transformations going both ways between human and animal. One of the story sketches he cut from 'Man in the Drawer' is about a horse who is a great reader of books, but is forced to turn to *Pravda* when his copy of Sholem Aleichem falls apart. But *Pravda* makes him lose his sight—which is only restored when he goes back to reading literature. Derived initially from Howard Nemerov's short story 'Digressions around a Crow', 'The Jewbird', which appeared in *Idiots First*, is a comic masterpiece, the talking bird claiming residence in the Cohen household, in squawking flight from 'Anti-Semeets'. All he wants is herring and an occasional look at the *Jewish Morning Journal*. In return he helps the slow son, Edie, with his homework: 'He's a good boy—you don't have to worry. He won't be a shicker or a wife beater, God forbid, but a scholar he'll never be, if you know what I mean, although maybe a good mechanic. It's no disgrace in these times.' But the old Jewish bird ends with a broken neck, thrown out by the resentful father. It is a tale in mute counterpoint with 'Angel Levine' because now, even amongst their own kind, there are Anti-Semeets (and not just Jews) everywhere. This again was Malamudian comedy 'spiced in the wine of sadness' (TH, 19). The sudden shift in possibility from one level to another, from one mood to another, from one register to another, was comedy's great challenge, its freedom, and also, as Mary Busch saw, its disguise.

It was 'Talking Horse' that Daniel Stern also particularly admired in his review of *Rembrandt's Hat* in *The Nation*, 3 September 1973. The animal, the comic, the fantastic together made 'the weapon in [Malamud's] artistic arsenal that has made it possible for him to treat of emotional situations, desperations of the heart and spirit, that would otherwise have been unbearably sentimental'. Abramowitz is a talking horse serving as a novelty act in a circus; on the other hand, his master, Goldberg, is ironically enough a deaf-mute who communicates with the horse only by tapping on his head (often very hard) in Morse code. He is another of Malamud's unansweringly cruel God figures. In the ring Goldberg asks a question in his indecipherable horse-like noises, 'Geee gooo gaaa gaaw?' The horse replies in beautifully timed English, 'To get to the other side.' There is an astonished silence, and then Abramowitz looks across and translates Goldberg's question: 'Why does a chicken cross the road?' And only then does the audience laugh.

But in himself Abramowitz has more serious questions: 'Q. Am I a man in a horse or a horse that talks like a man?' Sometimes he messes up the comedy act, changing the lines, and is beaten for it. 'I did it on account it made me feel free.'

A. 'A talking horse'
Q. 'What has four legs and wishes to be free?
At that nobody laughed.

He cries: 'Help! Get me out of here, somebody! I am a prisoner in this horse! Free a fellow man!' The sudden incongruous seriousness creates a silence 'that grew like a dense forest'.

For Stern, privately, this was Malamud himself crying strangely to be free—half-man half-beast, mind trapped in body, moral spirit in sexual appetite, half-comic half-serious, like some hybrid creature never fully at home in his audience's world. But in his review he wrote that Abramowitz 'becomes a kind of Everyhorse, seeking to bridge the gap between our animal and spiritual nature'. He ends transformed, in one of those transcendent moments of art in Malamud, achieved here through an act of animal violence, in the need to be free:

> He reared with a bray of rage, to bring his hooves down on the owner's head. Goldberg, seeing him out of the corner of his eye, rose to protect himself. Instantly jumping up on the chair, he managed with a grunt to grab Abramowitz by both big ears as though to lift him by them, and the horse's head and neck, up to an old wound, came off in his hands. Amid the stench of blood and bowel a man's pale head popped out of the hole in the horse. He was in his early forties, with fogged pince-nez, intense dark eyes, and a black mustache.

He is become a beautiful centaur cantering away, but still in comic middle age, with his youth lost, half-man, half-horse. Malamud himself was fifty-eight, but behold his latest disguise. 'As to the new,' wrote Malamud, thinking of the experimental fiction of Donald Barthelme, Robert Coover, John Barth, and his friend John Hawkes, 'I am limited. "Talking Horse" is the best I can do' (LC II 7.4).

Bennington

When Malamud returned from Harvard in 1968 he told Claude Fredericks of the 'viciousness' he found in Bennington now, compared with the 'graciousness' he and Ann had found in Cambridge: 'Something is deeply wrong,' he said (6 August 1968). The great years of Bennington were fast coming to an end, in the literature division at any rate. Howard Nemerov left for Brandeis in 1966. In 1970 Stanley Edgar Hyman died of a heart attack over his dinner at the Rainbarrel, the local French restaurant, at the age of 51. Kenneth Burke returned to Bennington for the wake: when it came to his turn to say something, he shouted, wild white hair flying, in agony, 'Stanley—Stanley—why did you leave us?'

But a little more than three weeks after the death, Malamud on 26 August took Claude Fredericks down the lawn, away from the Malamud house to say that Hyman had been a little monster, 'That's what he was simply, a little monster.' Three years earlier Malamud had said that incident after incident had deprived him of all respect and liking for Hyman: he thought poorly of the man even as a father, accusing one of his own children of stealing from his coin collection and calling in the police. Malamud had spoken to Claude Fredericks at greater length on 6 August 1970, the day after the memorial service, as Fredericks records in his journal:

> After lunch Bernard took me in his study and 'had a talk' with me. First he wanted to explain why he had fought and broken with Stanley. It had been weighing on his mind. It had to do with Ellen Stark. He was her tutor. One day he had pressured her, gently, to write. She had been upset, got drunk, told a friend he was pressuring her to do what she couldn't. The girl had called Stanley. Stanley had called Harry Pearson, the dean, insisting Bern be fired. That night Bern, learning this from a shamefaced Ellen, called Pearson and demanded to know the facts—explaining exactly what had happened. Harry was apologetic—but it was a year before Stanley and he spoke. That night, ironically enough, Ellen tried to kill herself. I wonder, though, if—as I've often heard rumoured—all this was not coupled with Bern's trying to seduce the girl. Surely there is more to the story than he told me. Stanley is not as irresponsible as—on merely that—to make such a statement to Harry. After a year Stanley sent Bern a book. Bern thanked him in a note but said it should have also had an apology—but knowing Stanley was, like some people, probably incapable of apology, he would still accept it. They spoke after this—but never amicably.

Claude Fredericks felt that in intimately giving him his version Malamud was 'as if dictating to posterity'.

Whatever the truth of the incident, it was certainly the case that until the mid-1960s Hyman had held together the alliance between scholars and writers on faculty. Thereafter there was increasing conflict. In his later years Malamud lamented to Stephen Sandy, Nemerov's replacement, that 'they'—the other people in the literature division—would not listen to him or defer to his advice on appointments. With Ben Belitt he was a senior member of the division, and the writing of them both gave the place distinction. But from his second year at Bennington he had restricted himself to teaching no more than one term a year and eventually just one course, and felt that as a result it was easy for him to be ignored. 'How strange Bern is,' Claude Fredericks wrote in his journal for 13 August 1967 after one of his dinner parties:

> he is a strange distant smiling little man. That little fixed smile, those faraway eyes—and then suddenly, pushing his way into the conversation, some vituperation about the isolation he feels at Bennington (which he thought was perhaps because people feared a famous man) or about something else. Is it

lack of force, is it saving himself, is it what—that keeps him so much on the periphery? He so often seems bored by an evening—and never more than last night.

Malamud would talk obsessively about himself and his work. Or he would read out loud—'and it is perhaps more amusing than it is touching'—a letter of fervent admiration from the morning's mail: 'His fan mail is of the greatest importance to him. How strange that this world-famous writer should need such confirmations still' (1 February 1971). But then he would also go along with Ann to catch a glimpse of the celebrated economist J. K. Galbraith: 'Bern was interested in "famous" people in a charming way, as if he were not probably the most famous man in the room' (26 August 1970). Claude Fredericks was rather snooty (and knew it) when he found an evening at the Malamuds tedious on account of the other guests: 'I suppose Bernard wants to know—ordinary people' (12 December 1968).

The famous and the ordinary: unpredictably lurching back and forth between humility and pride, Malamud was defensive in both. The first time the painter Philip Wofford met Malamud in Bennington, Wofford had just finished reading *The Tenants*, a book he immediately told Malamud that he thought did not ring true, particularly in relation to the black writer it attempted to portray. 'It didn't seem like you writing,' said Philip Wofford. 'I feel it worked,' Malamud shot back. But just because Malamud was a good writer, Wofford went on, he shouldn't assume he could imagine anyone so different:

MALAMUD: 'Who do you think you are?'
WOFFORD: 'Who do you think *you* are, God'?
MALAMUD: 'Yes.'[12]

Shep Levine, the professor of art in Oregon, had told Paul a similar story about Malamud in argument with a philosopher back at OSC, ending with Malamud insisting: 'Until you've tried to write something or paint something or do something where you have to structure a whole world, you'll never know what in hell that means.'[13] Malamud preferred it when John Gardner the novelist went round the room at a dinner party in Bennington drunkenly giving each writer present a lesson in what they should have done: when Gardner finally got to Malamud, watching in detached fascination a man who was his polar opposite, Gardner sat on the floor, crossed his legs, and said, 'And now master, you teach me.'[14] But Malamud told a colleague on another occasion: 'Whenever John gives you a piece of chocolate cake, it's filled with worms.'[15]

Increasingly, the literature division was a little world Malamud could neither control nor feel at home in. There were interminable arguments about new appointments. In 1968 Claude Fredericks felt himself almost without allies in his fight against the scholars Harold Kaplan, Barbara Smith, and Richard Tristman. He phoned Malamud on 23 August, concerning a particular candidate, Charles Thomas Samuels:

> When I'd called Bernard, he had suddenly said he was strongly against Samuels, I was delighted and asked why. He gave *The Fixer* a very unfavourable review, he answered candidly. 'Not only did he not like it, but he said I was writing the way Kazin was telling me to write. And afterwards he boasted to Frank MacShane that he'd "got one of the big ones."'

Yet thirty minutes later, Malamud characteristically called back: 'I don't want you to say what I just said, Claude. That's between us. I shall abstain from voting if Samuels is voted on. I will not let something personal stand between him and a job.' In fact, what followed was a meeting a week later at Richard Tristman's house, where Tristman broke out in fury against Malamud, 'saying the only reason he hated Samuels was because he gave him a bad review once'. Bern—reported Claude Fredericks with regret—'later dutifully voted for Samuels' (30 August 1969).

Stephen Sandy made notes of Malamud's frustrated remarks during another long ineffectual meeting of the literature division, at which they failed to decide on any candidate whatsoever for a vacant post. The notes became 'Vale of Academe: A Prose Poem for Bernard Malamud'.[16] Malamud sat at the meeting staring at the hands of the electric clock on the wall: 'But what did they want | but what did they want | who did they want'. At some point Malamud would provocatively bring up something he had read in the *New York Times* that day, presuming to remind Richard Tristman, Alvin Feinman, and others of issues from the larger world beyond. So many intelligent people were sitting around the table, entangled in college arguments, not writing or not publishing anything any more. Yet nothing stemmed the Latinate sentences of eloquent colleagues, the intelligent futility of their fine points:

> why did they spend such time those hours
> defending virtues in others
> hardships failings reputations of persons not
> under consideration, knowledge spread thinly
> around the table, persuasion thinly, art of suasion, not
> the knowledge of how, of why, whereunto.

Claude Fredericks had turned into an ally of Tristman at this later date, and at one point in the poem the Tristman figure says he'd like to hear what the

Claude Fredericks character would say if he were here. Exasperated, 'Bern cried: GO ASK HIM'.

When Camille Paglia arrived as a faculty member in 1972, ready to stir the place up, 'the college was still sailing on its clouds of past glory. Its distinction and uniqueness were in process of dissolution—partly due to the absorption of its innovations by larger universities.'[17] 'Bernard is *always* wrong,' Richard Tristman had told her. She remembered him uttering 'fulsome platitudes in department meetings. For example, "Literature teaches us what it means to be human." As an advocate of Baudelaire, Nietzsche, and Oscar Wilde, I found these pronouncements wearisome and reactionary to the point of nausea.' Amongst Camille Paglia's defenders, Richard Tristman told Malamud, 'This is a new kind of woman in history, and you'll have to get used to it.' But Malamud, old-fashioned and patriarchal, Paglia believed, only wanted around him traditional unthreatening women who would be his comforting allies. The faction to which Camille Paglia belonged believed that Malamud had pushed for the appointment of Phebe Chao, Janna Malamud's own resident advisor from Harvard, so that he would have a supporter.

According to Camille Paglia, Mara Maizitis was another example. Latvian by birth and with a heavy accent, she came from Yale to give a presentation to the department at Bennington as part of the interview process. Eager to please and good-natured, she offered a specialized academic competence in English Renaissance Literature. But she was by no means sophisticated or 'hip', and at Bennington it was felt, 'a cosmopolitan breadth was required'. Camille Paglia recalled the process:

> After [Marguerite] Stewart, I, and others had spoken in the negative, the sense of the meeting was distinctly away from Maizitis. Then Malamud stood up, aggressively and gratuitously went to the front of the room and launched a melodramatic defense.

He began to speak about the name 'Mara', with its biblical associations from the story of Naomi in the book of Ruth:

> It means 'bitter', he declaimed—the bitterness of the wandering, homeless stranger. So must we, Bennington, embrace the wandering, displaced Latvian and turn her bitter experience into milk and honey. By the end beatifically smiling, he was pink and glowing

Mara Maizitis was then appointed.[18]

Wherever he was teaching, Malamud had always regarded himself as the moral voice in the institution—often, like Camille Paglia herself, in beleaguered opposition. In 1967, for example, he had written to the President,

Edward Bloustein, concerning the case of his colleague Francis Golffing. Golffing had sent out a mimeographed letter to all members of the Literature and Language division complaining that he had not been given a salary increase because he was judged to be a 'mediocre' teacher. 'I am not entirely comfortable with the way Francis has chosen to counter this (to my mind false) judgment of his performance' and 'matters of salary are the administration's prerogative', wrote Malamud, but:

> I can't help thinking it was a mistake, as a rationale for not granting him a
> raise, to characterize his performance as a teacher and counsellor as mediocre
> and barely tolerable. Francis has taught at Bennington for almost twenty years.
> I imagine he is approaching sixty. He has been embittered by the frustrations
> of his writing career, which do not really reflect the quality of his work. He is
> thin as a board and not in the very best of health. It seems to me that he should
> have been handled with more patience and understanding, if not mercy. It is
> gratuitous I think to tell a man who has been retained in his job throughout
> the years, when it was possible to let him go, that his work is inadequate. And
> if a man is kept on, he ought to be paid a decent wage.   (HRC 3.11)

Malamud could imagine being this failed poet—with 'certain deficiencies of personality (whose mea isn't culpa?)'—subject to indignity, reacting clumsily, just as he could imagine being the Latvian outsider. Golffing's salary was so small, added Malamud, that to give him a raise each year until retirement 'would cost the College very little and might be a means of recouping for him some of the dignity and peace of mind he has no doubt lost as a result of this incident'. The authorities subsequently claimed there had been a misunderstanding.

But what Camille Paglia saw in 1972 was an ageing Malamud, hungry for adulation from males as well as females, going around Bennington with token sons, Nicholas Delbanco and Alan Cheuse, 'like three miniature musketeers'.[19]

Nick Delbanco had come to Bennington in 1966, aged 23 and about to publish his first novel, to replace Malamud while he was at Harvard. When Malamud returned, he would take Delbanco on his famous Bennington walks—a sign that someone had made it into the inner circle. Malamud would talk about his work, Delbanco recalled—not the particular problems he might be having with this character or that chapter, as John Gardner might, but more generally, at one remove: 'he would speak of the writer's life: the process itself, the habits of work, the problems of a draft, the issue of research, the degree of distance or intimacy that he was feeling with a project'.[20]

When Nicholas Delbanco married Elena, a former student at Bennington, in 1970, the Malamuds were at the wedding, held on Claude Fredericks's estate, to approve another addition to the extended family. The couple were Jewish, but it was not an orthodox synagogue wedding which traditionally would conclude with the groom's final celebratory smashing of a glass. Instead the civil service was conducted under a pine tree in Vermont by a justice of the peace who unluckily, Delbanco recalled, threw in as many references to the Father, the Son, and the Holy Ghost as he could summon. It was only in the toasts that followed that somebody by accident broke a champagne glass, and Malamud, turning to Delbanco's father, cried, 'At last—a Jewish wedding!'

It was Delbanco who was often trusted to find some document in the Bennington study when Malamud was writing away in New York: 'He'd call from where he wintered and say, "On the second lower shelf on the north wall of my study, three books in is one I want"; or, "In my file cabinet, seven folders from the rear, second letter, could you check a source?"'

Alan Cheuse arrived in 1970, was similarly adopted, and had his wedding at the Malamud's own house. But Cheuse's career ran into difficulties. There was no formal tenure at Bennington: instead after five years there was a putative tenure when a member of faculty was reviewed, and given a renewed contract or not. It was Malamud who fought for retaining an Alan Cheuse, or a Phebe Chao, when others were against them. He rehearsed the defence for Cheuse in note after note he made for himself in his private papers. It was not just a matter of scholarship or so-called 'quality of mind': there was also the commitment to teaching to be considered, and there was a person's character as whole. The principle should be, he said: stick with what you have chosen, unless there is good reason.

In 1974 he noted that he had supported Cheuse and would continue to do so, for 'our division does not support colleagues as they should' (HRC 4.13). In 1977 he writes of how 'the experience of humiliation' could produce 'a low-profile approach' and 'passivity in meetings' out of sheer 'self-defense' (HRC 4.13). Alan Cheuse recalled a fatherly Malamud giving him, during the worst of it, an indirect vote of confidence by drawing on the abandoned novella, ' The Man Nobody Could Lift':

At a time when my pride and ego were badly wounded—if enough people say bad things about you, you begin to believe some of them—he called me up one day in the middle of this and said, 'Could you come over?' So I came over. We went into the study and he opened his filing cabinet and he took out a manuscript and he said, 'This is something I've been working on for years and I can't get right. Could you read it for me and give me some help, make some recommendations?' It was just the most wonderful thing anybody could have done.[21]

Malamud pushed hard but when he publicly suggested that Alvin Feinman was not impartial towards Cheuse, he found himself in an unhappy quarrel. Feinman wrote privately to complain to Malamud that he needed jolting awake: Malamud was content to hurt feelings and reputations, providing it was for his own 'humane' purposes. In his moral zeal Malamud was arrogant in assuming that a judgment was not honest or honourable 'solely on the evidence of your difference with it' (HRC 1.2). In reply, Malamud detailed the reforms of procedure that he believed needed to be in place with regard to tenure, and then closed with careful balance: 'I am glad to be humane, and thereby to foster justice at the college. One is not always his best self even in a good cause, but I am not, in truth, an arrogant man, and I'm sure you know it' (21 June 1977, HRC 1.2). He went on to petition the then President of Bennington, Joe Murphy, who refused to intervene. In the end Alan Cheuse, with a young family, was offered one extra year, as a compromise, which in fact he did not take. His then wife, Marjorie Pryse, obtained a teaching post at the University of Tennessee, and Cheuse began to write fiction full-time.

Claude Fredericks thought that whenever Malamud resisted the firing of staff, it became almost a matter of class. He noted, 1 August 1980, 'He becomes the poor Brooklyn boy, whose mother went mad, whose immigrant father ran a corner delicatessen.'

But Joe Murphy himself had been a poor boy and always knew how to handle Malamud. He had taken over as president after Bennington had lost its first female president, Gail Parker, in 1976 in a scandal which had taken the college to a new level of sexual ridicule.[22] Irish-Jewish, himself a drinker and a womanizer, Murphy came from just as hard a background as Malamud, working his way up from a fifty-hour-a-week job in a New York bagel factory at the age of fifteen. He understood Malamud, as the loyal opposition, in all his continuing campaigns—while Murphy himself was warm, defiant, and charmingly witty in the rueful comic relish of his retorts. Thus he would write Malamud, as on 25 November 1981: 'I realize that your explanations are not intended for me so much as for a straightening of the divine record. Being morally coarse myself, it's so difficult to understand the subtleties of moral distinctions as you make them. But I admire the effort.' Or again, Murphy writing to Malamud at Stanford, 14 January 1982, where, it had been reported, there were great mudslides and rains: 'It did in fact cross my mind that the natural events may be in some small way connected with your propensity to encourage direct and unmediated conversations with God' (HRC 3.11).

19. Arlene Heyman
in 1965, age 23

20. Malamud and
Arlene Heyman at her
wedding, 1979

21. Malamud, daughter Janna, and cat, 1966–7

22. When he was writing *A New Life* in Oregon, Malamud had sometimes taken a room in the Frontier Hotel, on Second Street, Corvallis, where he could write all day undisturbed. There from a second-floor window he could see the sign of the local hardware shop of 'Jim the Fixer'. The photograph was taken by Tom Warren for the *Oregon Stater*, 1976.

"~~No," she said,~~ "It was the only way I could get in," ~~there~~ Raisl said.
reason I came is I came to cry." Her mouth fell ~~open,~~
lips contorted, she wept. Tears flowed through her
fingers as she pressed them to her eyes. Her
shoulders shook. She sobbed.
~~He watched.~~ He felt, as he watched her, ~~He watched~~ ~~He felt~~ what else could he do? ~~he felt~~
the weight of her blood in his heart.

The guard rolled another cigarette, lit it,
and smoked it slowly.

There is where we left off, the fixer thought.
The last time I saw her she was crying like this,
and here she is still crying. ~~Still crying.~~ In the
meantime I've been two years in prison without
cause, in solitary confinement, and even chains.
I've suffered freezing cold, fleas, lice, ~~and~~ the
degradation of those terrible searches, and
she's still crying.

"What are you crying for?" he asked.

"For you, for me, for the world."

She was, as she wept, a frail ~~person~~ woman. Who
would have thought this frail? ~~This was his~~
~~talent, to make her cry.~~ As she wept she moved
him. This was his talent, to make her cry.

~~"Here," she said after a while,~~ "What's there
to do but think, so I've thought," he said to her. "I've thought
about our life, and I can't blame you ~~for~~ more
than I blame myself. If you give little you
get less. I got more than I deserved. Also, it
takes me a long time to learn. Some people have
to make the same mistake twelve times
before they know they made it. That's my type
and I'm sorry. I'm also sorry I stopped
sleeping with you. I was out to stab myself,
so I stabbed you. ~~Who else~~ ~~someone else~~ ~~was so close to me?~~

The next day he is searched six times in the bitterly cold cell, standing naked
on the stone floor, each stone like a block of ice, as they poke their fingers into
his private parts. He is enraged but his rage keeps him alive. [He hungers to kill
them instead of himself.]

[If you're a Jew what do you do with it?

He has made up his mind he can't take his life, not because he is afraid of
suicide, or condemns it, but because there is no way of limiting his death, keeping
its consequences to himself. If he dies now, he kills the innocence of all Jews.
He makes them more vulnerable to mass slaughter. To the Christians what one Jew is
all Jews are. Their qualities, good and bad, their strengths, failings, "guilt" from
whatever source, if it belongs to one belongs to them all. Since the crucifixion the
crime of the Christ-killer is the crime of every Jew. "His blood be on us and our
children." The curse flows through the generations.

He pities the poor Jews, and their fate in history. Not all Jewish days are dark,
but the dark days are too frequent, and the horror is easily renewable. You wake up
innocently after sunlight in a black and bloody world. Overnight a madman-anti-Semite
is born who turns on rivers of blood. The innocent lose their innocence. Overnight
their lives become worthless. If they live their memories are pain. What can Yakov
Zack do for them? Very little. All he can do now is not make things worse for them.
They are bad enough. He is [not a man of God, therefore] only half a Jew, but Jew
enough to defend them. He can best do this by defending himself against the lies
and false accusations. He must somehow prove he did not kill Zhenia Golov. He must
wait for the trial and let them prove it for him. Their lies will prove it.

"I can't kill myself and I can't let the state kill me. I have no choice but to
wait, to go on living. It's all I can do but I must do it."

He is astonished and angered by what has happened to him. A whole society is

25. Malamud in his forties

26. Bernard and Ann Malamud, Oregon Coast, 1972, photographed by daughter Janna

27. Bernard Malamud with his wife, Ann, at their home in Old Bennington, Vermont, 24 August 1971, photographed by Jill Krementz. (Reprinted courtesy of the photographer)

with the road. The snow coming in gusty waves across the fields had
wiped it out.

He felt fright. He was, to his surprise, on a slope going down,
and turning quickly, ascended the incline, following his tracks--path
rather than tracks--but when he got to where the path disappeared in
the snow he was not on the road. He did not know where he was. Possibly in some farmer's field? He wasn't sure he had followed his own
path. Could it have been an animal's? Was a dog close by? What would
it be doing in the snow? The wild begins where you least expect it.
One step off one's daily course and it's down to basics, your life
may be in jeopardy. He had changed the black inner world for the
white outer, both perilous. What it amounted to is that Dubin was
imperilled, wherever he was. Man's fate, in varying degrees. Some
were more vulnerable than others. He had been wandering a little and
struck his boot the ground to see if he could determine whether
he was on the road or still lost in a field, but could not in the snow
tell one part of the frozen earth another. I am not the Inspector
of Snowstorms, that's for sure. I am master of the facts of his life
but not of his knowledge. I can't do what he could do though I love
what he did. Dubin thought he would wait for the wind to die down
so that he could see more than the snow surrounding him. But the
moaning wind continued to blow furiously. He turned into it, assuming
it was still blowing from the east and that he had gone off on the
western side of the road; to his relief he soon felt the level road.
Now he lowered his head and went forward again. It was not easy.
He had gone, with great expenditure of energy, at least an eighth of
a mile father on when he found himself trying to evade a clump of trees
blocking his way and knew he was off the road again.

28 a

28. (a) First and (b) second drafts of *Dubin's Lives* (Ch. 4)

minutes. Once he BEHELD saw int~~o~~ the distance, winter fields GROWING whitening,
a wall of WHITENING black~~ish~~ trees, and beyond them the rising ~~weiue~~ misty-white WHITE
f~~i~~elds flanking the snow-topped hills. Extraordinary s_ight: he
felt a moment of elation before it was gone. Dubin peered around
for a ~~farm~~house but saw none. ~~They~~ MUST OF TURN were behind him, towards the
middle of the long road. He would HOPED HE soon be ~~back~~ at the highway. & THE WIND CAME AT
Then ~~he~~ realized the ground had roughened, and he was no longer HIM AGAIN. HE
on the road. The snow, moving in veiled gusty waves across the STAGGERED
field, had w~~i~~ped out every sign of it. FORWARD,

He felt fright, an old fear: his mother frightened by winter;
himself, city boy, where he had no right to be. Dubin ~~~~
felt himself on a slope going downward. Turning HASTILY he diagonally
ascended the incline, following his tracks disappearing as he
sought them. The snow came down momentarily slowly, the flakes
ha~~n~~ging in the air before they touched ~~the~~ earth. HE ~~Dubin~~ was sta~~n~~ding
in a ho~~l~~low in an unknown field. As he tried to ~~puzzle out~~ THINK which
whitish
way to go he saw a rabbit skittering through the snow pursued by
AN ANIMAL. ~~a fox~~. The rabbit slid UP against a rock. Th~~e~~ fox pounced on it
screeching
and in a moment tore the rabbit apart. The snow was covered with
blood. Dubin ~~~~ STUMBLED ~~~~ away. The
"wild" begins WHERE ~~which~~ you least expect it, one step off one's daily
course. A foot off the road and you're flirting with death. He
had changed the black inner world for the white outer, equally
perilous. Man's fate, to varying degrees, though some were more
fated than others. Those who were concerned with fate were fated.
He struck his boot against the ground to determine where he was
now but could not tell one part of the frozen earth from another.
He could see nothing in the distance, had no awareness of direction.
DUBIN ~~~~ kicked up some threads of brown grass through the snow and knew
WAS OFF
he still ~~had not come to~~ the road.

28b

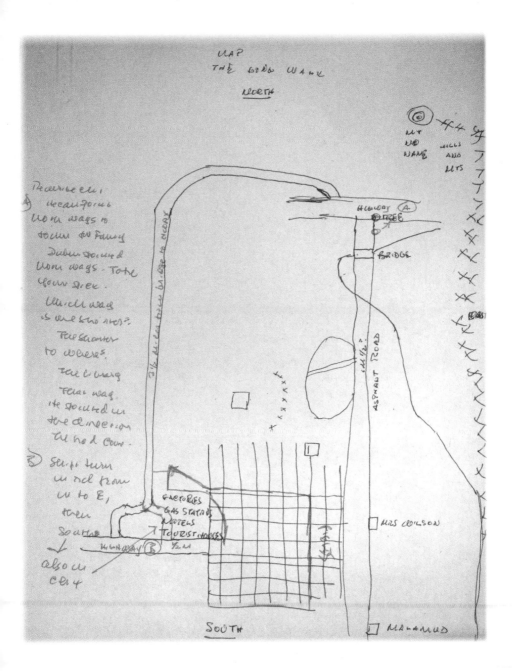

29. Malamud's drawing of Dubin's long walk

that well. He could be very hard on me.

Dubin said ~~that~~ he had understood that; he had
put it together from things she had told him about Nathanael.

Once he **hit** me, she confessed; he said he hadn't
meant to.

~~He~~ DUBIN muffled a laugh.

Would you hit me, William?

If you hit me.

She laughed ~~bitterly~~, later whispered, Please don't
ever leave me.

Q You ~~told me~~ SAID ~~once~~ it was about this time you got into
biography?

A He was still doing obituaries for the _Post_ and
book review, for _The Nation_. ~~Dubin~~ HE was tired of the obits but
stayed with ~~it~~ THEM because he ~~needed money and because he~~ liked
summarizing people's lives. The editor had asked him to
emphasize successful careers but /he sometimes managed to slip
in a failed life.

After Maud was born ~~he felt~~ DUBIN he had to make a better
living. Kitty, concerned about ~~money~~ THEIR FINANCES, suggested he go back to
practicing law. ~~Dubin~~ HE felt it made her nervous to think her
husband had given up ~~his~~ a profession. He'd consider it, he said,
if he could BE IN LAW ~~exercise~~ without being a lawyer. She then suggested
teaching. He doubted he knew enough to face serious students.
STET (What could he teach if he taught?) ~~I won't want to teach the law.~~

One morning as he was typing out the ~~obit~~ OBITUARY of a poet
who had killed himself by jumping from the George Washington
Bridge into the ~~ice-filled~~ ICY Hudson--~~an~~ FRAGMENT OF AN ide floe, like a bloody
raft, carried his body down the river--Dubin felt as he wrote

30a

30. On the biographer finding his vocation of _Dubin's Lives_. Third draft (Ch. 3)

that the piece had taken on great urgency. The dead man was terrifyingly real. He felt an imperious need to state his sorrow, understanding, pity--wanted with all his powers to preserve the man from
extinction. Dubin, you can't relight lives but you can recreate
them. In biographies the dead become alive. He was moved, tormented,
inspired, his heart beating like a tin clock, his head constricted,
aching, as though struggling to pop through the narrow neck of a
bottle in which it had been encased, imprisoned. He felt for a
brilliant moment as though he had freed himself forever.

Afterwards he knew he had shaken himself out
of sleep and discovered--affirmed--his true vocation: the lives of
others; there was no end to them. ~~He would write them as he learned
from his own and learn as he wrote them.~~ He sensed a more vital
relation between books and life than he had allowed himself to feel
in the past. He felt the fragments of his own poor life could be
annealed into a unity. He would understand better, be forewarned and
forearmed. He felt he had already deepened, extended his life. He
knew he had become Dubin the biographer.

That night he took out of his drawer two chapters of
short lives he had started to work on but had not completed. The
Schubert was the first Dubin finished. Kitty, when he showed it
to her, said it was a good piece of work. She went on to say she
hadn't known he was afraid of death. Dubin said neither had he.

04824   6   53   2638 0 0   10 26 78

MS. P. 317

SEE BELOW FOR THE BITS TYPED OUT

[A] THEY DIDN'T COUNT THE YEARS⊙

[A] "IF YOU'RE DEAD YOU'RE DEAD," FANNY SAID⊙

[A] SHE STARED AT HIM.

backwards. I don't dig death hanging over everything they do or created. Are you afraid of death?"

"Not of death but maybe what leads to it."

"Doesn't life lead to it?"

"I'm speaking of sickness, ~~and~~ accident, I'm afraid of the unexpected. ~~A/o~~ |¼ *BEING INCAPACITATED* ◊ *UNABLE TO* What I expect I can make my peace with. On the other hand ~~I wrote~~ those *RUN MY LIFE(;)* short lives ~~to~~ show how intensely and creatively life can be lived even when *THAT CAN BE* it is early aborted. In terms of years lived, they may have missed nothing." *WORSE THAN DEATH⊙*

"Nobody has to tell me what to do with life, only how to do it. I know all I want to about death. I don't want my nose rubbed in it."

"It's late," Dubin said, after a ~~moment~~, "let's go home." *MINUTE*

He helped her up, noticing she stood firmly on the cut foot.

Fanny promised to wash the blood out of his handkerchief and mail it to him.

He asked her where she had got the locket she was wearing.

She fingered it. "Harvey gave it to me about a week before his heart attack."

"A whole heart for a broken one?"

"He liked me a lot."

Fanny asked him whether Dubin would answer if she wrote to him once in a while⟨?⟩

He was not much a letter writer, he said.

Why waste what the winter had taught him?

As they were moving down the granite slope half a dozen black birds rose from the oak trees and flapped off toward the reddened sun. The dark rays of the dying sun touched the tips of the trees. Overhead, massive bronze clouds in long convoys were moving east. As Fanny and Dubin came out of the wood a softened early-evening light lay on the long field of wild flowers.

Fanny began to name them. "There's celandine, oxeye daisy, ~~Queen~~ *RED ROOSTER* ~~Anne's lace~~—what a ball those names are." Farther on she said, "There's forget-me-not, which I knew, and those bushes are bridal wreath."

She plucked a red trillium and thrust it into her shoulder bag, then began to collect a bouquet of daisies.

The clouds were crimson, those close to the hills were ~~violet~~ ships voyaging *PURPLE* to black mountains.

Fifteen or more billion years after creation, the biographer thought, here's this sea of wild flowers on earth and amid them this girl picking white daisies.

206

" I'm ~~speaking~~ of sickness, accident—being incapacitated, unable
to run my life; that ca^n be worse than death. I'm afraid of the
unexpected. What I expect I can ~~make my peace~~ with. On the other hand *DEAL*
these short lives show how intensely a^nd creatively life can be lived
even when it is early aborted. In terms of years lived, they missed
~~nothing~~; they weren't counting." *LITTLE*

"If y^ou're dead you're dead," Fa^nny said. "Nobody ha^s to tell
me what to do with my life, only how to ~~do it.~~ I know a^ll I want to *GET IT TOGETHER;*
a^bout death. I don't want my nose ~~rubbed~~ in it."

~~She stared at~~ him.

10-26-78

31. On Fanny's return (*Dubin's Lives*, Ch.9): Malamud still making changes even to his proofs

32. Malamud in the 1980s

33. Malamud with daughter Janna and first grandson Peter, 1984

34. Malamud in the 1980s

35. Malamud working on his short story 'God's Wrath', published 1972. Photographed by Jill Krementz and reprinted courtesy of the photographer.

36. Close-up of Malamud working on his short story 'God's Wrath', published 1972, photographed by Jill Krementz and reprinted courtesy of the photographer. The page in the close-up reads:

> 'The next day he tried to find her. Where do you look for your daughter who has become a prostitute? He waited a week for her to call, but when she did not he called information and asked if there has been a new number for a Lucie Glasser.
>
> ' "Not Lucie Glasser, but Lucie Glass," said the operator.
>
> ' "What is her address?"
>
> 'The operator gave her one on Third Avenue. The sexton put on his hat, his fall coat, and he took his cane.'

The same passage appeared in the published version as follows:

> 'The next morning he woke in the dark and determined to find her. But where do you look for a daughter who has become a whore? He waited a few days for her to call, and when she didn't, on Helen's advice he dialed information and asked if there was a new telephone number in the name of Luci Glasser.
>
> ' "Not for Luci Glasser but for Luci Glass," said the operator.
>
> ' "Give me this number."
>
> 'The operator, at his impassioned insistence, gave him an address as well, a place on midtown Ninth Avenue. Though it was still September and not cold, the sexton put on his winter coat and took his rubber-tipped heavy cane.'

But for Malamud Bennington had long since become a claustrophobic place, with too many reflections in too many mirrors. Claude Fredericks had confided to his journal for 6 August 1970 how Malamud seemed to have chosen Nicholas Delbanco as his 'son': 'But at lunch he'd spoken harshly about Nicholas. Nicholas is incapable of feeling, he said. His novels show it. He has no idea what love is. He simply apes and imitates.' On 15 August Malamud was confined in hospital recovering from an operation on his gall bladder, yet still talking harshly about Nicholas Delbanco as a 'phoney', flying about to a hundred different places with a thousand tangled friendships. 'His gall was gone,' wrote Claude Fredericks, 'and yet he was, still again, curiously nagging about Nicholas' flaws. He's fond of him and yet—perhaps it is somewhere an envy for those qualities—so opposite to Bern's—Nicholas so apparently has, for the boundless energy, for the extravagant & almost greedy hunger for innumerable experiences, the daring with which he risks new and strange things. I am in certain ways like both of them'. Delbanco, Malamud, Fredericks: in Bennington everyone was looking at everyone else, detecting hypocrisies, imitating, envying, shadow-boxing—and barely knowing when it was really themselves they were seeing or fighting.

In September 1972 Malamud returned from a three-week trip to Oregon where he and Ann had found ageing friends, whom they had not seen for years, in various kinds of difficulty or misery. He told Claude Fredericks that 'increasingly he began to yearn for solitude'.

Bennington and New York

In 1968 the Malamuds left the college-owned faculty house they rented in the Orchard, alongside seven other houses. The Orchard was mainly for new and younger faculty with children at local schools. Janna was now boarding at the Cambridge School and was to enter college in 1969, the year that Paul graduated from Yale. Ann wanted a house of her own and at her instigation the Malamuds paid just $35,000 for a fine white, 1930s colonial-style house set in two and a half acres in Catamount Lane, Old Bennington, with a view over the town to the Green Mountains.

In 1968 Malamud also spent an anxious month of engagements in Israel on his own, Ann being unfit to travel after having pulled some ligaments in her back at the last moment. In 1971 the couple took an apartment in Eaton Place in London for five months, where Malamud worked on the stories for *Rembrandt's Hat*. But, most significantly, in 1969 they had also begun renting an apartment in New York, and from then on would spend their winters there. On their return from London, they had leased and then bought a two-bedroom apartment at Lincoln Towers in New York in 1972. Claude Fredericks saw a change in the couple in their shift towards a New York life from 1970. Ann was somewhat 'grand', he thought (23 March 1970).

Malamud himself liked small suppers with one all-inclusive conversation which he orchestrated.[23] Letty Cottin Pogrebin listed the subject heads he dished out in New York:[24] 'If you could live your life over again, what would you do differently?', 'Is there such a thing as a Jewish writer or a woman writer—or just writers who happen to be Jewish or female?', 'Where would you rank art in humanity's hierarchy of needs?', 'Does it affect your reading of a poet's work if you know he was a bad person like Frost, or had bad politics like Pound?' Back in Bennington Joan Gardner, then wife to John, remembered Malamud urging everyone around her table to tell something bad about themselves, so he could use it, without names, in his next book. People began to go along with it: 'Cut it out, Bern,' she said.[25] Another time he told Joan Gardner she must have been a beautiful girl when young. She replied bluntly, to the effect that when young he himself must have been better endowed, and he backed away. But he had always pushed personal questions. When in 1963 Barbara Herrnstein married Tom Smith, recently divorced, Malamud came over at the reception and asked her how Tom's first wife felt about the marriage.[26] At the Bennington memorial service for Malamud, Phebe Chao listed some of his interrogations: when he was writing The Tenants, 'Have you ever had sex with someone of another race?'; of a woman married to an older man: 'What was it like when your husband first kissed you?'[27] 'I want to put this in a book' was the line Joan Gardner remembered him using, pen and notebook in hand, as he confronted some younger woman.

But then the tone might change to something very warm for people in trouble. At a dinner party at the home of Bert Pogrebin and Letty Cottin Pogrebin, Malamud, near the end of his life, asked the assembled company 'If you could instantly possess any body of knowledge, what would it be?' Louise Bernikow said that the knowledge that she herself wanted was to know why when one person loves another, the other does not necessarily return the love, and suddenly Malamud was moved by the pain. He said, for his part, that he wished he could memorize great literary works so he could have their company on his solitary walks, and that also he wished he had known how to have fun. On one of his regular New York Sunday walks with Bert Pogrebin, again late in his life, Malamud said completely out of the blue that he regretted not having known the love of several beautiful women. Bert

Pogrebin replied that that would have taken up a lot of Malamud's time: 'Which of your books would you have given up for these loves?' Malamud was silent for a moment and then said, 'None.'

Behind the social front, Malamud remained in a writer's difficulties. In the Malamud Papers in the Library of Congress there is a folder that contains miscellaneous fiction notes from the 1950s onwards. One page seems to come from the late sixties. On one side Malamud makes one of his lists, entitled 'themes of mine'. There are seven items:

1. The new life—that life is possibility.
2. Hidden strength—that the spirit is strength even when the man is weak, comic, farcical.
3. That the human, conscious of the best in itself, is precious. My work is in defense of the human.
4. The element of the Jewish is the element of the humanistic.
5. My ideas are ideas that persist in Western Literature—they express the Western esthetic and morality. There's nothing strange about my ideas though the Jews who fulfil them may seem strange to some.
6. I use the Jew as Jew, and the Jew as universal man (as Bloom in Joyce) and symbol of suffering man. All men are Jews, if they knew it.
7. The movement of the individual towards freedom—fullness of life.   (LC II 10.9)

None of these is a surprise. But turn over the page and on the other side is another list, untitled, concerning his problems:

1. Memory—meagre
2. Attention span—very short
3. Reading with anxiety
4. Inability to generalize
5. Timewasting through obsessive rituals—cleaning, straightening, neatening
6. The illusion of a whole self—the illusion of not knowing the nature of one's weakness
7. The spread of anxiety—a hidden awareness of the self's lacks—its weaknesses and a fear of self-exposure
8. Unawareness of the depth of (instinctive) lust
9. Unawareness of the mechanism of anti-lust, depression
10. The fear of being 'idealess'

It had taken years, Malamud told Claude Fredericks, for him to free himself of his mother's anxieties, and many of the anxieties that remained, listed here, had been with Malamud for much of his life. Nor was it altogether surprising that a writer who summarized his ideas so simply and frequently, outside their impact within a novel, should find himself worrying about being 'idealess' or lacking in the power of 'generaliza-tion'—though in other moods that last could be a useful disability for the novelist, like his having what he called a very *good* bad memory (LC II 1.5). But whatever the actual date of this list, the fact was that throughout the 1970s almost every item in it was causing him increased concern, as if what he had never resolved before was now worsening as a result.

Following the break-up of the affair with Arlene Heyman, he had long had a story idea he headed 'Depressed': 'Man who many years ago gave up a love affair to remain with his wife. In his old age (or fifties) becomes massively depressive. Caused by "failure" in the past' (LC II 7.5). Such was the subject-matter of later middle age: residual sorrows and illusions, a sense of declining mental abilities and a fear of their increased deterioration—and yet also the physical raging of an almost inappropriate, incongruous lust unslaked by an unsatisfied past. A further worry list, this time explicitly marked the 1970s, includes:

Questioning (at this age success, the value of art over life)
Inattention, fear of impaired equipment
Less amour propre
The masked self
Force of anxiety   (LC II 13.10)

At one point in 1975 Malamud was writing out passages from an article by the biographer, Leon Edel, 'The Madness of Art' in the *American Journal of Psychiatry* (10 October 1975). 'When the lament for passing youth is sung, the poet may survive to rage with Yeats upon his aging.' When the artist thus survives, 'the geriatric depression permits a towering rage like Lear's against the prisoning of great powers in senility of body and mind.' The most enduring works, Edel concluded, 'may be those of artists who lived through their sadness to experience and control their rage against aging—Sophocles, Michelangelo, James, Bach.'

Here, in his anxiety over premature ageing, was a Malamud worried about failure yet sceptical of success, fearful both of egoistic blindness and of the loss of 'amour propre', averse to self exposure yet hampered by the masked self, troubled alike by lust and the repression of it. It was not simply one thing or another: he felt caught between almost every alternative. It was the autumn of middle age, neither dead nor fully alive. It was the predicament of a talking horse, unable to be completely animalistic or fully moral. The most dismaying sentences in *Rembrandt's Hat* are from 'In Retirement' where the widower, formerly a doctor, is 'astonished—even thought of it as affronted, that this was happening to him at his age. He had seen it in others, former patients, but had not expected it in himself. The hunger he felt, a hunger for pleasure, disruption of habit, renewal of feeling, yet a fear of it, continued to grow in him like a dead tree come to life and spreading its branches.' It had never been a well-synchronized life, and he was increasingly caught between being puritan and cavalier. He told a friend, for example, the story of his involvement with an anonymous woman who, in the course of their relationship, once asked him, to his shock, to urinate on her. Raising himself to his more public posture, Malamud said that he had replied, 'I will not piss on another human being.'[28]

But in sudden reaction he could do other things to human beings, which seemed to some witnesses to be mere moralism. For months he refused to speak to one student, Christine Graham, who had acted as the Malamud house-sitter one winter, when he discovered she was having an affair with the professor of music at Bennington, Louis Calabro.[29] Only later when the two were eventually married, with children, was Malamud reconciled. Judy Feiffer remembered Malamud coming to her around 1974 shortly after her marriage with Jules Feiffer had broken up, to warn her not to hope for a reconciliation because there was another woman—the artist, Susan Crile—who was involved. Judy Feiffer felt that at that moment there were almost two men talking to her: the one who was Bern, a genuinely kind friend who never made any advances; the other who was Malamud the writer, carefully watching and noting her reactions like a scientist. She remembered she had been dumbfounded when he had come to her years before to ask her, 'Will you tell me about women, what they are really like?' Now in telling her about the other woman, it seemed he was still trying to find out.[30]

There are also from this difficult time curious, involved letters that Malamud kept in his private files which survive like fragments of stories not told or uncompleted.[31] From a woman who was a close friend of the family:

> I have love for you as a novelist that is as strong as any I hold of any sort. As a friend you are sometimes passing difficult. As a woman I know enough to always be poised for emotional defense in your company—but when I think of you as a novelist and you think of me as a reader—there is real love of the purest kind.

From a student in the late 1970s, looking back in 1983 at 'what you did for me when I was twenty-one':

> Between these walks I wrote you some letters. With you I was my best self—the one I was ever becoming—but in my letters, despite some small ability to turn a phrase, I was a depressed little girl and we were anything but 'equals', to use your recent term.
>
> Your old letters, if you want them back, are yours if that is now the price of friendship. My request is that we talk first; or what's the sense. You're invited, then, to my place, which you've never seen, for lunch, any day of the week, whenever you're ready.

Those letters of his which he wanted returned do not seem to have survived. But this letter, drafted by him to a girl of fourteen, though arguably kindly, caused her mother some concern:

> Dear K ____ , I have the feeling you are present often when I am although we haven't talked together at any length. I'm aware of the disadvantage of having older folks around, particularly some who often ask questions that you may think much this side of personal. The truth is that you and B ____ have become lovely young women, and I for one would like to know you better.
>
> Ann and I intend to come to the city in early November. I hope you will sometime take a walk with me so that we can talk about who we are
>
>   Yours with affection

Amidst unreliable gossip and encounters arguably innocent or misunderstood, some of the people involved will go on the record, and some not, to attest to amorous passes that Malamud made unsuccessfully and awkwardly. These include a member of Bennington faculty in her first year, the wife of a close friend, the wife of a near relative, a bereaved acquaintance, a publicity girl. They were approaches often accompanied by apologetic murmurs about an artist needing beauty or about a whole youth lost in work. The painter Pat Adams said that Malamud, drawn into one aspect of college behaviour, approached several of her friends on campus.[32] Those who do not wish to go on record say their reticence is for the sake of Ann Malamud's feelings or to prevent self-damage to Malamud's own reputation, twenty years after his death. But at some level the feeling, rightly, is that the foolish advances should not have occurred or did not quite happen. Sometimes, putting out feelers, Malamud did not know what sort of human contact he wanted or could get. Yet Malamud himself complained to Clark Blaise after a particularly high-minded lecture by Irving Howe that 'these old Jews never let on about their sex lives'. And 'Get his sex life' was what Beverley Sanders remembered

Malamud ruthlessly urging upon her scrupulous husband, Ronald, in the writing of his biography of Kurt Weil.[33]

But one genuinely concerned observer put it thus, regretfully, in relation to Malamud himself:

> He needed women to affirm his virility, to give him what even his writing and his family could not. He somehow or other was able to live with that in the tension of this deep contradiction of character. It was so much a secret part of him, compartmentalized, rationalized or denied. But if he had it all put on paper in front of him, he would not be proud. If he had not been a writer, it might have destroyed him to have seen all he had been implicated in.[34]

Within himself, he turned it into his fiction. Yet Ann Malamud recalled the persistent trouble that remained within the life:

> I was so annoyed with Bern that for the one and only time I packed my bags. This was probably in the last two years of his life. It was when we were in New York. I think Bern at that point was interested in seeing women more, having the *freedom* to have relationships of some sort with women, flirtations, taking them out to dinner, and so on. He had this idea that it would be very nice if I would go away for a while and he could just be alone. And he wasn't all that well, but he had this need, all of a sudden, this sense of 'I'd love to be free for a while'. 'Wonderful!' I said then, 'You want to be free, you go on. Why don't *you* go away, if you want a vacation.' But I was so angry that I packed a bag, and then he cried, and of course I didn't do anything. These things really were signs of someone who towards the end of his life must have felt in some way that he hadn't lived, you know, because they didn't make a lot of sense.[35]

But she always tried to make sense of it. Writing a consoling letter to Pat Adams years later, on the cycle of despair and elation in an artist's psyche, she referred to a psychology textbook which Janna had been using as part of her training in becoming a social worker. It was just such a work that Kitty cited to her husband, Dubin, in the midst of his unhappiness. It said that in the face of stress and desperation, where women would turn to sublimation, men 'are more likely to turn to physical relief—or booze'. Malamud himself had never been a drinker. But the artist, Ann Malamud concluded, always swam in some sort of 'muddle'—'until he climbs out to not an arid but a fertile ground.'

Both to make sense of himself and to find fertile ground, Malamud *had* to write *Dubin's Lives*—for all his fear of self-exposure. He wrote to Arlene Heyman, 6 October 1972, stoically insisting that he lived 'not badly': 'What supports me? My accomplishment in writing, a certain wisdom in life, an ability to relate to a few people who make me think I could be more loved than I permit myself to be. And perhaps the feeling that if I give myself time I will do things right, even those things that do not come easily from a nature such as mine.' He eventually gave himself five years to write *Dubin's Lives*, from August 1973 to July 1978, two more years than usual for a longer work. His wife had not wanted him to write it—'she kept persisting "Why are you writing this?"'[36] —and it did not solve his problems when he had finished it. But it was his last major work and in art at least it redeemed a life which at many levels in the 1970s had been going very badly wrong.

It was the book, he was to say at the end in interviews, which was to answer his question, What do I know up to this point? His parents, his mother in particular, had suffered in early middle age. This was the novel about middle age, about marriage, about once again realizing that he could make his disadvantages and difficulties, in both writing and living, into his subject-matter (CBM, 100). It was to be the great test of Malamud in the modern world.

9

⟨⟨◇⟩⟩⟩⟩

Dubin's Lives

'What Are You Going to Do to Make It Different?'

If *A New Life* was his springtime book, *Dubin* came out of the winter season. 'After a series of rather short books, *Dubin's Lives* was a big crisis book,' recalled Stephen Sandy, 'and he would tell you, "I'm having trouble writing this"':

> He had been in agony and one day I knocked on his room door in the Barn, concerned for him. It was in the winter and there wasn't anyone else around. He must have been lying on the floor because suddenly he loomed up, this little shape behind the frosted glass, and said 'I've finally got it: "He disappeared down winter's hole." I couldn't start the novel until I'd figured out how to begin it.'[1]

In the end it wasn't the first sentence, though on the novel's second page it becomes this: 'Dubin had uncovered bright-green shoots under dead leaves in February ... [He] felt change and could not bear it. He forbade his mind to run to tomorrow. Let winter stay in its white hole.' This was the sort of change that Malamud managed best in his imagination—the difficult, unsynchronized, almost involuntary coming back to life. It was always hard for him to follow the ancient advice of Dubin's hero, Henry Thoreau, to take everything according to its season.[2]

Dubin was Malamud's attempt at largeness, breadth, 'a fuller use of what I have to offer', in the tradition of George Eliot and Thomas Hardy (CBM, 117). There are two careful notebooks with the novel's working title, 'The Juggler', spanning 1970 to 1972: 'He is the juggler—he keeps several balls in the air at once' (HRC 19.4, p. 11). William Dubin, born a Jew but married a Gentile, is a fifty-six-year-old man juggling between life and work. What is more, he is involved in 'three kinds of love, wife, children, girl'—the last, a young woman thirty-five years his junior, who becomes his lover (HRC 19.3, p. 8). Early on, Malamud sketches various possibilities as to how his protagonist, perhaps a cellist, perhaps a poet, meets this girl: he is in hospital and she is a volunteer, and when visiting she masturbates him, thus commencing his obsession; she was a former student of his—there was nothing between them before but there might have been, or simply wasn't because she left to get married; she is a new arrival in town who wants to write and has come to be his protégée (HRC 19.3, p. 4). She is a product of the sexual revolution, freer than Dubin. 'One of the things that bothers me', Malamud warned himself in a third notebook which he began on writing his second draft, is that 'it is essentially—in these times—such a mild story' (HRC 19.5 p.26b):

> It's the story of an older man and a young woman. My god, how many millions of stories are there like that? ... What are you going to do to make it different?
> (TH, 124)

In the face of his own challenge, Malamud began writing the first draft in February 1973, but instead of the usual year, the writing of it took him three years, the first stage finally completed only in April 1976. He explained the process to Clark Blaise, 10 March 1974, at the end of his first year of writing: 'I've done something over a hundred pages—three chapters that comprise Book One. First I rewrote each chapter two or three times; then I felt the need to write them over as Book One; that will be done by April first. I shall then give myself more or less three years to complete the book. It is the kind of novel that grows in second, third, and fourth sights. I sit still and wait for bubbles to hit the surface. Each bubble is a new idea—hopefully a detail that is better than one I've already used; or a new invention to carry the story on.'

Extraordinarily, he began the first draft with a character called 'Malamud', a writer of fiction, meeting his friend William Dubin in the course of their separate walks. By the second draft 'Malamud' has become Greenfeld the flautist and the role shrinks. But 'Malamud' was an initial dramatic device he used to outwit simple confession and keep himself conscious of what he called 'point of view'. He meant the complex relation between narrator and protagonist. 'How to disinvent it?' he asked himself, answering: 'Make it seem imagined.' To avoid simple autobiography and prevent the monotony of personal woe, the novelist is turned inside the book to become character and witness, releasing other parts of himself for his protagonist. Malamud had initially described the problem to himself in a notebook entry for 11 November 1971:

Witness. I've never done that before and can get a tone of wryness and comedy. I feel I need a story of this kind. At the same time my (Malamud's) personal friendship for this man, poet and autobiographer, whom I walked, talked with, eaten with, listened to him playing the cello—will bring me up close, compassionately at the same time as I, the novelist, make the story as objective as I need. So we have distance yet compassion, sympathy. Could it be that *I* am interested in the girl when she appears a second time round.   (HRC 19.4, p. 8)

Malamud himself was juggling—between the objective and the inner, between ironic comedy and deadly seriousness, between himself and his protagonist. And what was more, in the process he was also splitting himself in order to re-arrange his experience in new combinations. The melancholy poet and autobiographer with whom he walked was in memory of Howard Nemerov, a private man confiding in his friend; but the cellist side of Dubin was the charismatic Bennington musician, George Finckel, who left his wife for a beautiful student and heiress called Connie Wallace. If William Dubin was to enjoy the relationship that Malamud had enjoyed with Arlene Heyman, it was also a passion fuelled by Malamud's own envy for George Finckel.[3] No wonder Malamud initially thought of having his persona at some point desire the same girl as Dubin. As he wrote to himself in a note, 'One must transcend the autobiographical detail by inventing it after it is remembered' (LC II 1.5).

Moreover, Malamud's careful chronologies make clear that the action of the novel itself takes place between 1973 and 1976, as close as can be to the time of composition. Where before in the writing of the major novels there had been much greater temporal distance, now in the imaginative immediacy there was an increased tension in the day-to-day writing in the midst of ageing, which further fuelled the urgent need for strategies of imaginative invention and varying distance. Asked to read a draft, Nina Pelikan Straus, writing to Malamud on 16 March 1975, recognized in her notes the varying shifts and movements—for example, 'William's looking at Fanny with the distance that Malamud is looking, and then suddenly embracing her with a closeness while Malamud is looking' (HRC 18.5).

'What are you going to do to make it different?' he had asked himself. In further response, Malamud came up with two formal inventions:

One was to invent Dubin's walk, so he walks, in his four-to-five-mile circle, after he does his day's writing for an hour, hour-and-a-half, or two hours ...

The second invention that opened the book was that instead of making Dubin a cellist (which was my first idea), I made him a biographer ... and therefore [the novel] becomes a life book—a book about lives.   (TH, 124)

Unlike Fidelman the failed artist and Lesser the failed novelist, Dubin begins as a success, albeit in a minor art, having recently won a medal of freedom from President Johnson for achievement in the art of biography, following his life of Thoreau. Dubin had begun as a writer of obituaries, but suddenly, writing of the death of John Berryman, the writing had come alive. Then he knew he did not want to summarize lives any more, he wanted to try to recreate them.

Dubin's idea of becoming a biographer came out of his wanting more lives for himself, a hunger like Malamud's own. Malamud's working notes set up the predicament and the test it constitutes. 'In biography he controls the life, in life he doesn't. In afterthought he is good' (LC I 13.4). But for all their shared love of secure compartmentalization and control, both Dubin and Malamud know this:

> There is no life that can be recaptured wholly; as it was. Which is to say that all biography is ultimately fiction. What does that tell you about the nature of life, and does one really want to know?   (*Dubin's Lives*, 20)

It is a question that Dubin is going to have to face, launched into Malamud territory. For as Malamud writes in his notes, there is in Dubin a 'sense of letdown after Presidential medal. Won't admit to himself he is not enjoying his success' (LC I 13.4). For his latest work, the biographer has chosen D. H. Lawrence as his subject. It may be a mistake, a wild choice ill-suited to his own cautious temperament, and eventually his wife urges him to let it go. But for better or worse it becomes a most terrible challenge—not only a challenge to his writing, but a challenge to the way he has led his life, which he faces both in the study and on his walks.

It also seems the trigger to his taking up with Fanny Bick who is twenty-two, only two or three years older than his beloved daughter, Maud. 'Old billy goat—these feelings at fifty-six, disjunctions of an ordered life,' says Dubin to himself (*Dubin's Lives*, 27). For in Dubin (again from Malamud's notes on point of view), 'Biography has given him a certain objectivity about life', including his own (LC I 13.4). It is as if he were his own biographical subject. 'He sensed in himself something resembling incest taboo once removed—you don't bed down a girl your daughter's age' (*Dubin's Lives*, 32). But Dubin, notes Malamud in an interesting distinction, is 'objective, not detached; he is involved. Sometimes the involvement is overwhelming, sometimes more than he can bear' (LC I 13.4). For all his objectivity, he is still caught within his needy self. Dubin becomes a man on a tightrope, on a borderline between almost everything in his life. And in his writing, he is at his richest when he is uncertain of the difference between seeing himself in his subject and his subject in himself. Malamud throws open the boundaries, goes for the creative mess, as Dubin launches into his adulterous love affair. Writing on Lawrence and his religion of sexuality, Dubin cannot tell cause from effect—whether his life is trying to learn more of the sex instinct for the sake of the work; or whether it is the work driving him towards Fanny for the sake of his life. 'You fear primal impulses'—Dubin hears Lawrence himself bitterly haranguing him—'Work which should be an extension of human consciousness you distort to the end-all of existence. You write muckspout lives because you fear you have no life to live' (*Dubin's Lives*, 319). The charge of timid hypocrisy was what Malamud himself would least have wanted to hear; which was why he—that workaholic whose art, he insisted, was always finally for the sake of life—deliberately put it to the challenge. Don't *write* of more lives, says his Lawrence, *live* more lives than the one you have become accustomed to call your own—or else the writing is just a fictive substitute. And this thought too goes into the writing of *Dubin's Lives*—as though the writing were checking against itself, knowing also that even such checking may not be sufficient—in those twists and turns of near-mind-bursting complexity that never quite worked in *The Tenants*.

Malamud was packing in to his work as many implosive contradictions as he could dare. It is itself Dubin's biography, without Dubin knowing it, and Malamud's autobiography hidden within it.

'I can't keep a complexity totally in mind,' goes another of Malamud's notes, 'though I can construct it piecemeal' (LC II 1.5). Piecemeal then, movement by movement, Malamud assembled the broad structures of the novel. Thus Dubin, desiring Fanny, invites her to join him in New York, but she fails to turn up. He then invites her to accompany him to Venice, but there he not only fails to make love to her but is sexually betrayed. Making a virtue of necessity, he resolves to give her up: what was he doing anyway miles away from his work on Lawrence, putting his fate in the hands of such a young girl? In chapter 4, towards the end of 1973, he returns home, back to work; only then to find that he can't work—and does not know whether it is more to do with the humiliation over Fanny, or the difficulties of Lawrence, or with himself in relation to both. 'In fooling with Fanny he'd allowed desire to overflow the workaday life. A pipe had broken, the psyche was flooded' (*Dubin's Lives*, 122). Dubin desperately keeps trying to write his sentences, then reads them over later to see what his writing is telling him: 'But the last sentence when he read it, said, "I am trapped." Dubin with a cry flung his pen against the wall. Disgust rose to his gorge and he fought the approach of panic. I've got to get out of here. I've got to get away from my fucking mind'

(Ibid. 148). That is when he turns most to Malamud's other invention—his walks—for help.

But in chapter 5, in 1974, just when he has given her up and is back on track, Fanny returns to his life, and taking this second chance, she and Dubin at last become lovers. There follows two chapters with Dubin caught between Fanny, his lover, and Kitty, his wife. But by chapter 8 he has lost Fanny again because he will not leave his wife. It is now 1975 and, as though circling back to chapter 4, he faces the same trouble with his book and with his marriage as two years earlier—except that in the meantime he has aged, not just through time, it seems, but through the effect of the repeated blow.

> Having gone, why didn't she go? What kept her imprinted like a burn on the brain? Yet his sense of loss was more than loss of Fanny. What you dug out of left a hole deeper than the hole. He disliked himself for having twice succumbed to her, and twice to this self-inflicted punishment.   (Ibid. 286)

'Twice': it is like the ironic structure of a Hardy novel, with the same mistakes, the repeatedly returning agonies, and Dubin finds himself wondering if he is not the sort of man who should have been writing the life of Hardy rather than Lawrence.[4] As he buries the family cat, nicknamed Lorenzo, after accidentally backing his car over him, he recalls secretly burying his daughter Maud's pet kitty in the same place years earlier: 'Why does every misery happen twice?' (Ibid. 287).

This too is what Malamud meant when he told Clark Blaise that it was the kind of book that grew at second, and third, and fourth sight, the novel continually turning back on itself in the search to uncover whatever it *was* that lay within the cumulative density of its experience. 'Whatever you learn,' goes another of Malamud's notes, 'you have to relearn; life changes' (LC I 13.4). Dubin does believe that lives have stories, patterns that can tell the people living them who they are. He knows he is two-thirds through his own story and in the dark looks for its later direction to purpose.

It is by these patterned repetitions of itself that, as ever in Malamud, the known becomes, oddly, ever more unknown. The struggling long winter walk, initially meant to get the man away from his writing block in the study and out of his subjectivity into the world, turns round on itself when it becomes a form of fighting himself on the road instead. If he cannot write, then he will run, put body in place of mind, 'compelling a willed experience to contend with another, unwilled that lingered' (*Dubin's Lives*, 158). 'The trick was to get into the winter world and out of within' (Ibid. 132)—but, as so often in this novel, nothing is ever quite so separate. To leave one predicament is only to find it reappearing in changed form within another. 'Ravenous for summer, for an end to the barren season, he hurried on thinking of the next rise or bend' (Ibid. 133). It is like running in space in lieu of time; even more frightening, it is like running through his own head.

If you stopped the run or walk for even a single day, Dubin warns himself, 'much you had accomplished—at last got used to—you had to accomplish again' (Ibid. 158). He must show the depression inside him that it is not all. But here in chapter 4, one day, in the midst of this tough routine exercise in displacement, the wind-driven snow falls harder and harder upon the known and habitual route:

> He expected he would soon reach the highway. The wavering wind came at him again. He stiffened, staggered forward, then realized the ground had softened; the earth had roughened, he was no longer on the road. The snow, blowing in veiled gusty waves across the uneven fields, had wiped out every sign of the familiar road.
>
> He felt fright, an old fear: his mother frightened by winter; himself stranger, where he oughtn't to be. Dubin found himself moving on a slope propelled downward. With fear in his gut he then diagonally ascended the incline, following his tracks disappearing as he sought them ... The wild begins where you least expect it, one step off your daily course. A foot past the road and you're fighting with death. He had changed his black inner world for the white outer, equally perilous. (Ibid. 149)

This is not merely 'symbolic' in some literary sense imported from outside: as in *The Fixer* Malamud characteristically immerses his man in the reality of protracted time until the deeper meaning it has for him is thrown up within the experience itself. It is typical of how the novel grows on second and third sight that the flashback to the frightened mother who tried to commit suicide is the extra layer that the second draft usually provides—playing off what Malamud called the vertical dimension, back and forward in time, against the horizontal onward movement (Illustrations 28a and 28b).

But still the walk goes on in the wild: 'Panic went through him in a lightning flash. He pictured himself running in circles, but managed to bring himself under control ... How can I keep from walking in circles? You can't if you live in them' (Ibid. 150–1).

> He went through a grove of knee-high pines, then beheld a stand of tall whitened Norway pines. Where were these trees? He was almost certain he had seen them close to the road before the bend to the highway where the road sloped on the right. But there was no downward slope he could feel, let alone see. Are these pines where I think they are? Am I where I think I am? What a mad thing not to have stayed home with my small stationary miseries. Now I

risk my life. He thought he ought not move until he could think of something
sensible to do next ...   (Ibid. 151)

In the shifts between present and past tenses, 'Where *were* these trees?'
(clinched in the third draft) is brilliant, as the mind works between what it
sees in front of itself and the map of the past it holds onto within. Inept
out in the open, this is a mind that finds itself lost, clearly has not known
what it was doing, and now knows it cannot trust itself to find its way back
to normality. 'Did I cross the road without knowing it? Why is it I don't
remember the high stone wall I just climbed? Has it always been there and
I have never noticed, or have I seen it but am too frightened to remember?
Is this the long hard-topped road I usually walk, or have I gone somewhere
I have never been before?' (Ibid. 153). Whichever or wherever it is, it is
experientially somewhere he has never been before. 'Am I where I think I
am?' is specifically geographical and psychological at once.

For this is what *Dubin's Lives* is about, formulated from the very first draft:
'The wild begins where you least expect it. One step off one's daily course'
(Illustration 28a). In a moment, at every level, assumptions that had seemed
familiar, courses that were merely ordinary, and signposts that were thought
reliable are suddenly become dangerous and risky, barely holding off the
chaos around or beneath them, and threatening sanity in their breakdown.
'Embarrassing to die so close to the road, like drowning in a bathtub', thinks
Dubin in a formulation again found from the very first (Ibid. 152). That
is what this novel is: a domestic bathtub that turns into an ocean storm.
It is the terrible version of what gave Malamud heart in Dubin's beloved
Thoreau—that the local could become the universal in a moment. Malamud
marked the following passage in his selection from Thoreau's journals:

> It matters not where or how far you travel—the farther commonly the
> worse—but how much alive you are. ... Every important worker will report
> what life there is in him. It makes no odds into what seeming deserts the
> poet is born. Though all his neighbors pronounce it a Sahara, it will be a
> paradise to him; for the desert which we see is the result of the barrenness of
> our experience. ... All that a man has to say or do that can possibly concern
> mankind, is in some shape or other to tell the story of his love.[5]

This was in defiance of the charge that the writer—Thoreau, Dubin, or
Malamud—was merely limited, old-fashioned, or provincial.

'Here's a mysterious thing happening to this man,' wrote Malamud in
another note, adding in a bracket '(he makes it happen)' (LC I 13.4). Indeed
sometimes, scarily, Dubin is making it happen without quite knowing that he
does: 'Did I cross the road without knowing it?' Determined to know more

of himself, Dubin resolutely goes back the following spring to that winter landscape, accompanied by his wife Kitty:

> At the end of the walk, close to where he had been lost in the snow, Dubin felt an urge to leave the road and attempt to retrace his circular wandering, wherever it had been; but one stone wall looked like another; and the woods were full of green trees and flowering bushes, the farmland growing grains and grasses. Where he had been was in truth no longer there.   (*Dubin's Lives*, 191)

That last sentence is like 'Having gone, why didn't she go?' or 'Am I where I think I am?': it makes the metaphysical break through the physical world in a burst of meaning lodged in the mundane but almost in excess of it. Dubin momentarily feels it again when Fanny comes back to him after their first failure and they walk together in the spring meadows: 'Fifteen or more billion years after creation, the biographer thought, here's this sea of wild flowers on earth and amid them this girl picking white daisies' (*Dubin's Lives*, 208). And it is something Malamud had felt before, in the writing of *A New Life*, as he put it in a letter to a Mrs Zolderman, 20 January 1959: 'The "fleeting glimpse" is the way of art. Those who move us most are those we hunger for, hunger to know. The fleeting glimpse is the way of life. Life is poignantly transient. But I try to say in the glimpse that man is everlasting' (LC II 1.1).

The sense of the everlasting within the transient: that is what the richness of language is paradoxically seeking to sustain. For so it is between the end of one paragraph and the beginning of another in Malamud's account of how Dubin found his vocation as a biographer (Illustrations 30a and 30b):

> In biographies the dead become alive, or seem to. He was moved, tormented, inspirited; his heart beat like a tin clock, his head aching as though struggling to pop through the neck of a bottle in which it had been enclosed, imprisoned. He felt for a brilliant moment as though he had freed himself forever.
>
> Afterwards Dubin knew he had discovered—affirmed—his vocation: the lives of others, there was no end of them. He sensed a more vital relation between books and life than he had allowed himself to feel in the past.   (*Dubin's Lives*, 98)

A lesser writer would have changed levels—from the 'forever' at the end of the first paragraph to the 'Afterwards' at the beginning of the next—in ways that were ironic and disillusioning, if not cynical. In Malamud there is a temporal break: the 'forever' of that moment which envisions the future must be taken up and worked out again at the level of 'afterwards'; but it is a recommitment of the glimpse of the everlasting *within* the mundane world and not its entire cancellation.

The Stitches

The mergence of one thing inside another is crucial to the very structure of *Dubin's Lives*. On 24 June 1960 Malamud, the great compartmentalizer, had written to Rosemarie Beck: 'I can't work with departments of being; I'm inspired by the human invention of freedom, the man who seeks to be whole, no matter what the odds against it, and though I am no Tolstoy, I'll try to make the best I can of the whole man and the good and evil thereof.' If in the crisis of *Dubin's Lives* there could not be wholeness, then there had to be that chaos of elements out of which wholeness was composed.

But it was a human mess that still had to be crafted, particularly in the revisions that took place in the writing of the second draft between May 1976 and September 1977. And that included bringing together all that was ostensibly ill-fitting. In terms of what he sometimes called the work's formal sculpture, it was Malamud's most challenging and mature work.[6]

In chapter 3, for example, Dubin goes straight from his failure with Fanny in Venice to seeking in Stockholm his estranged stepson, Gerry, a deserter from the army, just prior to being posted to Vietnam. Two sentences make the uncomfortable link—'Dubin wondered if he had come to see the boy so he could tell Kitty he had stopped off in Stockholm to visit him. He wanted her to be grateful to him before he lied to her about Venice' (*Dubin's Lives*, 95). That is what Malamud always wanted: the paring down that made transitions into electric shocks.

James Atlas, writing his biography of the poet Delmore Schwartz, was privileged to get a view of the galleys of Saul Bellow's Schwartz-based novel, *Humboldt's Gift*. When Atlas showed them to Malamud in 1974, Malamud recognized the prose's prodigal richness and lamented: 'He uses two words to my one' (HRC 31.6). But actually Malamud might have known that his way was precisely the opposite of Bellow's: 'My style springs. Every word ought to take the place of two' (LC II 13.11). He could not do everything—'Every sentence one puts down reduces his thought of one hundred sentences' (LC II 1.5). But what Malamud could do was refine what he had, and make it suggest more than itself. He loved it when in a journal entry for 22 August 1851 Thoreau complained of sentences that 'say all they mean'. Like Thoreau, Malamud wanted sentences that suggested 'a reserve of meaning, like a stutterer', had 'an atmosphere about them', and contained 'the seed of other sentences, not mere repetition, but creation'. That is also why Malamud much preferred the treatment his short stories received as austere libretti for operas by Marc Blitzstein, as compared to the proposed film versions, padded out with material he no longer considered his own.[7]

Dubin, wrote Malamud, 'loved sentences' (*Dubin's Lives*, 216), loved the 'stitches of biographical sentences' (Ibid. 261). Through his biographer, Malamud was taking on the whole of his own life, all he knew so far, and if he could move back and forth in time, he could also move backward and forward in his manuscript, looking for the seeds, creating the patches. 'Sometimes what saves you in a scene hard to work out', he noted in the record of his craft, 'is the good writing leading up to it' (LC II 1.5). It was mainly in the second draft that a series of piecemeal flashbacks were stitched in. Of the third draft of *Dubin*, he wrote to Robert Giroux, 'Ideally, I'd like to make four sentences out of every five' (LC I 3.7). The basic strategy was thus: shape and insert in the second draft 1976–7; then trim again in the third, which took him from December 1977 to July 1978.

In chapter 3, for example, the inserts in the second draft include all the matter that in the previous chapter Dubin had refused to discuss with Fanny in Venice—how he first came to be married to Kitty, after the death of her first husband Nathanael, left with one son; their early days together; the relation of family and writing work. On the latter in particular, the second draft contains interesting details that Malamud nonetheless cut from his third version. 'She complained he was too often silent at the table. If it weren't for me talking to the children there'd be no conversation.' After the exchange of Christmas–Hannukah gifts, for which he cares little, 'Dubin, to his wife's restrained anger, went back to his desk to construct and reconstruct his Lives' (LC I 7.2, pp 24–5).

Theirs was, Dubin recalls, an 'arranged' marriage, they arranged it: he picked up her lonely-hearts advertisement in the office of the newspaper in which he worked, just before she withdrew it in panic. All his life thereafter he has had to fight Kitty's thought that she had married him more out of fear than love; and that he had married her only as an act of will in flight from bachelor loneliness. In the final printed version it goes:

> If they had been in love, certain things would have been easier, might have gone better. There would have been fewer spats—bad for the children. We would have been gayer, certainly less tense. I was gayer with Nathanael. And more carefree in sex.
>
> Dubin doubted it: Love, once you have it, whether it comes with intensity and stays, or in slow building and stays, is love. He said he hadn't much use for the kind of honesty that crapped on experience because it had occurred one way and not another.   (*Dubin's Lives*, 102)

'Dubin doubted it' comes only in the second draft; in the first it was 'I think' in simpler reported dialogue. This is symptomatic of the fluidity Malamud has created in such places, with those marvellous seamless shifts from 'they' to 'we', from 'I' to 'he' and back again—making the whole of one little world available in all its varying perspectives and dimensions, moving fluently inside, outside, and between human beings. 'I get the impression,' goes another Malamud note of work in progress, 'I am working with pieces of a mosaic to create the impression of a raging river in flood' (LC II 1.5).

It is also in chapter 3 that Malamud first brings in those little question-and-answer sessions, first used in 'Talking Horse', that here come out of nowhere, like an interview conducted by an unseen biographer: 'Q: It was about this time you got into biography? A. He was still doing obituaries for the Post' (*Dubin's Lives*, 97). In a letter dated 11 April 1979 Clark Blaise, for one, realized that Malamud had found something new in his search for point of view—in the fluid movement between past and present, inside and outside, speech and thought, husband, wife and lover, first-person and third-person, omniscient narrator and indirect free discourse—and that this variation was part of the sheer life the book demanded of its principal character: 'All your other books are studies of a man not quite alive, they've all lived in isolation (technically, the way you've made a limited-third-person narration feel like omniscience is unique)' (HRC 3.13).

In this expansiveness *Dubin's Lives* is the sequel to *A New Life*: it gives up on automatic renunciation, it wants the life missed in the past to become a life for the immediate future. If the language of 'thou shalt not' means making life itself less than it could be, then the book will even risk challenging the old morality. It will do so even if all that is happening may turn out to be no more than the humiliating foolishness of a conventional mid-life crisis. Clark Blaise saw Lawrence at the heart of such an enterprise: 'The essential world of Lawrence is still the *figure* of all other life and art.' But what is at stake is also caught later in a little image of Dubin in Fanny's New York flat, overlooking a synagogue across the street. There, after making love or writing sentences, he can see in a small candle-lit room 'the elderly Jews reading or at prayer', white shawls glowing on shoulders (*Dubin's Lives*, 216). Dubin is Malamud's Jew now emphatically in the modern world. What now counts for him, belatedly a modern man, in contrast to those old Jews?

Like the juxtapositions, the flashbacks are part of this process in the massing and weighing of a life. Seeking Gerald in Stockholm, Dubin has time to remember that it was a big day for him when he came to love Kitty's nervous,

needy boy as though he were his own: it made the marriage. Later there was
a child of his own, a daughter Maud. Dubin remembers:

> Do you love me, the boy asked.
> Yes. You must know that.
> As much as Maud?
> Yes.
> He seemed to doubt it.   (Ibid. 104)

In the second draft, the second reply had been, painfully, 'As much as I love
Maud he lied.' Kitty tells Dubin in the first draft, 'You were a good father
to him too.' 'For a short time' he sadly replies (LC I 7.2). It was only a
short time because, abruptly, the boy had withdrawn himself in adolescence,
disappearing into utter silence. Dubin did not know how to speak to Gerald
any more and was left fumbling. Fearing his ignorance of someone living
in the same house, Dubin had measured his distance from Gerald to match
Gerald's distance from himself, worried too about Gerald's effect on Maud.
In all versions the third chapter ends stranded like 'My Son the Murderer':

> 'Gerry, a father is a man who treats you like a son. At least walk with me. I'm
> the only father you've got.'
> The youth took off in a heavy-footed run.
> Dubin awkwardly trotted after him,
> At the Skeppsbron bridge Gerald slowed to a fast walk. The biographer limped
> along behind him. It was a bleak night, the lights of the long bridge glowing
> foggily in the freezing drizzle.
> 'Wait up, Gerry. I can't go fast.'
> Gerald told Dubin he had passed his hotel a block back.
> I have to follow him, the father thought. It's the only way to be with
> him.   (*Dubin's Lives*, 111)

The lover having lost Fanny in Venice, the father finds another form of
loss in Stockholm. In the second draft Dubin remembers walking with his
unhappy stepson in the latter days of their time together: after a short while,
the boy would always stride on ahead of Dubin. It also reminds Dubin of
how his own father would sometimes walk on ahead of his disturbed wife in
the street (LC I 7.2). But on the back of page 6 of his 'Juggler' notebook for
1973, Malamud also wrote, not of all he was putting into his novel, but of
something that came back out of it—a dream of his son:

> Paul embracing me—a new Paul—I weep for a minute, then almost unbe-
> lievingly enjoy my new-found grace. Afterwards the one who embraced me
> is someone older than I, whom I thought of as a young person chrono-
> logically.   (HRC 19.5)

Malamud himself had long ago lost the young Arlene Heyman, in Italy; had lost his children to their own adulthood; had lost his brother Eugene to a heart attack on 30 October 1973, a death which itself led to a further, continuing exacerbation of Malamud's own coronary problems; and had lost, it seemed, so much of his marriage—leaving him often to imagine that in all this he had no one either older or younger to care for him.

In the face of such pain, there is a profound double alchemy going on in this book. One has to do with its *content* and the transmutations of what, I say, is virtually Malamud's whole life. For example, from the transcript of Robert Robinson's interview of Malamud for British television, to a question on the recurrence of the theme of second marriages in his work Malamud replies: 'My father had married twice, once after the death of my mother, and perhaps that had popped into my consciousness, obviously it did' (HRC 31.4, pp. 56–6). And, within the mix, it is also true that Dubin, like Malamud, feels like a late-bloomer—that everything that should have come to him at first is only coming the second time round. With Fanny or some other, Dubin wanted to be 'his bride's first husband' (*Dubin's Lives*, 162).

The other work of alchemy is more to do with the book's *form*—in particular, as we have seen, those painfully moving juxtapositions of life which are often the product of the second draft. They come in two forms. Either they are flashbacks, often with particular relation to Dubin's father and mother: 'He looked at his hands as he spoke. They were his father's' (Ibid. 66). Or, more painfully, they are the signs of the almost impossibly simultaneous double-life of adultery:

> At night they sat in opposing armchairs ... As they were reading, Kitty, a day behind with the day's news, read him humorous snippets from yesterday's papers.
>
> 'Don't,' Dubin said. 'I find it hard to concentrate.'
>
> 'Why bother?'
>
> Afterward she said, 'We used to talk about everything in the world. We talk about nothing now.'
>
> He got up to put on a record, not because he wanted to listen to it, but because he must think of Fanny. His thoughts of the girl were a gluey collage representing an unalterable desire to be with her.
>
> Why don't I tell my wife and maybe the misery will yield?
>
> It seemed to him he had not told her because Fanny was still possible. If he answered her letter they might meet.   (Ibid. 142)

The play-off of one paragraph sitting uncomfortably against another, the almost osmotic shifts between outer speech and inner thought—they are like a bitter parody of marriage's proper closeness, juxtapositions finally nearer to insanity than to simple hypocrisy. 'Mad, Dubin thought ... He was, in his thoughts, living with Fanny' (Ibid.). He had wanted to live more than one life at a time. Polygamy was the thrilling sexualization of that imaginative desire—the lives at once kept separate from each other and yet secretly combined. 'The biographer, as he read the newspaper, hefted and measured guilt, yet managed to sidestep it. I'm not twenty, nor forty—I'm fifty-seven. Surely these years entitle me to this pleasure. In life one daren't miss what his nature requires. Only the spiritually impoverished can live without adventure' (Ibid. 210).

What is more, amidst all this work of mergence, these two alchemies of life-content and novel-form could also fluidly interact. In Venice, Dubin thinks he sees Maud with an older man, just as he himself is there with a woman young enough to be his own daughter: 'Could Dubin despise an aging man who desired the company of a young woman—endless insistent hunger? ... Life responds to one's moves with comic counterinventions' (Ibid. 64–5). It is in its own terms a powerfully ironic juxtaposition—but also, it is itself connected with two elements taken from Malamud's own experience. One is the unconsummated affair with an older man, her white-haired English teacher, which Janna Malamud Smith frankly describes in her memoir. It was in late 1968, early 1969, and she was turning seventeen: 'I did not flee him until autumn when I began my freshman year in college. He, having left his wife, transformed before me into a grotesque, incestuous apparition. Sensing my sudden shift, he became frantic, wrote long letters, telephoned weeping from a phone booth, and turned up unannounced at my dormitory room, pleading' (MFB, 237). In the novel itself, Maud's lover is made into her Spanish teacher instead, a married black man by whom she becomes pregnant. But the second half of the amalgam came in part from Arlene Heyman. Her award winning college story, 'The Priest', was based on a relationship, before ever she met Malamud, with a defrocked priest who had introduced her to Spanish poetry. After she left Malamud at the end of 1963, towards the end of her Fulbright-funded year in Spain, she also had a brief relationship with a serviceman in Strategic Air Command, a black man in his thirties, and had written to Malamud about it. The hidden sign of this extraordinary mental composite in *Dubin's Lives* is the double use of a phrase of Arlene Heyman's from the notes and letters Malamud had kept: once in a loving note from *Fanny* to Dubin: 'Lover, father, friend—love me, I love you' (*Dubin's Lives*, 262); then again when *Maud* gives her account of her own parallel affair: 'It became a sort of mythic thing in my mind that he was more than lover—he was father, friend, and lover—that there was something extraordinary in our relationship, that it had been happening since man appeared on earth' (Ibid.

340). It felt strange enough to Janna reading *Dubin's Lives* when it came out
in 1979:

> Were Dad alive he'd prefer to think of my still too-troubled reaction as simply
> documenting the power of his fiction (I initially typed 'faction') ... But he
> would be being cagey, as he so often was when queried about the literal basis of
> his work. He defended his artist's prerogative ferociously to anyone who tried
> to finger the place where creative transformations started and ended. Yet to a
> family member, some fictions feel like a view through a misaligned stereoscope,
> where two separate images overlie each other, never reconcile, and leave you a
> little queasy.   (MFB, 242)

Malamud was mixing, and risking, everything.

Dubin's family thought the writer so very self-sufficient when really he was
vulnerable. In both men, Dubin and Malamud, day by day the writing and
the living go on alongside each other in a paradoxically close distance across a
dangerously narrow mental boundary. Malamud's travel diaries, for example,
show that he went to Stockholm in October 1973 to check on the bridge he
was to describe in chapter 3, then took Ann to Venice with him to check
on the streets and sights of his imagined adultery in chapter 2 (HRC 27.8).
At a trial reading at a Poetry Center, Malamud introduced Kitty Dubin as
aged 50: 'This is the second draft of my book. In my third she'll be 51,' he
joked, 'which shows how tough I get as I go on' (HRC 27.5). Actually, the
boundaries between the work and the life, both inside and outside the novel,
were becoming extraordinarily porous.

Claude Fredericks wrote in his journal that it was a remark of Malamud's
that helped him better to understand and like Ann Malamud: 'Ann was
above all things honest' (12 December 1968). Too often Fredericks had found
her rigid, disappointed, not liking anything, a moralistic 'nay-sayer'. But 'as
Bernard said in the car leaving,' he noted 28 October 1968, there was also 'her
refusal to accept any kind of lie, her determination harshly to look everything
square in the face.' In the notes and drafts of *Dubin*, it is a version of that
honesty that Malamud examines in Kitty. 'She is terrifyingly honest because
she is afraid of illusion' goes one note. But she also lives on above her own
fears: 'She has to have a quality greater than her psychology.' Another note
states: 'She is a fanatic about honesty—hurts him, but his work is better.
When he writes something she thinks is not honest she grows cold' (LC I
13.4). Then Malamud writes in the first draft of chapter 4: 'Kitty defended
the real, she had to, as though a living lie might wreck her world' (LC I 4.4,
p. 7). It is precisely that insecurity which Dubin risks in himself when, seeking
more from reality, he begins to lie to her.

'Kitty happens to be easy to lie to,' he tells Fanny, 'which makes it harder to do. I don't like not to be honest with her' (*Dubin's Lives*, 58). But he lies, he says, to protect her. 'Ultimately he was able to lie with less guilt' is his terrifying achievement: as juggler he 'had to protect his relationship with Fanny, at the same time not hurt Kitty' (Ibid. 241). Before Fanny, he had already split himself, however unevenly, between his family and his study; it seemed only a variation on his capacity for secret inner working to split himself another way. Kitty and Maud see him off on his journey to New York, ostensibly to do research in the public library, actually to meet Fanny:

> He wished, considering the circumstances, they hadn't insisted on taking him to the train, but they knew he disliked buses. Well, life isn't ideal. He loved them both and tried to put them out of mind. They returned at once through predictable doors and windows. One can't easily dispense with the actors of his personal history. The biographer, as he read the newspaper, hefted and measured guilt, yet managed to sidestep it: I'm not twenty, nor forty—I'm fifty-seven. Surely these years entitle me to this pleasure. In life one daren't miss what his nature requires (Ibid. 210)

Things will not stay separate: thrown out the front door they immediately return through the back. That 'and' in 'He loved them both *and* tried to put them out of mind' is one of Malamud's quietly telling moral conjunctions at the heart of a human sentence. Or again, when Kitty asks him if a divorce wouldn't make him happier: ' "No," he said, *but* his heart was gladdened by the thought' (Ibid. 255, my italics). Or when Kitty admits to an infatuation with her library boss, triggering Dubin's own much-belated confession: 'That he had told her what had happened in Venice only *after* she had confessed her feeling for Roger did not seem to bother Kitty, *but* Dubin regretted he hadn't told her long ago' (Ibid. 187–8, my italics).

Quietly shocking in similar fashion is the beginning of chapter 7: 'They made love on a sunny Sunday morning, the moving white curtains enfolding warm light.' It is only in the next sentence that the reader discovers who 'They' is: 'Afterward Kitty, lying on her side, said'. The fourth sentence then contains the implicit idea: 'He had made love with her, trying not to think of Fanny.' He had wanted to spread the love around, like some sixties' youth. But he is inwardly ashamed to be secretly thinking of Fanny whilst with Kitty—thus seconds later:

> Forgive me, he thought.
> 'What for?'
> He asked after a minute, what he had said.

She laughed to herself. 'What shall I forgive?'
'Who I am.'

(Ibid. 226)

This is the technique Malamud had taught himself in 'My Son the Murderer': the thin but vital boundary between thinking within and speaking out. Freud terrifies Dubin when he says that no-one can keep a secret forever but must blurt it out someway: 'If his lips are silent his fingertips give him away' (Ibid. 238). Things leak and merge across bounds in *Dubin's Lives*. 'Do you think I might be deceiving you?' Kitty later asks her husband; 'I wish you were', he thought (Ibid. 240). His is the dishonesty of an honest man seeking more than honesty, the painful complexity of someone who needs simplicity but not reduction. Yet whatever his motivation in defying truthfulness and fidelity, he has to stop thinking of himself as a truthful man. In the silence of the marriage, the would-be juggler hardens into becoming both what he has done and what he has omitted to do:

> He had nothing to say because he hadn't said it when it was his to say. What you don't say grows into not saying. … He was, in his silence, elsewhere. He was not who she thought he was.
> (Ibid. 143)

On the face of it, this domestic hell does not have the stature of suffering in *The Fixer*. Dubin has done it to himself, and what he has done also seems grubby. Yet like being lost in the snow, the situation is more than itself, without ever ceasing to be itself. Something of huge import is trapped in this modern story, within but also beyond its theme of a failing marriage. 'He was elsewhere; not who she thought he was' is like the strange metaphysical turn the language suddenly takes concerning the increasingly distant Maud:

> Yet every so often the father had the feeling he had lost or misplaced his daughter at a specific time in another country, a foreign experience. Had he, indeed, lost her in Venice, although he did not, in truth, know whether she'd ever been there?
> (Ibid. 168)

It is that final 'although' clause which is brilliant, sending the mind spinning into a realm beyond fact.

'If a man needs his daughter so much, Dubin thought, maybe he needs somebody else more' (Ibid. 129). It is words such as that 'else' which are always a clue to what is mysterious or unknown in *Dubin's Lives*—'he was elsewhere', 'he needs somebody else'. For this is a novel going *beyond* that language of ordinary explanation which would make it just another story of a failing marriage, like a million others. 'I want my life to tell me what it knows,' Dubin says. But what the great writer does, Malamud noted, is 'create a mystery at the same time as he unravels it ... solving a mystery that leads into a mystery' (LC II 10.9).

Why *Dubin's Lives* is so powerful is in that sense mysterious: as though modern forms cannot contain or satisfy what rages within this book. Writing in his notebook about Thoreau, Malamud struggles with the idea of a super-charged realism: 'The "real" plus hypothesis of more than is real—what?' (HRC 19.3, p. 39). But this novel, which is never less than realism, will not stop asking what the reality within it is really about. The consequences of the experience within Dubin himself—writer's block, impotence with his wife, thoughts of suicide, insanity, or divorce—together with the power of the language that registers them point to something in excess of the forms in which his life finds itself.

The book leaks secrets. 'What it amounts to, the biographer thinks, is that one may be able to mask dishonesty but not its effects: the diminution of libido, ebb of feeling for a woman, love for her' (*Dubin's Lives*, 242). And another effect is a sudden sense of mental deterioration and blankness. Increasingly Dubin cannot remember the details of Lawrence's life, gets lost in his notes and his writing. He has long tried to forget his mother, but now, attempting a memoir of his parents, is shocked to find how sparse and brief it is, as though in nemesis. He has even tried to forget that love in his marriage has not come to that fulfilment of which Lawrence had so demandingly preached. But with Fanny gone a second time, he now turns to his wife to try to make out what they have made of their life. 'So it was a bad marriage?' he asks Kitty. 'Not much of one,' she replies, 'Not any more. I have to be honest.' Dubin 'damned her honesty, felt at a loss, had not wanted to fail in marriage' (Ibid. 336). But no one, not even the partners, can now sum up this marriage, in the confusing density of life's relativism: 'He wasn't certain what he was saying, that he was telling the truth about the past. He was trying to but it seemed, in their quarrel, impossible to recall exactly; to say what had truly happened to them. Or exactly what was happening now' (Ibid. 255).

Somehow, Dubin suspects, all that he has tried to forget, together with his repeated failure to be fully present in the present, is wreaking a mental revenge. Now, as though in sudden premature ageing, the mind of a writer cannot recall the words which are its very lifeline:

> You had this thing to say and the words would not come ... Usually when he forgot words he would wait for them to seep back into consciousness like fish drawn up to the hungry surface of a stream. He would remember the initial letter of the forgotten word or sense sounds in it; soon the word reappeared in an illumination. Now words rarely returned when Dubin needed them.   (Ibid. 310)

What had he done to himself? Trying to be younger had only made him older. 'Dubin forgot what he read as he was reading it'—even St Augustine's *Confessions*:

> Augustine had discovered God in his memory: he had left Him there, abandoned Him, and there God had remained. ... He feared telling Kitty what was happening to him, although she sometimes looked as if she knew. Had guessed? What are you forgetting? her eyes seemed to ask. You, Dubin thought, I am forgetting you. What one forgot conceived a further forgetting: a hole unraveling. Unweaving Fanny, he had unwoven the tapestry of their experience.   (Ibid. 311)

Augustine could leave God in his memory and God would come back. For Dubin there is neither faith in a God nor trust in his faculties. There seems nothing left. *The Natural* had spoken of a second life, maybe a third. 'William Dubin's in his last life, no longer those one lives to learn with' (Ibid. 299).

The novel ends with Dubin going back to his wife with an erection borrowed from seeing Fanny. It ends once again with a bibliography of works by William B. Dublin which seems to indicate that in the future he completed his life of Lawrence, wrote all he knew about writing lives in *The Art of Biography*, and finished with a life of Anna Freud, the great man's daughter, written in collaboration with Maud, now apparently married in bearing the Spanish name Perrera. But it has no ending as such. It is, rather, a resonant holding-ground for, a saturated solution of, all that seeks resolution and fulfilment in modern life and cannot find it. 'You've made something that incorporates the world,' said Clark Blaise (HRC 3.13). Malamud himself underlined Thoreau, 26 February 1841; 'I cannot tell you what I am ... What I am I am, and say not. Being is the great explainer.' In *Dubin's Lives* it is that unappeasable 'being' which is created.

Aftermath

'Bern was giving the new novel to his publishers in December,' Claude Fredericks wrote in his journal for 23 October 1977—though this could only have been the second draft, for consultation. 'I think it will be his masterpiece, I said. I certainly hope so, Ann said a little doubtfully.'

It had not helped Malamud's confidence that Ann repeatedly told him that though a good writer, he was not a great writer such as Faulkner or Joyce. But on 23 August 1978 he wrote in his notebook, 'My book is done, five years ... three drafts, connections, connected connections, I've begun to relax, and understand how massively I had set myself to work. It was a hard book to write but I think I've done well' (HRC 19.7). The first printing from Farrar, Straus and Giroux was his largest ever, 50,000 copies, with an advance of $150,000. At the launch party thrown by Roger Straus, Malamud said quietly, referring to the famous line from F. Scott Fitzgerald about there being no second acts in American lives: 'There *are* second acts.' *Dubin's Lives* seemed to mark the end of a more than ten-year period of abeyance since the success of *The Fixer*.

Reviews were generally respectful. In particular Mark Shechner in *The Nation* (17 March 1979) argued that the novel in its 'heightened sexuality' and its 'mayhem' marked a move on from 'the old ethics', in an attempt to cut through to something else not resolved by the novel's close. But in retrospect both Robert Giroux and Robert Boyers felt that the novel never quite got the recognition it deserved: if it had, 'it would have supplanted an earlier idea of Malamud as a very limited writer, a merely historical figure, and done much for his reputation in the longer run'.[8] Saul Bellow in a letter of 25 March 1979, expressed his admiration, adding wryly that he had perhaps known too much of the book's sexual sorrow to be able to judge it reliably (HRC 3.10).

As ever Malamud denied autobiographical equivalence in interviews, and in his notebook wrote in preparation for such questions, 'Dubin's history isn't mine. He and I may share similar experiences but we are different people. Put a man in fiction and he becomes fiction' (HRC 19.7) But Malamud also told Bert Pogrebin on one of their New York walks, 'If you know *Dubin's Lives*, you know me.' [9] Among Malamud's friends who knew the story behind the story, the response was ambivalent. One relative was said to have called it a disgrace to the family. Gloria Stern was upset to find small personal details reproduced in the book, to do with being a widow and having a son prior to her marriage with Dan, which she had refused Malamud permission to use; later she believed he had simply forgotten the refusal. Bernadette Inkeles admitted, 3 March 1979:

> In my initial reading I was not able to transcend the environment and many conversations which have been part of our mutual lives for so many years. I am *not* saying that I thought I was reading autobiography; but I kept seeing *your* walking route, *your* very old mountains and indeed kept seeing *you* walking. I could not distance myself from the sleepless nights, the time Ann didn't sew on a button, the many times I used to make Alex drive back to make sure I hadn't left the iron connected, the stove burning ... We have all talked together so often over the years about so many of the themes that appear in one guise or another in *Dubin's Lives* that Dubin awake was you awake, and Kitty awake was Ann awake.

But on a second reading, she reported, she saw more clearly how it dealt 'with questions of burning interest to the contemporary person' and felt it more as 'the independent entity I know that it is': 'This morning about 2.00 a.m. I was tossing around sleeplessly in bed, and I groaned, "Oh, I'm doing a Kitty." And I thought of Kitty, and not of Ann' (HRC 11.5). Back in Oregon, Sue Hovland, who had never quite forgiven the writing of *A New Life*, noted Malamud's belief that the personal was the stuff of creation, and acknowledged that only the artist could know just where to draw the line—but she concluded sadly: 'Whereas I originally felt that we understood each other without any need to "explain ourselves"—I now have the feeling that you may not understand us at all. I feel almost a will to mis-understand' (HRC 11.1). 'It's all there,' she wrote.

But as so often in all areas, it was Nina Pelikan Straus who, having read some of the novel in draft, was the one most to recognize the rich, fearful venture that *Dubin's Lives* had constituted on the verge of bedlam. During April 1975, she wrote Malamud: 'I am anxious. It is almost as if there were a choice of which levels one could live upon. Sometimes there appear so many. Happiness is perhaps the simplicity of one—work or motherhood, or some abasement to Circumstance. Is there a place for the merging of confusions in fiction? Who has written such? Do you perhaps, when Dubin is in Venice?' But she adds ruefully in her next paragraph, 'You are, however, too sly for me' (HRC 18.5).

Replying to Nina, 1 June 1975, Malamud speaks of having just received a letter from her, at the very moment he is writing of Dubin receiving a letter from Fanny. Malamud copies out for Nina the passage in question, saying of Dubin: 'He is not doing well. He is about to walk alone at night. It was as though you had entered the fiction. You may keep it.' Earlier, on 26 April, he had written Nina that she was 'a little like fiction to me', adding 'in the best of all possible worlds we would all be so to each other: that heightened sensibility, insight, expressiveness'.[10]

Too often, outside his writing, Malamud felt himself cut off, the emotions turning back inwards. But in *Dubin's Lives*, he created what Nina had rightly called a full, emotional 'merging of confusions'. And these confusions were lodged in that place *in between* literature and life, which the writing itself seemed to occupy at the very moment of its composition. Always Malamud was a practical, ordered man who wanted to know if he was *here*, or if he was *there*; but at his best, within the study, he created places where he barely knew where he was, and yet wrote out of them.

The realism of *Dubin's Lives* was like a great maddening circle, made up of wild oscillating movements in desperate search of balance. This was a man in danger of sacrificing so much of life, precisely in order to write about it. His was an art almost in contradiction of itself, using all its power to create within books the sense of a reality greater than the books which sustained it. And yet even in his art's service to life, nothing perhaps was ever perhaps quite so deep or wide for Malamud as what he created in fiction. That did not feel how it should be. In a 'juggler' notebook, Malamud copied out Auden's saying: 'The feeling that life is essentially inadequate to the human spirit, and yet that a good life must avoid saying so' (HRC 19.5, p. 58).

Shortly after her husband's death, Ann Malamud wrote Karl Schrag that Malamud's constant, commonplace 'leitmotif' had been 'Life is sad'.[11] Fiction was the best of all possible worlds for Malamud not because it escaped the disappontment of the unwritten world, but because it incorporated the expression of it. Take away that art, and people were again more separate, more emotionally hidden than Malamud believed that they ought to be.

When Kate Hickler, one of his favourite students at Harvard, set off for Cuba in 1969 in search for something bright and positive in the world, Malamud had told Jay Cantor that 'really what she was talking about was love'.[12] He did not mean that this was merely politics in compensation for personal relationship. For Malamud, love meant a form of belief, a personal passion seeking some object or individual in the world outside the self to charge with its force—and then the arduous education in life that was involved in following that through. It was like the young student in 'The Magic Barrel' taking his chance with the lost young woman who looks whip-lashed with understanding. When Kate Hickler and Peter Hayes, another of that talented batch of would-be writers from Harvard in 1966, got together in 1970, Malamud wrote them, 'And now, for Godsake, make love last.' No one, said Kate Hickler, was more aware of death, of ephemerality and loss than was Malamud, from his early days onwards. But love as bond or commitment was the perilously attempted antidote—knowing nonetheless that often it too did not last, that moral duty had often to serve as the human substitute. The only object that did not let one down was writing: whatever it demanded, it could in return bear his perfectionism; transform ordinary truths into felt experience; fulfil his need for a clinching moment of transcendence, whatever followed thereafter. It was a sort of religion.

Later, Peter Hayes went to visit Malamud in his apartment near the Lincoln Center in New York some time after the publication of *Dubin*. It was not a good time in Hayes's life and he went to Malamud as 'the closest thing to a wise man I knew', in search of solutions to his problems. 'He asked me if I'd had any "victories" and I told him no, not recently. He responded

by saying, "That's too bad. Writers need them in order to keep writing."'
Malamud at the time seemed to have won many victories of his own:

> He had taught me fiction at Harvard and had won National Book Awards. He
> was a writer of great economy and powers who, from the humblest beginnings,
> had reached the pinnacle of his profession and been rewarded with accolades,
> wealth, and fame. And yet, as we talked that Sunday afternoon, I realized with a
> sinking heart that he was no happier than me. His health was bad; his marriage
> shaky; and whatever answers he had discovered were all his own ...
>
> Then he asked me what I thought was the meaning of life. The answer I
> gave was patently mystical, something about the one Being who looks out of
> all our eyes and about our recognizing our identity with Her or with Him. He
> surprised me by nodding his head when I was through, and saying something
> to the effect of: 'Yes. Well, you got that right.'[13]

The terms were manifestly not his own, but in his own way Malamud
knew he was only arbitrarily himself—albeit inescapably so too. He knew he
was trapped in a subjectivity which fiction alone relieved and widened and
deepened. He knew that however much he could see more, imaginatively,
in the whole of Life than the part he occupied, he was enclosed still within
limitation—within his self, his life, and his relationships, and still, even at
the higher level, within the capacity of his books. In a first draft of chapter 8
of *Dubin*, Malamud had had his man standing in a graveyard, feeling that he
knows the living hardly better than he knows these dead:

> The subjective self yields only so much of ultimate subjectivity. Only love
> carries into another's consciousness but mainly for your own uses. I've nev-
> er been one for metaphysics but how may strangers come together, man
> being the subjective miser he is, except in God's self, God's mind, if there
> is a God.   (LC I 5.3, p. 66)

Dubin himself 'played God to some who had once lived: he entered their
lives.' Authorship gave him the glimpse: it was an imperfect, fictive version,
the best he could achieve. Do you believe in God? Fanny asks Dubin in that
first draft. She says that *she* does, and in this version tells him that she too is
Jewish. 'Not in God,' he replies, but—'in the idea of God.' What good is
that? she demands. 'It's good for me,' he replies (LC I 4.1, p. 45).

IN HIS LAST LIFE

10

❮❮❧❧❧❯❯

'As you are grooved so you are graved'

'A Sixty-Year-Old Smiling Public Man'

One day in 1980 Ellen McCulloch-Lovell, a graduate of Bennington in 1969 and now chief of staff to Senator Patrick Leahy, was surprised to find Malamud in Washington, DC doing the rounds of the congressional delegation. He was there on behalf of PEN (the American Center of Poets, Playwrights, Editors, Essayists, and Novelists) in support of the National Endowment of the Arts. 'A famous writer in his later years', this man who was never willing to waste a moment of his time had travelled to DC to sit waiting in the offices of congressmen. 'When I asked him why, he answered: "Because my work alone is no longer enough." '[1]

Of *Dubin's Lives* Malamud told Danny Myerson, 'The song of my youth is gone, but I have other compensatory qualities.'[2] That novel in particular had aged him, as though in writing it the whole of his life had caught up with him and made its demands. It was now almost entirely the winter season for Malamud. Ann Malamud well knew how, like his man Dubin, Malamud had loved Schubert: 'I remember his saying "Schubert writes the heart." Bern had a particular feeling for one of Schubert's great song cycles, *Winterreise*— A Winter Journey. The slow movement of the great C-major quintet was played at Bern's memorial service.' 'How moving a simple song is,' thinks Dubin, 'How often they go to sadness' (*Dubin's Lives*, 137).

Again and again in the later 1970s there are letters describing the loss of a capacity for surprise or change. On his walks, Malamud wrote Karl Schrag, even as one season changed again into another, 'change now holds little surprise': 'It's change because it happens, not because we know it will.'[3] He felt he knew too much now. Sometime in 1979 he wrote Nina Peilkan Straus: 'It seems to me I am not conscious of the magic of writing; at this stage, more

of a prosaic self at work. There must be such a thing as knowing too well
who one is.' 'The surprises no longer surprise me,' he told her (HRC 18.5).
On 4 September 1978, he wrote to Karl Schrag and his wife Ilse:

> Yesterday morning I went for my walk and noticed how thin summer had
> become. The day was weightless, limpid, very still, and once more I remembered
> the nostalgia I felt as a child at this time of the year—summer's end, the loss of
> the season of freedom; and yet at the same time I felt then a stir of anticipation:
> school beginning, that multifarious excitement fed by rich experiences of the
> classroom, very few of which I could duplicate at home.

He was thinking about writing memoirs of his father and of his mother,
disappointed about how little he could recall. But as he wrote to the Schrags,
he felt no boyhood feelings, felt 'light' instead, 'as though the brain had lost
weight' now that he had at last reached the end of *Dubin's Lives*:

> It took me five years and five months and finally it's done. It was a day by
> day affair and had to be done almost forever. I walked a tightrope, trying not
> to look down. Hardy was afraid he would die before he finished *The Dynasts*.
> Anyone in his sixties would have that fear. Now, except for the galleys, my
> work is done and my fears can go to the next book.

But for once there was not only the next book. 'I like what I am doing at
P.E.N. I like being used in my age,' he wrote Nina Pelikan Straus on 25 June
1980. Malamud had been elected President of PEN American Center on 6
June 1979. Only a former student of his from the Harvard summer school
of 1961, the novelist John Bart Gerald, voted against. Ann Malamud was
disturbed because he seemed to be accusing her husband and his publishers
of some sort of conspiracy, but Paul Malamud simply went over and sat
quietly beside him. John Bart Gerald believed that PEN was increasingly bent
towards government agendas and that Malamud, for all his literary eminence
and compassion, was not sufficiently an activist to combat this tendency or
to fight for the less prominent among the world of writers.[4]
    In his presidential address to his fellow-writers, Malamud did express a
wry provincial surprise at this institutional turn in himself:

> I live most of the year miles away, in a small town in Vermont, where I write
> full-time and teach in the spring. Who wants to come running to New York
> City, leaving a world of fields and flowers, to chair institutional meetings in
> Manhattan? I have a book to begin and stay with until it says what it must.
> You know the feeling. I was not, therefore, thinking of assuming a task of
> communal responsibility two hundred miles from home. To assure me that it
> could be done without seriously getting in the way of my work, a former PEN
> president told me on the telephone, 'Malamud, I guarantee you, we will not

interfere with a single paragraph of your prose.' But we agreed to wait until I had finished a long book. That was about four years ago.

Dubin's Lives was now launched. He was planning the writing of a shorter fiction again, *God's Grace*.

> I agreed to serve and here I am because I want to be. I may lose a paragraph here, a paragraph there—without regret in a good cause. On my return I will say, 'Good morning, paragraph, I have not abandoned you.' 'Good morning, comrade, I have lost weight but not faith.'   (LC I 60.4)

PEN's defence of writers' liberties was a cause that naturally appealed to Malamud's liberalism. When Solzhenitsyn famously defected to the West in 1974 Malamud had sent him a telegram in West Germany: 'I am grateful to you for enlarging my freedom.' Malamud had himself experienced, as a sort of equivocal compliment, Voerword's apartheid-driven proscription of *The Tenants* in South Africa. But in its minor parochial way, the banning of *The Fixer* in 1977 by ordinary, decent American citizens, sitting in ignorance on the Long Island school board, reminded him of how lucky he had been in general. '*The Fixer* does not defend me. I must defend it. And PEN supports me in that defence. I must, with other writers, support PEN' (LC I 61.3). One of Malamud's favourite quotations was Tolstoy on censorship: what worried the great novelist was the suppression not so much of what he had written as what he might have written. Malamud was therefore willing to serve PEN, because, as his presidential address finally declared:

> I am past sixty and have long reflected on what being a writer is and entails. I believe in a fellowship of writers, more or less informally constituted, aware of how deeply and complexly we are concerned with, and foster, literature as a civilizing force in an unstable world; a literature that gives flesh, bones, and perhaps a brain to the politics that assail us; a literature that entices us to understand and value life, and act as though we value it, before it is gone. I approve the idea and endeavor of PEN and feel I owe it a more active service than I've given it in the past.   (LC I 60.4)

But in the initial negotiations, he had given Karen Kennerly, the executive director, a careful list of his conditions. He would concentrate on the Freedom to Write Committee and the Events Committee. There would be monthly meetings at most, and unlike those at Bennington, they would be conducted speedily. He would use different coloured paper for different sorts of business. 'I told her that I wanted plenty of time to make decisions asked of me. I did not want to make impulsive decisions on matters of PEN . . . . I said I liked the responsibility of being responsible. She understood' (LC I 61.6). He was a prestigious catch.

The American membership consisted of 1,600 writers, but the organization was running at a $20,000 deficit. Malamud immediately contributed $1,000 himself and wrote to other writers and some publishers asking for a similar donation in order to keep the organization going. He also gave money for a PEN translation award out of the belief that literature should never be a solely national endeavour. He raised staff salaries and worked hard at improving some uneasy staff relationships. American PEN's campaigns for writers' freedom included interventions for Vaclev Havel and the Charter 77 human rights group in Czechoslovakia. Among the writers on whose behalf protests were lodged were Nadine Gordimer, on the banning of *Burger's Daughter* in South Africa, Andrei Sakharov the physicist under constant surveillance in Russia, Kofi Awoonor in Ghana, Kim Chi Ha in South Korea, and also the underground publisher Miroslaw Chojecki in Poland. Malamud led the fight against American visa restrictions when Dario Fo was denied admittance for being 'a leftist'. He appealed to Castro, via Edward Kennedy, to let Herberto Padilla, the Cuban poet, join his wife, family, and ailing mother in America. All this was bound to be of serious concern to the writer of *The Fixer*, noted Tamas Ungvari, another PEN stalwart, quoting the sentence that Malamud himself quoted from Sanhedrin (the ancient Jewish supreme court) in *God's Grace*: 'He who saves one life, it is as if he saved the world' ('The Flood', 6).[5]

Within America itself, PEN under his presidency continued to support writers' freedom of expression, in particular in the cases of Gwen Davis, who was being sued by her own publishers in the face of an alleged sexual libel, and Frank Snepp, a former CIA employee who had turned Vietnam whistle-blower only to have his book earnings sequestered by the government. PEN led a successful fight against the imposition of taxes on publishers' warehouse holdings which would have led to the pulping of millions of copies of books. Less successfully, it sought funding for a libraries-in-prisons project, initiated by the organization's treasurer, Joan Crowell, and entitled 'Books Behind Bars'. In January 1980 Malamud led a symposium of publishers, writers, and booksellers to discuss the conglomerization of the American book business, in both publishing and bookselling, and the resulting emphasis on best-selling blockbusters to the detriment of serious writing. In particular he took on Richard Snyder, the tough and powerful president of Simon and Schuster, deploring the ever greater emphasis being placed 'on what can be characterized as making a buck'.[6] In his own childhood home, whatever the poverty, 'I never heard a word in praise of the buck' (TH, 12).

Karen Kennerly called Malamud 'the last moral man'.[7] But he was also like a little boy, she said, coming to her excitedly to report, 'Guess what I did today.' His biggest coup was to persuade Norman Mailer to serve as his successor.

He told her: 'I said, "Norman, when you get to a certain age, it's time to *give back*."' By then Malamud had already decided to serve a second year. He said it was a shame to leave just when he had learnt enough to be more effective. 'It is satisfying as a cause—an opportunity to work off in some worthy way the desire of the writer to get out of his room and do something helpful to someone else, to a good cause. The sense one has of using a reputation—such as it is—for a purpose other than to sell books, worthy purpose though that is' (LC I 61.6). Moreover, he loved being part of the team of workers, work for him being normally so lonely. He also liked appearing to be up to date and in the know. For years, Karen Kennerly and Miles Davis, the legendary jazz musician, had been lovers. Karen remembered a party that Malamud held at his own place at which he turned to her and said slyly, in his most well-prepared style, 'And how is Duke Ellington?' 'Oh, you mean Miles Davis,' she replied. He aged in a moment, again behind the times. 'He was so deflated.'

PEN was one of three institutions to each of which Malamud left $10,000 in his will. The others were Bennington and Yaddo, for which Malamud served as a Board Director from 1981 until his death, in 1983 acting in emergency as temporary president despite poor health. He felt continuing gratitude for the time he had had at Yaddo to write so much of *A New Life*.

It was the season for honours, given to what Malamud's beloved Yeats in 'Among Schoolchildren' had wryly called 'a sixty-year-old smiling public man'. Malamud had been made a member of the American Institute of Arts and Letters in 1963, then was promoted into the American Academy, and in 1983 received its Gold Medal for Fiction. In Vermont, in May 1980, Malamud received the Governor's Award for Excellence in the Arts; in 1985 there was the prestigious Premio Mondello prize in Italy; and so on. Malamud seemed not displeased but often diffident, the recognition too late, he would say, to be of much help to him. But whenever he received an award, his cousin Murray Malament would write him, as though in continuance of the memory of Malamud's father Max, his own 'uncle Mendel'. At the presentation of the Jewish Heritage Award in 1977, where Malamud gave the broadest of answers to the question what is a Jew, Murray recalled the old grocer 'kindly and smiling, selling trayfe [non-Kosher food]'. In 1983 he quietly alluded to the reconciliation that eventually followed the rupture of Malamud's marrying a gentile: 'the picture of my sweet, gentle Uncle Mendel, greeting Ann and touching baby Paul' (HRC 33.6). On 25 June 1979 Malamud himself wrote to Nina Peilkan Straus of his relationship with his son Paul:

We were cut off for a while but have been coming together, have whittled our way back into each other's affection. His, for me, has grown; when he was a little boy we were very close. I think I have always loved him, even at his most disaffected—when he couldn't make it with himself.

It was the tradition described in *Life Is With People*: 'Human relations are expected to endure. There is seldom a final end to anything.'[8]

It was also a time to mark the milestones, on those celebratory family occasions from which small tokens survive. There is a poem from Dan Stern to Ann to mark the thirtieth wedding anniversary, the text being from St Paul on its being best not to marry, though better to marry than to burn. 'Saint Paul has nothing to teach dear Ann | Since years ago she found her man | And can give the Apostle a lesson to learn: | It is better to marry—and to Bern' (HRC 18.3). Another poem was by Ann herself, in comic ruefulness, to Malamud on his sixty-fifth birthday in March 1979, illustrated by Paul:

> This has been a day of papers;
> (Better, far, have cut some capers!)
> Letters, bills, to toss, to file?
> (Better, far, have sailed the Nile!)
> But writers' brides must tend the nitty-gritty;
> (Better, far, to dally with the witty!)
> Now pause I must to write this hymn of praise;
> (Better, far, if I could get a raise!)
> To sing my song of monogamous love and thanks;
> (Better, far, to have indulged in pranks!)
> For my dear spouse's 65th fiesta;
> (No better far than he; Bern is the besta!)   (HRC 37.8)

There had always been those underlying reservations, not always so happily negotiated as in these mellowing years. On holiday in Capri in 1979, Malamud noted in his travel diary how Ann had said she felt ambivalent about *Dubin*, that the book made her nervous: 'She said she realized she was a very nervous woman' (HRC 28.3). Malamud had often characterized the marriage as 'nervous'.[9]

But increasingly beneath everything, what was making Ann more nervous was the problem of Malamud's deteriorating health. 'Sometime in the 1960s,' Janna Malamud Smith reported, 'his doctor warned him that he was "a candidate for a heart attack", and admonished him to change his habits; so he did. He started taking daily walks, eating less, and losing weight'. (MFB, 9). At one point, Ann Malamud recalled, he was told to lose 20 lbs because of his high blood pressure. In the first draft of *Dubin's Lives* the diet becomes another way in which the writer seeks to discipline himself: 'The paunch symbolized useless growth, fat, formlessness—disorder. He was in a way pregnant with the burden, the memory of Fanny' (LC 4.4, p.17). But the stress of writing, particularly from around the time of *The Fixer*, was itself part of the problem. Malamud took medication for his blood pressure, but in the later 1970s the heart condition was worsening, and he began to experience increased breathlessness when walking, the symptom of increasing exertional angina. In January 1981 he wrote to Alex Inkeles from New York that he could usually manage his short morning walk of eight blocks with ease, unless there was a wind blowing or he had eaten too much the night before; but the twenty-to-thirty block afternoon walk depended on his taking nitrostat as medication. His physician described him as 'severely limited' (HRC 11.5).

By November 1981, during his time as a fellow at the Center for Advanced Study in Behavioural Sciences at Stanford, Malamud was consulting Dr Donald Harrison, the head of the department of cardiology, and his resident, Dr Bruce McAuley. In a special medical notebook which, characteristically, Malamud had started in 1974, he wrote: 'McAuley says he heard a slight murmur, "nothing to worry about"—the first time I heard this. Dr Harrison also examined me, listened to the history of my angina and recommend-ed angiography and possibly [an] operation.' What was proposed was a three-vessel coronary bypass operation, requiring two weeks hospitalization and two months convalescence, for the following reasons—as listed by Malamud:

1. If I have a heart attack I will probably drop dead. (He put it less dramatically but that's the point.) He gave me a 6 or 8 per cent chance of having the worst attack within a year.
2. The angina produces anxiety and worry.
3. The medication destroys mental clarity.
4. There are physical (including sexual) limitations.

The chances of dying during angiography, he noted, were 1 in 1,500; the chances that the operation would fail to end the angina were 10 per cent. In the meantime Dr Harrison advised a change of medication to Atenolol because 'Inderol produces depression', and told his patient carefully to watch out for pain at rest, night pain, longer duration of angina pains, or missed heartbeats. But the characteristic statement on Malamud's part is this: 'I said I couldn't have the angiography until I finish my book.' Dr Harrison agreed 'and thought a by-pass operation should come soon thereafter, possibly in February' (HRC 25.8). But as ever the book came first.

God's Grace

In June 1973 in a notebook of story ideas, Malamud had already been thinking of the novel to follow 'The Juggler': a fantasy which was to be 'a larger and deeper try at a talking animal story'. It had been in his mind even earlier, when undertaking *The Tenants*. But he felt further encouraged in the enterprise when in 1978 Claude Fredericks produced for him a fine limited edition of the animal stories, 'The Jewbird' and 'Talking Horse': it was 'to help me feel, when I had doubts about the almost unreal enterprise I was about to embark on, that I had already taken the first step towards its completion and could not fail to take the second' (LC II 8.15).

'The Tribe' or 'Surviving', as it was originally called, was to be a story about a chimp and a chimp doctor. From the first Malamud linked it with Abraham and the sacrifice of his son, Isaac; but this time it might work in reverse, so that through the sacrifice of their fatherly teacher or doctor, the chimps 'begin to approach the human experience' (HRC 22.1). Gradually the tale also became associated in Malamud's mind with thoughts of the Nazi Holocaust and fears of a Nuclear Holocaust: historically, it now seemed, his whole life had been lived out in small uneasy safety between the Camps and the Bomb. In his journal for 21 June 1980, Claude Fredericks noted a Malamud again troubled by a new work but this time with a poignant difference: 'I don't want, he said sinking into the front seat of my car, to write a pessimistic book, I don't want a pessimistic book to be my last.'

Again and again towards the end of 1979 and at the beginning of 1980 Malamud would write out his list of the book's themes. In a note on 'point of view', dated 11 January 1980, he writes 'Don't make it a time story; make it an event story' (LC I 25.5). *The Fixer* and *Dubin's Lives* had been time stories, living with duration; but this book felt different from Malamud's usual mundane obsession: '[Cohn's] watch had stopped, he would not wind it up. It extended time not to hack it to bits and pieces. Perhaps this was closer to the Lord's duration' (*God's Grace*, 'Cohn's Island', 46). It was a fable to be written, noted Malamud, more like the Bible, succinctly, in chapter and verse. 'You are engaged', he told himself, 'with locale and fantasy more than with developing characters (one is, therefore, not heavily into people).'

Indeed the novel opens with just a single man left on the planet—a scientist called Calvin Cohn, the lapsed son of a rabbi, who, conducting his researches at the bottom of the ocean, while all the rest of mankind had been wiped out in a thermonuclear war, has survived by sheer accident. With him on the deserted ship is a chimp he names Buz (descendant of a brother of Abraham), to whom his late colleague the Germanic Dr Bunder seems to have taught a sign language. It also turns out that Bunder has recently operated on Buz's larynx. Cohn completes the procedure by twisting together two copper wires hidden under the healing bandage of the chimp's neck cloth, and at once Buz speaks. They make it together to a desert island, inhabited by other apes. Cohn is the didactic father-figure, not only a Robinson Crusoe but a Noah and a Moses—though Buz has been heavily Christianized by the sinister Bunder. What follows is an experiment in biology and culture, in the attempted recreation of civilization. When Alex Inkeles ventured to remark that the environment of the island was rather a strange mixture, Malamud retorted, 'It's my island! I made it up! I have a right to this island!'

For once, Malamud's main reading list for the project survives. It consists of Genesis and Deuteronomy, together with commentary by Rashi, and Shalom Spiegel's account of the sacrifice of Isaac in *The Last Trial*; *Gilgamesh* and *The Odyssey*; and the literary criticism of Eric Auerbach's *Mimesis* and Frank Kermode's *Sense of an Ending*. There is Freud's *Civilization and Its Discontents*, Christopher Lasch on mass consumerism in *Narcissism in America*, John Searle's *Speech Acts*, Walker Percy on language on a desert island in *The Message in the Bottle*, and George Steiner's *After Babel*. Wolfgang Kohler's *The Mentality of Apes* and Jane Goodall's work on chimpanzees, *In the Shadow of Man*, are both important, supplemented by magazine articles and careful note-taking trips to Central Park Zoo. Malamud also mentions the explorer Thor Heyerdahl, and further reading in novels such as Saul Bellow's *Henderson the Rain King*, George Orwell's *Animal Farm*, Defoe's *Robinson Crusoe*, John Updike's *The Coup*, Hardy's *The Dynasts*, Bulgakov's *The Heart of a Dog*, Georgi Vladimov's satirical account of a Soviet camp guard-dog, *Faithful Ruslan*, and Hugh Loftus' *Adventures of Dr Doolittle*. The neo-allegorical twist to the story has origins in Melville and Hawthorne.

There is also later on file 'Yossel Rakover's appeal to God', a cry from the Warsaw ghetto by one 'forsaken by the God in whom he believed unshakeably', with notes on the theme of the suffering servant in the Jewish tradition; clippings on the Darwinism of Stephen Jay Gould and the anthropological studies of Louis Leakey; an essay by Rabbi Irving Greenberg, 'After the Holocaust', with substantial annotations; and very extensive notes on Edward O. Wilson's work in socio-biology, *On Human Nature*.

In these researches it is clear that Malamud was working at once from the two great directions of Creation: from top-down through the workings of the God of the Old Testament, and from below upwards in terms of Darwinian evolution. It was the final extraordinarily ambitious development of 'Talking

Horse', taking Malamud's sense of his own double nature into the very nature of the universe. For *God's Grace* was to deal with that strange hybrid called man, in his bungled and partial emergence from the apes:

> Cohn then noted man's ambivalent nature, the no-in-yes, evil-in-good, death-in-life, illusion-in-real, the complex, joyous-heart-breaking way it had worked out. Was the basic split caused by body–soul? Or was it God's withdrawal from His own presence? How would that go? Freud, an unbeliever, spoke of a secret trauma in His mind, converted to pain Everywhere.
>
> (*God's Grace*, 'The Schooltree', 132)

Daniel Stern knew how powerfully Malamud felt this mixture of contradictions in the nervous system. When Stern played the cello in an amateur performance of Schubert's C major quintet in his own home, Malamud came up to him afterwards and told him, 'Danny—you don't know what we felt sitting there, listening to the music, *tormented by joy*' (MWB, 30). When Malamud was doing the research for one of his last stories, 'Zora's Noise', he asked Dan Stern what it was like to play the cello, an instrument that Malamud felt came closest to the act of writing. Stern replied in terms of the sort of rare integration through art that Malamud loved: 'Performing on a cello is a little like sculpting out a piece of clay that is already there—so that one of the great pleasures is sensing the gradually shaping of something beautiful that pre-exists but that has not been made palpable (audible, visible?) until the instant of playing .... It is an odd combination of a physical and spiritual pleasure that is absolutely indivisible as it occurs' (LC I 50.7).

But in itself human nature, according to Edward O. Wilson, was a mishmash of special genetic adaptations appropriate for an environment now largely vanished, the world of the Ice Age hunter-gatherer. This evolutionary process, noted Malamud, left in human beings an intellect that 'had taken over more than it was meant to—with what result?' It made for an accidentally overevolved mind in amalgam with an animal body: 'In a sense,' Malamud quotes Wilson, 'love was added to sex.' The language Wilson used to describe his theme was familiar to Malamud in his own account of art—thus, according to Malamud's own notes: 'human nature is *not* the purely cultural artifact we assume it to be: *the basic clay is genetic*, even though *culture shapes the form*' (LC I 26.1). Marxism, in contrast, was based on a distortingly one-sided interpretation of human nature, ignoring its genetic foundations. What fascinated Malamud, in what must have felt like the conceptual culmination of his own career, was the question as to how far the human creature could change itself. How completely, for example, it could graft the altruistic onto the selfish. 'Genes for possibility?' Malamud asked, 'Some people are able to do more with the possible than others?' Yet Malamud took from Edward O. Wilson a strong sense of innate limits: 'In fiction you can't invent a soul. Those without souls write soulless fiction.' Still, there was no sharp boundary between the inherited and the acquired: only by experiment, of which writing was a version, could one find out what could or could not be invented, what could or could not be modified.

Officially, Malamud's position was always that of the secular, liberal Enlightenment, the civilized modern man rationally seeing through all the veils of superstition and intolerance. But when Wilson claimed that his account of religion as a product of evolution would remove forever its power as an external source of morality, then Malamud wrote in the margin of his own notes, 'I am not sure I want that to happen.' Wilson's book and the world it envisioned was 'cold', Malamud thought, 'No mention is made of feeling.'

Irving Greenberg's article, 'After the Holocaust', was in this a counter-weight. In the liberation of mankind from centuries of dependence on God and nature, and the concomitant development of secular belief in autonomous logic, Greenberg saw the hubristic creation of the conditions for the Holocaust itself. The sovereign power of reason was still lodged in what was an ill-assembled creature. If that creature believed it was capable of producing a wholly man-made world, it could sweep away all traditional limits and restraints in the name of its own new freedom. It was a thought that took Malamud back to reading *King Lear*. 'It will come. | Humanity must perforce prey on itself | Like monsters of the deep' was originally one of Malamud's epigraphs for *God's Grace*.

It was Anne Roiphe who brought the essay to Malamud's attention when, she said, 'he was struggling with the issue of God's destructiveness' and needed to reimagine the Jewish tradition of 'finding God wanting'.[10] For Greenberg, after the Holocaust the covenant with God was broken. Nothing could be said about Him or about why He could have allowed it. Yet Greenberg offered two thoughts that manifestly interested Malamud in his notes and underlinings, and which were useful to him in the only way that ideas could be to a man of his nature—they released in him what at some level he already knew or needed (LC I 26.1). One was to do with the decision still to bring children into a world where Auschwitz was possible:

It takes enormous faith in ultimate redemption and meaningfulness to choose to create or even enhance life again. In fact, faith is revealed by this not to be a belief or an emotion, but an ontological life-force that reaffirms creation and life in the teeth of overwhelming death. One must silently assume redemption in order to have the child—and having the child makes the statement of redemption.

Whatever you supposed you thought or felt, it was what you *did* that revealed what you really believed. The Malamuds, for example, had actively decided to have children: it was a small conventional decision, doubtless of mixed motives, but one taken, in implicit faith, despite the genetic and psychological family threats.

In *God's Grace*, Cohn fathers a child upon a female chimp, Mary Madelyn, one of his students. There is no planning in it, there may be sin in it, and it causes jealous uproar in the community, but he cannot resist her affection. Afterwards he thinks:

> Whatever happened thereafter was uncertain, but the beginning—without which nothing began but God himself—would have begun.
>   In sum, a worthy primate evolution demanded, besides a few macroevolutionary lucky breaks, a basis of brainpower; and commencing with a combination of man–chimp child, the two most intelligent of God's creatures might produce this new species—ultimately of Cohn's invention—an eon or two ahead on the molecular clock.   (*God's Grace*, 'The Virgin in the Trees', 165)

Perhaps even this, fantastic or mad as it is in fooling around with evolution, may be part of God's purpose, if He now regrets His second great Flood. Cohn will never know: 'The future was beyond invisible reach, and he would never know what he had stirred up' (Ibid. 167). Extraordinary catastrophes are not met by routine ethical responses; only extraordinary risks in life and creativity can match them. Malamud had noted Greenberg's account of Lot and his two daughters, the sole survivors of the fire-and-brimstone catastrophe of Sodom. According to Jewish tradition, the daughters had seduced their own father in an act of drunken incest—even in that not only saving the race but conceiving the future Messiah. 'It is quite a contrast to the Immaculate Conception, but it is truer to human reality and redemption out of the human condition. In the welter of grubby human reality, with evil and death rampant, with mixed motives and lusts, the Redeemer comes out of the ground of new creation and hope.' After the Second World War, Greenberg added, 'the highest birth-rates in the world prevailed in the displaced-persons camps, where survivors lived in their erstwhile concentration camps.'

The other thought that struck a chord with Malamud came from Greenberg's use of Martin Buber and the idea of 'moment theology'. To Buber, whatever God is is known only through moments of encounter with the presence of life at its most vital. But this knowledge is interspersed with long spells of normal, self-contained, routine existence. Malamud liked this sentence in particular from Buber: 'The difference between the skeptic and the believer is frequency of faith, not certitude of position.' All Malamud's work was to create and recreate, even through hours of revision, those moments of life commitment, whatever they meant or wherever they came from. For the novelist in Malamud knew very well how it was that different positions were necessary at different moments: 'Faith is a moment truth,' he read in Buber, 'but there are moments when it is not true':

> This is certainly demonstrable in dialectical truths, when invoking the truth at the wrong moment is a lie. To let Auschwitz overwhelm Jerusalem is to lie (i.e. to speak a truth out of its appropriate moment); and to let Jerusalem deny Auschwitz is to lie for the same reason.

That is why even in his remonstrances with God, Cohn is reunited with the language of paradox that was so powerful in *The Fixer* in particular, and in the Jewish tradition of the suffering servant, in general. 'Survive is what we have to do. Thus we protest our fate to God and at the same time imitate him .... My father said survival was one way we shared God's purpose' (*God's Grace*, 'Cohn's Island', 86).

'He was no Martin Buber and the apes no Hasidim' (*God's Grace*, 'The Schooltree', 129). But Danny Myerson, who had helped on the Jewish theological background to the story, delighted Malamud when he told him that 'only a deeply crazy person could have written *God's Grace*'. For the book offers a stunning mix of wild and ruefully comic inventions. It opens with God Himself explaining to Mr Cohn that the scientist's survival is an embarrassingly minor mistake, 'nothing to do with your once having studied for the rabbinate, or for that matter, having given it up' (*God's Grace*, 'The Flood', 4). Once this God sets things in motion, it is not always possible even for Him to predict where they will move: that is how, like some super novelist, he has arranged his own mind, to give Himself a few surprises. But it is with utter deliberateness that He has angrily let man, in his destructiveness, destroy himself. 'God is love,' says the indoctrinated Buz: 'Cohn wasn't sure but didn't say so' (*God's Grace*, 'Cohn's Island', 73). God is God, Cohn says later, fearing rather than loving Him.

For the sake of the human race Cohn recites Kaddish, the prayer for the dead, on behalf of one hundred representative souls chosen at random from a surviving Manhattan telephone directory. What is human? Buz asks him—receiving the didactic reply that in life would often set Malamud's own auditors innerly groaning: 'Cohn said he thought to be human was to be responsible to and protective of life and civilization.' Then Malamud adds: 'Buz said he would rather be a chimp' (Ibid. 70).

There is also among the chimps a solitary gentle gorilla named George. He sits on the periphery of the group, listening to Cohn's lessons on how the island's chimps may evolve into a species like man, or perhaps even better. At the end of the oration, while some of the chimps applaud, 'George dropped out of his cedar like a long lump of putty, as if dismayed he hadn't heard a gorilla mentioned once, and loped away' (*God's Grace*, 'The Virgin in the Trees', 165).

Malamud had always moved between fantasy and realism, not dividing the two between different books but sliding from one to the other within the same book. In *God's Grace*, the comic fantasy rides upon an underlying horror. Moreover, it is just when the world seems to have become renewed, in the most unlikely of circumstances, that the old biological story begins to repeat itself. When violence breaks out, Cohn is as enraged by warring of the apes as was God by the destructiveness of man. Cohn had tried to redeem the animals, precisely in lieu of God redeeming man. And when morality was failing, he had attempted—even without sufficient belief or feeling—to reinvent a God. But instead, he finds in the end an almost human beastliness in his betrayal by Buz and the murder of his baby daughter. In angry despair, Cohn withdraws his teaching and his leadership, lets the apes lose their human language, and destroys Buz's larynx. 'I can still hear the disheartened tone in his voice,' Danny Myerson recalled, 'when he read me parts of the book, his exhaustion—a line like "Esau resumed eating the yummy brain"—and his voice filled with bitterness.' Finally Cohn is destroyed by Buz himself—his throat cut by the son in an act of sacrifice which is also a testimony to failed paternity:

> Cohn lay still on the floor of the cave waiting to be lifted onto the flames. By the golden dark-light of the fire he could see that his long white beard was flecked with spots of blood.
>
> 'Merciful God,' he said, 'I am an old man. The Lord has let me live my life out.'   (*God's Grace*, 'God's Mercy', 223)

Malamud told Claude Fredericks 'a secret' which 'I must tell no one, the idea that had made the new novel at least viable in his own mind':

> He'd be pained to be writing about a God so cruel he could only scorn him, who'd take the life of the last surviving man on earth without compunction ... But suddenly in a flash it had occurred to him that what God would do—in those few months he was pursuing his prey—was make him grow old. The man would suddenly discover he had a long silken beard,

he'd have grown old without knowing it—and this was God's mercy, taking his life only when he was old. It's a beautiful idea'.   (31 July 1980)

It is then at the very end of the book that George, the pariah, suddenly begins to say Kaddish for Cohn—the prayer he recalls from the long-since shattered gramophone recording of the voice of Cohn's father, the rabbi. That is the only grace. Fredericks told Malamud that through the big, gentle, and unlikely figure of George it was as though 'first the gorillas and then all the animals and even the trees and flowers were learning to speak, to be kind and good. "That's it, that's it," he said quietly' (1 July 1983).

Claude Fredericks believed *God's Grace* was Malamud's masterpiece. But he also feared that the last chapter was almost evil in its despair, Malamud taking a sledge hammer to his world's renewal:

> The novel takes a sudden—and unexpected—turn in the last chapter. Was it perhaps written in haste—or was it written when he knew he must have an operation he dreaded? The next night he conceded that he had not known this would happen. He had somehow thought that large, silent, mysterious gorilla would be a savior.

'It is as if the world had had a third chance and then utterly and miserably and entirely failed,' he concluded, 'and it seems all the more evil and irresponsible if the vision had grown out of Bernard's sense of his own impending death' (27 August 1982). Yet Howard Nemerov told Ann Malamud that he thought Malamud deserved the Nobel Prize for *God's Grace* alone. Pat Adams believed that, as an investigation into the 'very ground of things', into the evolutionary future for 'the stuff that remained', 'The urge-to-say in Malamud transcended whatever were the problems of its embodiment.' It was Malamud's final 'ache for the furthering of humanity'.[11] The book was also touchingly praised by Arthur Sackler, the philanthropist, in a review for the *Medical Tribune*, in which he recalled Malamud from their days together in Brooklyn, at Erasmus Hall High. But Malamud himself feared that somehow he had always resisted this book. On 2 January 1981 he had written:

> It is hard to 'join'—no feeling to share, to empathize with. It is a kind of jeu, of joke. Afraid of a willed book, or something like the tone of *The Tenants*—a book I can't live in as I did with *Dubin*. Perhaps I can enter this *imaginatively*. Call it a dance and dance with it so long [far] as I am able to.

But at the end of the attempted dance, he was disappointed that his publishers printed only 30,000 copies, 20,000 fewer than the initial printing of *Dubin's Lives*. He had always been anxious about reviews, had often professed not to read them, and would usually get Robert Giroux to send them in one bunch so as not to have to bear them one at a time. But a review by John Leonard in the *New York Times* (23 August 1982) particularly upset him: Malamud, said Leonard dismissively, was 'heavy on the symbolic potatoes, not quite the flying Chagall'. 'Bern confessed to me how depressed he had been by the reviews,' noted Claude Fredericks, 4 January 1983, 'how, in spite of a few friends, he had come almost to believe what they said. It was a vulnerable moment for him, it is true, but I was surprised in his lack of faith in himself and in what he does.' Later, again according to Claude Fredericks, Malamud began to hope that it was after all one of his three best works, after *The Assistant* and *Dubin's Lives*; that once again it was *The Fixer* rather than *God's Grace* which was the great disappointment (1 July 1983).

In his notebook Malamud simply quoted the Hassidic saying: 'There is no heart so whole as a broken heart.'[12]

Health

The bypass surgery took place, after the completion of *God's Grace*, on Wednesday 10 March 1982, the operation performed by Dr Bruce Reitz.[13] Malamud had been invited to Palo Alto to take up a year's fellowship at the Center for Advanced Study in Behavioral Sciences, through the influence of his old friend Alex Inkeles who had a permanent position at Stanford and wanted the scientific and sociological community to include a novelist. Malamud wrote to Nina Pelikan Straus on 30 October 1981, shortly after his arrival, describing the beautiful environment offered to the fellows and his own newly adjusted routines:

> My office is easy to work in. We sit at the top of a fairly high hill with a view of the bay, and beyond the water, a table of long low hills extends from San Jose to San Francisco. Above them lies a parallel mess of boiling white, or golden clouds rising taller than the mountains. Closer to me the calligraphy across the sky is the rough broken-backed arms of a live oak. I write all morning, as I usually do, though lunch comes half an hour earlier, and that's not bad because I eat less. We eat in sunlight on the terrace, a warm noon after a cool morning, and [I] listen when the facts are more than I know, and talk when I am in the mood, beginning 'I've been reading a good book lately and wonder if some of you know it?' We have read different books so I hold forth for a while, then go back into my office and read the paper for an hour and then do correspondence for a while before walking a long path down the high hill and then to Campus Drive and home.

But there was also a new worry. Since the death of her husband, Ann's mother, Ida Barbieri, had been a regular visitor to the Malamud household in Bennington or New York: now she was diagnosed as having lateral sclerosis, Lou Gehrig's disease, and would probably need to go into a nursing home. 'One becomes troubled,' he went on to Nina, 'an old person is human and begins to be treated like a thing, no matter the true affection and the terrible guilt one feels. I would rather have the Eskimo ice floe than the home for the aged.' It was ordinary but characteristic Malamud: the unblinkingly honest admission of aversion, the sympathetic as well as guilty desire to behave well, the imaginative identification with his own future.

The poet Josephine Carson wrote to the Malamuds jointly on 2 November, thinking of the recent slow death of her own mother.

> If one can become the helpful witness of one's mother's dying and feel one's way through it along parallel sympathetic lines exactly the way you, for instance, must have had to do with your children so as not to interrupt the proper sequence of their learning (the syntax is everything, I think, in all learning)—if one can find a way to do that, then one can learn a profound lesson about our lives that doesn't come so dramatically or convincingly in any other situation.
>
> (HRC 4.10)

A parent, she said, should not have to die alone and secretively, as though in haste, with the communication waves jammed.

Ida died in January 1982. Malamud wrote to Nina again on 14 February:

> Ann needs time to recover more fully from her sincere (and to my mind, good) mourning for her mother. She saw her to the end with grace and courage, and I am moved by it, though Ann, as Ann, never gives herself credit enough for her performance. That's when it pays to have someone around who can say, 'You did it well. I was there. I know.'

But, as it had been after the death of Eugene, Malamud's own health took a turn for the worse after the death of his mother-in-law. Some friends were opposed to his risking an operation. But for all his hypochondria, he was clearly a tired and dying man.

Stanford had a large medical school and hospital, and was a leader in the development of heart surgery. Just before Malamud underwent surgery, the chief of medicine invited the novelist to give an evening reading at his own house for the faculty. Malamud was seated on the floor, Bruce McAuley recalled, and read 'The Loan', written back in 1952.[14] It was the story of the baker forbidden by his wife to give money to the old friend who had never paid him back the last time, though he swore he had. Kobotsky needed the money to buy a headstone for his late wife's grave. It ended: 'Kobotsky and the baker embraced and sighed over their lost youth. They pressed mouths together and parted forever.' It was good to have such a famous writer on campus, but Alan Cheuse believed the reading took place because the head of the team 'wanted them to know how important it was to keep this man alive'. He also remembered how Malamud read *Dubin's Lives* in Bennington when it first came out: 'It was like watching a composer conduct his own work. He knew exactly what he wanted to emphasize and what not.'[15]

The surgery itself was apparently uneventful. But once it was determined that the paralysis of the limbs in the recovery room was not simply the result of the anaesthetics, it was clear that Malamud had suffered a stroke on the operating table. He was put in a respirator in critical condition, and Claude Fredericks in a journal entry for 16 March 1982 recorded Ann's phone call: 'that the night before was the nadir of her life, that Bernard—enduring now a second operation, having suffered perhaps "brain damage"—will probably live.' Janna saw her father a few days after the operation:

> He was alive but not yet coherent. "What is your name?" a nurse asked him.
> He confabulated, 'William.' She noted that he was disoriented. 'How old are
> you?' 'Fifty-seven.'   (MFB, 35)

He was actually sixty-eight. His mind had reverted to William Dubin, his biographer.

The stroke seemed to have affected his right rather than his left hemisphere, but as he recovered consciousness and struggled to find words, he feared he would never write again. He told Ann that if he could not write, he would not want to live.

Marjorie Pryse, married at the time to Alan Cheuse, visited Malamud in his hospital bed soon after. She brought with her a copy of a poem by the Old Bennington poet, Robert Frost, to whose grave Malamud would often walk. 'I wanted to communicate with him by literature,' she recalled. The poem she chose was 'The Oven Bird' and she slowly read it to him:

> There is a singer everyone has heard,
> Loud, a mid-summer and a mid-wood bird,
> Who makes the solid tree-trunks sound again.
> He says that leaves are old and that for flowers
> Mid-summer is to spring as one to ten.
> He says the early petal-fall is past,
> When pear and cherry bloom went down in showers
> On sunny days a moment overcast;
> And comes that other fall we name the fall.
> He says the highway dust is over all.

> The bird would cease and be as other birds
> But that he knows in singing not to sing.
> The question that he frames in all but words
> Is what to make of a diminished thing.

'After I finished reading the poem, he smiled and said, "Sweet girl." '[16] He had still to try to make something of himself. But it was also the last two lines that offered Malamud the word he would often use to describe what he felt like thereafter, and what his gift seemed like to him: 'diminished'.

Recovery was slow. Lew Krakauer, Malamud's old friend and doctor from Corvallis, wrote Malamud on 10 April that the chance of the return of total function seemed to him very good:

> How you can ever tell when creative functions really come back has to be hard especially when there is a normal slow-down, but I surely hope that the signal will be present. I will say further that I am personally impressed by the effects of self discipline and will power on retraining any muscle including the brain and if there is anybody who strikes me as a disciplined person, it is you, which gives one further hope.   (HRC 8.3)

What was involved in the task of relearning becomes clear in letters from other friends. Josephine Carson wrote on 5 May, 'I feel good about your having begun to read, even in large print' (HRC 4.10). At the end of August, Don Early, from the old days in New York, was writing: 'You sounded fine on the phone, and I am properly awed that you remastered the multiplication tables—a feat I never accomplished in the first place' (HRC 8.3). 'Speriamo', Malamud had said to Ann when he got back from the hospital in mid-April—Italian for 'we hope' (HRC 31.6).

God's Grace had come out. By August Malamud said, almost formally to Ann, in front of an interviewer: 'I realize how dependent I've become upon you, and I'm grateful for all you're doing. I'm not ashamed to say it.' 'All in a day's work,' she had replied (CBM, 117). In the same month a letter from Richard Popp, professor of cardiology at Stanford School of Medicine, gives a glimpse of the raw distress, despair, and anger the couple had struggled with over the first few months of recovery:

> Yours was an unusually difficult road with unforeseen obstacles, but you are quite unusual people to come through it so well. You have finite time to prepare and polish your thoughts and control your emotions when you banter at a party, or teach a class, give a talk or write a piece. You draw on experience and are in relatively comfortable areas. But the situation was so new, the experiences so intense and the stakes so high in the situation you found yourselves in after surgery that you had no choice but to react and be yourselves in an elemental

way. Clearly you both feel your emotions deeply and with wide range, but also
you both are very solid, very strong.   (HRC 9.3)

The professor's comparison with situations which allowed time for preparation or redrafting was apt, for this was an exposed Malamud now without
the power to revise himself.

In December he underwent a stress test and did well, in the ninetieth
percentile for people his age. But he was experiencing subtle difficulties with
reading, akin to dyslexia, also with his handwriting, and with spatial awareness.
It is sad to see in the archives photocopies of passages from his books in large
print, designed to help him through the public readings of his later years.

But the neurologist's report at the beginning of February 1983 was hopeful
that the eyes would recover and that the right arm would at least get stronger:
'I probably will have trouble typing,' Malamud recorded in his medical
notebook (HRC 25.8). In a letter to Howard Nemerov on 12 February, he
explained the nature of the stress tests on the treadmill, undertaken at increasing speeds up a rising incline, equivalent to a hill of ten to fifteen degrees.
Now he could manage eight and half minutes, he reported, where before the
operation it was barely three (HRC 14.9). Nevertheless, friends could see other
differences. Marian Seldes recalled her daughter Katherine telling her that
the most noticeable change in Malamud after his stroke was that 'his focus
wasn't ever sharp again and his mind seemed to drift off from whatever was
going on' (HRC 31.6). Alex Inkeles had known a man precise and articulate
in his language: 'instead what you had was a person who was struggling to
say a single word, or losing track and not able to keep going.'[17] He had lost a
cruel amount of verbal memory. He would be struggling terribly for words,
but Ann, anxious and impatient, would say sharply, 'You *know* that word!'

In the Library of Congress there is an undated notebook, a mere A4 writing
pad, that tells something of the inner story of these continuing difficulties
(LC II 13.4). In it Malamud speaks of a 'dim sense of being unable to keep
up, not competent in the way I was—overdistanced'. 'What more can I do
for memory?' he asks, 'How much aphasia. What to do about rebuilding
vocabulary. The effect of anxiety on meaning and vocabulary.' It is as though
the mental deterioration he had described in *Dubin's Lives* was not only a
report of what was already ailing him but a prediction of what would be
worse. 'How can I help myself to make more progress?' he asks himself, the
lonely man with the page in front of him. He turns to reference books and
dictionaries; he laboriously writes down the meanings of words he used to
know, a list of words such as 'fetish', 'baffle', 'skimpy', 'phoenix', 'garnished',
'imperious'. He tells himself he is 'going on with my writing which is ok but

diminished by some anxiety. Sleep is not good, interrupted—new diuretic gets me up 3 times a night'. He has sad secret fears about social life, the awkwardness he had always felt now exaggerated almost to crisis-point, yet still witnessed with that third eye of the novelist-diagnostician:

> Ann feels we are being put aside partly because I treat myself carefully and am limited in what I can do. She feels bored. I feel myself shrinking. What can I do to extend experience. At dinner parties I feel limited. I doubtfully participate. I don't seem to know how to engage unless I challenge people to answer questions—to be involved with me.

For all the remarks about Malamud's intrusive search for copy, over all the years previously, perhaps that was what his insistent questioning had mainly been about, after all—getting the people 'involved with me'. Perhaps too that need to belong, which he had identified in his late youth and again suffered all the more now, was what had led him to create his own version of what it was to be a Jew in modern America. Whatever was the unattainable truth of his condition did not matter quite so much before, when there was always the work that came out of it. But now the justifying work was in danger, and sitting at his desk, Malamud kept writing to himself alone. 'I still have the small white 3 by 5 notepad that was on his desk the day he died,' wrote his daughter, 'In green ink: "I am difficult" and "Who else can I confide in? I can no longer listen to myself"' (MFB, 251).

By October 1983 Malamud had at least acquired a secretarial assistant to help with the physical demands of the writing. Bob Dunn was an aspiring writer who had known Paul Malamud when they were both working at the *New Yorker* in 1976. He had visited Malamud in the hospital at Stanford in 1982, and had visited both the Malamuds again in Bennington in the summer of 1983 just after their return from a trip to Cambridge, when he found Malamud faced with a stack of mail. Malamud was frail and anxious, and every time he forgot something, as anyone else might, he instantly blamed it on 'the damned stroke', Dunn recalled, 'rageful' at what he called 'my fate'.[18] From then on, over the next three years until Malamud's death, Bob Dunn helped him in the Lincoln Towers apartment in New York—two afternoons a week, Tuesdays and Fridays, mainly typing out the 'humps and clusters' of Malamud's handwriting, doing errands, filing and photocopying, but also providing company. Promptly at 2 p.m., tuna sandwich finished, Malamud and his apprentice would begin with the letters:

> And here was the classic Malamud response. He'd ask me to read him again what he'd dictated, setting his hands before him, rolling his shoulders forward, lowering his gray eyebrows—he would assume a very quiet, concentrated,

almost prayer-like position—as I read from my notepad: he'd try out my suggestion, as if tasting each word—hmmmn—and then he'd shake his head and completely redo the letter his way.   (HRC 31.6)

Bob Dunn kept the notes he made at the time: 'One day I changed a light bulb. Malamud is so often tired and anxious in the afternoon. Sometimes his hand shakes. Sometimes he sits back in his chair with the spirit whammed out of him. But rarely does our work slow beyond the methodical or brisk pace he likes. We have to "get through it".' When they had got through the work, they would sometimes spend time together. Once the two of them went to see Billie Whitelaw in Samuel Beckett's *Rockaby*. Her great ending cry, 'More, More, More, More', before she slumped forward, left Malamud saying ruefully, 'There's no reason to die now' (HRC 31.6).

But there was more to do or try to do. He began writing very short stories, first about Virginia Woolf, later about Alma Mahler, which were like brief collages assembled from reading their biographies. The fascinating method he proposed, in a note written in 1983, was to take a scene from the real life of his subject, explicate that as fiction, then put the fiction back into the context of the work and the life. 'You come out, or should, with an *invention forward as story*, limited but carrying the meaning of the life as a short story.'[19] Bob Dunn noted the completion of the Virginia Woolf story:

> November 12 1983: last Thursday when I finished typing 'In Kew Gardens' and reading it back for errors with its author Bernard Malamud, he turned to me and said, 'That's a distinguished piece of work', and for the first time in the nearly three weeks I'd been working for him as a two-to-three-day-a-week afternoon assistant, he relaxed. 'It's so damned disturbing. That's what I mean,' he said referring to the aftermath of the stroke he'd suffered a year and a half ago, 'but I can still do good work. It's there.' His face was at ease, his eyes still.

He was willing himself, nonetheless, to believe it. For this was work in miniature which was an adaptation to his condition, in the struggle to sustain long acts of connected attention. Bernadette Inkeles said it was like what happened to a sculptor of her acquaintance when she could no longer carve in alabaster, heavy stone, or redwood and turned to making paper collages instead: 'He was trying to find a new medium.'

Malamud of course had become ever more interested in biography during the writing of *Dubin*, and, at Arlene Heyman's suggestion, in 1976 he had joined a biography group technically affiliated to the New York Psychoanalytic Institute, which met monthly at the home of Bernard Meyer. Malamud had even given a paper on Walter Jackson Bate's life of Samuel Johnson—quoting Bate on 'the immense reassurance Johnson gives to human nature, which needs ... every friend it can get'. In Johnson, said Bate, 'we have a hero who starts out with everything against him' but the centre of Bate's biography, said Malamud, was 'the moral drama of Johnson's middle age'. Bate himself, noted Malamud, suffered a mid-life crisis in his forties because he had 'burned up his youth in hard work' (LC II 11.4).

The group included the psychoanalyst Stuart Feder, later the biographer of Mahler, to whom, remarkably, Malamud turned on his own behalf, from 1983 onwards, for help in fighting his depression:

> He had consulted another psychoanalyst, but he was very put off because it was somebody who didn't talk very much. Bern was not about to go into psychotherapy. I questioned the appropriateness of my seeing him as a patient, because he was a friend. I can't think of another time when I saw a friend as a patient. I did it for three reasons. One, he asked me to. I guess I was flattered, but I also could see that it wasn't easy for him to ask for that kind of help. Number two: I disagreed with anybody who didn't pay him the respect of giving a lot of feedback. Third, my own view of late depression in one's fifties, sixties and seventies is that it is of a somewhat different nature from depressive episodes earlier in life. It becomes physical later on. I attributed his to the physical effects of the stroke. I treated him with medication and saw him occasionally. He got a moderate result and he wasn't on his own with handling the depression.[20]

But what Malamud was doing in his work had still to be dependent on the help he could generate from himself. For the moment that self was borrowed from his own character, William Dubin again, as he described in an undated postcard on holiday in Como to his old friend Doris Milman: 'I am trying to create a short life of Virginia Woolf, as Dubin used to before he devoted himself to major biographies.'

In the midst of this struggle, *The Stories of Bernard Malamud* was published, being the author's own selection of his shorter fiction. Most unusually, Malamud had felt he needed to ask Bernadette Inkeles for help in deciding the final running order of the tales in the volume. She felt she had somehow let him down when she found him hurt by her natural refusal to accept any payment. When the selection was published, it was a representation of all he had been able to do in the past, before his debility. But it was suddenly spoiled for him by the reception given the book in *The New York Review of Books*, 19 January 1984. Again Bob Dunn was the private witness:

> Bern is quite disturbed by a review by John Leonard, a strong direct attack. I think it's all a sneer. Leonard sees some aspects of Bern's work clearly but makes them out to be negatives, where I or anyone else would be more complimentary. The piece is also disjointed and in parts incoherent ... Bern hasn't read it yet.

He's heard about it from Giroux and others. He had a walk a week ago with Harold Brodkey and they talked of it. Nonetheless, Bern's upset, 'depressed and feeling despair'.

Leonard said it was as if in the reissue of these tales, many of them relics of the fifties, 'some vital principle had died'. The writer's 'liberal optimism' was insufficient, even to himself, 'and Malamud wants us to stand outside in the rain and snow.' At night Malamud would lie awake making mental lists of the people he feared would damage his future literary reputation. But even at the time, Bob Dunn believed the trouble really lay elsewhere:

> I think he's more worried about his own work. The Alma Mahler piece isn't coming together and this review just seems an unnecessary blow. I'm sure he'll be over it soon. He does tell me of a few occasions when he believed he slighted Leonard but they are tame, and someone—Leonard or Malamud—would have to be paranoid to make anything of it .... Giroux thinks it might harm his reputation for a while. I, and evidently Janna, pooh-pooh this. Still Bern seems more worried and unsure than usual. We both agree this is bothering him more than it should.

The routine went on, because it had to. In the course of it, Bob Dunn noticed that Malamud would not throw away a single sheet of cheap yellow paper if only one side had been written on. But once he had turned over the pages, reused them for a draft of the Alma story, and had them typed up, Malamud then threw them into the wastebasket: 'The so-and-sos [meaning professors, interpolated Dunn] would love to get their hands on this but I won't let them.'

Nina Peilkan Straus tried to write encouragingly to Malamud about his 'Alma Redeemed' on 28 June: 'I know you have things to be depressed about, but I assure you that diminished powers of writing are not among them as a fact, although as an anxiety this may be.' She tried again on 15 August:

> I'm frankly worried about you, not because I have doubts about your writing, but because I know that your own doubts cause you some anguish and themselves interfere with writing. What I think you have now, as meditation and work, is perhaps not as broad a range as you would like, but a capacity to essentialize—to generalize in images—that may transist into a new voice. The memory you have used as a source may not be in the same condition as it was before, yet I have a sense that there may be another part of the mind available to you—that this deep, narrow well has its possibilities and challenges for the writer that has perhaps been overlooked by many. I think of Mann's *Joseph and His Brothers*, I think of many books like Jean Rhys's *Sargasso Sea* (characters from *Jane Eyre*) that have been created from other books and writings, that have a doubleness about them which is itself an exotic richness. I cannot solace your anxiety, but I can think that there are many ways to write. You have had a divorce from your

old self and you mourn it, yet another life, another voice must come. After all, Bern, you are fundamentally a writer. Nothing can change that.   (HRC 18.5)

Nothing could. Another temperament might have been able to call the writing career to a final halt. But 'old men should be explorers,' Malamud had told Bob Dunn, quoting T. S. Eliot. From 1984 Malamud was also determined to try to write a new novel, *The People*. He told Stuart Feder, nonetheless, that he was concerned that he had been compromised by his stroke and that he was worried about the flatter quality of the writing.

The People had begun improbably with a joke told by Don Early back in the forties. It concerned the Jewish dietary laws which required different cutlery and utensils for the eating of meat products and milk products. It began in a way that immediately tickled Malamud: 'There was once a Jewish Indian'. This Jewish gentleman, it went on, was part of a Red Indian tribe that was desperately short of food and vainly hunting for buffalo meat—when suddenly a herd appeared. The Jewish Indian grabbed his spear, leapt to his horse, galloped towards the kill, then as he raised his arm realized, 'My God, I got the *milkhik* tomahawk.'

It is not so amusing to examine the folders upon folders of research and drafts for *The People* held in the Malamud archive at the Library of Congress. It was to be the story of a tribe of native Americans, unjustly forced from their land by the superior power of the U. S. government. It was to tell of their resistance under their unlikely new, white, Jewish chief named Jozip—successor to the failed leader Cohn in *God's Grace*. Its historical source was the story of Chief Joseph, the man of peace who had to become the so-called 'Indian Napoleon', and the epic 1,400 mile journey of seven hundred men, women, and children of the Nez Perce Indians, in 1877, out of their homeland in the Pacific Northwest to a new promised land in Canada. They were like a lost tribe of the Jews led by a new Moses, trying to live by a version of Gandhi's passive resistance, but forced into violence and, ultimately, bloody surrender. Their chief died of a broken heart.

Malamud's numerous notes to himself are full of worried doubt: 'How can I go on with the novel'; 'Do outline so I know where I am going—won't get "lost"'; 'Anyway just continue with the outlines. Collate them before there get to be too many. Type a new one. Make the latest one count. Throw away the others.' 'Sidestep outside opinion', he tells himself, 'to say what is in me to say, just as I please (interior laughter).' He tries to think of new moves: 'Put it on a social plane, which is good, suits me better at the moment'; 'Obvious next step—but difficult for personal reasons'; 'The right thing to do but difficult to do'. But he is afraid there are no new moves left in him: 'The purpose of life to live it out. I've done all I can with that. I need a replacement of ideas'; 'The need for new experience (What's left to say?)'; Is the book worth doing?' Malamud knew he had all of these doubts before: 'Have begun reading—same old resistance problems as to Fixer' (LC II 5.5). What he did not know was whether he could find in himself the magic of language he had hitherto been able to deliver. Jozip himself struggled alongside his author:

> he had not spoken as well as he would like, yet he heard dignity in the words he had said. 'If you speak with your heart,' he told himself, 'the words will fix themselves together in the right way. They will say what you want them to say.'
>
> (*The People*, 46)

But on the whole the writing was sketchily drawn out along the horizontal: there was little of that old Malamud ability to grab the sentence in the middle and stretch it vertically. The gift for crystallization by compressed metaphor or sudden symbol—the sort of figure that would 'simplify experience at the same time as it makes it complex' (LC II 10.8)—had been partly wiped away. The human sentence had been diminished.[21]

Malamud wrote his former Bennington friend, the novelist Steve Becker in April 1985, thanking him for his birthday wishes: 'A warm word warms. Not much of new for me except I go on writing and the writing goes on in surprising sentences. They surprise me simply by being there. That was a massive wound in the head I took. I'm lucky so many sentences survived' (HRC 3.8). So here he was, he wrote his former student Karen Wunsch, in July 1985, 'trying to write a book with diminished eyesight and handwriting I can almost not decipher' (HRC 18.17).

It was a mistake, Ann Malamud believed, ever to have shown the work in progress to Philip Roth, and she had advised against it. It was in July 1985, in Bennington, and after lunch Malamud read Roth his opening chapters, 'a few typewritten pages shaking in his frail hands'. In Malamud's 'The Letter' a poor madman gives a visitor to the hospital a letter to post on his behalf, only there is nothing in it, the pages are blank. As he listened to Malamud's latest, Roth found in what he heard if not nothing, then nothing much: 'He hadn't got started, really, however much he thought otherwise.' Yet this was two years of work, struggling with incapacity. 'I didn't want to lie to him,' wrote Roth. He tried to say noncommittally that it was a beginning, then asked him what happened next:

> But he wouldn't let go of what he'd written, at such cost, as easily as that. Nothing was ever as easy as that, least of all the end of things. In a soft voice suffused with anger, he replied: 'What's next isn't the point.'

In the silence that followed, he was perhaps as angry at failing to master the need for assurance that he'd so nakedly displayed as he was chagrined with me for having nothing good to say. He wanted to be told that what he had painfully composed while enduring all his burdens was something more than he himself must have known it to be in his heart. He was suffering so, I wished that I could have said it *was* something more and that if I'd said it, he could have believed me.[22]

Philip Roth published the account a few weeks after Malamud's death. The family, in particular Ann Malamud, found it thoughtless, cruel, and humiliating. Roth, for example, had not failed to notice or to mention the crumbs scattered around Malamud's chair after lunch, the result of the hand-tremor even in eating. Distressed himself, Roth told James Atlas, ruefully, 'I stepped in dog-shit again.'[23] He wrote to Ann Malamud on 27 July insisting that he did not believe the author of *The Assistant* or *The Magic Barrel*, concerned as they were with the themes of 'struggle, hardship, disappointment and loss', would have found anything humiliating in the account of his own struggle (HRC 16.5).[24] But whatever Malamud felt at the time, and whatever Roth himself might or might not have found to say to Malamud immediately after the unhappy reading—the fact was that Philip Roth was basically, sadly right about *The People*. It was not really there. And what came through his account was a judgement that was not so much his, as life's own.

Malamud loved quoting Thoreau on the power of revision: 'The men and things of today are wont to lie fairer and truer in tomorrow's meadow' (TH, 15, 35). But almost every day, even as he carried on writing, Malamud knew there might be no such tomorrow for *The People*. He told Gloria Stern that he did not think he was going to live to see the book finished. What his estate and its executors would do with it was up to them. In their last conversation together Malamud recounted to Giroux a story he had heard from Claude Fredericks concerning the ageing Verdi, struggling to work at *Falstaff*: the composer had 'all his energies for that single hour each day in his eighties' when 'he was up and at his desk' (23 March 1986). But Alex Inkeles felt two fears on his friend's behalf: 'One, that the progress was of necessity so slow that it wouldn't get finished. The other, which I feared more, was that when it was finished it would seem not to be Malamud; that it would be a broken thing, which would be very painful to him, and painful for everyone else, not knowing what to do with it.'

Over dinner on the evening of 17 March 1986 at the house of Roger and Dorothea Straus, Malamud was able to report that he was within three or four chapters of completing his first draft and would have that finished by the fall. He died the next day.

Grooved, Grieved, Graved

Dated July 1980, there was a little double poem Malamud wrote, entitled 'You Write About What You Write Best', to which he kept referring in his later years. It was a two-columned piece about his limitations. One column began, 'As you are *grooved* | by wind, by tooth, | so you are *grieved*', and it was finally dated 18 July. The other version alongside it went, 'As you are *grooved* | by wind, by tooth, so you are *graved*', and it was dated ten days later. Michiko Kakutani quoted Malamud in the *New York Times* for 15 July 1980, when he was clearly in the midst of writing the verses:

> As you are grooved, so you are grieved. One is conditioned early in family life to an interpretation of the world. And the grieving is that no matter how much happiness or success you collect, you cannot obliterate your early experience—diminished perhaps, it stays with you.

The early griefs and grievances grooved him, left marks, and cut channels in his psyche, and those grooves, once established, caused him a further sense of grief that would never leave him until the day he was graved. But both versions of the poem go like this towards their end, still making all they can out of those pains and diminishments

> Your song survived
> by dint of breath.
> Having been grooved
>
> now breathe, be moved
> to sing the depth
> of music saved.
>
> What tongue has lived
> gives tune its worth.

Played off against 'grooved', 'be moved' was always what saved and gave worth. Then one poem ends: 'As you are grooved | so you are grieved'; and the other: 'As you are grooved, | so you are graved.'

One of those grooves meant that, as he moved grave-wards, Malamud's worries came out in terms of measurable material concerns. In the early days it had been necessary for Malamud to keep careful accounts: money was tight, the teaching work came from different sources, tax returns needed to be accurate. But the handwritten process of listing continued long after Malamud was already receiving detailed figures from his agent and his publishers. He copied them out again, to the very cent, and kept all his records together, to give himself the sense of maintaining control. He would ring his agent or his publishers when the figures did not seem to tally—usually because he had not taken into account books that had been returned unsold by the bookshops. Tim Seldes, his agent after the death of Diarmuid Russell, eventually said to him one day that all this querying of his royalties was just 'horsing around', an odd obsessive way of relaxing, and Malamud admitted it.[25]

Certainly he had had good earning years throughout the 1970s, averaging nearly $70,000 gross per annum, rising to over $150,000 in both 1978 and 1979. Often he would forego his income from Bennington in the interests of the college, particularly as his duties became increasingly nominal, in terms of occasional readings and seminars. Film rights from the making of *The Fixer* in 1968 eventually earned him around $200,000. But with regard to film options, though potentially lucrative, Malamud had always hated the negotiations, the uncertainties, and the final product if ever there was one—particularly since 1969 when he had spent months writing a whole screenplay for *The Assistant* without final purpose.

Just as bad, in 1973 he became reluctantly embroiled in a lawsuit when Elliott Gould and his associates went broke and could not make the payment for the proposed filming of *A New Life*. Eventually Malamud's lawyers, Shirley Fingerhood and Joel Camche, settled for just over $39,000. It was an unhappy ending because Malamud had loved it when at the beginning of the project he had met Barbara Streisand, at the time Gould's wife, and found she too was a graduate of Erasmus Hall High. But Malamud had been glad of the services of Shirley Fingerhood from the late sixties onwards. Originally she had prepared a contract for him in the course of work on behalf of Farrar, Straus and Giroux. To her amusement, Malamud told her he had copied this contract and, in admiration, had reused it in a number of subsequent deals—freely, without further fee.[26]

When the film of *The Natural* appeared in 1984, starring the American golden boy, Robert Redford, Malamud had long since sold the original rights. But he did get a percentage of the second sale, worth around $125,000, when the rights were bought up by Redford himself. He did not seem, at least, to mind much that he had not made a fortune. He was flattered by the idea of Redford doing it, miffed that he was never consulted or contacted by the director Barry Levinson, but finally quite enjoyed the film—as long as he could sit there in the dark, he said. With its optimistic ending, it was not *his* book, he emphasized, but he hoped they would turn it into a musical before too long (HRC 21.7).

In short, in a list of estate made in April 1984 it was estimated that Malamud was worth a total of $1,143,944 plus $54,000 of art and jewellery (HRC 24.6). But after the stroke, for reasons that were part practical and part displacement, he was clearly worried about his future earning-power and the situation of his wife and family after his death. There is a note for 19 December 1984:

> Ann and I talked after a difficult day for me. I asked her help to keep me on even keel and as much able to work as I can.
> We talked about our finances: we will continue to make a living but the money won't exactly flow in.   (HRC 6.7)

In the same file there is a note to Ann, concerning negotiations over paperback deals and worries as to whether Roger Straus was doing his best for them. 'Baby, Obviously I had forgotten too much of the contract. But now I see our earnings will be *small* for next year unless I take whatever we can get .... We have money. We are not in difficult straits. But we will have to take advantage of all sorts of offers that may arise.' But what Malamud would never do was leave his old publishers, in particular because of his relationship with Robert Giroux. At one point Ann Malamud remembered him turning down an offer of something like $350,000 to change firms.

Amongst the debilitating changes which followed from the stroke that took away Malamud's gift, there was one, however, that had good in it. Malamud became at times a much more openly affectionate man. It was partly to do, perhaps, with slowly saying his goodbyes, for it was a sweetness that he had always had, albeit often warily hidden in reserve. But to Nina Pelikan Straus he wrote just before his operation, 5 March 1982, that now he was privileged 'not only to feel friendship more broadly and richly—like a narrow brook breaking up and flowing in full rivulets through the lush grass—but also to love without excuse or definition.' His art had always been more than just a species of defining. He ended: 'A bypassing we will go, because the heart is apparently whole, and I must keep it so.' 'I feel almost as though I taught you to sustain me,' he wrote her on 3 July 1984, 'and you have the grace to do it.'

Near the end, he also said to Dan Stern, 'If I had my life to live again, I would make more time to be with you.' He wrote to Clark Blaise in 1986, 'Dear Clark, you are a very good man to know. I am not embarrassed to say I love you.' 'Not embarrassed' or 'not ashamed' was now a more customary locution. Bob Dunn's notes recall one Christmas dinner back in 1983: 'A slight something. I forget what caused it. Ann gets a little huffy. Bern: "Ann, I'm your friend, your husband, I'm on your side." "Yes, yes, dear, I know," she replied.' There were still the marital bickerings. But there was also this, 14 June 1984, while Ann was visiting Janna in Boston, and Malamud was preparing his autobiographical lecture 'Long Work, Short Life' with Bob Dunn's assistance:

> Tonight we viewed slides Bern took in '56 or '57 in Rome. He wanted to see them because he's using Roman memories for a Belitt lecture. And what was most touching was the way he left his seat and got close to the wall projection when a picture of Ann came on. 'What a handsome woman,' he said, 'she was so young, it breaks my heart.'

On 18 July of the same year he had written to some old friends on the struggle for reconciliation that was going on with one of their family:

> Something astonishing has to be done that not all are capable of. I am reminded that I once apologized to a woman who, through a false accusation, had done me harm. I figured, after hearing later that she was remorseful, because she thought she had destroyed her husband's and my friendship, that it was *not* in her nature to apologize to me; therefore I must apologize to her in order to keep that friendship alive. I did, she accepted, perhaps accepting that there was a metaphorical message for her in my action. Perhaps not. At any rate her husband is still more or less my friend, and I think his wife would like to be although she knows I am wary of her.
>
> I'm not sure this makes sense to you but let's limit it to the thought that you must search out a metaphor that will appeal to [X] and inspire her to an act of generous acceptance of you as people different from her. (HRC 9.4)

Again it was all he knew of art, used in the service of life: not limiting definitions or cut-off points, but metaphors as ways forward. Without metaphors, he said, he felt naked in his art. What he needed was to be creative. Right up until the very end, it was worth believing it was never too late to avoid or outwit a final ending.

On 18 March 1986, Ann Malamud was out having lunch with a friend. Bob Dunn came to knock at the apartment door just after lunchtime, but there was no answer. It was a beautiful spring day, and Bob sat downstairs in the lobby and waited for almost an hour. Ann Malamud recalled the rest vividly:[27]

> I think Bob was supposed to accompany Bern that day to the doctor, because Bern had been having high blood pressure again. Bob sat in the lobby thinking

that maybe Bern had gone out on his own. And Bern never showed up, so Bob left.

He had died during lunch hour. There was still one gas unit on—maybe he was going to pour some coffee or tea for himself—but he had moved the water kettle away from it. He had had his lunch and he must have felt ill because there were two chairs over-turned in the dining room, right adjacent to the kitchen, and Bern was on the floor near there. He must have not felt well and grabbed the chair.

I came home at about four—because I did a couple of errands. And I went upstairs and I found Bob Dunn had left a note on the door, 'Bern I was here ... ' So I thought, well, Bern must have gone off to the doctor by himself or something. I went into the apartment and facing the door was one wall of the living room where I had that little table—you see that one in the corner—and on it I saw his wallet. And I said, 'Bern, Bern.' There was no answer. And I thought he might have gone out and forgotten his wallet. I went in and I walked through the little hall. The kitchen was to the right and the dining room area, and then the rest was the living room, and ahead was another little hallway that went to the bedrooms and the bathroom, so I walked right across the living room, noting the wallet, and I went into his study. I said, 'Bern, Bern.' I checked the bathroom, I checked his study, he wasn't there, and then I turned to the right where our bedroom was in this little corridor area. 'Bern, Bern.' I checked hesitantly the other bathroom, thinking he might have fallen, then I turned around and retraced my steps. And as I emerged from this little back corridor, in front of his study, I looked ahead, where I could see the dining area of the living room and his body was lying on the floor. And I remember saying, 'Oh my God, oh my God.'

At some point she left the apartment:

And I went downstairs to see if our doorman Victor was there, thinking I could get some help or something. I realised he was dead. I went down in the elevator with a couple of other people. It was all I could do just to control myself and just get down there. And Victor had left the door. There was a kid there who was his replacement. Victor had gone off somewhere so I came upstairs again. And my neighbor was there. I told my neighbor, the poor woman, I said, 'I've just found my husband dead on the floor,' and I sort of put my arms around her. She was not someone who was a friend of mine. She said, 'Have you called 911?'[1] Then I went back in the apartment and I had to call Security: we had our own security people in this development of Lincoln Towers. There were three of them, I think, two men and a woman. By which time I was sitting on the floor, holding Bern's hand which was still soft. I think they brought out a sheet from the linen closet and eventually covered him. But I sat there holding his hand, and sort of rocking back and forth. Then I also called friends. I called Ruth and Bernard Morris who by that time were living in a building on the way. They came over in a very short time. And a couple of neighbors came. I called Farrar Straus and spoke with Roger and Bob who were stunned because the night before we had gone to dinner at the Strauses. I said 'Who shall I call? What funeral parlour?' Roger said, 'I don't know, call Campbells.' So I called Campbells, and I remember when I said it was Bernard Malamud the woman must have been aware of who he was, because she sort of gasped. I called the doctors to explain that he had died and that he couldn't keep his appointment. I called my children. My daughter came that night with the baby because she was breast-feeding Zachary, the new baby. This was March and Zach her second child was born in November. Paul came the next day.

It was Ruth Morris who had first introduced the Malamuds to each other in 1942. She saw and heard Ann's distress.

Tim Seldes remembered that on the day Malamud died, for the first time ever, a bird flew into the New York offices of the agents, Russell and Volkening, as though it were the jewbird. Ann Malamud was left with a different image:

Bern had been lying on the floor, not on the rug. The body I think sweats—gives forth fluid after. There was a mark of his bone structure. He was thin then. An imprint of the hips and the back—there was some kind of mark left on the floor. I know I got one of the men to go over the floor and wax it but that imprint was there for a long time. Very strange. It was light.

Two weeks before her husband's death, Ann Malamud told Claude Fredericks, they had been out walking: 'and she, leaning heavily on his arm, had said, Papa, I need you to lean on even when I walk now. You'd better stick around for a while. I intend to, he had said firmly ... ' (Journal, 23 March 1986).

Malamud was cremated, his ashes buried in Mount Auburn Cemetery, in Cambridge, Massachusetts. A small stone lozenge marked the place, inscribed in Hebrew, and bearing the words from Malamud's introduction to the selection from his stories that was published in 1983: 'Art celebrates life and gives us our measure.'

But Malamud had always been unsure of his own measure. In 'Long Work, Short Life', the Ben Bellit lecture he gave at Bennington on 13 October 1984, he had closed by saying:

I don't regret the years I put into my work. Perhaps I regret the fact that I was not two men, one who could live a full life apart from writing; and one who who lived in art, exploring all he had to experience, and know how to make his work right; yet not regretting that he had put his life into the art of perfecting the work.   (TH, 35)

It had been a lonely life, working in the dark with words and associations. But in struggling to find the right words, he had told Michiko Kakutani, 'the feeling you feel can be just as strong as the worries of life, of love and family.' For deep moral and emotional reasons, Malamud would have liked to balance the two existences, the art and the life, and be the best that he could in both. Because he could not do so, he vainly wished for two lives instead. But he did not leave his family and for the sake of his art take off, like Gauguin, for Tahiti. Part of him wanted and needed to live like the ordinary man he never quite was. And what he actually had was the compromised sacrifice of one life for another in art. It was in any case a life he might never have been able to live properly in the first place, without his hard-earned gift as writer. But out of the pained botching and blurring of that failed, uneven compromise between his life and his art, there came, paradoxically, the very best of Malamud's work.

But in the end he himself did not know what he had done or if it had been worth doing it. Ann Malamud recalled finally:

> I remember, not long before he died, in the last year or so, he said to me, 'You know, I think I wouldn't want to live beyond 75.' It had become a struggle. He said that for a man who had a limited talent, he had done the best he could. But in the last year of his life particularly, he was depressed and felt that he hadn't accomplished enough. He felt insecure about his legacy and how much after all he had really done in his life. I used to say to him, 'Bern, you don't know how fortunate you are. How many people get to live the life they want to live and to accomplish what they wanted to—at least as much as you have accomplished?'

This was a major writer of the twentieth century. But he was aged seventy-two and still uncertain.

'At what an expense any valuable work is performed!' wrote Thoreau in his journal for 11 April 1852, 'At the expense of a life. If you do one thing well what else are you good for in the meanwhile?' Malamud marked it in the margin of his own copy. Also against 28 February 1841: 'Every sentence is the result of a long probation. The author's character is read from title-page to end. Of this he never corrects the proofs ... Our whole life is taxed for the least thing well done.'

Among the lives of the artists, there are dramas of greater heroism and greater turpitude and simply greater interest than Malamud's; but few so close to an ordinary sense, in an extraordinary man, of the uses of and costs to a life in the service of a serious vocation. Maggie Scarf was emotionally close to this powerful sense of a man in the process of turning the ordinary into the extraordinary, and dealing in both, when she recalled a telephone conversation she had with Ann Malamud shortly after the end. After some words, Ann said, ' "But of course he wasn't a simple man." We were silent again. "Well, maybe he *was* a simple man, in a way," Ann said reflectively' (HRC 31.6).

It was just after Malamud's death, when Ann had gone out of town, that Dan and Gloria Stern borrowed the Lincoln Towers apartment. In Malamud's desk they saw a line and a half from a poem:

> The work of life, which is so long to do,
> and so soon done.

It was by Howard Nemerov, who died in 1991.

In the Malamud archive in the Harry Ransom Center of the University of Texas at Austin, there are other items which were found in the desk on the day of Malamud's death. One is an article by Martha Wolfenstein, 'Loss, Rage, and Repetition', on the effects of the loss of a parent in childhood or adolescence. It was given to Malamud by Arlene Heyman, to whom there remains the draft of an unsent note: 'Thank you for letting me read your paper. It was like being allowed to look into a forbidden room. I saw more than I had meant to.' The effects had gone on to the very end. There is also in the folder on a tiny white slip the last of those notes to himself which Malamud had written all his life, which was found by Paul Malamud:

Don't be fragile
Don't be fragile
Don't be fragile
Don't be fragile   (HRC 34.34)

It said, 'Today is Tuesday February 18'; it was March 18.

But the true end was in the characteristic last words of the interview Malamud gave to Daniel Stern back in 1974.

DS: Is there something I haven't asked you that you might want to comment on?
MALAMUD: No
DS: For instance, what writing has meant to you?
MALAMUD: I'd be too moved to say.   (TH, 24)

Notes

CHAPTER 1: The Inheritance

1. Mark Zborowski and Elizabeth Herzog, *Life Is With People* (first published 1952; New York: Shocken, 1962), 294. Hereafter cited as *Life Is With People*.
2. Notes made by Bernard Malamud around 1976 on his family history, in the possession of Janna Malamud Smith; hereafter cited as 'Family History'.
3. I am grateful to Ann Malamud for access to the correspondence between herself and her husband.
4. Interview with Curt Leviant in CBM, 48.
5. Mrs Mickey Levine, e-mail to Janna Malamud Smith, 26 April 2006
6. When they were younger and the children little, then sometimes they ventured out, as Malamud described it in the first draft of *The Assistant*: 'on Jewish holidays, they dressed their best, locked up the store, and ventured forth into the open. They travelled to Second Avenue to see a play, Sholem Aleichem's Tevye, Hirschbein's Greene Felder, or I. J.Singer's Yoshe Kalb. And they visited old friends, landsmen, or if not landsmen they had been immigrants together, and knew each other's history. They would sit, while the children ran free, relaxed, drinking tea with lemon, munching sponge or honey cake, tasting nuts and raisins, as they exchanged news of dear friends, or with sweet pleasure reminisced of the old days' (LC I 1.5, p. 192). Tevye became popularized as *Fiddler on the Roof*; *Greene Felder* (Green Fields) is the story of a young man leaving the synagogue for the open world and ending up in a small farm in the country; *Yoshe Kalb* (Yoshe Calf, also known in its English translation as *The Sinner*) by I. J. Singer, the older brother of Isaac Bashevis Singer, tells of the downfall of an Hasidic community as a result of the erotic passion of a sensitive young man. 'Landsmen' were those who had come to America from the same town or village.
7. Personal interview with George Martin, 2 July 2003.
8. Letter to Bernard Malamud, 11 January 1946, HRC 12.8.
9. Personal interview with Charles Kopelman and his mother Jean Haber, 13 July 2003.
10. Personal interview with Herb Wittkin, 11 July 2003.
11. Telephone interview with Reinhard Mayer, 17 July 2003.
12. From correspondence in the possession of Ann Malamud.
13. Personal interview with Ann Malamud, January 2003

CHAPTER 2: The Long Adolescence

1. Philip Roth, *Shop Talk* (London: Vintage, 2002), 123. The chapter 'Pictures of Malamud' first appeared in the *New York Times*, 20 April 1986.
2. 'Notebooks 1930s–1940s', in possession of Janna Malamud Smith; hereafter cited as 'Notebooks'.
3. Personal interview with Bernadette and Alex Inkeles, 28–9 July 2003.
4. Miriam Lang, 'The Young Malamud: Age of Innocence' (unpublished); hereafter cited as 'The Young Malamud'; given to me on behalf of the author by Doris (Milman) Kreeger.
5. Personal interview with George (Markowitz) Martin, 2 July 2003.
6. Telephone interview with Linda Lowell, 13 November 2005; hereafter cited as 'Lowell'.
7. Personal interview with Herbert Wittkin, 11 July 2003; hereafter cited as 'Wittkin'.
8. Personal interview with Nina Pelikan Straus, 20 July 2003.
9. I am indebted to Doris Milman, now Kreeger, for access to her correspondence with Malamud here and in the rest of this chapter.
10. Personal interview with Doris Milman Kreeger, 11 July 2003.
11. Ted Solotaroff, *First Loves* (New York: Seven Stories Press, 2003), 236; hereafter cited as 'Solotaroff'.
12. Unpublished 'Reminiscences' by Hannah (Needle) Broder.
13. Personal interview with Harriet and Larry Lustig, and Burt and Betsy Rush, 15 July 2003.
14. Personal interview with Susan Shrag, 8 July 2003.
15. *Bernard Malamud: The Complete Stories*, ed. Robert Giroux (New York, Farrar, Straus and Giroux, 1997), 7–8.
16. I am indebted to Ellen Belton, the daughter of Vivian and Alan Rothenberg, for copies of her letters.
17. For what follows I am indebted to a personal interview with Ann Malamud held throughout January 2003 (hereafter cited as 'Ann Malamud'). Copies of letters between her and her husband were also given to me by her.
18. In a letter of 15 August 1951 Paul Schrag recalls the occasion: 'the knowledge [is] still fresh with me that I hurt you when my observations on 'The Light Sleeper' sounded harsh and crude. … If in the mood of the moment I uttered these conclusions dismally and so hurt you—it is positively the last thing I could ever wish to do' (HRC 9.4).
19. Excerpt from the unpublished journals of Claude Fredericks, 26 August 1970, kindly provided by the author and with the kind assistance of Marc Harrington. Acknowledgement is also made to the Research Institute of the Getty Centre in Los Angeles where the manuscripts are kept.

CHAPTER 3: Oregon

1. Personal interview with Ann Malamud, held throughout January 2003 (hereafter cited as 'Ann Malamud').
2. I am indebted to Professor Joel Salzberg for access to these memoir notes.
3. See Suzanne Clark, 'Bernard Malamud in Oregon', *The American Scholar* (winter 1990), 67–79 (OSC 13.4).
4. Interview with Chester Garrison, conducted by Paul Malamud, in MWB, 14.
5. James Groshong, e-mail communication, 19 June 2004.
6. Joan Norris Boothe, an excerpt kindly sent me from her memoir *Faith Grigsby Norris*: 'In the puritanical Oregon of 1947, it wasn't even possible to buy a bottle of liquor in town.'
7. Paul Malamud, 'Malamud in Corvallis', in MWB, 4.
8. Elizabeth Henley, 'Boom Town' in *To Hear Unspoken Things* (Portland, OR: Press-22, 2000). I am grateful to her son John Henley. 'Boom Town 'refers most particularly to the Bellingham, Washington, of her childhood but equivalently poems such as 'Water Music' are clearly about Corvallis.
9. John Ericksen, 'A Class with Mr. Malamud', *The Salem Statesman* (25 February 1983) (OSU 1.52)
10. Tom Bennett, *Oregon Stater* (June 1996); hereafter cited as 'Bennett'.
11. Personal interview with Victor Erlich, 18 July 2003. For what it is worth, the story went on with the announcement in a German accent: 'All ze people who know how to shvim, please sit on the right-hand side. The people who don't know how to shvim, please sit on the left'—followed by the Captain's voice, on hitting the ocean: 'To ze people on the right-hand side, start shvimming. To ze people on the left, thank you for flying Lufthansa.' Iza Erlich continued to serve dinner on a casual basis.
12. Lorena MacCafferty from a letter to myself, 1 December 2005.
13. Videotaped interview with other Oregon colleagues, 6 April 1988 (OSU Malamud Papers).
14. To Eugene Malamud, 22 April 1959 (HRC 13.2); to Rosemarie Beck, 21 August 1959 (Berg Collection of English and American Literature, New York Public Library).
15. Delmar Leaming, *Newton Iowa Daily News*, 21 June 1958.
16. Telephone interview with Danny Myerson (a freshman at Bennington in 1967), 5 February 2006: 'It was at the end of the story that the claims of the logically practical fell apart, and there was no longer an insisting on narrowly personal rights, however reasonable.' Thus at the end of 'The Mourners' (or later 'The Elevator' or 'The Last Mohican'), one who is self-righteous, and in narrow terms right to be so, suddenly feels remorse or generosity by finding that winning in one way was a form of losing in another, larger sense..
17. I am indebted to Powers' daughter, Katherine A. Powers, for access to this correspondence.

18. Copyright retained by Paul Malamud. With this as with the rest of his writings, while granting his permission, he retains full copyright of his original materials, including the right to sell, publish, alter, or reprint the texts in any language in America, England, or any other country, in whole or in part, and in any medium, print, or electronic, and retain all subsidiary rights in such mediums as film.

19. Compare Janna Malamud Smith: 'For his forty-sixth birthday, in April 1960 … my brother bought Dad a hunting cap, and I bought him a fishing rod and tackle box, knowing he'd never use them. … We teased him for living indoors, for always writing; by then we grasped how out of place he was' (MFB, 135).

20. Telephone conversation with Pam Metz, 20 November 2005.

21. William James, *The Varieties of Religious Experience* (1902), lectures 6 and 7 ('The Sick Soul').

22. Thus: 'an egregious failure', William Du Bois, *New York Times*, 23 August; 'pretentious mish-mash', *Columbus Dispatch*, 28 August; 'Flashbacks Mar Baseball Story', *Lexington Herald Leader*.

CHAPTER 4: *The Assistant*

1. Personal interview with Robert Giroux, 13 July 2003.

2. In *Malamud: Three Elegies*, 20 April 1986, printed by Glenn Horowitz, p. 7.

3. See, for example, *The Downtown Jews* (New York: Harper and Row, 1969) by Malamud's friend, Ronald Sanders.

4. Personal interview with Alan Cheuse, 30 July 2003.

5. By kind permission of Katherine A. Powers.

6. LC I 1.5 'p.70 insert' on Frank's creative accounting: 'He was doing them a favor, at the same time encouraging himself to stay there and help them further. Stealing this was a kind of creativity. It was a way of showing how much you had to give.'

7. Personal interview with Nelson Sandgren, 25 July 2003.

8. See Victoria Aarons's excellent 'A Kind of Vigilance: Chiastic Suspension in Malamud's Fiction', in MWB, 175–86.

9. Telephone interview with Bill Potts, 21 May 2004.

10. Personal interview with Nina Pelikan Straus, 19 July 2003.

11. Jay Cantor, *New York Times Book Review*, 28 September 1997.

12. Reprinted by permission of Philip Roth.

13. The charge is repeated in Ruth R. Wisse, *The Modern Jewish Canon* (first published 2000), where, remarkably, Malamud is excluded from the modern Jewish canon—as Roth himself remarkably is not—because the 'conflation of victim with "chosen" is characteristic of Malamud, who identifies the Jew exclusively and ideologically with the archetype of the sufferer and on this basis imagines the Jew as the ideal Christian' (Chicago: University of Chicago Press, 16).

CHAPTER 5: Because I *Can*'

1. Malamud to Rosemarie Beck, 13 July 1959. I am indebted to the Berg Collection (Astor, Lenox and Tilden Foundations), New York Public Library for permission to quote from the Malamud–Beck correspondence. All scholars are indebted to Joel Salzberg's work on this archive, most readily available in MWB, 43–56.
2. Personal interview with Bernadette and Alex Inkeles, 28–9 July 2003.
3. Personal interview with Nelson Sandgren, 25 July 2003.
4. Personal interview with Bernadette and Alex Inkeles, 28–9 July 2003.
5. I am grateful to Doria Hughes, Rosemarie Beck's granddaughter for further access to 'Becki's' letters and for excerpts from her journal. She writes of the friendship, with justice: 'Because she has not achieved his stature as an artist, she is frequently dismissed as merely a minor painter who saw an opportunity to curry favor with a great man. This perception constitutes an injustice to both of them—it makes a fool and a poor judge of character of him (which, from reading his letters, he does not appear to be), and a self-serving opportunist (or worse) of her (which from reading her letters and journals, she does not appear to be). … She recognized in him a kindred work ethic, the same kind of dogged determination, that same relentless need to serve the Work which drove her until death took her. She recognized in him a true fellow artist.'
6. After his death, Rosemarie Beck gave the letters Malamud wrote to her to the New York Public Library and asked Ann to add in Rosemarie's own letters kept by Malamud, although she was worried about how emotional her own were and feared they could be misinterpreted. 'They say that emotionalism is a sign of weakness,' she had written Malamud, 19 March 1961, quoting Puccini, 'but I like to be weak! To the strong, so-called, I leave the triumphs that fade, for us, those that endure.' Ann Malamud recalled the discussion about the fate of these letters: 'Well, at that point I said, "Rosemarie, it was all so long ago, what difference does it make?" She was saying, "I just sound that way and I know it's awful because it's misleading." Well, I was not entirely misled. I think she had a small fling with Bern at some point. I was only trying to reassure her to say, "Look, kiddo, at this point in our lives, who the hell cares?" ' (Personal interview with Ann Malamud, January 2003).
7. In his article 'The Magic and the Dread' Kazin was troubled by Malamud's need for symbolism and fantasy. Why like so many other new writers arising out of minorities downtrodden in the Depression, did Malamud take Dostoevsky for his patron saint, always searching and searching for the meaning of life, instead of valuing it for its own sake? 'Unlike those who are abstract because they have only their own cleverness to work from, Malamud is abstract out of despair: despair of the world itself, which can no longer be represented.' In fear of his own desire to compensate for this despair at the flimsiness of his under-privileged human material, Malamud 'has to outwit his own possible sentimentality' (*Reporter* 18, 29 May 1958; reprinted in *Contemporaries* (New York: Little, Brown, 1962)).

8. Richard Stern, *One Person and Another* (Dallas: Baskerville, 1993), 92 (hereafter cited as 'Richard Stern').

9. *New York Review of Books*, 9 October 1997.

10. 'Suddenly, in each of Malamud's best stories, something surprising happens: it is as if the speed of the movie reel were crazily increased, as if the characters leapt clear of the earth, as if a Chagall painting snapped into motion and its figures, long frozen in mid-air, began to dip and soar. The place is familiar; but the tone, the tempo, the treatment are all new' (LC I 30.1). In a notebook entry for 8 March 1954 Malamud first sketched out the 'feeling' for the story before the 'idea' of it—a feeling for a return to 'the poetic, evocative, singing' and thus essentially symbolic short story, closer to the visionary painting of Chagall than to the short realistic pieces he has been writing for a while (LC II 1.9).

11. The marriage broker, Salzman, first appeared as a peddler both in Malamud's destroyed first novel 'The Light Sleeper' and in 'The Cost of Living'. Even the tomato he asks for—though Malamud only alludes to 'a detail from childhood'—is actually the beefsteak tomato that in 'A Lost Bar-Mitzvah' Malamud's unkind and toothless Hebrew teacher got from Malamud's mother, even as she complained about the use of the ruler on her son's hand. Malamud connects the protagonist, Leo Finkel, a substitute-teacher, with himself in 1939, a teacher-in-training unhappy in his rooming house, who one day received a list of prospects from a matrimonial agency, with phrases such as 'well-Americanized', 'owns Dodge car', 'her father is a dentist'. There were literary sources too. It was Mark Twain who fell in love with his wife-to-be when he saw her picture in her brother's possession, though it could also have been Dostovesky's Idiot or Hardy's Jude. And in particular there are two comic anecdotes from the Yiddish collection *Royte Pomerantzen* which Malamud was invited by Irving Howe to translate for an anthology. One is about a young man who insists he only wants a love match and the marriage broker who triumphantly replies that he can 'get him that kind too'. Another is about nothing making any 'difference' to the young man in the face of the ever-increasing list of deficiencies in the bride on offer—because (he finally tells the broker) he won't have her in the first place.

12. Personal interview with Nina Pelikan Straus, 16 July 2003.

13. In the Malamud archive in the Library of Congress (I 53.5), there are fourteen small envelopes, now empty, each with a summary of the chapter they represent on the cover. Inside used to be the small white notes he assembled.

14. Personal interview with Robert Giroux, 13 July 2003.

15. E-mail received via the younger son, John Henley, 5 May 2006: both Elizabeth and Avis had a scarred breast.

16. Short, beautiful, and exuberant, Kathy Kohner (now Zuckerman) was known amongst her fellow surfers as the Gidget (girl midget): her father, to whom she confided all her sexual adventures, made her the basis for a novel and then a television series. She told Malamud, another Jewish father-figure, of her encounter with a member of the Literature division who had asked her,

seated beside him in his car, whether they should be 'decorous or venturesome' (telephone conversation, 15 November 2005). Another model may have been a Carol Lewis (Henley).

17. Personal interview with Maggie Scarf, 18 July 2003.

18. Soren Kierkegaard, *Fear and Trembling*, trans. by Alastair Hannay (London; Penguin, 1985), 52.

19. Telephone interviews with Bill Potts, 21 May 2004, and Ed McClanahan, 16 November 2005. Ann Decius' husband Jack had tears in his eyes, she simply reports to the Malamuds, when he read *A New Life* (HRC 8.3).

20. Friendly correspondents writing to congratulate Malamud were often anxious about words such as 'lay' in passages often otherwise rhapsodic (Robert Heilman, 25 December 1951, HRC 1.2; Ed Smith. 8 October 1961, HRC 9.4). But the tonal shift is to do with Levin's testing of himself in the midst of things, to see if what he feels is more than biological alchemy.

21. Malamud spoke of 'the necessity of making one thing two (every object a possible symbol)' and equally of 'the necessity of making two things one; all things revealing the single form' (LC II 13.12).

CHAPTER 6: The Beginning of the Middle Years

1. Interview with Clark Blaise, 21 July 2003. A similar version of this incident is given in *Resident Alien* (Penguin, 1986).

2. E-mail from William J. Cooper, 6 October 2005.

3. Telephone interview with Sara Witter, 12 November 2004.

4. To Nina Pelikan Straus, 10 October 1975: I am grateful to her for access to these letters.

5. Personal interview with Ann Malamud, January 2003.

6. E-mail correspondence from Anne Waldman, 7 June 2006.

7. Phebe Chao writes of Ben Belitt: 'He was one of several children of a Russian Jewish immigrant whose husband had died (I think before she left Russia). The only way she saw to support herself was to remarry here. Which she did. And she had more children. At some point, the decision was made that the children from the first marriage had to be sent to foster homes. I'm sure that in itself was wrenching for Ben, to be sent away, but the situation was exacerbated by mean or uncaring or abusive foster parents. He was sexually molested at one of his homes. I don't know how he managed to live through all that. But he did get away to college, I believe to the University of Virginia. He was a brilliant student, supported by scholarships and fellowships, and encouraged to go to graduate school. He did all the work for the PhD but for one reason or another he didn't complete his dissertation. Anyhow, he went to New York City. He had found his own sexual orientation by then. He knew Lorca in NYC. And the dancers Martha Graham and Martha Hill, both of whom later taught at Bennington. He was part of the literary scene, beginning to be published; part of the Key West crowd that included

Elizabeth Bishop. He travelled to Europe, to Mexico. He always said that like a
spider making a web, a person only needed three anchoring points—by middle
age, he'd settled on Bennington (Vt), Cuernavaca (Mexico), and Block Island
(off Rhode Island). Ben was really Mr. Bennington. He was there for decades,
he had a hand in every re-invention of the department, he loved the place. By
the time I knew Ben in the 70s, he wasn't very active in the gay world; he was
stoic about his aches and pains (from the wear and tear of age). There are some
wonderful poems and translations from the Spanish, though his style is somewhat baroque compared to the deliberately flat language of many contemporary
poets. Ben made peace with the idea that he wasn't considered among the
foremost poets of his age, certain that fame would come to him after he died.
The college didn't make much of a fuss about him when he retired—that hurt
him. At the end, the college disappointed him' (e-mail 15 May 2006). In his
journal for 8 August 1981 Claude Fredericks speaks of Malamud's visiting 'lonely
ailing Ben' every day in the hospital, taking him to the movies every fortnight
and says that Malamud cultivates such acts of duty 'as seriously as a monk'.

8. The only manifesto Malamud thought sane, when the place went through a
   whole series of internal arguments in the mid-seventies, was one which simply
   insisted on the primacy of the personal: 'if YOU are talking to ME, it's YOU
   and ME, not some philosophy, or some "ism", or some abstraction.' If this
   was not learnt, said the pamphleteer, then 'things are just going to keep getting
   more bent and more out of shape', Malamud to Arlene Heyman, 2 June 1975
   (quoting David Whiteis).

9. Personal interview with Alan Cheuse, 30 July 2003.

10. Personal interview with Nina Pelikan Straus, 20 July 2003.

11. Howard Nemerov Papers in Special Collections, Washington University in St
    Louis, Series I, 2.h, Bay 37, Folder 175.

12. Telephone conversation with Danny Myerson, 5 February 2006.

13. Jay Cantor, 'Remembering Malamud', New York Times Book Review, 28
    September 1997.

14. Telephone interview with Bharati Mukherjee, 21 July 2003.

15. R. S. Baker, letter to New York Times, 18 May 1986.

16. Philip Roth, The Ghost Writer (Penguin, 1980), 19.

17. Journal entry by Claude Fredericks for 3 September 1985, towards the end of
    Malamud's life.

18. From the Malamud–Heyman correspondence recently deposited in HRC and
    uncatalogued at the time of writing.

19. Personal interview with Roger Straus, 10 July 2003.

20. Personal interview with Robert Giroux, 13 July 2003.

21. Telephone interview with Letty Cottin Pogrebin, 19 July 2003.

22. 'Put some gypsy in him', 'Bach had the declamatory quality of a Jew', letter to
    Arlene Heyman, 27 July 1962.

23. Telephone interview with Kate Hickler, now White, 18 November 2005.

24. Arlene Heyman had a friend, a fellow-student who was poor girl from a poor family who had married a man from rural Vermont, had had a child, and never had any money. She did not like Malamud—'she valued the spontaneous, the mystical, the easy enactment of one's genuine feelings, and so she disliked Bern for writing every day, whether he felt like it or not, and for trying to do the right thing, whether he felt like it or not'. She felt he was a pompous goody-goody. But when she had problems with her teeth and needed a hundred dollars to get them fixed, Malamud gave the money to Arlene to give to her, knowing she wouldn't accept it from him. Later she ended up with Malamud as her senior thesis advisor, because he would take her when no one else would, though he knew full well that she did not like him. She was writing short stories but was unable to finish the third story for her thesis and left without her degree. Malamud spent ages after she left, trying to get that last story out of her—'any story of any length'—until finally he got her the degree. There was some relation in him between compassion and putting himself to one side, even to the point of anonymity (personal interview with Arlene Heyman, 22–3 July 2003).

25. Personal interview with Nina Peilikan Straus, 16 July 2003.

26. Personal interview with Arlene Heyman, 22–3 July 2003.

27. Arlene Heyman, *Lovers and Ghosts*, unpublished manuscript reprinted by kind permission of the author.

28. From the Nemerov Papers in Special Collections, Washington University in St Louis (WTU00089).

29. I am indebted to Claude Fredericks for access these hitherto unseen excerpts. The original manuscript is in the Claude Fredericks archive at the Research Institute of the Getty Centre in Los Angeles to which acknowledgement is also here made.

30. Personal interview with Daniel Stern, 20 July 2003.

31. Janna Malamud Smith, 'My Father Is a Book', in *The Threepenny Review*, no. 94 (summer 2003).

32. Personal interview with Bernadette and Alex Inkeles, 28–9 July 2003.

33. Personal interview with Chester Garrison, 24 July 2003.

34. Personal interview with Paul Malamud, 31 July 2003.

35. Telephone conversation with Karen (Jackel) Wunsch, 4 September 2005.

36. E-mail from Paul Malamud, 20 March 2006

CHAPTER 7: We Need Some Sort of Poverty in Our Lives'

1. Personal interview with Stephen Sandy, 7 July 2003. The poet Anne Waldman said that, nonetheless, Malamud in 1966 was encouraging her to read Modernists who were not consistently taught at Bennington—including Pound (whose anti-Semitism was usually held against him there), Williams, Stein, HD, as well as the Beats and the New York School of Ashbery and O'Hara (e-mail correspondence, 3 April 2006).

2. E-mail correspondence with Peter Hayes, 6 February 2006.
3. Telephone interview with Katha Pollitt, 20 November 2003
4. Jay Cantor, 'Remembering Malamud', *New York Times Book Review*, 28 September 1997.
5. Telephone interview with Pam Metz, 14 November 2005.
6. Telephone interview with Karen (Jackel) Wunsch, 4 September 2005.
7. Personal interview with Nina Peilkan Straus, 20 July 2003.
8. See *A Howard Nemerov Reader* (Columbia: University of Missouri Press, 1991), 161–75. Form, said Nemerov, 'is (1) allied with religion, for it is against "the tempest of passions" and thus in favor of control, discipline, askesis, renunciation. But it is (2) opposed to religion, for it is also against "the institution", that is against church, state, dogma, or any fixed habit of the mind. Finally, it is (3) against something in its own nature, called "the art", against, perhaps, the idea of form itself' (p. 165).
9. Telephone interview with Linda Lowell, née Feldman, 13 November 2005.
10. E-mail correspondence from Barbara Herrnstein Smith, 8 March 2006.
11. Personal interview with Paul Malamud, 1 August 2003.
12. Letter from Arnold Cooper, MD, 19 January 2006.
13. Details of verbal parallels were given on http://MendelBeilis.com, which is currently not available.
14. According to the Beilises, whose case deserves to be heard, Malamud was a hypocrite who wanted privacy for his own family whilst exposing theirs. In an interview for the *New York Post* in 1967 he showed what the interviewer described as 'a highly developed sense of privacy' in respect of his own family: 'He veered off sharply from questions about his wife, his son and his daughter. "Please don't use my children's names," he said. "I don't care for them to have any attention they haven't earned. And I don't care for people to have personal knowledge of my kids. In *any* way." ' Years later Janna herself wrote an article in the *New York Times Book Review* (5 November 1989), doubting she would ever make public her father's private letters and journals because 'today, it seems that a biography's capacity to make a profit or boost an academic career matters much more than how it will affect either the subject's family or the reader's experience of the fiction.' Noting these concerns, Jay Beilis added 'Would that Bernard Malamud had possessed his daughter's sensitivity when writing *The Fixer*'. Yet *The Story of My Sufferings* was a published work, albeit one out of copyright.
15. 10 July 1965, Clark Blaise Papers, University of Calgary Library.
16. Robert Boyers, *A Book of Common Praise* (New York: Ausable Press, 2002), 174.
17. Quoted in a review of *The Fixer* by Herbert Kenny, *Boston Sunday Globe*, 25 September 1966.
18. Howard Nemerov to Malamud, 30 December 1965, after reading the second draft, spoke of the way that *The Fixer* was like Kafka's or Dostoevsky's version of the detective story. 'The detective story, in which hero and reader are

detecting and suffering at once, as in King Oedipus, is to me something like the ideal narrative form' (Special Collections, Washington University in St Louis).

19. In the possession of Ann Malamud.
20. Charles Thomas Samuels, *The New Republic*, 10 September 1966 (LC I 16.2).
21. I am indebted for permission from Claude Fredericks to use hitherto unseen excerpts from his journals.
22. Personal interview with Maggie Scarf, 14 July 2003.
23. Telephone interview with Tamas Ungvari, 28 June 2006.

CHAPTER 8: From *The Fixer* towards *Dubin*

1. Robert Alter, 'The Jew Who Didn't Get Away: The Possibility of an American Jewish Culture', repr. in Jonathan D. Sarna (ed.), *The American Jewish Experience* (New York: Holmes and Meier, 1986), 272.
2. Morris Dickstein, *Gates of Eden* (Cambridge, Mass.: Harvard University Press, 1997 edn), 50.
3. Personal interview with Herb Wittkin, 11 July 2003.
4. Personal interview with Robert Giroux, 13 July 2003.
5. From the Howard Nemerov papers in Washington University in St Louis. The final quotation is taken from Martin Luther in his protest at the Diet of Worms: 'I can do no other.'
6. On this see, for example, Joel Salzberg, 'Of "Autobiographical Essence" and Self-Parody: Malamud on "Exhibition" in *Pictures of Fidelman*', in *Genre* xxiv (Fall 1991), 271–95.
7. Philip Roth, 'Pictures of Malamud' (1986), repr. in *Shop Talk* (London: Vintage 2002), 123.
8. Roth had earlier argued in 'Writing American Fiction' (*Commentary*, 1960) that Malamud's tales of suffering and regeneration were insufficiently lodged in contemporary reality, his old Jews invented metaphors that spurned the modern world. Malamud made careful notes on that essay too (LC II 13.10).
9. Telephone interview with Jules Olitski, 2 February 2006.
10. Cleophus Thomas Jr was a young black student who wrote to Malamud in appreciation of his work: he was moved by Malamud's African-American characters and also in his own way knew what Malamud meant in saying that all men were Jews. Malamud wrote back: 'I'm glad you like the Magic Barrel stories and am very much pleased that my Jews seem black to you. That is empathizing. I'll leave it at that. It doesn't at all bother me that you create your own magic in reading the book. One hopes for that' (9 May 1980, by permission of Cleophus Thomas Jr).
11. Malamud to Nina Pelikan Straus, 24 April 1971 (by kind permission of the recipient): 'I do, unfortunately, agree with you about Irene. She is too much the daughter of plot; I gave her only so much as the story requires and not enough to create a woman of broader human quality. However, I have broadened her

in recent revisions. She can now say at the very end, "I am more important than your book." And mean it because has learned some thing about herself that I wish I knew earlier in the game. If I felt I could do more with her I would go through a fourth draft, but she has been wounded by my treatment of her and does not respond to my urgings. And I think she confuses me with Lesser.'

12. Telephone interview with Philip Wofford, 24 July 2003.
13. Unpublished interview with Paul Malamud.
14. Personal interview with Alan Cheuse, 30 July 2003.
15. Quoted by Professor Camille Paglia to whom I am grateful for writing a brief memoir of Malamud and Bennington, 29 May 2006, for the purposes of this book.
16. *Vale of Academe* (Holocene Publishing, 1996) by kind permission of Stephen Sandy.
17. The provocative nature of Camille Paglia's bold interdisciplinary dissertation, the now famous *Sexual Personae*, deterred prospective employers till Harold Bloom recommended her to Alvin Feinman when a faculty member left Bennington for Oxford at the last moment. She writes as background to her eight years there:

'I don't mean to defend my extreme behavior in the 1970s—the pranks and stunts, the abrasive confrontationalism and indefatigable intrusiveness into every aspect of Bennington life. I often say I grew up at Bennington. That is, it was the first time I was forced to confront the disjunction between my arrogant 1960s ideals and the humdrum realities and requirements of institutions. I shared the impatience and delusionalism of my generation—in my case caused not by drugs (I didn't take them) but by hubris.

'However, many others at Bennington—not in the puritanical Social Science Division but among the arts faculty outside the factionalized Literature Division—were more sympathetic to my public performance side and saw the novelty and promise of my interdisciplinary ideas, which they recognized as embodying Bennington's maverick intellectual tradition. Feinman and Tristman used to remark that if Stanley Edgar Hyman (who had written on Frazer and Freud, two major influences on my work) hadn't died prematurely at the age of 51 in 1970—shortly before I arrived—I would have had a powerful protector against my enemies at the college, including Malamud.'

18. Camille Paglia wrote thus of the aftermath: 'I felt, as the department was stampeded into hiring Maizitis, that nothing good would come of it. By taking the charity route with this candidate, we had lost an opportunity to add to Bennington's national stature, which was slipping. Mara Maizitis was yet another of the deferential, dependent women with whom Malamud wished to populate the world.

'During her first year at Bennington, Maizitis seemed well-liked by students, but as time passed, she began to struggle. Complaints multiplied—she was too nervous; she talked too rapidly with an incomprehensible accent; her courses were too narrow and academic and not tailored for Bennington. And of course she wasn't "hip"—not by a long shot. She seemed to lack natural authority.

'I played no role in her fate, which culminated after I had left Bennington. But I heard of her desperation when she was confronted with these accumulating problems. There were open tears, and the situation became emotionally wrenching. It was evidently conveyed to her that she was unlikely to be promoted or retained on "presumptive tenure". She was humiliated, and her suffering was overt.

'Several years (four or five?) after her arrival at Bennington, Mara Maizitis was suddenly stricken by a brain tumor and incapacitated. Fortunately, the college provided disability insurance to faculty, so she would have medical coverage and a means of support. But she was gone from the college and, as far as I know, was unable to work again.'

19. For a fictional account of Malamud in relation to a more predatory or parasitic version of the figure of the writer-son, see his satirical short story, 'An Exorcism', published in *Harper's Magazine* in 1968 and revised for the selected *Stories* (1983) but finally not included by the author.

20. Personal interview with Nicholas Delbanco, 4 July 2003.

21. Personal interview with Alan Cheuse, 30 July 2003.

22. Janna Malamud Smith describes it thus: 'The first female President, during the 1970s, Gail Parker, got herself drummed out of the job (and featured in *Esquire*) for her very public affair with a history teacher (not even a student). Some male Presidents also had affairs, but more discreetly. Parker's in-your-face gender reversal, and the couple's bad taste—stripping off sweaters in the class they co-taught to reveal on each of them a scarlet *A*—must have felt way too mocking to the board of trustees—who fired her. But the couple were merely buffooning into high relief the school's ethos' (MFB, 185). In the *Esquire* article Camille Paglia was quoted as saying that in Bennington nobody was paying attention if you were doing it with a dog. It was said that she had kicked a young male student three times for parodying her Uzi lecture style; afterwards she claimed that the kicks were parodic, too. Malamud was shocked by female aggression and also told Paglia, on the basis of his wife's heritage, that he knew of no Italians like her.

23. In Daniel Stern's 'A Hunger Artist', Brandauer tells one of Malamud's own well-rehearsed stories about a Japanese businessman who suspects his wife of infidelity in his absence. Three times the Japanese businessman confronts his wife about 'affair with Jewish gentleman'; third time, sick of hearing it, she shrugs her shoulders in disgust: 'Ach' she says, 'the bubbe meisehs!' It was (unfortunately) the Yiddish for grandmother's tales, total lies. But Brandauer himself 'was like a Japanese visitor, without the language, trying to join in a light-heartedness he did not quite understand but longed to experience.' Arlene Heyman also recalled his set-piece about a Frenchman who suddenly had the urge to make love to his lady-companion and took her under his car. Then a gendarme arrived. 'What's it to you where I make love?' says the husband. 'Monsieur, I do not care where

you make love, but your car has been stolen.' Stanley Eskin, a colleague from Bennington, recalled other ribald set-pieces (e-mail 25 July 2006): 'A man tells his friend about this girl he's met who offered to make a corned beef sandwich on his penis and eat it. "She put it on a slice of rye, spread mustard on it, put in lettuce and tomato, then a hefty portion of first-rate corned beef, then a big sliced pickle." Friend: 'Then what happened?" "It looked so good I ate it myself." ' 'Then there was a French teacher of English who asks her pupils to use the word "Pro*babl*ee" in a sentence. The first says, "My fazer come home from work; he put on heez slippers; he lights heez pipe; and he open heez newspaper. Pro*babl*ee he eez going to read ze newspaper." Teacher: "Veree good. Next." "My mozaire peel potatoes, boil zem, and zen take out potato masher. Pro*babl*ee she eez going to make mashed potatoes." "Veree good. Next?" "I com home and my seester eez having her piano lesson. Her skirt eet eez up over her waist. The teacher, he has heez pants off. Pro*babl*ee zey are going to sheet in the piano." '

But in 'A Hunger Artist' the company's spontaneous laughter and the noisy commentary get louder and louder and more and more out of hand until suddenly, in a sort of panic, Brandauer pounds his hand on the table for quiet: 'A god of large and small universes, he was accustomed to being able to control them' (*Twice Upon a Time* Houston, Tex.: Rice University Press, 1992), 8–9).

24. 'Bernard Malamud: A Reminiscence': available at http://randomhouse.com/boldtype/0597/pogrebin/essay.html
25. Telephone interview with Joan Gardner, 2 November 2005.
26. E-mail letter from Barabara Herrnstein Smtih, March 2006.
27. Reprinted in *Quadrille* (for Alumni and Friends of Bennington College), Fall 1986, vol.17, no.1.
28. Personal interview with Daniel Stern, 20 July 2003.
29. Telephone interview with Christine Graham, 10 July 2006.
30. Telephone interview with Judy Feiffer, 5 April 2006.
31. HRC 16.4, 7.7.
32. Telephone interview with Pat Adams, 26 July 2006. His approach to her, which she considered as one arising out of mutual admiration, was: 'You and I are going to be in each other's biographies.'
33. Telephone interview with Beverley Sanders, 3 March 2006.
34. Telephone interview with Letty Cottin Pogrebin, 19 July 2003.
35. Personal interview with Ann Malamud, January 2003.
36. Personal interview with Chester Garrison, 24 July 2003.

CHAPTER 9: *Dubin's Lives*

1. Personal interview with Stephen Sandy, 7 July 2003.
2. In Malamud's copy of *The Heart of Thoreau's Journals*, edited by Odell Shepard, there are pencil marks against entries for 5 December 1856—'I love best to have each thing in its season only, and enjoy doing without it at all other times. It is the

greatest of all advantages to enjoy no advantage at all. I find it invariably true, the poorer I am, the richer I am'—and 26 October 1857—'These regular phenomena of the seasons get at last to be—they were at first of course—simply and plainly phenomena or phases of my life. The seasons and all their changes are in me.'

3. Nina Pelikan Straus knew of the Nemerov connection (20 July 2003); Phebe Chao, the Finckel–Wallace relationship, as well as the physical resemblance of Connie to the shapely Fanny (22 July): 'At a party Bern went up to Connie and said, "You know, contrary to what they say, [Fanny] wasn't modelled after you." The denial was so unexpected and revealing. Everybody thought, "O my God, what has he just said!" There are autobiographical things and some that are fantasy. Connie got real angry of course because she said, "I never thought I was but now I have to think I am."' On her own involvement at the level of detail—including aviator glasses, a few dark hairs under the chin, contact lenses—Arlene Heyman wrote Malamud, 4 March 1979: 'The things to do with me I was very tickled by—that clothes line, my dear God. And the wild spring outfit in the Fall. (That last may be pure invention on your part, but I remember my yellow and white polka dot wash-n-wear dress.) The VW and the half-eaten apples or some mess anyhow and the myopic discontented eyes.... The opening meeting with Fanny is excellent, as is the sad waiting and waiting for her. (Though I never didn't show, I've kept you waiting plenty, for which I apologize. It's less now, for which I'm glad.)'

4. Malamud wrote Nina Pelikan Straus commending her for proposing to teach a course comparing the two writers, 26 September 1979.

5. Entry for 6 May 1854 in *The Heart of Thoreau's Journals*, ed. Odell Shepard (New York: Dent, 1954), 130, from the books retained by Ann Malamud.

6. As part of his reading for the novel, Malamud had come across an essay by Elliott Jaques entitled 'Death and the Mid-Life Crisis', concerning what happened to artists in middle age (*The International Journal of Psychoanalysis*, 46 (October 1965), 502–14). Creativity in early adulthood was typically precipitate: it poured out of the young artist as sheer inner expression. But in mature adulthood, creativity was more sculpted, was given more externality as an object to be worked over again and again. In that sense, of course, as in so many others, Malamud had never been young. But the article did provide him with the carving metaphor he used to so often as an analogy for his art.

7. I am greatly indebted to Leonard J. Lehrman and his excellent *Marc Blitzstein: A Bio-Bibliography* (Greenwood Press, 2005). There he explains how after working on *Sacco and Vanzetti* in 1961, Blitzstein visited Israel, reawakening his sense of Jewish identity. Blitzstein, a teacher at Bennington in 1962–3, subsequently befriended Malamud and decided to compose a series of one-act operas to be called 'Tales of Malamud', including 'The Magic Barrel' and 'Idiots First'. He was completing the music when he was beaten to death in Martinique in 1964. Lehrman completed 'Idiots First' and went on to compose a version of 'Notes from a Lady at a Dinner Party' entitled 'Karla';

Elie Siegmeister created versions of 'Angel Levine' and 'The Lady of the Lake'. Lehrman noted how Malamud's 'Yinglish' (Yiddish-English) created a singing dialogue ideal for opera (e-mail correspondence 8 April 2006).

8. Telephone interview with Robert Boyers, editor of *Salmagundi* and director of the writing programme at Skidmore College, 22 July 2003.
9. Telephone interview with Bert Pogrebin, 17 July 2003.
10. Letters in the possession of Nina Pelikan Straus and reprinted with thanks.
11. Ann Malamud to Karl Schrag, 2 August 1987. I am much indebted to Schrag's daughter, Katherine Wangh, for access to the correspondence.
12. Telephone interview with Kate Hickler White, 18 November 2005.
13. E-mail correspondence with Peter Hayes, 6 February 2006.

CHAPTER 10: 'As you are grooved so you are graved'

1. E-mail correspondence from Ellen McCulloch-Lowell, 13 April 2006.
2. Telephone interview with Danny Myerson, 5 February 2006.
3. Letter to Karl Schrag, 6 September 1976, by kind permission of Katherine Wangh.
4. E-mail correspondence from John Bart Gerald, 1 April, 22 July 2006.
5. Telephone interview with Tamas Ungvari, 28 June 2006.
6. Quoted in *New York Times*, 1 February 1980.
7. Telephone interview with Karen Kennerly, 20 November 2005.
8. Mark Zborowski and Elizabeth Herzog, *Life Is With People* (New York; Shocken, 1962; first published 1952), 304.
9. Letter to Ann Malamud, London, 26 July 1963, by kind permission of Ann Malamud.
10. E-mail letter from Anne Roiphe, 25 July 2006.
11. Telephone interview with Pat Adams, 26 July 2006.
12. Taken from Malamud's notes on Irving Greenberg's essay, quoting the Hasidic Rabbi Nachman of Bratzlav (LC I 26.1).
13. Dr Reitz writes in an e-mail, 3 August 2006: 'It was a triple bypass utilizing the saphenous vein from his right leg to bypass the LAD, a branch of the circumflex, and the distal right coronary artery. The description of the findings states "The patient's heart was moderately enlarged and there was a small amount of left ventricular hypertrophy. There was visible and palpable coronary disease throughout the LAD, but most of the palpable disease ended after the first third and the LAD was bypassed in its midportion at a point where it was approximately 2 mm in diameter. The ramus intermedius coronary vessel was extensively involved with atherosclerotic disease". This is a fairly typical description of some one with hypertension and atherosclerosis. He had a fairly routine operation.'
14. E-mail correspondence from Bruce McAulay, 9 April 2006.
15. Personal interview with Alan Cheuse, 30 July 2003.

16. E-mail correspondence from Marjorie Pryse, 10 June 2006.

17. Personal interview with Alex Inkeles, 28–9 July 2003.

18. Personal interview with Robert Dunn, 12 July 2003.

19. Quoted in Robert Giroux's introduction to *The People and Uncollected Stories* (London: Chatto and Windus, 1990), p. xv.

20. Personal interview with Stuart Feder, 17 July 2003.

21. Philip Roth loved Malamudian sentences such as this, near the end of 'The Bill': 'He tried to say some sweet thing but his tongue hung in his mouth like dead fruit on a tree, and his heart was a black-painted window.' Or there was the opening of 'Idiots First', which Daniel Stern so admired: 'The thick ticking of the tin clock stopped. Mendel, dozing in the dark, awoke in fright. The pain returned as he listened. He drew on his cold embittered clothing'—the 'thick' ticking, the play-off between 'in the dark' and 'in fright', the 'return' of something before the 'stopping' of the beginning, the daring of 'embittered' clothing. Marjorie Pryse showed an unpublished essay of hers to Malamud in 1979 or 1980, entitled 'The Malamud Sentence': 'In its logic, the Malamud sentence exists in part to create pattern, or to assert that meaning must transcend the narrow boundaries of syntax and semantic choice. Because many of the sentences are brief and terse, the ponderousness of their meaning often seems to overburden or outweigh the language, as if the Malamud sentence imprisons the meaning of the work. The tension creates an inverse relation such that the tighter the form, the more resonant the meaning. In a style which the reader might accurately describe as magical, at times the Malamud sentence is so compressed that it almost seems to disappear.' Malamud in response said, 'Your writing is gnomic.' The Malamud sentences are also interestingly described in a powerful review by S. K. Oberreck of *Idiots First* (*St Louis Post-Dispatch*, 22 September 1964): 'The prose is so tight one hardly feels an urge to pry apart a paragraph and slip in between the lines, the usual job of someone paid to swim around in the "deeper meaning". Perhaps Malamud consciously makes that critical picking and probing difficult. He mentioned last year, when he read at Washington University, that one can't discuss a story by moving off into the ideas the story generates. The meaning is in the fiction and the fiction is the meaning, he dogmatically told me' (LC I 27.4).

22. Philip Roth's 'Pictures of Malamud' was first published in the *New York Times*, 20 April 1986 and reprinted in *Shop Talk* (London: Vintage, 2002), 120–30. The quotations above are taken from pp.129–30.

23. Telephone interview with James Atlas, 8 November 2005.

24. Reprinted by permission of Philip Roth.

25. Personal interview with Tim Seldes, 25 November 2005.

26. Telephone interview with Shirley Fingerhood, 27 July 2006. From then on Malamud employed Shirley Fingerhood as his legal advisor until her appointment as a judge made it impossible for her to continue.

27. Personal interview with Ann Malamud, January 2003.

Index